Janet
and
Jackie

The Story of

a Mother and Her Daughter,

Jacqueline

Kennedy Onassis

JANET *and* JACKIE

Jan Pottker

ST. MARTIN'S GRIFFIN
NEW YORK

JANET AND JACKIE. Copyright © 2001 by Writer's Cramp, Inc. All rights reserved. Printed in the United States of America. No part of this book may be used or reproduced in any manner whatsoever without written permission except in the case of brief quotations embodied in critical articles or reviews. For information, address St. Martin's Press, 175 Fifth Avenue, New York, N.Y. 10010.

www.stmartins.com

Design by Kathryn Parise

Library of Congress Cataloging-in-Publication Data

Pottker, Janice.
  Janet and Jackie : the story of a mother and her daughter, Jacqueline Kennedy Onassis / Jan Pottker.—1st ed.
      p. cm.
  Includes bibliographical references and index.
  ISBN 0-312-26607-3 (hc)
  ISBN 0-312-30281-9 (pbk)
  1. Auchincloss, Janet Lee, 1907–1989. 2. Onassis, Jacqueline Kennedy, 1929–1994. 3. Mothers and daughters—United States. 4. Celebrities—United States—Biography. 5. Presidents' spouses—United States. I. Title.
CT275.A884 P68 2001
973.922'0922—dc21   2001041617
[B]

First St. Martin's Griffin Edition: November 2002

10 9 8 7 6 5 4 3 2 1

To my mother,
Olga Somenzi Pottker

Contents

Acknowledgments

The greatest influence on Jackie Kennedy Onassis was her mother, Janet Auchincloss. While I was researching and writing *Janet and Jackie*, the critical role Janet played in shaping Jackie became clear to me. The Kennedy family, larger than life, has dominated the stories of Jackie, even though she was married to Jack Kennedy only eleven years of her life.

Janet had a long life; alas, Jackie did not, dying after a short illness at age sixty-five. Janet had died only five years earlier: Jackie's mother was clearly the most constant guide in her life. Yet Janet has stayed unknown to most people.

Janet and Jackie puts a stop to this nonsense and supplies the missing pieces to the jigsaw puzzle of Jackie's life. I could not have written this book without the help of Janet Auchincloss's children and friends. First, I would like to thank Yusha (Hugh D. III) Auchincloss, Janet's eldest stepson—the man who, as a teenager, welcomed Janet, Jackie, and Lee into the Auchincloss family and who remained a constant presence throughout their lives. Yusha oversaw Janet's care in her last decade when she suffered from Alzheimer's disease, and his kindnesses to her during her life were many. Yusha was generous to me also, spending long hours sharing his reminiscences during my three trips to Newport. At his Castle residence on Hammersmith Farm, he arranged for me to spend time with the woman who was Janet's caregiver over her last decade, Elisa (Mrs. Joseph J.) Sullivan. Elisa's patience in sorting through Yusha's massive collection and pointing out special items was incredible, and I thank her. Most important, Yusha generously supplied me with correspondence from Janet and about her, giving me access to precious Auchincloss documents.

Yusha also introduced me to his wonderful daughter, Maya Auchincloss, Janet's grandchild and Jackie's niece. She kindly provided me with anecdotes and memories about both women and, especially, told me what it was like to be a grandchild in the environment Janet created for her large family.

Jamie (James Lee) Auchincloss, Janet's only son, was pivotal to my understanding both of his mother and of her relationship to Jackie, his half sister. I deeply appreciated Jamie's political sense and his ability to home in on the similarities between the women.

Lewis Rutherfurd, Janet's son-in-law (he was married to Janet's third daughter, Janet Jr., who died of cancer at thirty-nine), who lives in Hong Kong, was helpful in our several brief telephone conversations, especially regarding the influence of Janet's father, James T. Lee, on Janet and subsequently on Jackie.

John H. Davis, the first cousin and biographer of Jacqueline Kennedy Onassis (*Jacqueline Bouvier: An Intimate Memoir, The Bouviers: Portrait of an American Family,* and *The Kennedys: Dynasty and Disaster, 1848–1983*), provided his memories of a young Aunt Janet Bouvier when she was married to her first husband, Jack, and of Janet's larger-than-life father. John Davis was also Janet's godson. His adult observations on Janet and Jackie provided insight to the women and their relationship with each other.

Maude Davis also gave me her memories of Aunt Janet and how the intricate family relationship—shaped by the Janet and Jack divorce—played out sadly in later years.

Kathleen Bouvier, who is the widow of Jackie's first cousin Michel Bouvier, supplied fond remembrances of Jackie's father. She also understands the traditional values that formed Janet's own behavior. And she wrote *Black Jack Bouvier: The Life and Times of Jackie O's Father,* which fills in a part of Jackie's history that other writers have missed.

Mimi (Mary-Lee) Cecil, who is Janet's niece and Jackie's first cousin, graciously hosted me over a three-day period and contributed anecdotes about Janet and Jackie, as well as stories of her beloved grandfather, the developer and banker James T. Lee. Mimi Cecil is married to William A. V. Cecil, who is responsible for establishing his grandfather's Asheville, North Carolina, property, Biltmore Estate, as this country's largest privately owned estate that is open to the public.

Jock (John F. Jr.) Nash, whose grandmother Esther (Mrs. Norman) Auchincloss Biltz was the elder sister of Janet's second husband, was of great help and gave me previously undisclosed information about the Auchincloss family.

Margaret (Mrs. Robert L.) Kearney spent days and days with me talking about Hugh D. Auchincloss and his large family. As Hughdie's personal secretary for more than two decades, she was able to provide details about the family and their lifestyle that could have come from no other person.

Marta Sgubin was governess to John Jr. and Caroline for the pivotal years of their lives and the one who gave them stability during their mother's marriage to Aristotle Onassis. After the children grew up, she became Jackie's family cook and, after Jackie's death, wrote *Cooking for Madam*. Sgubin knew Janet before she ever met Jackie and often took the children to Hammersmith Farm sans Jackie; she saw with a keen eye the nuances of similarities and differences between Janet and Jackie, and between Janet and Rose Kennedy. I believe that Janet's insistence that Jackie hire Marta is, at least in part, the reason for the sound character formation of John Jr. and Caroline.

Letitia Baldrige, Jackie's first White House social secretary and a longtime friend to both Janet and Jackie, provided her perspective on the Auchincloss family and their social group. She was supportive of my idea to celebrate Janet's life and gave me two lengthy interviews while she was on deadline herself. Her recent book, *In the Kennedy Style: Magical Evenings in the Kennedy White House,* is a valuable look at the nighttime celebrations she planned so carefully with Jackie.

Thanks go to those who shared memories of their professional relationship with Janet and Jackie. Mary Barelli (Mrs. Raymond A.) Gallagher worked first as Janet's personal secretary and then as Jackie's. After Jackie moved to New York and later married Ari Onassis, Gallagher wrote *My Life with Jacqueline Kennedy* as a way to explain to a surprised world who Jackie really was. Gallagher kindly shared her fond memories of Janet and some of her thoughts on the mother-daughter relationship.

Michael Dupre, who was Janet's personal chef during the 1980s, contributed his memories of Janet's last years and of Jackie's visits. Michael now is the innkeeper of Rhode Island House, one of Newport's finest B&Bs, which hosts a guest room named for the Auchincloss family. Prominently placed in the inn's entry is an outdoor garden sculpture from Janet's estate, given to him by her grateful family.

The story of the sale of Merrywood, the Auchincloss estate in Mc-Lean, Virginia, is a snapshot of Jackie in action. Several players in that episode gave me their memories. Thanks go to the Honorable Stewart L. Udall, Secretary of the Interior under President John F. Kennedy, who told me of both Jackie's and Bobby's push to stop Merrywood's development.

C. Wyatt Dickerson, who later purchased Merrywood, told me many colorful stories about the brouhaha over the planned sale and development, as well as what it was like to renovate and refurbish the Auchincloss estate.

I am grateful to Marie (Mrs. Walter T.) Ridder, who was an opponent of Merrywood's development. She told me about this controversy as well as what she observed as a guest at Jackie's wedding to Jack.

Tom (Thomas W.) Braden was a friend to both Jackie and Jack, as was his late wife, Joan. He freely shared crucial memories of events in both Washington, D.C., and Newport.

Ben (Benjamin C.) Bradlee, vice president at large of the *Washington Post*, was kind enough to share his perspective of the Auchinclosses during the Kennedy White House era and give me leads to others.

Betty Beale, a terrific journalist who traveled in the same social circle as the Auchinclosses and was therefore trusted by Janet, contributed her memories and her perspective on Janet and her children. In addition, her columns "Exclusively Yours" in the *Washington Evening Star* were invaluable for their exclusive interviews of Jackie's mother.

Charlie (Charles L.) Bartlett, who with his wife introduced Jackie to Jack, talked to me about the couple and their visits together to Hammersmith Farm.

The Honorable Claiborne Pell, former senator from Rhode Island, and his wife, Nuala, spent an afternoon with me in their historic Georgetown home and told me about their long friendship with both Janet and her husband Hughdie, and with Jackie and Jack.

The Honorable J. Carter Brown supplied a dual perspective of Janet and Jackie: initially, from his vantage point as a boy growing up so close to Hammersmith Farm that he shared the same view of the bay to, later, the outlook of a man who became celebrated in his own right as the director of the National Gallery of Art. Not only were his parents close friends with Janet and Hughdie, but he was witness to the arc of Janet's life in both Newport and Washington, D.C.

Many thanks to Robert Berks, the internationally renowned sculptor of the head of John F. Kennedy that graces the John F. Kennedy Center for the Performing Arts. Bob spoke about his sculpture and Jackie's vision for her husband's memorial. Todd Berks, Bob's archivist and wife, was a fount of information about that period.

Eileen (Mrs. John Jermain) Slocum of Newport graciously gave hours of her time to talk about her dear friend Janet and Janet's daughter Jackie. Janet confided to her close friend about every aspect of her life as mother to a blended family of seven children, and Mrs. Slocum kindly passed on her keenly remembered conversations with Janet.

John R. Drexell III of Palm Beach and Newport and his wife, Noreen, were dear friends of Janet and Hughdie; Mr. Drexel told many stories about Janet and Jackie that he had never discussed before. I appreciate the candid insights he shared.

Candy (Mrs. James H.) Van Alen received me on short notice and told me of her friendship with Janet that lasted from Janet's divorce from Jack onward. Her stories were fascinating.

Nancy (Mrs. Edward F. Jr.) Cavanagh recounted her Newport friendship with the Auchinclosses and her memories from East Hampton of both the Bouvier and Lee families.

Ella (Mrs. Poe) Burling of Georgetown was invaluable in filling in the portrait of Janet during her first decade of marriage to Hugh D. Auchincloss, as well as later. She also knew Hughdie's first two wives, and her comparison of the three women was extremely helpful.

The Honorable R. Gaull "Ricky" (Mrs. Lawrence H.) Silberman told me stories of Janet's last days in Georgetown in the house on Volta Place. Many thanks go to Ricky for taking the time to chat with me.

Rosemary Reed, proprietor of Washington's delightful Dupont Circle shop Toast & Strawberries, gave me important information about Anne Lowe, the woman who designed Jackie's wedding dress when she married Jack.

William Steinkraus, equestrian Olympic gold medal winner, provided invaluable information on the riding circuit he shared as a child with Jackie.

Thanks to Carter Horsley, NYRealty.com, who provided his expertise on the Manhattan buildings of James T. Lee.

A special thank-you goes to those who helped me characterize James T. Lee. Verne Atwater, former chairman and president of Central Savings Bank, which became the Apple Bank, supplied invaluable firsthand information. Raymond T. O'Keefe, who voluntarily oversees the James T. Lee Foundation, Inc., told me what his father had said about Mr. Lee and generously explained the good work of the foundation. Florence (Mrs. James) Bloor, whose husband was a close business associate of Mr. Lee's, related his characterizations of James T. Lee over the years.

Although my research skills were honed while earning a Ph.D. at Columbia University, I could never have researched Janet's Lee forebears as well as a professional genealogist. I want to thank R. Andrew Pierce for his exhaustive work in finding Janet's Irish American ancestors. In addition, many thanks to Joseph M. Silinonte, who picked up the trail in Manhattan when needed. To both men goes the credit of destroying the rumors that Janet was "half Jewish." Instead, they proved that she was all Irish in ancestry and that Jackie was thus more Irish than French. I would also like to thank Gary Boyd Roberts of the New England Genealogical Society for his information on the Kennedy-Fitzgerald line.

Thanks go to those at Fort Adams, who are Hammersmith Farm's next-door neighbors: Dick Masse, Fort Adams State Park superintendent, and Frank Hale, president of the Fort Adams Trust. Thanks also go to Donald McGee of the Newport Book Store.

I appreciate the help given by the staff of the Rhode Island Historical Society in Providence. I would also like to thank Jennifer Hazard of the *Providence Journal-Bulletin,* who spent several days pulling clip files and photographs from the newspaper archives. Alice Raguso of the *East Hampton Star* also took hours away from her deadline-pressed work to assist me.

Sonya Bernhardt, publisher, and Robert Devaney, editor in chief of *The Georgetowner* newspaper in Washington, D.C., were especially welcoming to me when I reviewed their archival collection.

Many thanks go to Sharon Cole, production assistant of the American Horse Show Association. She was consistently helpful over a period of weeks and gave me leads to organizations and people in the world of show riding.

Thank you to Kathleen Kelly, public relations, John F. Kennedy Center for the Performing Arts, and to Kate Gorecki, operations director of the National Symphony Orchestra, which is located at the Kennedy Center.

Biographies could not be written without good libraries, both public and private, and I was fortunate in being able to use some of the best while researching *Janet and Jackie*. I would like to acknowledge the New-York Historical Society and the Local History and Genealogy Room of the New York Public Library in Manhattan. Thanks also to Elizabeth Ellis, collections access associate of the Museum of the City of New York. In Long Island the Pennypacker Long Island Collection of the East Hampton Library was invaluable. I am indebted to both Dorothy King and Diana Dayton of this collection for spending three days advising and assisting me.

In regard to Newport, my gratitude goes to the Newport Historical Society and its librarian, Burton Lippincott, whose perspective on Newport families was invaluable. For those who wish more detail on the early days of Hammersmith Farm, the spring 1994 bulletin *Newport History* can be obtained from the society at 82 Touro Street, Newport, RI 02840. The Newport Room of the Newport Public Library and its librarian, Pat LaRose, were very helpful. In addition, the Redwood Library and Athenaeum has a lovely collection that would be difficult to find anywhere else. There, I was aided by Wendy Kieron-Sanchez and Robert Behra.

At the John Fitzgerald Kennedy Library and Museum in Boston, June Payne, Kara Drake, Moira Porter, and Ron Whealan have my thanks. Special thanks to James Hill of the audiovisual staff, who found numerous photographs for me, most of which had never been requested before.

In the nation's capital, it was the wonderful collection of the Washingtoniana Division of the Martin Luther King Memorial Library, District of Columbia Public Library, that allowed me to see the possibilities of the story of *Janet and Jackie*. Dr. Susan L. Malbin, its chief and the former librarian/archivist of the Peabody Room of the Georgetown Regional Branch, D.C. Library, deserves special thanks.

I would like to thank the staff of the Library of Congress, Roger L. Stevens Collection, for giving me special permission to see the Stevens correspondence before the 107-box collection was completely processed. I would also like to thank the prints and photography collection staff for their patience in helping me access the Toni Frissell collection of Jackie and Jack's wedding.

Invaluable also was the Virginia Room, Fairfax City Regional Library, Fairfax County Public Library, Virginia. Thanks to Carol S. Bessette of the Washington Tour Guild, for pointing me toward Fairfax County research offices that surveyed Merrywood.

The library of Stratford Hall, the ancestral home of the Lees in Virginia, was very useful, and Judy Hinson, librarian, turned up relevant documents from its archives about Janet's directorship.

The staff at university and school libraries were especially helpful. At Columbia University, I thank Jocelyn K. Wilke, Honor Library Archives; Whitney Bagnall, Law Honors archivist; and John Kelly, director of public relations at the School of Law. Yale University's Chris Baird deserves thanks for her attention to Yale graduates Jack Bouvier and Hugh D. Auchincloss.

I would like to thank Elizabeth Daniels, Vassar College historian, for explaining what being a student at Vassar was like in the 1940s. At George Washington University, where Jackie received her B.A., Jane Lingo, assistant director of university relations, was of great assistance. The staff of the library archives at Long Island University were helpful, as were the archives staff at La Salle University in Philadelphia. I thank David Blount at Sweet Briar College and, at Groton School, Gage R. Stockter, who provided the right information at the right time.

Hope Dellon, executive editor of St. Martin's Press, brought her best judgment and wisdom to *Janet and Jackie* throughout all its stages. She is simply terrific. I appreciate the good work of her assistants, Kris Kamikawa and Tanya LaPlante. I also want to thank John Murphy, publicity director of St. Martin's Press, for his belief in this book and its possibilities.

My agent, Pam Bernstein, is top-rate. Pam's perception and incisiveness moved this project from proposal to book. Thank you, too, to her assistant, Jonette Suiter.

Without the encouragement of my family—especially my husband, Andrew S. Fishel, and my daughters, Tracy and Carrie Pottker-Fishel— I might not have been able to slog on to get those interviews or spend another day in front of a microfilm reader. I would also like to thank Tracy for the work of her company, Fishy Design. My sister, Mary Helene Pottker Rosenbaum, read and critiqued with her editor's eye every word of this book and made invaluable suggestions at crucial times. Thanks also for the support of my brother-in-law S. Ned Rosenbaum and my sister-in-law Diane Fishel Bialick. The dedication of *Janet and Jackie* to my mother, Olga Somenzi Pottker, needs no explanation.

Where would we be without friends? First, thank you to Cathy O'Donnell, who was supportive during this project and who also pitched in her incredible administrative skills during the weeks preceding my deadline. I want to thank M. Kathleen McCulloch, Steven Brady, Eleanor Baker, Cynthia Vartan, Susan Schmidt, Barbara Harr, Marilyn McDermett, Scott Bernstein, Karen Seals, Jane Graf, Mark Woodland, David Blum, Larry Dickter, Lolly Esham, Elizabeth Rios, David Hochberg, Dave Cutler, Anne-Marie Groome, Tom Killmer, Jill and Victor Zacherie, Marty Reid, Kathy W. Snyderman, and Jack Weisner for their interest and encouragement.

Writer friends are especially important. Deep thanks to Kristina Arriaga de Bucholz, Judith D. Pomerantz, Doreen Conrad, Fiona Houston, Bob Pack, Dan Moldea, Bob Speziale, Dotson Rader, Pam and Ron Kessler, Larry Leamer, and Diane Leatherman. Thanks to Ed Klein for his encouragement, and to Charles Higham for his anecdotes.

You may think that you know everything about Jackie and the people who shaped her character. Because of the kindnesses of the people acknowledged here, you will learn fresh stories and gain a deeper understanding of how Janet's strength allowed Jackie to become the woman we know. Again, I thank them for allowing me to tell this story, *Janet and Jackie.*

$\mathcal{P}$rologue

Janet and Jackie: the first a private woman, and the latter a public woman. During her lifetime, we knew Jackie as Jackie Bouvier, Jackie Kennedy, and Jackie Onassis. As her life drew to a close, she acknowledged her legend and accepted the name that most people identified her with: Jackie Kennedy Onassis.

Jackie's last names represented, of course, the men in her life. Each of these men — Jack Bouvier, Jack Kennedy, and Ari Onassis — influenced her and helped shape her personality. But each was with Jackie only briefly.

- First, there was her father, Jack Bouvier. She lived with him for only eleven years, and he died when she was twenty-eight.
- While married to Jack Kennedy and through the drama of his assassination and its aftermath, she became an international icon. But the time arc from their first date through the final disaster spans a mere eleven years.

1

- Jackie shocked the world when she married Ari Onassis, but he also was in her life for only eleven years—from when she cruised on his yacht after her baby died until Ari's death.
- The last man in her life, Maurice Tempelsman, was a serious presence for, once again, about eleven years.

On the other hand, Jackie's mother, Janet—the greatest influence on Jackie, more important to her character than any of the men in her life who came and went—was there for a full sixty years, from Jackie's birth till Janet's death.

So, for sixty of the sixty-five years that would be allotted to Jackie, Janet Auchincloss was her daughter's permanent anchor and lifelong guiding spirit. Who was this woman, and how did she influence the woman who would define an era?

In the decades when Jackie grew up—the 1930s and 1940s—American parents dreamed of their daughters becoming First Lady. They believed that to be the wife of the President of the United States was a noble and worthy goal. Only later—after cynicism about political leaders and more equal ambitions for girls and boys alike took hold—did they turn from this ideal.

If a mother's highest dream was to see her daughter on the Inaugural stand in front of the Capitol, then Janet achieved what others aspired to. By that measure, Janet's upbringing of Jackie was a success. No one questioned Rose Kennedy, after all, when she said that her greatest accomplishment was being the mother of the President. In fact, a survey of college historians rate Jack and Jackie Kennedy equally: of the Presidents and First Ladies, both Kennedys are ranked number eight. The only other couple held in equal esteem are Franklin and Eleanor Roosevelt, who come in at number one.

If Janet hadn't had the strength to walk out on a drunken, womanizing Jack Bouvier and take her daughters with her, their childhood would have been even more difficult than it was.

If Janet hadn't married Hugh D. Auchincloss Jr.—or a man like him—she never would have had the resources to raise Jackie as she wished. The expensive ceremonies, the debut, and the wedding reception at Hammersmith Farm were not so important to Jackie in themselves but were the pillars that supported the life she was brought up to lead.

And if Janet hadn't raised Jackie to speak French fluently (it was the language spoken every night at dinner), enabling her to study at the Sorbonne and live abroad; if Janet hadn't nurtured in Jackie the strength and discipline it takes to become an excellent rider (Janet was a top-notch equestrian herself, winning the hunter championship three times at the National Horse Show); and if Janet hadn't encouraged Jackie to develop her writing, her drawing, her love of literature and the arts (even if Janet herself was not artistic or intellectual, she admired those traits in others)—then Jackie would not have caught the eye of a canny Joe Kennedy, who vetted the marital candidates for the son he had such ambitions for.

Moreover, if Jack Kennedy hadn't married Jackie, he arguably would not have become President. Although her appeal was interpreted (by mostly male reporters) as one of dress and style—she drew larger crowds than Jack from the start—she added to the campaign a substance that went largely unrecognized at the time. Her radio spots in Spanish, for instance, which drew tens of thousands of voters to her husband, are acknowledged as among the most effective political advertisements of all time.

Despite the hundreds of books, thousands of magazine articles, and myriad newspaper stories on Jackie, Janet's role in her achievements has gone unacknowledged. Does the aura of the Kennedy name shine so bright that anyone outside it is eclipsed? Janet seemed invisible during the White House years and after. There's a wire-service photo of a group of women watching Jack Kennedy's State of the Union Address. The ladies pictured are Janet, her daughters Jackie and Lee, and Joan Kennedy. The caption says, KENNEDY WOMEN IN FULL FORCE. In other photos—for example, at Caroline's graduation from Concord Academy—Janet posed for the cameras with Jackie, Caroline, John, and Ted Kennedy but was cropped out before the photo service sent the image over the wire. It is as if she didn't exist.

In fact, this writer, requesting a photo of Janet at the White House with Lady Bird Johnson at the 1965 commemoration of the Jacqueline Bouvier Kennedy Garden, was told by the LBJ Library audiovisual department, "Oh, so that's who that lady is with Mrs. Johnson! We never knew."

It's time to put to rest the old myths in which Janet plays a marginal role in Jackie's life. Is there *any* mother who could be reduced to such a small role—particularly the mother of one of the world's most celebrated women? The truth is that Jackie's greatest ongoing influence was Janet.

This is what Janet instilled in Jackie: charm and flirtation; reserve and privacy; manners and consideration; creativity and artistic endeavor;

patriotism and hero-worship of military leaders; individuality and a strong sense of self; a passion for helping where it is needed; love of riding and horses; love of art; a belief that the finest things in life are necessities rather than luxuries; and, underpinning it all, the recognition that money is needed to support these undertakings.

Jackie, in turn, wanted to emulate and please her exacting mother. And Janet was there in times of crisis: whether Jackie was nearing the end of a troubled pregnancy and her husband was in Capri with his mistress or whether she needed her mother's tacit approval of her marriage to a Greek tycoon, Janet stood by her daughter—whatever her own doubts.

"Janet was much misrepresented in the press. The stories were really inaccurate," says Letitia Baldrige, Jackie's White House social secretary.

Janet was made out to be some kind of wicked fairy godmother who made an occasional appearance only to cast a spell on the beautiful princess. The most common characterizations of Janet are "cold" and "social climber." Yet paradoxically, everyone who knew her—even her detractors—in the next breath speaks of her charm and warmth. As for social climbing, while she did get silly about her putative ancestry, using her maiden name Lee to claim a relationship to General Robert E. Lee when there was none, that is hardly an uncommon or heinous crime. In fact, Jackie did the same thing when she gave the impression that her background was French, even though she was actually mostly Irish.

And it is true that Janet would not have married Hugh D. Auchincloss if he had been a poor man. To be fair, however, she had no skills, only two years of college, and an alcoholic ex-husband whose younger brother had already died of acute alcohol poisoning. What would the future have held for her two young daughters if she hadn't married well? Janet did what she knew she had to for them as well as for herself.

She did it well. Her second husband, Hugh D. Auchincloss, loved her, and his friends accepted her immediately. Had Janet been a social climber, social Newport—seasonal home to the most prominent names in American high society—would have spotted her in an instant and rejected her. It's unjust to dismiss her as a mere climber just because she married a man with money, particularly given her own impressive grandfather and father, James Lee and James T. Lee.

Then, too, Janet handled her daughter's fame appropriately. She was there when needed—which was often—but she did not intrude. This very reserved woman, married to a man who "hated" publicity, managed to acclimate to her daughter's metamorphosis from a naive twenty-four-year-old bride to the country's most celebrated First Lady in a mere seven years. Not only did Janet adapt to the transformation, but she kept her balance as the more mannerly white-gloved society coverage of the First Lady still in force at the end of the Eisenhower administration gave way to the incessant tabloid culture that devoured her daughter with such a voracious and ruthless appetite.

Janet Lee Auchincloss was a remarkable woman who passed her unique traits on to her famous daughter. To understand Jackie, you must understand Janet.

Here is a portrait of Jackie's life that you have never seen before. Here is a tale of Jackie from a perspective that you have never read before. This is the story of Janet and Jackie.

Chapter 1

AMERICAN
DREAMS

Janet Lee's story begins and ends with lush grasslands. First there was the verdant kelly green of Ireland; at the story's end, there was the sea-green lawn leading from the shingled house at Hammersmith Farm down to Rhode Island's Narragansett Bay. The ancestors of Janet Lee Auchincloss and her daughters traveled—from potato-famine Ireland to the social enclave of Newport—up a golden road lined with many thousands of dollar bills, some lettuce-fresh and others old money's worn olive.

Although Janet's narrative must start in Ireland—for all her forebears are Irish—during her lifetime she wanted nothing more than to escape from what she felt was her ethnic taint. She held no nostalgia for shamrocks, wee leprechauns, or Tara's heroes. In fact, Janet denied her Irish heritage, falsely claiming to be entirely English Catholic. She maintained this harmless fiction all her life and took care to select husbands whom she appraised as being a few rungs up the social ladder from her own Lee family.

Janet would have three husbands in all: John (Jack) Vernou Bouvier, the father of her daughters Jackie and Lee; Hugh D. (Hughdie) Auchincloss, the father of her daughter Janet Jr. and her only son, James; and a last, brief marriage to Bingham (Booch) Morris. Neither her first marriage nor her last made her happy. Hughdie would turn out to be the only man for her. *This* was the successful marriage: the one that lasted thirty-four years, from 1942 until Hughdie's death in 1976. Janet's daughters Jackie and Lee affectionately dubbed their mother's husband "Uncle Hughdie," and he, in turn, became their benevolent surrogate father, offering stability and a coddled childhood that their own father could never have provided.

Janet met Hughdie when she was still recovering from that awful first marriage. Hughdie was Jack's opposite in character and wealth, and he bested Jack at ancestry, too. Although Janet had thought her marriage to a Bouvier—who touted his own mythical lineage—had brought her a full league from her Irish origins, Hughdie's solid Scottish Presbyterian progenitors were even more attractive to her than the Bouviers had been.

Hughdie's ancestor Hugh Auchincloss was born in Paisley, Scotland, in 1780. (The name Auchincloss is an ancient Ayrshire patronymic, meaning "field of the stone.") He left for America at age twenty-three. Hughdie would be his great-grandson.

This first Hugh Auchincloss sailed on the *Factor* in 1803 to found a branch of his family's dry-goods business in downtown Manhattan. In 1806 he married a young woman, Ann Anthony Stuart, from a comfortably off family in Philadelphia. Her father was a slave owner who left, on his death, a "Negro wench" to his daughter. By 1808 Hugh had a dry-goods business in New York City in his own name and was living at 14 Gold Street. He had also become a founding member of the Fifth Avenue Presbyterian Church.

Unfortunately, Hugh had not thought to renounce his British citizenship as fervor grew against England's treatment of American warships. When the United States declared war against Great Britain in 1812, he had to obey President James Madison's proclamation for aliens to move "forty miles from tidewater so that [they] might not be able to render aid or give comfort to the enemy." Taking advantage of his position as best he could, he hitched mules to a wagon packed tight with dry goods, went west, sold his goods, and returned to New York after the war more prosperous than before.

Hugh and Ann Auchincloss had thirteen children, yet only one of their sons produced male heirs—so the entire clan named Auchincloss is descended from this one man. He was born in New York City in 1810 and was named John. In 1835, when John was twenty-five, he married Elizabeth Buck, age nineteen. He continued in the family firm in Manhattan—by now, his father had achieved the presidency of the American Wholesale Dry Goods Association—and lived with his wife at 11 West Fifty-seventh Street. However, Elizabeth's father, also a merchant, had established a fine residence on Newport's Liberty Street, so in 1851 John and Elizabeth Auchincloss demonstrated their success by escaping the noise and hubbub of Manhattan and setting up a flourishing summer home in Newport.

John and Elizabeth and, eventually, their nine children summered in a Newport house a few blocks from town on Washington Street, facing Goat Island and the deep malachite water of Narragansett Bay. The house—still standing, although modified—was a largish but rather ordinary-looking two-story frame structure with a basement and attic and generous front and side yards fenced to separate the property from surrounding farmland. In that Newport house one summer day, on July 8, 1858, Ann gave birth to Hugh Auchincloss Sr., who would be Janet's father-in-law.

But long before Janet met any of the Auchincloss family, she had married into the Bouvier family and given birth to two Bouvier daughters, Jackie and Lee. Michel Bouvier—great-grandfather to the Jack Bouvier who would be Janet's first husband—arrived in the United States from France in 1815, says John H. Davis, his descendant and biographer. Michel went to Philadelphia rather than New York, where the Auchinclosses had been settled for twelve years as solid middle-class retailers. Michel, a skilled laborer, resumed the cabinetmaking and carpentry he had learned in France. Across the Delaware River on the banks of New Jersey, Joseph Bonaparte was fashioning a new life for himself following the defeat of his younger brother Napoléon at Waterloo. Bonaparte hired Michel to do carpentry on his great estate and, when the property burned to ashes, charged Michel with the task of reconstruction. Michel's fee put him on solid ground and allowed him, eventually, to invest in real estate.

Michel's sons saw that they could do better for themselves in New York City, where money was more important than lineage. John Vernou Bouvier Sr., Jack Bouvier's grandfather, founded a stock brokerage firm and increased the Bouvier holdings. His brilliant son and namesake, John Vernou Bouvier Jr., who was to be Jack Bouvier's father, was uninterested in financial success. Instead, he graduated valedictorian from Columbia University in 1886 and received an A.M. degree in political science in 1887. Bouvier Jr. went from graduate school immediately to Columbia's law school, earning his law degree in one year (two years was then the norm) and passing the bar at the same time, in 1888. He specialized in trial work and eventually made a name as one of New York's most distinguished attorneys.

He married Maude Sergeant in 1890. A year later their first child was born. The boy was John (Jack) V. Bouvier III, who was to marry Janet and become father of Jackie and Lee. By 1893 John and Maude had moved from Manhattan to a rented house in Nutley, New Jersey. The young attorney didn't mind the commute into Manhattan, and his wife enjoyed the country, so they built an estate in 1895 that they named Woodcroft.

Another son was born, and a daughter. Then, more than ten years later, Maude gave birth to twin girls, Maude and Michelle. Maude roundly spoiled the children at home; even the German governess couldn't mitigate her indulgences. Jack was high-spirited, and whenever his teachers disciplined him, his mother would tell him he wasn't to blame—rather, she denounced the "bad French blood" inherited from his father's side. As Davis tells the story, one day Jack's father found him in the barn, pricking his finger and squeezing out drops of blood. "When asked what he was doing," Davis writes, "he replied that he was trying to squeeze all the naughty French blood out of himself."

Despite the French line that came through the Bouviers, Jack's daughters, Jackie and Lee, would be mostly Irish. Jackie's Irish majority was camouflaged by her French maiden name Bouvier and her well-known love of all things French. But Jackie was faux French and, instead, authentically Irish. On the other hand, the clan Jackie married into— the Kennedy family—has throughout the years loudly ballyhooed their Irish heritage.

Coincidentally, the same potato fungus (*Phytophora infestans*) that had tainted thousands of acres of Irish farmland with black rot brought to America the four families that would eventually intersect at some of the most memorable ceremonies of the second half of the twentieth century. Janet's great-grandparents the Lees, her grandparents the Merritts, and both Rose and Joe Kennedy's great-grandparents the Fitzgeralds and the Kennedys all came to the United States from Ireland to escape the potato famine. The legacy of these families, along with that of the Bouvier family, culminated in Janet's grandchildren Caroline and John Kennedy Jr.

Some believe that every year is cruel to the Irish, but the years 1845 to 1850 were especially sadistic. In 1840 this overpopulated country, with its millions of unemployed men, was fed chiefly by the potato crop. Potatoes were Ireland's fundamental nourishment; in fact, potatoes were often the only food on the table. The consequence of a potato blight that mysteriously began spreading in 1845 was catastrophic: one million Irish dead from starvation or from the diseases that ravaged a famished population.

Families were so desperate for food that they fed their children grass or, if they lived near the water, seaweed. Emigration to the United States was for the lucky ones who could afford passage. Others arrived in the new country because they had been evicted by crop-poor landowners who were given the right to send their tenants to America, much as they would have transported—in better times—sacks of potatoes. Ship captains witnessed starving Irish embark with mouths stained green from eating grass and subsequently watched only two-thirds of these voyagers disembark, the rest having been buried at sea after succumbing to diseases below decks. For good reason, the vessels bringing Irish immigrants to New York and Boston were dubbed "coffin ships."

But the stronger passengers survived. The proportion of immigrants streaming into America from Ireland alone jumped to one-third of all newcomers. The greatest number, including the Kennedys, traveled to Boston or other parts of New England. Others, like the Lees, landed in New York. With no money, these immigrants stayed where they were and sought jobs. Very few traveled south, and fewer went west.

Survival, to most who arrived, was their highest goal: Ireland had ingrained in them a sense of hopelessness and fatalism, and they carried this dismal philosophy with them to the new country. Very few Irish immigrants had the motivation and talent to dream and plan.

As Manhattan's merchant-class Auchincloss family was summering in Newport and as the Wall Street Bouviers were prospering, the Lees— and the Kennedys—were fleeing the potato famine. Janet's great-grandfather Thomas Lee was born in County Cork, Ireland, in 1810. He married Frances (Fanny) Smith, and their first child, Mary, was born in Ireland. The couple arrived in the United States in time for the December 20, 1852, birth of James Lee, Janet's grandfather. Throughout their marriage, Thomas and Fanny lived in Newark, New Jersey, a city with a large Irish immigrant population. Thomas Lee was a laborer who worked for the India Rubber Company, which imported crude rubber from such regions as Indonesia, Eurasia, and South America, as well as India.

Since the 1700s, rubber had been used to waterproof shoes and clothes, but the drawback was its stickiness. During the 1820s, Charles Macintosh, a Scottish chemist, found that spreading a coal-tar solvent on top of rubber and placing the combination between two layers of fabric prevented clothing from becoming tacky. He opened a factory that manufactured double-textured, waterproof jackets known as mackintoshes. In 1839 the American inventor Charles Goodyear discovered vulcanization, which kept rubber products from softening in heat and becoming brittle in cold, problems that impaired the mackintosh raincoats and boots worn by New Englanders. Although Thomas Lee's specific task at India Rubber is not known, vulcanization (still the basis of rubber manufacturing) requires workers to eliminate rubber's undesirable characteristics by treating it with sulfur and then boiling the foul mixture. Toiling in a rubber factory certainly was not only unpleasant but dangerous.

Thomas's labor at the factory did not keep him from establishing an active family. He and Fanny had six children in twelve years of marriage. Although Mary's birth date is not certain, she was probably born in 1851. James was born the following year in Newark. The couple's remaining children were also born in Newark: Thomas (his father's namesake) was born in 1857, Fanny (her mother's namesake) in 1859, Teresa in 1861, and Joseph in 1863. Thomas Lee, like many other Irish, did not fight for either the North or South in the Civil War but instead remained in Newark, sweating in the fetid rubber factory, seemingly unaffected by the conflict.

When the "green mouths," as the impoverished Irish grass-eaters were dubbed, entered the United States, they brought cholera, consumption, and typhus with them. Thomas and Fanny were more fortunate than many of the era's parents because they lost only one child, young Fanny, before she was eleven years old. But the couple's other five children thrived.

Mary, the eldest, was put to work in a cotton factory when she was in her teens, but James was far luckier. As a firstborn son, his parents had high expectations for him. James was a smart boy, and his mother and father—unlike many other working-class immigrants of the mid-1850s—stressed education for their sons. Thomas and Fanny stretched his meager income to cover private tuition for James and his younger brother Thomas at Cathedral School, a Newark parochial high school.

After graduation, James enrolled in Philadelphia's La Salle College, established by the Brothers of the Christian Schools and named after the organization's seventeenth-century French founder, John Baptist de La Salle. There, James read the writing of Brother Azarias (Patrick Francis Mullany), a distinguished Catholic philosopher and professor of literature. Brother Azarias had actually left La Salle a few years before, to help establish Rock Hill College (no longer in existence) in Ellicott City, Maryland, and the brother's magnetism drew James down to Maryland. James enrolled in Brother Azarias's pedagogy classes and was electrified by the new thoughts on teaching that characterized that part of the century. During the young man's coursework, he discovered the writings of the progressive educator Horace Mann, who had founded the country's first state-sponsored normal (teaching) school in Massachusetts in 1839 and later established a college in Ohio called Antioch. James absorbed a reverence for the process of learning, expounded by Brother Azarias and demonstrated by the teaching order of the Christian Brothers.

Indeed, James was also shaped by the influence of the Religious Society of Friends (Quakers), who had founded both Philadelphia and the tiny community of Ellicott City, Maryland, in the Patapsco Valley. When James arrived at Rock Hill College, he found the town recovering from a disastrous flood that had swept through, killing thirty-six residents and destroying many buildings. It must have been difficult for him to adjust to this rural environment after having lived in Newark and Philadelphia. At least James could travel easily—first by train from Newark to Baltimore, and from there to Ellicott City—because his college town was the last stop on the Baltimore & Ohio Railroad.

Education was an exciting field in the mid-1800s, and James became its proponent at Rock Hill, receiving a teaching certificate upon graduation. James continued to focus on education and learning; after earning his undergraduate degree, he came back to the Newark area and continued his schooling in New York City, receiving his M.D. at Bellevue Medical College, New York University.

How and why James met and fell in love with Mary Theresa Norton of Troy, New York, is unknown, but they were married in Troy in 1875, when James was twenty-three years old. Mary had been born in New York in 1852 and, like her husband, was the daughter of Irish immigrants escaping the potato famine. She was twenty-three when she married James: marriage at that relatively late age was typical for her class, partly because so many immigrant daughters were working in factories to help support their parents and siblings. Three years after their marriage, James's father, Thomas, died, and his mother, Fanny, left Newark to move into a boardinghouse at 104 East Twenty-sixth Street with James's brother Thomas, by then a civil engineer in New York City.

On October 2, 1877, James and Mary had their first child and only son, James (Jim) Thomas Aloysius Lee, who would be Janet's father. Mary purchased the infant's elaborate lace and lawn christening gown, with its minuscule puffed sleeves intricately embroidered with tiny bouquets. The family's home was at 62 Third Avenue in Manhattan. Five daughters followed Jim's birth: Florence Mary was born a year later in 1878 (now the family lived at 868 Lexington Avenue), but the next daughter, Genevieve, wasn't born until 1892, followed by Madeline in 1893, Amy in 1894, and Evelyn in 1896.

As his family was growing, James Lee built a distinguished career in both education and medicine in New York City. For a short time he was employed solely as a general practitioner of medicine, but by 1881, when Jim was four years old, James was hired as a teacher by the New York City public schools. Showing a prodigious appetite for work, he taught during the day and continued as a private physician in the evenings and on weekends. To make it easier to combine his professions, he saw patients in his home: first at 251 East 110th Street and then, by 1885, at 235 East 124th Street. No doubt his fluency in German and Italian helped him treat patients, for both his residences were located in the Harlem neighborhood then home to many middle-class immigrant and second-generation families. The area had changed from its initial Dutch population—Haarlem is a city in the Netherlands—to Irish. (Later, Jewish immigrants settled here, and by the 1920s, it had become an African American neighborhood.)

A hundred years later his granddaughter Janet would say that he received his medical degree in order to help a crippled son. Because the only son born to James was Jim, and since there is no evidence that Jim was ever disabled in any way, Janet's statement is perplexing. Was Jim crippled by illness during childhood, and had he overcome this handicap by the time anyone who had known him as a boy was still alive at the end of the twentieth century? Because he was tutored at home by his mother, it does appear that he might have had an illness of some type—especially as his father was a public-school teacher and therefore unlikely to have kept him out of school, save for a compelling reason. In any case, none of his descendants or business colleagues ever remembered his mentioning a childhood disability. However, everyone does agree that his five sisters doted on him. Obviously, he was precious to them: perhaps they perceived that he needed care, or maybe it was merely a case of sisters spoiling their only brother.

By 1890, when Jim was thirteen years old, James was promoted to associate superintendent of schools, a challenging job because of the huge number of immigrant children, many non-English-speaking with illiterate parents, enrolled in city schools. Throughout the nation, fewer than 6 percent of Americans eighteen years old or older had earned high-school diplomas. In a scant forty years, the city's population had risen tenfold. It was also a time of major change in the public schools, which later would be described as the "great school wars." The city was gripped by educational reform—reflecting the new thinking that had led college-age James into education—and the thrust was toward a decentralized school system. Despite the professional and political demands of James's position as one of eight men supervising thousands of teachers in hundreds of schools, he continued his medical practice.

Each generation of Lees possessed an unusual sense of drive. Jim, for example, was prepared to start college at age fourteen, but James and Mary thought he was just too young. So he spent a year studying the violin before entering, in 1892, the City College of New York (CCNY), where he was a fifteen-year-old engineering major. No doubt his uncle Thomas influenced his choice of major. Despite his youth and the level of coursework he must have encountered, Jim found time to play football and to work, at seventeen, as a law clerk. He also joined the fraternity Delta Kappa Epsilon. In 1896 he graduated from CCNY with a B.S. in engineering.

Jim immediately enrolled in a master's program at Columbia University in political science and economics, earning his A.M. degree within a year, in 1897. He then entered Columbia's law school and earned his LL.B. in two years, by 1899. (Coincidentally, ten years earlier John V. Bouvier Jr. had followed the same academic fields in the exact sequence as Jim Lee.)

By twenty-two Jim held an undergraduate degree in engineering, a graduate degree in politics and economics, and a professional degree in law; he had just been admitted to the New York state bar. His violin studies lent an air of culture to him as well. Jim Lee was a very impressive young man who seemed to exceed even his father's high expectations.

His father, James, still maintained his own dual career of school administrator and physician. Although he was a high-level administrator, he was also a school reformer and saw strength in organizing—by the 1870s half of the unions of the American Federation of Labor were Irish-run.

In 1898 James was elected president of New York State Teachers Association and presided that year in Rochester over its fifty-second convention, the largest to date. Although this organization was not, strictly speaking, a union, for its members were professionals, James served as president for two years and aggressively organized teachers' associations in every county in the state. He was one of New York's most important players in basing teacher salaries on length of service and in paying teachers of either sex the same salary, thus removing the taint of spoils from the civil-service teaching force. That same year, the five boroughs were organized into one unit, necessitating organizational changes in the public schools that eventually gave James the title he would hold until his retirement, district superintendent of schools.

Life at home was busy, too, for the Lees' unmarried adult children still lived with their parents. The first to marry and leave home was Florence, the eldest daughter. The rest of her siblings remained in a tight-knit unit. All the younger girls—Genevieve, Madeline, Amy, and Evelyn—became teachers and continued residing with their parents. To his sisters' delight, Jim also lived with the family after becoming an attorney in private practice in 1901. He relocated his law office a number of times within the decade but centered his work addresses on Broadway. No matter what stories they brought home from the classroom, Jim's work as a new attorney propelled him into a far more exciting sphere.

It seems likely that Jim's sisters introduced their brother to a fellow teacher named Margaret A. Merritt—who would become Janet's mother—for these two young people fell in love and married on October 7, 1903. They were twenty-six and twenty-four years old, respectively.

Margaret had been born in New York City in 1879 to Irish immigrants: Thomas (born in 1845) and Maria (Mary) Curry Merritt (born in 1851), who had emigrated from County Clare. Margaret's father, Thomas, had come to the United States on the ship *Queen* and worked as a laborer, eventually moving up the occupational ladder to become a grocer. He lived briefly in Savannah, Georgia, but had returned to New York City by the time he married on June 6, 1875. He and Mary raised their children — Margaret had an older brother, Samuel, and a younger brother, Thomas, who died as a child — on the Lower East Side of Manhattan, first at 107 East Twelfth Street (a predominately Italian neighborhood) and then at 296 Henry Street, near the Henry Street and the Jacob Riis Settlement Houses. This neighborhood was among the worst of the Lower East Side tenements, where as many as a thousand immigrants per acre were crammed into poorly constructed, windowless apartments. At least by 1879 a tenement house law imposed space and ventilation standards. (A toilet in each apartment wasn't mandated by the city until 1901.) But conditions must have been dreadful, especially after Thomas's death in 1893 forced his widow to bring up the two younger children by herself.

To help support her family, Mary would hold teas at her house, inviting ladies to whom she would sell buttons, pins, and thread. It was a socially acceptable way for a woman to earn "pin" money from her home. Through this small income, she was able to pay Margaret's tuition at a Sacred Heart school.

Margaret Merritt's ancestry made her a first-generation American, while her husband was second-generation. As the Lees and the Merritts demonstrate, even one generation's difference can translate into a large economic gain. Jim's immigrant grandfather was a rubber worker. Margaret's immigrant father began as a laborer and retired as a grocer. Yet the first American-born generation of Lees and Merritts shows that both were ambitious; James Lee was both a high-level school administrator and physician, while his daughter-in-law, Margaret, was a teacher. Margaret's marriage to Jim — with his two degrees beyond the college level — was a high step for her to ascend. She accomplished the move but not without later difficulty for herself, her husband, and their daughter Janet.

While Janet Lee's ancestors were settling — indeed, were thriving — in the United States, there were two other families also in America whose descendants' lives would merge with Janet's — and, later, Jackie's — own history. Their surnames were, of course, Fitzgerald and Kennedy.

The most striking parallels in ancestry are between Janet's family and the one that her daughter Jackie would marry into. The first of the

Kennedys to come to America was Patrick Kennedy, arriving in 1849, three years before Thomas Lee's immigration. Patrick Kennedy would be the paternal grandfather of Joseph (Joe) Patrick Kennedy, the father of President John F. Kennedy. In 1857 another Irish immigrant named Thomas Fitzgerald married and began a tribe whose lineage would include his granddaughter Rose Fitzgerald, the President's mother. The Fitzgeralds, the Kennedys, and the Lees became successful members of the middle class. Their status put them ahead of other Irish Americans: for even among such second-generation Irish as District Superintendent Dr. James Lee, 17 percent of second-generation Irish worked at unskilled or semiskilled jobs.

What marked the difference between the Lee and the Kennedy families was the New York family's stress on education and financial success versus the political involvement of the Boston dynasty. Rose and Joe both were children of ward bosses, and Joe would say of his own offspring, "None of my sons gives a damn about business, that's for sure."

And that difference in focus underlined the contrast between the families of the Lees, Auchinclosses, and Bouviers and members of the Kennedy clan. The former wished to thrive in privacy, while the Kennedys would broadcast even their most personal milestones.

Forty years later, when the families met, how could there not have been a cataclysmic clash?

Chapter 2

NEWPORT
SUMMERS

Hugh Dudley Auchincloss Jr. — the name given at his birth would say a great deal about his character: stodgy, yes; old-fashioned, yes; but also cliff-rock solid. The nickname Hugh-die would be his for life, an affectionate sobriquet used by all three of his wives as well as by men with such industrial-strength surnames as Rockefeller and Vanderbilt. He came into his exceptionally privileged world at 103 Washington Street in Newport, Rhode Island, on August 28, 1897. The winter residence of this fragment of the large Auchincloss clan was New York City, and by late September infant Hughdie was back in Manhattan with his family. Janet had not yet been born, although that same year young Jack Bouvier, six years old, was living across the Hudson River in middle-class Nutley, New Jersey. But whereas the Bouviers would soon be summering in rented houses in East Hampton, by the time Hughdie was born, construction was beginning on a fairy-tale country home called Hammersmith Farm.

Hughdie's father, Hugh Sr., born in 1858, had taken every

advantage of what the prosperous Auchincloss family had provided him and had also put to good use connections in their rarefied East Coast Protestant extended circle, which was growing in size and importance. Upon graduation from Yale College in 1879, he chose to take not the gentleman's tour of Europe but instead—showing the love of country that is second nature to this family—a hunting trip out West, to the pioneer land of Colorado. After returning, he joined the cotton buyers Muir and Duckerworth in Savannah, Georgia. This career move was no accident: his father had dispatched him to Savannah, showing an unusual insight for the era. He was providing his son firm grounding for the family dry-goods-commission business by giving him experience in a separate yet complementary company. After two years in Savannah, Hughdie's father returned to Manhattan and was named partner in his father and uncle's firm John and Hugh Auchincloss (later, Auchincloss Brothers) of New York. He was twenty-four years old.

What cemented the position in society of this Auchincloss family—and that of the generations to follow—was Hugh Sr.'s auspicious marriage in 1891, when he was thirty-three, to Emma Brewster Jennings of Fairfield, Connecticut. Miss Jennings was not only a descendant of Aaron Burr but also the daughter of Oliver B. Jennings, a partner of John D. Rockefeller and brother-in-law to William Rockefeller.

Two decades earlier, in 1870, John D. Rockefeller had abolished his original oil partnership and replaced it with the Standard Oil Company (Ohio). He fueled this new firm with $1 million, an amount of fresh capital never seen before in the United States. (A single dollar in 1870 would be worth over thirteen dollars today.) This cash guaranteed the oil company's success. Originally, Standard Oil had 10,000 shares, with each share priced at $100. Rockefeller, of course, held the most with 2,667 shares; his former partners Samuel Andrews and Henry Morrison Flagler had another 1,833 each; Stephen Harkness took 1,334 shares; and John D.'s brother William took one share fewer than Harkness's stake, at 1,333. The last 1,000 shares went to Jennings, the group's first business outsider—even though he was well known as William's brother-in-law. Jennings was able to invest $100,000 in Standard Oil because he had made a fortune in California during the gold rush of 1849: not by mining gold but by supplying prospectors with equipment and provisions.

Perhaps his daughter Emma followed in his adventurous path by marrying a man without the type of fortune held by her father. Certainly there would have been no Kennedy wedding in 1953 on the grounds of a vast estate when the wind so memorably whipped the dark-eyed bride's veil and gown if it had not been for the dowry-rich Emma. So many of the events that followed in the next century stemmed from the wealth created from those original 1,000 Standard Oil shares. With his wife's personal fortune as well as her connections, Hugh Auchincloss Sr. began weaving the core dry-goods business into a small empire that would grow to include banking, mining, manufacturing, and transportation.

Ten years before Hughdie's 1897 birth, his uncle John Winthrop Auchincloss (the middle name, with its colonial origins, came from his mother's side of the family) had begun constructing a good-sized dwelling. He surrounded it with a working farmstead and named this ninety-seven-acre property, finished in 1892, Hammersmith Farm. The twenty-eight-room house was shingled in the New England fashion, using a combination of stone, brick, and wood that turned dark brown over the years. The house had gables, dormers, and turrets, but its most distinguishing feature was the large windows with spectacular views of the rolling lawn leading to Narragansett Bay.

It was because of the fallout from a family feud that John sold Hammersmith Farm to Hughdie's father. The Auchincloss dry-goods business had risen in stature when John and Hugh's sister Sarah married James Coats, of the Scottish thread-manufacturing family J. & P. Coats, and the American company became agents of the Scottish one. However, Sarah and James wanted their son-in-law brought in as full partner to the family firm. John and Hugh said no, for the young man lacked experience. Out of pique, James withdrew his family's business association with the Auchincloss firm, an action that brought temporary instability to the company. Hugh could ride it out—after all, he had married a Jennings—but John knew that he would have to give up Hammersmith Farm, especially when the depression of the 1890s hit his Wall Street investments hard. After owning Hammersmith Farm for two years, during which time he was barely in residence, John sold it to his brother Hugh, Hughdie's father, who wanted the farm as a summer residence for his growing family.

There was no hint during its construction that, half a century later, Hammersmith Farm would become nationally famous. Although Hammersmith seemed—and still seems—impressive, the estate had tough competition from neighboring properties. For in 1880, less than a decade before construction began on Hammersmith Farm, a catalytic decision by a New York lady shaped social history: Mrs. William Backhouse Astor would summer in Newport.

Mind you, it wasn't as if Newport was unknown. Following the Civil War many New Englanders began traveling there each summer for the moderate seacoast climate. In addition, well-off families from Virginia and South Carolina had learned to appreciate Newport's sunny beaches, refreshing breezes, and low humidity. They stayed in summer hotels: Aquidneck House, Bellevue House, Whitfield's, and Ocean House. The opening of Ocean House in 1845, declared one observer, "reduced Saratoga to being a hotel while Newport was a realm."

The town's picturesque scenery also brought artists—over the years, they included Gilbert Stuart, John Singer Sargent, and John La Farge—and intellectuals such as Henry James, Julia Ward Howe, Henry Wadsworth Longfellow, Dr. Oliver Wendell Holmes, and Edith Wharton. The town's draw was so strong that one summer it attracted the gloomy Edgar Allan Poe, who, it must be noted in all fairness to the limitations of even Newport's cheerful demeanor, was apparently able to resist its charm, as he never returned.

As immense wealth was amassed from railroads, oil, and real estate during the Industrial Age, these riches threatened to overflow even Manhattan's possibilities. The city's wealthy—particularly the ladies—needed an outlet for their newfound lucre. And just as Philadelphians were the first to migrate to Palm Beach in the winter, New Yorkers turned to Newport for the summer.

If there had been any doubt about Newport's status, it was resolved with Mrs. Astor's decision to summer there; after all, she alone had the clout that would later enable her to establish the Four Hundred list of New York's social elect. Her self-importance was such that while at Newport during "the season," she insisted on being referred to as "*the* Mrs. Astor, Newport" to differentiate her from the other ladies in her husband's family with the same last name, a written form of address that resulted in a fracas with the U.S. Postal Service. (*The* Mrs. Astor won.) Beechwood is the name she gave her "cottage"—the proper nomenclature for a summer house, whether humble or grand.

From thinking it merely amusing, the rich came to realize that it was an absolute necessity to set up a permanent summer household in Newport. By 1900, three years after Hughdie's birth, Newport's summer estates provided half the city's tax revenue. The coveted address was Bellevue Avenue, Atlantic Ocean side. August Belmont, who represented the Rothschild interests in the United States (although he himself had converted from Judaism to Episcopalianism after his marriage to a Newport native), might have been the prototype for Veblen's theory of conspicuous consumption. The story—perhaps apocryphal, but does it matter when a tale rings this true?—goes that maids all over town tirelessly and unfavorably compared their own places of employment with Belmont's splendiferous By-the-Sea. "He keeps liveried footmen!" one parlormaid would exclaim to her mistress. "He keeps twenty servants!" another would breathlessly divulge to her envious employer. Finally, one lady grew weary of this continual litany of the maids and responded sharply, "Mr. Belmont keeps everything but the Ten Commandments!"

Where the Ten Commandments were being preached, at Newport's Episcopal Trinity Church, the parishioners were sure to have their box pews upholstered in the same shades as their liveries. Occasionally, a family would order its entire pew removed and replaced with more comfortable tapestried swivel chairs. Why should anyone be less grand at church than at home?

Newport's Gilded Age was hallmarked in 1888 by the construction of a magnificent $11 million house ($208 million today) overlooking the ocean. William K. and Alva Vanderbilt built the mansion: he, of course, was heir to the steamship and railroad fortune established by his grandfather, "Commodore" Cornelius Vanderbilt. Tons and tons of gleaming white marble traveled by ship from Italy to Newport's deep, sheltered Narragansett Bay, where it was unloaded and hauled from the dock to Bellevue Avenue. As the mansion was being built, high fences hid it from view; its construction team, nearly all European men with specialized skills and artistry, were kept sequestered from townspeople so that they could disclose no detail of its grandeur before the dramatic unveiling. A brigade of Chinese artisans traveled all the way to Newport to construct a red-and-gold lacquered teahouse on the lawn of Marble House, facing the ocean. Unfortunately, the equipment necessary to make tea was forgotten in the teahouse's design; the only solution was to build a miniature railroad from Marble House's pantry to the teahouse to bring liveried footmen jammed into tiny cars, holding silver platters with teapots above their heads as they traversed the great lawn.

In the period from 1890 to 1914, the William Vanderbilts set the pace for those who aspired to lead society, and everyone rose to meet the standard or—sometimes—raise the bar. The Cornelius Vanderbilts, William's own brother and sister-in-law, reached new heights, for they erected a cottage—The Breakers—that eclipsed Marble House. The Breakers' grand style was Italian Renaissance; the seventy-room house included a central Great Hall that was forty-five feet high.

Eventually, nearly a hundred splendid cottages lined Bellevue

Avenue, Ochre Point, and seagirt Ocean Drive. When ballrooms became commonplace in private Newport homes, one lady ordered her house built with two. Another cottage was constructed with three separate front entrances, making it easier to allow three carriages — later, car-loads — of guests to be disgorged simultaneously. Two hostesses boasted that they could invite a hundred guests for dinner without having to hire extra help. These cottages carried such names as Chateau-sur-Mer, The Elms, and Rosecliff. Mixing with the ocean breeze was the odor of new greenbacks.

In contrast, Hammersmith was a true working farm. This being New-port, it must be defined by what it was not. It was not built to establish the Auchinclosses' place in society, for they were far more secure than the other New York people were. Nor was it constructed to attract at-tention. After all, it faced Narragansett Bay rather than the ocean. In size and decoration, the house did not compare to such estates as Marble House. What was important about Hammersmith is that it was a home and that it became Hughdie Auchincloss's only true home, no matter how many other houses he resided in or owned.

Hammersmith Farm and Hughdie grew together; their histories min-gled. The year would not begin for Hughdie until May, when it came time to travel from his parents' New York City brownstone on East Forty-ninth Street to Hammersmith. Initially, little Hughdie journeyed contentedly with his elder sister, Esther, who had been born in 1895, and their nurse, Mary Riley. Hughdie's mother had hired Riley with the assurance that she actually had taken formal training to become a baby nurse, a fact that guaranteed the nurse's status and that of her charges among the other nannies and governesses.

One lady, a childhood contemporary of Hughdie's who had lived across the street from the Auchinclosses, remembered her mother closely observing the neighbor's household. "Mrs. Auchincloss," her mother would say, "has a *hospital-trained* nurse for little Hughdie. And when you see that nurse take little Hughdie out in his carriage, I want you to tell me exactly what she has him dressed in."

It wasn't until Hughdie was school age that he gleefully began to anticipate the magical summer place called Hammersmith Farm. By then he had a younger sister, Annie Burr Auchincloss, born in 1902 — an en-tirely different century! — five years younger than Hugh and seven years younger than Esther. Of course, there was no way that a mere Irish nurse could take care of *three* young Auchincloss scions, so a Swiss governess more befitting the elder children's higher status was assigned to Esther and Hughdie. Each May the three children traveled to Hammersmith with the two adults in charge.

In the early 1900s the trip from the Manhattan house was made in multiple stages. The long train ride north ended for the young Auchinclosses and their attendants at Wickford Junction, Rhode Island. From there, they took a several-mile-long shuttle train to Wickford Landing. Then they boarded a steamer that crossed Narragansett Bay, passed between Conanicut and Prudence Islands, and docked at the pier in Newport. Hughdie and his sisters would jump off the steamer, on the lookout for the horse-drawn Auchincloss carriage, which would take the party down Thames Street and into the countryside of Harrison Avenue. Soon a competition developed among the children as to who would be the first to cry out, as Esther would later remember exclaiming, "I see it! Hammersmith Farm!"

As they ran into the house after giving a few quick pats to the excited, barking dogs, the first smell that greeted them was not the freshwater breeze that came up over the sloping lawn into the airy deck room with its large screened windows overlooking the bay. Nor was it the southwest sea breeze, called the "sailor's delight," coming in through the dining room that signaled summer to them. Rather, it was the crisp odor of recently painted rooms, fragrant to the children, as the sharp scent ironically signified the promise of the languid summer about to begin. The young people would be greeted by the half-staff contingent that had arrived earlier to open the house and prepare it for the Auchinclosses. There would be no awkward moments for *this* family of "Where are the extra blankets?" or "This window is swollen shut!" because it was as if they had stepped onto a perfect stage set, expertly run; Hammersmith Farm seemingly operated on autopilot — seven in staff present, six still to arrive — and all for the pleasure of the five-member Auchincloss family.

As twilight segued to night, the children were tucked up into their beds. Mary Riley would bring them a bedtime snack of toast with home-grown mushrooms, cooked in butter and seasoned with a little pepper on a small gas stove conveniently located in the hallway. "So good!" Esther would remember many decades later.

Eventually, everyone settled in for the night. During the summer season, there were thirteen servants in all: besides the two for the children, there was also a French maid for Mrs. Auchincloss and a valet, John

Mahan, for Hugh Sr. and any gentleman houseguest who might be staying overnight. The valet's extra duties included waiting on table and polishing silver. There was a parlor maid for the downstairs rooms—including the deck room, parlor, dining room, and hallway. She also helped at table when there was an especially large number of guests. Two chambermaids cleaned the ten bedrooms, evenly split between the second and third floors. One worked neatening the sleeping quarters of the master and mistress on floor two, while the chambermaid assigned to floor three not only had the extra flight of stairs to climb many times a day but also was responsible for scrubbing the back hall.

A laundress kept the multilayered costumes of the era freshly washed, starched, and ironed. She had to work in the basement, keeping watch over the small range with its large pots of boiling water, into which she would drop individual items of clothing and stir them with a long stick. Another pot contained the boiling starch mixture for Mr. Auchincloss's collars and dinner shirts. The stove also heated the irons: when they were good and hot, the laundress would wrap a round cake of brown beeswax in a clean cloth and run it over the flat, hot surface of the iron before she began pressing the line-dried clothes.

For cooking the meals there were two staff: one cook to prepare meals for the five family members and another to feed the thirteen house servants. And, of course, a butler, Vincent Scully, coordinated the entire household of help and reported directly to Mrs. Auchincloss.

Hughdie's parents had high expectations for their servants; at the same time, they were considerate and thoughtful employers. The three children learned from their parents how to treat staff, and although they gave the help little attention—children being children, even in that more disciplined time—they knew that their attendants were adults and that they, definitely, were not. So there was nearly an equalizing of roles between the young Auchinclosses and those who worked for their comfort.

But the young spent no precious summer daylight hours ruminating over the ins and outs of status in the Auchincloss household. When day broke, the children were off and running. There were toys to be greeted—summer toys that stayed at Hammersmith year-round and hadn't been seen for a full eight months. Then the longing to touch and hug the beloved farm animals overwhelmed even the joy of familiar toys, now left scattered on the floor as the three ran out to the farm to greet old friends: first their own pony, then their parents' riding horses, the carriage horses, and the workhorses—even the equine inhabitants were differentiated by rank. There was also the livestock: the two teams of oxen, the sheep, the Jersey cows, and the pigs. The fowl, too, deserved some attention: guinea hens and bantam hens, geese and pigeons.

Pets were an important part of life at Hammersmith Farm. Wee lambs born in springtime followed the children, begging to be fed milk from bottles. An Irish terrier had puppies under the stable; Annie's pet piglet shadowed her as she played, and if the piglet lost track of the girl, he'd run around squealing until she reappeared, much to everyone's amusement. A white pigeon was Esther's own bird and would sit on her shoulder as she held lengthy conversations with her dolls. Rough, the English sheepdog, was beloved for his foible of running and hiding from thunderstorms. These animals were as much a part of Hammersmith as its brown shingles.

Most days the children took off for Hazard's Beach. They were driven in a pony cart when younger; when older, they were allowed to ride their bicycles to meet their best friends, Anita and Teddy Grosvenor. Hughdie and his sisters envied the Grosvenors' bright red bikes since their own were a sober dark blue to match the household conveyances (including, eventually, a dark blue open Pierce Arrow with blue leather seats and an isinglass windshield). Even after the exciting purchase of the new car, the family continued using its horse-drawn dark blue carriages, with coach- and footmen's uniforms to match.

Besides coveting his friends' bright red bikes, Hughdie also wished that his parents had ordered the family's new phone — "an oak wood box on the wall in the back hall," Esther remembered — a little earlier so that they didn't have to use the cumbersome three-digit number 307. After all, the Grosvenors had reserved their phone more promptly and were given the number 59. (The last four digits of the personal phone number of Hughdie's eldest son, currently living on the grounds of Hammersmith Farm, remain — a hundred years later — 0307.)

Other bikes — although not necessarily dark blue — were left leaning inside the garage by the gardeners who rode out from town every morning. These men were important to the household since, in addition to the vast outdoor gardens, there were six specialized greenhouses: two each for grapes and nectarines, one for orchids, and the last filled with cultivated flowers, for fragrant and colorful bouquets decorated every room in Hammersmith.

After mornings at the beach, the children would go back home for lunch, eating in a separate room from their parents, who often dined with their own friends. The food was nutritious and savory, made more tasty by the knowledge that it all—every bite—came from their own farm, for Hammersmith was self-supporting and had to bring in only such items as sugar and salt. The farm even included a windmill to bring up well water. And every glass of milk, pat of butter, and dollop of Jersey cream—so thick that it needed to be spooned from the pitcher— came from Hammersmith's own dairy. Everyone indulged in desserts after each meal: homemade crullers at breakfast and ginger cookies or corn bread with butter and molasses at lunch. On Sundays, for the large dinner that followed church, there was always ice cream churned in the bucket filled with cream and flavorings, set into crushed ice and rock salt.

After lunch—and a dreaded nap for the younger children—playtime would recommence, often with the Grosvenors, who would drive over with their German nurse in a pony cart. Or perhaps Hughdie and his sisters would go over to Roslyn, the Grosvenor house. The children played simple games in their playhouses while their nurses watched and chatted together. Fortunately, Mr. Auchincloss's new superintendent had a young son the same age as Annie, so Hughdie and Esther and their friends didn't have to include the youngest sibling in every activity. A snack was tangy yellow lemonade and sweet sugar cookies, served out- doors.

Hughdie was content to play with his doll Jackie or make a tempo- rary trade for another child's doll. Esther remembers that Hughdie "was always good and even-tempered," even if she was not. Esther was the one to get into scrapes and adventures, which were annoying to her parents but made her a heroine in the eyes of her little brother.

These children had no concept that their lives were idyllic in com- parison to others', for everybody has fears, even the offspring of the rich. Hughdie's were of the dangers pointed out by his parents and governess. First, there was the newly present threat of automobiles, which would zoom by the children's pony cart; it was a rare driver who would slow down or stop to let the children pass.

Fire was a less frequent threat, but when storms crashed along the seashore and lightning set the farm's haystacks ablaze, it seemed as though the gods were hurling thunderbolts. In case a bolt of lightning hit the combustible shingles of Hammersmith, or the oil lamps that lit the parlor and deck rooms should overturn, each third-floor bedroom had a rope ladder to be thrown out the window for quick evacuation.

Of course, Esther—always the ringleader of mischief—threw her ladder out the window one day when the children were feeling bored, in order to "practice" in case of a real fire. The experiment left Esther swinging and swaying in the wind, terrified at her own audacity. She had the good sense to hold the rope ladder taut as Hughdie descended, making a safer and easier downward climb for him.

Farms, no matter how bucolic their image or picturesque their appearance, carry their own dangers, especially for curious children. Esther and Hughdie were warned away from the "witches' house" on the property. When they were older, they realized it was the machinery in this pump house that the adults wanted them to avoid.

Other dangers proved, in time, not to be as perilous for these cosseted children as their elders had imagined. Moving pictures, which any middle- or working-class child who could coax a nickel from his or her parents could see, passed by Hughdie and his sisters completely. Their mother forbade them to see a silent picture, for she feared that the fast, flickering images might cause permanent damage to their eyes. The children's media excitement was limited to listening to Morse code come over the new "radio machine." The children had no idea what the audible dashes and dots signified, but they were awestruck, especially since they naively believed that the signals were being transmitted through "outer space."

Newport in August was especially festive, when the town was filled with spectators watching America's Cup races. To see the regatta, Hughdie's Grandmother Jennings, with Aunt Annie Burr Jennings, would visit on their yacht, *Tuscarora*. What a treat for the children to board this vessel. It was difficult to live in Newport and not love sailing, and Hughdie's father passed on his appreciation to the children by taking them fishing on his "cat boat" or out on his sailing yacht, *Katrina*. As fall approached, they'd throw out a line with several hooks and fish for mackerel off their dock. Often the family ate lobster, caught in the pots secured in the water offshore.

The bay and ocean offered Hughdie daily opportunities to swim, sail, and enjoy the sea's bounty at evening meals. The water also gave him a taste of militaristic pomp and an emotional rush of sheer patriotic thrill, for this small boy could fantasize about the adventures taking place next door at Fort Adams, which was one of the largest bastioned forts in the nation and had served as the bay's guardian since 1799. The Naval Training Station and Naval War College, which he could spot across the bay, were established in the 1880s and had served as the U.S. Naval Academy during the Civil War. At this time, it was the principal anchorage for the entire Atlantic fleet.

From his sloping lawn leading down to the sea, Hughdie could watch the battleships, white with orange trim, sail in and out of the harbor. Since any craft sailing to Newport had to pass Hammersmith, the water offered an ever-changing scene. One time Hughdie got a chance to visit aboard a warship, and the strongest memory held by this boy who loved the farm was of the naval ship's mascot: a goat, of course. And the lawn was the perfect place to retreat after the excitement of a good Fourth of July parade in town, with soldiers and sailors in formation.

Later that night, after dark, the adult males would be assigned to light the rockets and firecrackers. And the beloved world that was known to Hughdie would be illuminated briefly, only to disappear with the blink of an eye into absolute and final darkness.

These memories stayed with Hughdie when he left Hammersmith Farm for Groton, a school whose headmaster, Endicott Peabody, had become legendary since founding it in 1884. An ordained Episcopal minister from an old Boston family of some wealth, Peabody modeled his boys' school on the English public (to Americans, private) schools, with an authoritarian and hierarchical system based on uncompromising moral standards and a future duty to public service. The three-hundred-acre wooded campus, located forty miles northwest of Boston, contained a school in which conformity was praised over independence and in which its tall headmaster cast a long shadow. A few years before Hughdie arrived at Groton, another of its students, Dean Acheson, who later became Secretary of State, wrote his father of the rector, "You know he would be an awful bully if he wasn't such a terrible Christian."

Perhaps Acheson was referring to the punishment system of "boot boxing," in which a boy would be crammed into his boot locker and made to endure hours of being doubled over until let free. "Pumping" was the other sanctioned punishment; it consisted of its victim being held under an open water spigot until he was close to drowning.

The Groton environment was a shock: after all, not only had Hughdie known the comfortable life at Hammersmith Farm but—for short winter weekends away from Manhattan—his parents had a home called Dormy House on Sasco Hill in Fairfield, Connecticut, where Emma had been raised. When a change of pace was needed to escape the tedium of these three residences, the Auchinclosses would take off for Jekyll Island, off southern Georgia, where they would socialize with the Carnegies and Rockefellers.

So to Hughdie, Groton was a figurative as well as a literal dose of cold water. To Hughdie's parents, this toughening up was partly the point of sending Hughdie away to school. They worried about him, sandwiched between two sisters with no other boy in the family. Furthermore, they hoped that Groton would help him grow out of the slight stutter he had developed. His older sister, Esther, was already at Miss Porter's, in Farmington, Connecticut, where his little sister, Annie Burr, would eventually also enroll. But it was a rude awakening for Hughdie to leave his spacious sunlight-filled bedroom at Hammersmith Farm to live in a six-by-ten-foot nook with only a fabric curtain to close for privacy from the dormitory's long hallway. The warm bath drawn by his governess that had begun his day was now replaced with a communal cold shower, followed by chapel. The Groton weekday continued with academics and sports and concluded, after dinner, with another bout of chapel and a study period before lights-out.

Even though Hughdie's older first cousin and Groton alum Dr. Hugh Auchincloss arrived to walk Hughdie through his first day personally, Hughdie found Groton a difficult place, especially since a large part of its program emphasized sports and skills on the playing field. Intellectualism was considered dangerous; when the mother of another boy, Joseph Alsop, who later became a syndicated columnist, bragged of his bookishness, Peabody replied, "We'll soon knock all that out of him."

Both by inclination and by physiology, Hughdie was not good at sports. He had allergies and asthma and continually caught whatever bug was going around, ending up in the infirmary and out of class. Moreover, his rapid growth caused knee problems throughout his midteens, which often kept him out of sports. His mother, Emma, remembered, "When he was at Groton he had so much trouble with his knees that he was continually trying to catch up with his studies and he could not play football and baseball like the other boys."

When he was only sixteen years old, Hughdie lost his father from a stroke after three years of illness. The death was expected, and Peabody allowed Hughdie to travel to the Manhattan brownstone to be with his family at his father's side when Hugh Sr. died on April 13, 1913. Although Emma remained in excellent health and there were no money worries—for the estate was estimated at $1 million, or $17.4 million today—he felt strange having no father and no paternal grandfather (his grandfather had died several decades before Hughdie was born, of an apparent heart attack while on a fishing trip at the Restigouche Salmon Club of Canada) to visit him.

Emma was deeply concerned about her son being odd man out and spoke with Peabody about Hughdie's many disappointments. "This will all make for the development of his soul," Peabody responded.

It is true that Hughdie developed an instinct that was both kind and thoughtful, and he carried this with him when he enrolled at Yale University in 1916. As with Groton, Hughdie (nicknamed Houch by his fellow undergraduates) was one of a long line of Auchinclosses who attended Yale: besides his father, there were four uncles and four cousins who had preceded him and another cousin in his own class. The young men in the class of 1920, however, were both privileged to sit out World War I in an ivied classroom and also frustrated at missing out on the chance to fight in the Great War.

Hughdie did want to be prepared for the eventuality of a long war, though, and enlisted in the Naval Reserve, at Newport, in 1917. He had already been commissioned as an ensign when the Armistice was signed. He was discharged in late 1918.

While at Yale, Hughdie apparently realized that he had enjoyed Groton after all, because he became president of Yale's Groton School Club. He also joined the Sappinpaws, the University Club, Psi Upsilon, and the Elihu Club. He was not asked to join the best clubs but was a successful undergraduate and received the "second colloquy" learned discussion honor his junior year. He also had outgrown his knee problems and rowed for the class squad all four years. In addition, he had picked up a love of shooting from his father and belonged to the University Gun Club.

If his activities at Yale do not stand out, it would be hard to criticize him too harshly for being unremarkable, as his classmates were an unusually distinguished group of young men — even by Ivy League standards — who included such talent as Henry Luce, who was a member of the secret society Skull and Bones. Bones was founded in 1832; and if one organization has more status than the others, it is Bones. At this time at Yale, fellowship burned brighter than scholarship, and Hughdie must have regretted not being asked to join either Bones or its closely ranked second, Scroll and Key.

Hughdie and his classmate Luce had another thing in common besides being Yale men. They were both stutterers. Hughdie's was slight, though he would have it all his life. Luce's was severe when he was a child, but he had mostly tamed it by adulthood. So the men became casual friends, always comfortable in conversation.

Both men left for Europe for a gentleman's tour after graduation in 1920. Hughdie spent the summer traveling in France and, while in Paris, bumped into Luce, who had just arrived from Wales, where Luce had paid homage at the tomb of Elihu Yale. Hughdie needed to be back in England by October to attend King's College at Cambridge University, but he still had a month of vacation left.

Hughdie and Luce decided to travel together, and in September the men bought tickets for the Orient-Express and traveled to Constantinople. Luce took the lead as they journeyed through the Balkans, stopping at American embassies to be briefed on the political pulse of each country. In Budapest Hughdie and Luce found the hotels fully booked and asked for advice from their driver, who suggested spending the night in a bordello. Instead, the men pleaded their homelessness at the Ritz and were allowed two bathtubs as sleeping quarters.

Yale and the friendships he had made left an indelible impression on Hughdie that would influence him all his life. Of course, the college had changed greatly since his father's day and no longer stressed religion, public service, and Western literature but, rather, Wall Street. And although Hughdie wasn't conscious of his own predilections at the time, the Street is precisely where he eventually headed.

$\mathscr{C}$hapter 3

BUILDING THE
FACADE

When Hughdie was ten years old, Janet Norton Lee was born. The date was December 3, 1907. Like Hughdie, she was a middle child: she had an elder sister, Marion Merritt Lee, born in 1905; a younger sister, Margaret Winifred (Winnie) Lee, born in 1913. When the girls were young, Margaret and Jim lived at 669 West End Avenue near Ninety-third Street in a pleasant row house. However, the family would not stay at this address for long. Jim's aspirations were clear: the law was not to be his life's profession but rather the foundation for his chief business interest, real estate development. Jim's commercial enterprises would shape Janet's life — not directly, for she was never interested in business, but rather because they ingrained in her a subtle belief that a man's worth is measured by his worldly success.

Her father set a high standard that Janet expected other men in her life to meet. Yet, unlike real-estate developers of a later era, Jim reached a remarkable level of attainment without feeling the need to showboat. This attorney with no money of his own showed toughness, intelligence, and independence by his spectacular move into real estate. Even as a young man, he commanded respect. At home, he was "the family patriarch," according to his granddaughter Mary-Lee (Mimi) Ryan Cecil. Certainly no one except family or close friends called him Jim Lee. To others in business, he was always referred to by his full first and last names and his middle initial. Men in the city would call his office and ask for "Mr. James *T.* Lee."

Opportunity abounded for ambitious men at the turn of the century, and Jim took full advantage. New York City was not a unified political entity until 1898, when the five boroughs were consolidated into one enormous municipality. Until its "H" system opened in 1918, taking its name from the shape of the routes imposed on Manhattan, the city had no interconnecting subway line. According to stories Jim told about his exploits, he had kept his ear to the ground in the early 1900s for news of potential realty investments. When he heard of a proposed Seventh Avenue subway, he invested in land along its route. When news of the subway became public, he flipped these parcels for high profits, which he then invested in stocks that eventually were valued at $2 million ($36.5 million today). But his thirtieth birthday was an unpleasant wake-up call regarding the transitory nature of paper profits: he lost everything in the panic of 1907.

Jim was thrifty—how else could a young man with a new law practice have bought land along Seventh Avenue?—and his family had always lived well below their means. He had structured his household so that when the millions disappeared, the Lees' day-to-day living was not affected in the slightest. Jim himself was stoic about his losses and soldiered on.

By the time Janet was a toddler, Jim had become a partner with another lawyer, Charles R. Fleischmann, in the firm Lee & Fleischmann. Their first real-estate project was the twelve-story Peter Stuyvesant apartment house at Ninety-eighth Street and Riverside Drive. Later, their partnership became Century Holding Company (the word *century* was as widely used in the early 1900s as *millennium* would be a hundred years later). By 1910, just three years after losing his shirt, Jim would take a gamble on a new concept.

Starting in the 1890s, a building boom had begun in Manhattan's midtown area. (This was the same time that summer mansions lined Newport's Bellevue Avenue and that Hammersmith Farm, on the opposite side of the island, was constructed.) Ambitious men were looking toward real estate to make their mark. They knew that such industrialists as copper magnate Guggenheim and oil tycoon Rockefeller, and such retailers as F. W. Woolworth, were putting up palatial dwellings in Manhattan to house their families. It was fashionable to move north to live along Central Park on Fifth Avenue. Soon the area was dubbed Millionaire's Row.

Men with lesser fortunes followed suit. Smaller town houses—built for the merely well-off—were going up on the numbered streets off Fifth, as far east as Lexington Avenue, stopping before Third Avenue to avoid the El, the noisy elevated train system that ran up Third.

Canny Jim Lee would have had to wear blinders like the horses pulling carriages along Fifth Avenue not to have seen a new world being constructed before his eyes. But his vision was unencumbered: he saw rickety three-story frame row houses, each one identical to the next, on Fifth Avenue at Eighty-first Street, and envisioned in their place a great luxury tower. He ordered the row houses torn down to make way for a sumptuous apartment house. This was the first important building in which his partnership invested: the address was 998 Fifth Avenue, facing Central Park. Others were taking advantage of Manhattan's growth, too, but many of them were speculators who put up poorly designed and shoddily constructed buildings. Jim built his structures to last. The building at 998 Fifth was the first of three great towers Jim developed during his career.

The residence was to appeal to families who were living farther downtown in large brick houses. At the time, it was considered déclassé to live under the same roof as others, even those of one's own kind; buildings that housed multiple families were associated with the tenement houses and railroad flats of the Lower East Side. The wealthy stubbornly adhered to their mansions; those of middle income clung to their row houses. Apartment buildings were not yet socially acceptable; indeed, fifty years earlier it would have been scandalous even in a private home to put a bedroom on the same floor as a parlor.

Manhattan's very first "apartment house" (the phrase was not even coined until the 1870s) didn't go up until 1869—for how could there be apartment buildings before a new invention called the elevator was accepted by the general population? Builders, too, were reluctant to accept such new inventions as steam-powered cranes (boom derricks) to hoist the steel needed for these towers.

Many of the rich did not desire luxury apartment houses—not until
Jim Lee became involved, that is. In 1910 he hired the world-renowned
firm McKim, Mead & White to design a floor plan for 998 Fifth. (Stanford
White, of course, had been dead for four years, shot by Harry K.
Thaw in a great scandal of the day.) The twelve-story building was built
around a court: single-floor apartments, each taking three-quarters of
one whole floor, looked out on Fifth Avenue. The duplexes, which were
joined by combining the remaining quarters of two floors, faced Eighty-
first Street.

The apartments were huge. One entered a foyer that led to a reception
room, which was fourteen feet by thirty-six feet. From there, one could
go into the salon, dining room, or living room—the living room alone
measured twenty-one feet by twenty-four feet. The other rooms were the
pantry, kitchen, four bedrooms, and six servants' chambers. The master
bedroom was eighteen feet by nineteen feet; the far smaller servants'
quarters were purposely isolated in a different section of the apartment
to maintain the "upstairs, downstairs" tradition. Additional servants'
quarters were available up on the roof, in the event that a family had
more than six live-in staff.

The building's basement held generators in case the New York Edison
Company lines should be unreliable. Each floor had mechanical ventilation and a central vacuum-cleaning system. Jewel and silver safes were
set inside the walls.

Despite these new amenities, 998 Fifth was slow to catch on with the
upper class when it was completed in 1912. Its rental agent conceived a
notion: if one well-known man moved in, then others would follow suit.
He offered a special deal to Elihu Root, then the Republican U.S. senator
representing New York who had been Secretary of War and Secretary
of State. Root, who was living in midtown in a large brick mansion, had
recently been in the news because he had been awarded the Nobel Peace
Prize for his services as president of the Carnegie Endowment for International Peace. To entice Root to move into Jim's new building, he
was offered a year's rental of $15,000 ($260,000 today) instead of the
going rate of $25,000 ($435,000 today). For this price, Root was given
a special several-unit combination apartment composed of twenty-two
rooms and eight baths. The gimmick was New York's first rental "loss
leader" and attracted such other tenants as the Guggenheims and the
Vanderbilts, who were having difficulty finding enough staff to maintain
their elegant midtown mansions and who were stunned by the imposition
of an income tax.

Jim's first large-scale venture was thereafter a great success. The Italian Renaissance–style building—designated "the finest" in New York City in 1974 by the Landmarks Preservation Committee—remains one of Manhattan's best addresses. Now it is a cooperative, and in 2000 its sixth-floor apartment sold for just over $16 million. The building also set the pace for other Fifth Avenue builders of the 1920s and helped change the social structure of Manhattan by making apartment living acceptable. In time, the growing propensity of the well-off to live in city apartments helped kick off the custom of a house in the country for weekends.

Only a tenacious outsider like Jim Lee would have had the gumption to buck the commonly held belief that wealthy families would never agree to live under the same roof with others. Manhattan's future growth and social structure could never be attributed solely to one builder, but if it were, Jim Lee is as strong a candidate as any.

A few years later Jim put up a troika of commercial buildings around Grand Central Terminal. One was the Berkeley Building at 19 West Forty-fourth Street, down the street from the Algonquin Hotel (later famed for its literary circle) and the Harvard Club, and across the street from the Penn Club. By 1913 Jim had also developed the Century Building at 25 West Forty-fifth Street.

As Jim concentrated on building a career, he found that he gained greater pleasure from making deals than from the details involved in his law practice. He was such a success as a builder that by 1916 he had withdrawn from the law to devote his full energy to real estate. He focused on putting up the National Association Building at 25 West Forty-third Street, which was twenty stories tall and housed Lee's company. Its striking detail was that it receded at the thirteenth and eighteenth floors, making for a truncated pyramidal building. This building was one block from the new traffic light installed in 1920—the first in the city—which had become a tourist destination in its own right. The light went up at Forty-second Street and Fifth Avenue, shortly before Lee finished the Forty-third Street building.

As the threatening war turned into reality, the Lees acted to support the country. Jim's father led Liberty Loan drives and signed up for special training to recertify himself in emergency medical procedures—just in case the talents of a sixty-four-year-old man were needed locally or overseas.

Jim, too, was a strong believer in self-improvement, whether financial or intellectual, and at the war's end he felt it time to improve his physique. He hired a personal trainer—this, in the early 1920s—to come to his office each afternoon and teach him to box. He was also president for seven years of the New York branch of his college fraternity, Delta Kappa Epsilon, whose nationwide members included several U.S. Presidents and Supreme Court justices. He kept up his membership in the Academy of Political Science and enjoyed staying current with trends in political thought.

Jim, like other developers, took advantage of the midtown Grand Central Terminal having buried its train tracks under Park Avenue soon after the beginning of the century. With the trains underground, the wide avenue with its green median strip was now convenient for residential development. Here men put up tall (usually fifteen stories), solidly built apartment houses, some on buried supports over pavement that formed a ceiling for the underground train tracks. Jim built here, too, and in 1922 constructed 420 Park Avenue, between Fifty-fifth and Fifty-sixth Streets. He moved his family from the West Side that same year, when Janet was fifteen years old, and ensconced them in 750 Park Avenue, in one of the building's duplex apartments.

In 1923 *The New York Times* estimated the wealth of James T. Lee at $23 million (those were inflated, pre-Depression dollars) and called his buildings part of "the new social power of New York." In keeping with this newfound status, that year Margaret rented a summer house for herself and the girls on Jones Road in East Hampton, Long Island. By 1925 Jim was joining them: Margaret would take their daughters to stay in East Hampton for the season; Jim would drive out for weekends and occasional short vacations. Again, this annual sojourn to the Hamptons was another sign of how far the family had distanced itself from Margaret's childhood in the tenements of the Lower East Side.

When Jim was back in Manhattan, he founded a second real-estate development firm, called the Shelton Holding Company, in anticipation of a building he would call the Shelton Hotel, located between Forty-eighth and Forty-ninth Streets on Lexington Avenue. It was completed in 1924. This important project, designed by Arthur Loomis Harmon, is now the New York Marriott East Side. Jim had once again anticipated social change and built for the upcoming shift in community norms.

In the case of the Shelton, Jim saw that for the first time young unmarried adults were moving out of their parents' houses to live alone. In order to maintain propriety—for how could unrelated single men and

women live together under one roof respectably? — separate residential
hotels were constructed for each sex. The Barbizon later flourished as a
residence for women; however, the Shelton Hotel, Jim's bachelor lodging house for men, was less successful.

There were vacancies at the Shelton because of Jim's ill-conceived
notion of a men-only building. However, these empty apartments gave
him a chance to talk his ailing father into moving into the hotel. Jim's
mother, Mary, had died a few years earlier, and his father had married
Margaret A. Gubbins. In 1923, at age seventy-one, James retired as
district superintendent. Jim used the excuse of needing tenants to convince his father and stepmother to move to the Shelton, although his
real purpose was to keep an eye on his father's health.

Within a year, the Shelton's twelve hundred rooms were open to both
sexes. In fact, artist Georgia O'Keeffe and her photographer husband,
Alfred Stieglitz, moved into a top-floor suite in 1926, and in the next
three years O'Keeffe would paint fifteen cityscapes of their balcony view.
Stieglitz took advantage of the site, too, and his photograph *From the
Shelton, Looking Northwest* shows the partly built Waldorf-Astoria Hotel.

However misguided Jim's original thought that unmarried men would
flock to a separate dwelling, the hotel as a structure was a great success.
The Shelton — Jim's second outstanding building — was the first post—
world war skyscraper and the tallest hotel in the world at thirty-four
stories. And, unlike other skyscrapers that were designed with an eye
toward minimizing size, the Shelton's architect celebrated its height by
accentuating it, bulging out the structure as it rose higher. Harmon
added wonderful gargoyles that looked as if they were protecting their
huge edifice. In fact, one of O'Keeffe's works, *The Shelton with Sunspots*,
emphasizes the hulking mass that characterized the building.

The Shelton's design — which won several top prizes for its architect —
was a transition from classical allusions to anticipating the lines of Art
Deco soon to be engraved on skyscrapers throughout Manhattan. Most
important, the building jump-started Lexington Avenue as an area for
moderately priced midtown hotels, as it was the first major midtown
building following the city's 1916 zoning changes.

Nineteen twenty-six was a boom year for bank building, and Jim got
in on that game as well. All the money being made on Wall Street had
to be deposited somewhere; new banks were going up north and south,
east and west. Century built the ten-story Farmer's Loan and Trust Company at the southeast corner of Fifth Avenue and Forty-first Street,
across the street from the New York Public Library. Perhaps the bank's

location was prescient of the depression looming ahead; it had been the site of a rocky precipice on which General George Washington watched the retreat of his army after the disaster of the Battle of Long Island. (It was also a block from the Colored Orphan Asylum, which burned to the ground during the draft riots of 1863. Although more than one hundred New Yorkers were murdered by mobs — composed mostly of Irish immigrants, perhaps some who had arrived in America on the same ship as Thomas and Fanny Lee — all but one of the two hundred orphaned children and their matrons were evacuated to safety to a nearby police precinct before the rioters torched their home.)

Jim made a pivotal decision in 1926, joining the Chase National Bank as its real-estate adviser. As a real-estate developer and a banker, he never wasted time mulling over possible mistakes. He stated his philosophy: "Better a bad decision today than a good one three weeks late."

As part of his work for Chase, he developed its bank building at 20 Pine Street, at the intersection of Nassau Street. Once again he backed an unusual design; each story at 20 Pine Street was its own rectangular box, and the stories became smaller as the building rose. In 1928 Jim was named to Chase's board of directors and by 1929 was elected senior vice president. (Many decades later, in 1961, he helped plan Chase's location at 1 Chase Manhattan Plaza.)

Jim also built One Gracie Square in 1926, hiring Rosario Candela, an architect who would become one of Manhattan's legendary talents because of his buildings' diagonal and broad views. That year Jim also purchased several plots of land, one facing the Shelton on Lexington Avenue and one a block down from the hotel.

Meanwhile, Jim was developing a magnificent bank building, which was completed the same year as One Gracie Square. The Central Savings Bank — until 1918 it was called the German Savings Bank, and ultimately became Apple Bank for Savings — was a Florentine palace built on Broadway between Seventy-third and Seventy-fourth Streets. Its architects, who had built the city's Federal Reserve Bank of similar design, conceived a trapezoidal building to take advantage of the avenue's diagonal thrust. Although some of its interior has been reshaped over the decades, the office of its president remains the same — an elaborate replica of a room within the Pitti Palace, the fifteenth-century grand ducal residence in Florence.

Just before the Depression hit, Jim finished an apartment house that would stay in first place throughout the entire twentieth century and into the next millennium. The seventeen-story building — 740 Park Avenue, at Seventy-first Street—was the ultimate in extravagance for the time. Nearly all the apartments at 740 Park were duplexes; the one rented by John D. Rockefeller Jr. was a *triplex of ninety rooms!* (Now the building is a cooperative and, in 2000 the *roi* of the *riches*, Saul Steinberg, sold his thirty-four-room apartment, formerly part of Rockefeller's home, for $37.5 million, the highest price ever in the city's history.) Its architect, Rosario Candela, designed buildings that "were the grandest of the decade that was itself the greatest," according to architecture historian Elizabeth Hawes. Candela's limestone facade and granite entrance merely hinted at the beginnings of Art Deco style, as Jim realized that no one living on the East Side would want their gracious building to resemble a modernistic West Side structure. This was Jim's third great building.

So James T. Lee was, in the vernacular of the day, a big noise. By the end of his career he would have put up more than two hundred residential and commercial buildings. Although his name is generally unknown today, his works were never transitory. Manhattan's most socially acceptable residences of their day, built by James T. Lee, still stand as some of the city's best addresses.

As Janet and her sisters grew, Jim was busy and out of the house much of the time. After all, someone had to build Manhattan. Margaret established a life separate from Jim's—she rarely saw him at home—and the diversion she loved best was playing the ponies. The care of Janet and her sisters fell to the help, who went along with Jim and Margaret's unwise characterization of their daughters: Marion was the smart one; Janet, the pretty one; and poor Winnie was known as the "dumb" one because her schoolwork wasn't at her sisters' level.

Despite, or perhaps because of, Jim's absences during long workdays, he was nearly mythic to his middle daughter. Most young children are impressed by their fathers' importance: when they're older, they understand their actual statures. Janet was a typical child in this regard. She idolized the father whose time with her was limited. And when he did arrive home, she had to share him with her two sisters.

Jim, unfortunately, lacked the ability to shrug off his hard-driving personality as easily as he did his overcoat when he stepped through the front door of his home. He was no softer at home than at the office in the National Association Building, demanding the same high performance from his daughters as he did from himself. Another wife might have been able to moderate his unrelenting personality, but the couple's differences were so great that Margaret, by nature a whimsical free spirit, withdrew. Because Jim saw himself as the one best suited to shape his girls' characters, Margaret's position in the family became almost ancillary. As a result, the girls — especially Janet — perceived that their mother, their natural role model, was marginal. And if she counted for little, how could they ever measure up to their father? Janet felt inadequate; her father's accomplishments in both academics and business convinced her that she could never be his equal. No matter how hard she tried to please him, Jim acknowledged her efforts sparingly. Later, Janet's son would say that his mother was "desperate for her father's goodwill — she never knew what she could do."

The frequent visits of Janet's aunts also blocked her from her father's attention and approval. Four of her five aunts were still unmarried, and they would sit and listen, wide-eyed, to stories of their brother's latest success. Jim took their vicarious admiration as his due. Surrounded by women — five sisters, three daughters, and a wife, not to mention three female servants — Jim became increasingly confident in his abilities and the correctness of his opinions, which he didn't hesitate to voice. As his wealth increased, so did his self-satisfaction.

Jim did not seem to comprehend how his sisters were undermining his marriage. He was their big brother and was all theirs, the sisters thought. As a result, they caused Margaret "sixty-six fits," according to Mimi Cecil, and she resented their ham-handed involvement in her family life. The women's presence widened the gap between her and Jim. But Margaret was outnumbered.

When the girls grew old enough to see what was going on, they disliked their aunts, too. Years later Janet would tell her children that she "hated" her aunts, according to her son, Jamie. "She didn't like them at all," confirmed Mimi Cecil, whose mother, Marion, felt the same way about the women.

If the aunts' goal was to drive a wedge between husband and wife, they were successful. By the time Janet was fifteen, her mother and father had stopped talking to each other. Literally. Instead, the couple used the two elder children as go-betweens: when they would eat together as a "family," Jim would say, "Marion, please ask your mother to pass the salt."

Marion then would have to ask, "Mother, may Father have the salt?" And Margaret would hand the shaker to Marion, who would give it to Jim.

Jim and Margaret would not divorce, they said, until the girls married. Perhaps they secretly enjoyed this emotional pugilism and liked making each other miserable. But memories of the toxic air at these mealtimes stayed with Janet all her life, and she never forgave her parents for turning their daughters into pawns. It was particularly painful for the sisters when their girlfriends came to visit. The pride that Janet felt in living in a wonderful duplex at 750 Park Avenue—across the avenue from her father's luxurious 740 Park—was undermined by the embarrassing conflict between her parents. What made it worse was that her father moved into a bedroom on the lower floor so that he could avoid her mother except at meals. Janet and her sisters lived on the upper level with their mother.

Nevertheless, the experience toughened Janet. She learned to mimic her father's style: she never minced words or opinions, which was an unusual trait for a girl of that time. She did pick up something important from her mother, which was a love of horses. The difference between Margaret's childhood and Janet's, though, was that Janet's father could afford to give her riding lessons in Central Park. All three girls learned to ride astride rather than sidesaddle, which was progressive for girls in that decade. Janet, who was more athletic than her sisters, took to it naturally. (In the same year that ten-year-old Janet Lee was riding in Central Park, a baby named John F. Kennedy—who would become her son-in-law—was born in Brookline, Massachusetts.)

Janet and her sisters soon entered the Spence School, a day school for girls, then located in midtown on West Forty-eighth Street. Janet learned a classical curriculum and imbibed Spence's values of strength of character and spirit. She already spoke French wonderfully, thanks to the French governess who had taken care of her and her sisters since Marion's birth.

Janet's most important extracurricular activity was riding, and she took advantage of Central Park to improve her skill. But she also picked up the social niceties from her mother, who, for example, enrolled her daughters in dancing lessons at the Plaza Hotel. Janet was as successful at flirting as at riding and was remembered as the belle of the ball at the pre-debutante classes of Miss Robinson.

To Janet's displeasure, in 1920 yet another female relative was added to the mix of sisters and aunts who were always dropping by. A few years after Janet's grandfather Thomas Merritt died, her maternal grandmother, Maria, moved in with the Lee family. Teenage Janet felt that the last thing she needed was another woman in the house, especially one with such old-world ways. Janet's circle of girlfriends from Spence and the young people she was meeting at equestrian events giggled to one another when they realized that the coarse old lady dressed in black with an Irish brogue was actually Janet's *grandmother*. How awful for her!

Having spent her entire life working hard, Grandmother Maria didn't know how to stop. Unfortunately, "helping out" did not ingratiate her to the household. Despite there being three staff, Maria insisted on doing whatever housework she could, and her daughter encouraged it: perhaps she figured this served the double purpose of keeping her mother occupied and lightening the staff load. Others were more critical: Janet's nephew John Davis said that the family used her as an unpaid servant.

Jim hardly noticed his mother-in-law; such nuances of family life escaped him. Besides, he felt that his duty toward her ended with his financial support. So as this upwardly mobile family went about their increasingly swank activities — Janet, riding; Margaret, off at the track with friends; and Jim, making a name for himself in real estate — Maria was left at home, sequestered in her room or doing chores side by side with the help.

The old woman must have sensed that she was out of place. Although Jim did not object to his wife's mother living with the family, her companionship was another thing. She had little in common with them. So she stayed hidden when guests were in the house. Only occasionally would a visitor catch a glimpse of an old lady in black, head down, quickly scuttling out of view.

$\mathscr{C}$hapter 4

THE BLACK SHEIK

Janet walked into the Lees' living room of their Park Avenue apartment to greet her date, Jack Bouvier.

"Who was that woman?" asked Jack as a black-clad crone scurried from the room.

"Oh," Janet replied, "I guess it was the maid."

The relationship between Janet Lee and Jack Bouvier, the man who would be her first husband and the father of their daughters, Jackie and Lee, was counterfeit from the beginning. However unkind the young, insecure Janet's disavowal of her grandmother Merritt, it pales in comparison with Jack's later brazen infidelities. Their courtship started off on a false note, and the relationship remained corrupt throughout their lives.

But none of that was immediately apparent to an interested bystander or even to family members, with the possible exception of Janet's father. True, Jack Bouvier had a reputation as a ladies' man, but Janet, in a naive way that was not surprising for a woman just out of her teens and still living at home, thought that his interest in her was a testament to her femininity and charm. She was only twenty years old, after all, and Jack was thirty-six, with an apartment at 375 Park Avenue, nineteen blocks down from her family's, and an East Hampton summer home his parents owned. (The Bouviers' twelve-acre estate, Lasata, a word from the Shinnecock tribe meaning "place of peace," was legendary for its opulence.)

Jack's initial interest in this vivacious twenty-year-old was understandable. Although no great beauty, she was a pretty girl with a well-toned body and flashing dark eyes and auburn hair. The force of her personality camouflaged her nose, which was too long, and her chin, which was slightly sharp. Although she had a quick tongue and didn't hesitate to use it, Janet could also use her verbal skills to flatter a man and make him feel as if he were the most important person on earth. A narcissist like Jack Bouvier was sure to be attracted to her.

Certainly Jack's family lineage appealed to Janet. His grandfather, the first John Vernou Bouvier, had excelled as a stockbroker and was accepted by the best of families, having been listed in the first national social register in 1889. Jack's father, John Vernou Bouvier Jr., was a hardworking, successful attorney whom future U.S. Supreme Court Associate Justice Benjamin Cardozo termed "one of the ablest and most brilliant lawyers in the state of New York."

Unfortunately, Jack inherited little of his father's intellect. One friend of the family, Letitia (Tish) Baldrige, commented bluntly that "Jack Bouvier had an IQ of zero." In addition, he was devoid of ambition. He felt that life should be about enjoying himself while looking terrific. His clothes were tailor-made to his preferred European style. He eschewed the tweeds worn by other Ivy Leaguers. There was another, more subtle difference between his clothing and other men's, and that was the sensuous note he added to his dress: the silk handkerchief in his jacket pocket; the patent-leather opera pumps worn during the day, sans socks; and the tightly cinched waist.

Jack was well aware of the handsome dark looks that gave him the nickname Black Jack. This moniker was originally coined for General John J. Pershing—the dashing commander of the Buffalo Soldiers—who had led the African American cavalry regiments through skirmishes out West and in San Juan. Black Jack Pershing sported a mustache and sat tall on his horse, wearing custom-made black leather

E. Vogel riding boots; Jack Bouvier did not mind sharing his leader's nickname.

An additional tag for Jack, in double reference to his dark complexion and his reputation with women, was the Black Sheik. Another was the Black Orchid. The message was clear, but rather than being embarrassed by these monikers, Jack was proud of them.

"Style is not a function of how rich you are or even who you are," he would say. "Style is a habit of mind that puts quality before quantity, noble struggle before mere achievement, honor before opulence. It's what you are. It's your essential self. It's what makes you a Bouvier."

Was this philosophy archly humorous or self-deluded? Certainly Jack was shallow, self-centered, and frivolous. And to fuel his quest for "quality," he needed money. Envying his enormously wealthy great-uncle Michel Bouvier, he probably wished his father had a little less learning and a little more green stuff. He may also have been sensitive about his flimsy accomplishments (inevitably compared with his father's precedent-setting legal cases) and understood how deficient in substance he seemed. Perhaps his frivolities were a reaction to an authentic sense of inferiority. But Jack's mother encouraged his indulgences and sense of entitlement. She was as soft as his father was sober. This sweet-natured lady did not help build her eldest son's character but, rather, unknowingly undermined it.

Jack, whose nickname at Yale University was Bove, graduated in 1914 without distinction. "Instead of studying, he threw parties," said his niece Kathleen Bouvier. Yale's yearbook squib makes reference to Jack's obsessive interest in clothing: "As proper a man as ever trod upon neat's leather." Jack belonged to the Book and Snake Society and to the Cloister Club, neither of them top social organizations. He did graduate—although a year older than his classmates and at the bottom of his class—four years before another Yalie, Hughdie Auchincloss.

Cole Porter was a classmate of Jack's, and the composer was said to have been quite taken by Jack's good looks. Porter had met Jack through the university's Glee Club. The men were members along with Dean Acheson (later Secretary of State) and Averell Harriman (later governor of New York and ambassador to the USSR, as well as a political mentor to Jack Kennedy). Porter and Bouvier were to remain friends for life.

After Yale, Jack joined his brother-in-law's brokerage firm. Then war broke out and Jack left the brokerage in 1917, when he joined the U.S. Navy. That was too tough for him; he managed to get himself transferred over to the army. He himself wrote that he had fought his "toughest battles in the smoke-filled honky-tonk back alleys and brothels of North and South Carolina, waiting for this dirty little war to end."

Jack flaunted his shabby behavior during a war that claimed the lives of 10 million men and disabled 20 million more. While Jack was hanging out in back alleys and brothels, his father, on the other hand, was commissioned as a major in the army's Judge Advocate General's Office.

At his discharge in 1919, Jack took a position as a Wall Street stockbroker, buying a seat on the New York Stock Exchange for about $115,000 (about a million dollars today) with loans from Uncle Michel. With his family connections, he did well. After all, the Bouviers had by then intermarried with such old-line families as the Drexels, the Ewings, and the Sergeants, which augmented the Bouvier wealth but helped dilute Jack's French heritage. Jack's grandmother, the former Caroline Ewing, was honorary president of the New York Foundling Hospital, which came to be known for its care of unwed mothers and abandoned babies. (In fact, its mission of placing babies in foster homes resulted in the well-known "orphan trains" that were begun in 1854 and lasted until 1930. This effort to find good homes for thousands of immigrant children who lacked responsible parents — on the recommendation of a parish priest, a child would be sent west with an accompanying nun via train to be raised by a Catholic family — was generally considered a success.) In Manhattan, Jack was a member of the Racquet and Tennis Club, the Sons of the Revolution (through the Ewing line), and the Yale and University Clubs. Life was full of promise.

Jack first became engaged in 1920 to Miss Eleanor Carroll Daingerfield Carter of Baltimore. Her name references her descent from the Carrolls after whom Carroll County, Maryland, was named and also from the Carter family of Virginia. (Carter's Grove near Williamsburg is open to the public and remains one of the state's most impressive estates, originally comprising 300,000 acres and, 150 years later, some 1,000 slaves.) Miss Carter's father was a diplomat, and her first cousin was Lady Acheson of England.

It is said that Jack was gun-shy and couldn't face the responsibility of marriage. Or perhaps Miss Carter — or possibly her parents — decided she could do better. In any case, the engagement was broken, and Jack seemed none the worse for wear. At the time, Jack's failed relationship had no impact on Janet: he was twenty-nine, and she was only thirteen years old.

During the early part of the century, the Hamptons were becoming solidly established as *the* place for New Yorkers to summer. A traveler
would voyage due east from Manhattan to Westhampton, the town that
begins the Hamptons. Next would come Quogue, Hampton Bays, Southampton, Bridgehampton, East Hampton — a hundred miles from Manhattan — Amagansett, and Montauk. The long trip and paucity of resort
amenities kept the Hamptons from becoming popular until a railroad
was laid in 1844, although it was possible to travel overnight by packet
boat or in a three-passenger stagecoach. Among the first to discover the
pastoral Hamptons, in the 1870s, were the artists Winslow Homer, William Merritt Chase, and Childe Hassam, causing *Lippincott* magazine to
dub it "the American Barbizon," in reference to the French artists'
colony.

The chief colony became East Hampton, sought initially because it
was beyond the reach of the railroad, which traveled east only as far as
Bridgehampton. One 1868 guidebook mentions East Hampton as a
"place where the blasé tourist won't find all the parvenus"; five years
later the first summer home was put up. By 1895 the train line had made
it to East Hampton, whose residents caviled, "Soon the shriek of the
locomotive will wake the Rip Van Winkle slumber of the past." It surely
woke up local farmers, who began to ship their white potatoes, grown
on some of the East Coast's most fertile soil, into the city.

But it wasn't until a tunnel opened under Manhattan's East River
that travelers could make the trip in one phase rather than having to
ferry from Thirty-fourth Street across the river to Long Island to catch
the train. The shorter travel time increased the number of summer residents, who, in turn, superimposed a playground of beaches and ponds
on Long Island's farms and fields. Until the end of the century, most
men worked six days a week — the five-day workweek would need to be
established before there could be weekend retreats for the middle class.
The families who sought a quiet summer haven were those of prosperous
men who could spend weekends or even the whole summer in the Hamptons.

Then, too, in the Hamptons there was little lodging for transients —
unlike Newport, for example — so one had to be well-off to rent or buy
a summer home. Also unlike Newport, there is no sheltered bay on which
to sail: East Hampton faces the Atlantic Ocean, where it is more difficult
to manage a small boat. Fishing, too, is poor. So the key interests that
remained were golf, tennis, swimming, and riding.

As taller buildings were going up in Manhattan, built by such men as James T. Lee, East Hampton's homelike ambience was especially alluring to city dwellers. The houses had a cozy cottage appeal: brown-shingled or clapboard saltboxes, built in shambling American style, with long roofs sloping from two stories in back to one story in front. Rose-bushes covered white picket fences, and elms stood tall over the spacious yards. Hook Windmill, built in 1805, still sits in town, which is also the location of the big white church — where in the 1600s Goody Garlick was tried as a witch — that still receives worshipers. So the picturesque town enticed city dwellers.

While Jack Bouvier was working on the Street in the early 1920s and Janet had been living in her parents' new duplex on Park Avenue for only a few years, Jim Lee started to set down roots in East Hampton for the summer season. The Lees took an immediate liking to the colony. The girls, first Marion and then Janet, were given for their birthdays new cars that blasted distinctive horn melodies, and they enjoyed driving their friends around the Hamptons. Jim Lee was no pushover, though; when Marion insisted on having her own car, he told her that she would need to know how cars functioned before he would buy her one. Marion promptly retired to the garage in East Hampton and began dismantling her father's Rolls-Royce. Fortunately, in the summer Jim always took the train into the city, and by season's end, she had successfully replaced the Rolls's inner workings. Jim made good on his word, and she got her car. He had also learned a lesson and did not make the same demand of Janet.

Janet had graduated from the Spence School in 1925 in its college-preparatory program. The commencement was held at the Waldorf-Astoria Hotel. She debuted at a dinner dance the Lees gave at Sherry's, a well-known supper club. Janet was always popular: at a Lincoln's Birthday dance at St. Paul's School in 1924, her dance card was literally filled, with dance numbers one and ten, as well as supper, by Bingham Willing Morris. Janet had indicated that she would attend Vassar College but changed her mind in favor of Sweet Briar College in rural Virginia.

At Sweet Briar well-mannered young ladies wearing pearls valued friendliness over academics. Families chose the college in part because the dormitories with hardwood floors and fireplaces smoothed their daughters' transition from home to college. In the fall and spring, fresh-men would walk ceremonially with lanterns around the campus quad-rangle, singing songs with newly invented lyrics to upperclassmen.

During the 1920s Sweet Briar placed at least as much emphasis on how to be a Southern belle as on book learning. When Janet was asked if she was related to the state's icon, Confederate general Robert E. Lee, she found it easy to say that she was. After a year at Sweet Briar, she moved back home and transferred to Barnard College. Janet had not developed any real academic strengths or intellectual interests—she would have that in common with her future husband—and studied only two semesters at Barnard, leaving at the end of the spring term.

Instead, she focused on the buzz in the Lee household over the approaching nuptials of her twenty-year-old sister Marion. In January Marion was to marry John Ryan Jr. of Troy, New York, a town with a large proportion of Irish Americans to which Janet's grandmother Mary Norton Lee had emigrated from Ireland. Marion's fiancé was in the textile business and doing very well.

Jim Lee found a reason not to be pleased with his eldest daughter's engagement. "Ryan!" he exclaimed when Marion told him that she was serious about the young man. "How can you marry someone with as common a name as Ryan?"

Marion challenged her father and wagered that there were more Lees in the New York City phone directory than Ryans. To prove her point, she showed him the long columns of Lees and the relatively shorter list of Ryans.

Jim, who knew his real estate, recognized many of the Lee addresses. "These Lees live in Chinatown," he said. "They're not related to us!"

The young Mr. Ryan eventually passed muster despite his name. Janet served as the couple's maid of honor, with Winnie as one of the bride's attendants. The reception was held at home. Later, Marion's children would feel that her marriage was partly motivated by the desire to get her out of the house and away from the tension between her parents.

By summer Janet and her family were back in East Hampton, and Janet was tooling around town with her friends, including the red-haired twins Maude and Michelle Bouvier, who were her age. She was thrilled to see the great actor John Drew in summer residence, especially when he hosted his famous niece Ethel Barrymore. At Drew's death in 1927, he was honored by the village green's flag hanging at half-mast for three days and was eulogized by Jack's father—who became nearly as well known for his oratory as for his lawyering—at the Maidstone Club's Saturday night dinner.

Both Jack's and Janet's fathers were members of the Maidstone, East Hampton's most social country club, located on Old Beach Lane. Its name derives from East Hampton's earliest English settlers, who had named the entire area after their home in Kent. Although many claim that the Bouviers were founding club members in 1891, they were not, having first summered there in 1910. (In 1912, while Jack was at Yale, his parents had given up their home in Nutley in favor of a move to Manhattan.) However, their membership dates earlier than that of James T. Lee, who joined in 1925 after several years of seasonal privileges that conveyed with his summer rentals of members' houses.

The Maidstone was the gathering spot for the summer colony—and still is. The grounds overlook Hook Pond, the dunes, and the ocean, with the Maidstone's current clubhouse, an English stucco building with a long veranda, situated on the dunes. The club offered three of the most popular summer sports—swimming, tennis, and golf—all in one membership. Tennis was the first sport of interest to club members, most of whom were members of East Hampton's private Lawn Tennis Club, founded in 1879. The Beach Club was built in 1928 below the clubhouse and included a pool and cabanas.

Maidstone's golf course had a tricky hole 17, about which Jack's father said it was "guarded by the river Styx, upon whose turbid bed, lost pars and lost balls co-mingle." Of course, no golfing was allowed on Sunday until the afternoon, when church services had ended. The Maidstone's only shortcoming, according to many members, was its early prohibition against liquor. In fact, for the club's first few decades, nothing more exciting than "oatmeal water" was served at the tennis courts. On that, too, there was a strict prohibition—for health's sake, members had to wait a full ten minutes after the match ended before quaffing the refreshing mixture.

But other places on Long Island offered stronger stuff. As soon as the Eighteenth Amendment went into effect in 1920, Long Island felt the nation's terrible thirst; it became the capital of bootlegged liquor. Yachts and commercial ships would pick up cases of liquor from the Caribbean or from the French islands south of Newfoundland and bring them just to the edge of international waters, just over three miles from Long Island's shoreline. Soon the coastline was nicknamed Rum Row. Fast-moving contact boats would lie low until dusk, waiting for a sign hung from the ship's mast to signal that the area was free of law enforcement.

The illegal activity was perfectly orchestrated: to prove you were who you said you were, you would show half a torn dollar bill, whose jagged edge would be matched to the half already on board. Cash was the only form of exchange, and if the Coast Guard arrived, liquor was thrown overboard. Otherwise-law-abiding Long Islanders would wait onshore to form human chains that hoisted cartons, one man to another, to trucks that traveled to New York in convoys with machine-gun escorts. There were some losses, though. One East Hampton newspaper reported in 1922 that the *Madonna V* had broken up offshore. Its cargo of liquor was "being salvaged by willing hands," including those of several church deacons.

When federal agents stopped cars and trucks to search for contraband, traffic was jammed for miles. But few arrests took place: the easy money had filtered to court clerks and telephone operators who tipped off bootleggers when the federal agents—more than three thousand in Suffolk County alone—planned arrests.

Kathleen Bouvier tells of the time Jack was in a Montauk casino that was operating illegally yet openly. Next to him was New York City mayor Jimmy Walker. When a vice squad smashed the door in, both men dove out a great bay window overlooking Long Island Sound.

It was during this boisterous era, at the Maidstone, that Janet saw the handsome Bouvier brothers again. She was looking for a break from the funerals of the year, for she lost both her grandmother Maria Merritt in 1928—the grandmother she had passed off as a maid—and her grandfather Dr. James Lee. Dr. Lee was living at the Shelton at the time of his death and had served New York City schools for thirty-three years. The funeral took place at their duplex at 750 Park, and a requiem High Mass was held two days later. Now Janet and her sisters had no living grandparents.

For Janet, these deaths brought home how fleeting life is. It was only natural that she wanted to enjoy herself while there was time. When she first met the Bouvier men, she had been more attracted to Jack's younger brother, Bud (William Sergeant) Bouvier, who had a gentler manner than Jack. The drawback to Bud—and it was a major concern, particularly for a Roman Catholic—was that he was divorced. It was also known that he had a drinking problem, in an era when drinking was rarely considered a problem. Janet's flirtation with Bud only whetted Jack's interest in the young woman whom he frequently saw socializing with his sisters at Lasata.

Of course, Jack's twin sisters wholeheartedly encouraged the romance. "They thought it was a hoot their brother was struck by their kid sisters' friend," remembers Janet's niece Maude Davis.

But Janet's father objected to her flirtation with Jack. She ignored his advice: after all, as Mimi Cecil recalls, Janet knew Jim Lee felt that no man was good enough for his daughters. Over the years many people have asked what would attract a straight arrow like Janet Norton Lee to a man of such weak character. "Why would such a sweet young girl marry a man like Jack Bouvier?" tennis ace and Newporter Jimmy Van Alen remembered people asking.

Her own family eventually realized that, as with Marion, Janet needed to escape her parents' unhappy household. For an Irish American woman at that time, marriage was the only way out—save for the convent. Given a choice between the Black Sheik and a black veil, who could blame Janet? After all, she was barely twenty-one years old while Jack was by now thirty-seven: she must have been easily taken in by Jack's infatuation. In fact, the typical age difference between wives and husbands in 1930 was three years, compared with this couple's sixteen-year difference.

But what would lure Jack to Janet? When he began flirting with her, he was a sophisticated man making $75,000 a year, which would be ten times that today. He also had accumulated nearly three-quarters of a million dollars through good investments in a bull market. Of course, Janet's vivaciousness and youth must have appealed to a man who was already jaded. Kathleen Bouvier believes that Jack realized it was time for him to marry; after all, the average age for a man to marry the first time in this boom economy was twenty-four, a full thirteen years younger than Jack. Mimi Cecil says the family later joked that womanizing Jack knew the only way he could get anywhere with Janet was by marrying her!

Another reason for the marriage is that Janet was a Roman Catholic, and Jack—despite his own transgressions—would not think of marrying outside his religion. "Whether he was a good Catholic or a bad Catholic," muses Kathleen Bouvier, "he was still a Catholic."

But Janet's nephew and godson John H. Davis has the most interesting take on Jack's interest in Janet: "Old Man Lee's money. Jack Bouvier always could smell money."

Although there was no single reason for Jack's interest in Janet, the numbers support Davis's theory: despite Jack's impressive income, he was in debt. In fact, he was always to be in debt; no matter how much money he made, he spent more. And by this time, Jim Lee was very wealthy.

If there was any doubt about that, the burglary removed it. While Janet and her mother attended the Ladies' Village Improvement Society fair, their home was invaded and jewelry valued at $20,000 was stolen. The *East Hampton Star* reported: "The thief or thieves had entered two master bedrooms on the second floor, presumably by means of a ladder. Jewel boxes on two dressing tables were taken. Upon investigation, an empty jewel box was found in a nearby rose garden and another in the gutter on the second story roof." A watch, vanity case, and signet ring were among the items taken.

Rather than leaving capture to the small-town police, Jim hired a private investigator and placed an ad in the *Star*: $1,000 REWARD FOR RETURN OR INFORMATION LEADING TO RETURN OF JEWELRY MISS-ING FROM RESIDENCE ON DUNEMERE LANE, EAST HAMPTON, ON JULY 23, 1926. COMMUNICATE WITH B. H. BECKER, 25 WEST 43RD STREET, NEW YORK CITY.

Both the burglary and Jim's snub of the local police electrified the town. The buzz only increased when his hiring a private detective proved successful. The detective caught two thieves when they tried to fence the jewelry to private detectives hired by the National Jewelers' Crime Com-mittee, whose head, conveniently, was the assistant district attorney of New York. They were convicted and sent to jail for three years.

All this excitement left tongues wagging.

"There's Mr. James T. Lee," his fellow members at the Maidstone would say as Jim entered for his ritual daily swim, chewing on a wet cigar, recounts Davis. Then their voices would fall to a whisper. "He's *very* rich."

His image swelled when he made a sizable donation to the Maidstone soon after joining and when he rented a more impressive house: W. H. Woodin's estate on Lily Pond Lane called Avery Place. At that point, members charitably reevaluated his gruff manner and characterized him as "a diamond in the rough."

Jack Bouvier had summed up the tangible assets of Janet's father. He hoped that, as a son-in-law, he would be given her father's millions to invest in the market. Remembers Davis, "Mr. Lee was always a gold mine he could tap."

Or so thought Jack.

July 7, 1928, dawned sunny—warm but not hot—with a blue sky punc-tuated by fluffy white clouds. St. Philomena Roman Catholic Church in East Hampton was jammed with the rich and the social. (The church is now called Most Holy Trinity; ironically, in this story of true love coined of counterfeit metal, it turns out that Philomena was decanonized after a review of saints.)

That day, oblivious to the shaky ground she trod, the bride shimmered in her bias-cut dress of white satin accented with Irish lace and crystal-and-pearl embroidery, with the dark and dashing mustached groom her shadow image. Janet's sisters looked charming in their summery apple-green chiffon dresses and butter-yellow horsehair hats, and Janet's mother was so ebullient that she could have floated all the way up to the cottony puffs wafting in the sky. She thought that Jack Bouvier, with his social standing and his French name—not to mention the family's money—was a real step up for her middle daughter. After all, Bud Bouvier had married blond, blue-eyed Emma Louise Stone, whose family had once owned thousands of Chicago acres and who was a niece of the poet Edgar Lee Masters. And Jack himself had once been engaged to a girl of impeccable Southern credentials. Adding interest were the tales of Jack's frequent engagements and disengagements, although these romances were most likely exaggerated by his sisters, according to Kathleen Bouvier.

The groom's family, too, was pleased. Jack was finally marrying, and to a girl of innocence and wealth. To cap off the day, their beloved Bud had been released from a Connecticut sanitarium, after being temporarily dried out in order to take part in the ceremony.

There was one man in the church, though, who was steaming, and it was the one who had just walked the bride down the aisle. There was little that Jim Lee liked about the Bouviers. He ridiculed their social connections: the very linkages that the women in his family revered, he mocked as "sassiety," and he despised Jack for being a reprobate and a dilettante broker who would have few clients if not for his family connections. Just the sight of Jack wearing those dandified outfits repulsed Jim, who had hoped that the April engagement would be broken just as Jack's first engagement had been. But the wedding had been set a mere ten weeks in the future, and there were not enough days for disillusionment to take its course.

The day was so lovely that the couple received their five hundred guests standing between two small blue spruce trees on the lawn of the Lee house on Lily Pond Lane. As the guests ate a wedding breakfast from small tables on the terrace and danced outside to the music of the Meyer Davis Orchestra, Jim fumed. His dark mood deepened, in counterpoint to the gaiety around him. He watched Bud manfully resist the flowing champagne while his new son-in-law—he could barely tolerate the thought of being in that relationship to Jack—flirted with the female guests.

His ill temper mounted. When Jack made a frivolous comment, Jim started shouting. At first the crowd thought they were hearing exuberant voices; then, as they realized that an ugly argument was taking place — between the bride's father and her new husband, of all things — they hushed their chatter, which only isolated the yelling between Jim and Jack. The sound rose all the way to Meyer Davis, the bandleader. He raised his chin and cupped his left hand upward, motioning his players to step up the volume.

Luckily, the couple was soon off to Manhattan to spend their wedding night at the Savoy. The next day they arrived at their stateroom on the *Aquitania* to greet friends who had boarded to see them off. Jack got a strong head start on the booze brought by their guests, and by the time their friends disembarked and the ship blasted its horn, Jack himself was six sheets to the wind.

Jack was pleased to see that Doris Duke, heir to a tobacco fortune, was on the passenger list. He had met her a few times and knew of her family's great mansion in Newport. When Janet returned to their cabin to bathe before the evening meal, Jack struck up an easy flirtation with Duke, which irritated Janet. Years later some people believed that Jack and Duke consummated a romance on that ship, but relatives never heard of any stories at the time, and Duke's age — only sixteen years — makes the gossip less credible.

Janet was also annoyed at the time Jack expended playing roulette and poker. (He did avoid betting at blackjack, because of its name.) When he confessed to her that his extra spending money was lost at the gambling tables, she marched to the casino and won it back. Their relationship was a house of cards: Janet was pleased at replacing their money, Jack was angry that he had been bested by his own bride, and then Jack's reaction infuriated Janet because of his lack of appreciation for what she did for him. Disagreements over money and Jack's behavior with other women first surfaced on their honeymoon voyage and would continue to plague the marriage in years to come.

Money and other women: the tip of the iceberg that would wreck their marriage first surfaced on their honeymoon voyage.

Chapter 5

LIFE WITH
JACK BOUVIER

Janet and Jack Bouvier were adapting to marriage in their new apartment at 790 Park Avenue near Seventy-third Street. Two blocks down, at 750 Park, Janet's younger sister, Winnie, fifteen years old, was having her own adjustment problems. She was the only child left at home, and her parents made it clear to her that despite their refusal to speak to each other, they would not divorce until she married and was out of the house.

To Margaret and Jim's astonishment, Winnie announced that she—unlike her sisters—would not be pressured into a wedding. "I'm not going to marry until I'm good and ready," she said. According to her niece Mimi Cecil, she also told her parents, "And I am not asking either of you to pass anything at the table unless it's something that *I* want."

"That's the end of that!" she proclaimed of their childish and acrimonious behavior. And it was. From then on, Margaret and Jim managed to choke out whatever few words they needed to communicate with each other.

But they were still able to dominate Janet, who especially heeded her father. Jim Lee continued to despise her husband and used whatever excuse Jack gave him—and there were many—to criticize him. Janet took her father's words to heart; she evidently hadn't learned from watching her five aunts undermine her own parents' marriage. Jack, in turn, would carp about her father, whom he called Old Man Lee behind his back. To his face, of course, Jack would address him respectfully as "Mr. Lee," just as Marion's husband did.

Also a heavy presence in the marriage was Jack's mother, Maude, who continued to side with Jack—in her eyes he could do no wrong. The senior Bouviers' apartment at 765 Park Avenue and Seventy-second Street was only a block from the young couple's. Although it was fairly typical in those days for parents to be participants in their adult children's marriages, both the Bouviers and the Lees were "a little more so," according to Kathleen Bouvier. And it was easy for the older generation to be involved: in a borough of close to 2 million people, the newlyweds lived about two streets up Park Avenue from the bride's parents and one street up from the groom's.

Still, there was room for Jack and Janet to enjoy themselves. Despite Janet's inborn quietness and reserve, the couple was immensely social; entertaining friends was their pleasure. Janet had adopted the mannerisms of a Southern belle at Sweet Briar, and men, reacting to her charm, swarmed around her. She used her marriage to further her ascension in society. In fact, a Southampton man named James Parrish Lee—with a name so like her father's and who actually *was* a descendant of the famed Lee family—bolstered her fantasy that she, too, might be a relative of the Confederate general. By contrast, Jack just wanted to have a good time and didn't give a fig about a person's studbook. He would spend a short day on Wall Street while Janet organized whatever supper party they were throwing. They might, in East Hampton, attend the Devon Yacht Club, where there was always a big band and sometimes a party with a speakeasy theme.

Risk-taking Jack would fly to East Hampton in a high-wing monoplane, strutting from the field in aviator goggles and a brown leather jacket. He nearly invested in an early version of the helicopter, an autogyro whirlybird. (His brother, Bud, missed an opportunity to stake the operation that became Pan American Airways.) Jack's flying days ended when, seconds after taking off, his helicopter crashed ignobly into the potato field his father-in-law owned off the house on Further Lane, writes John Davis.

Jack was a gambler on the floor of the Exchange, too, favoring spe-
cialty stocks. To ensure that he had enough shares for customers, he
would stockpile them and even buy excessive amounts if the price
dropped. It was a hazardous manipulation, but Jack thought nothing
could go wrong in the sizzling market. After all, buying stocks on margin
was now an accepted practice: volume had increased nearly 300 percent
between 1926 and 1929. Everybody was taking chances and accumulat-
ing profits—so they thought.

Jack spent his winnings as quickly as they came in. He owned four
cars, including a black Lincoln Zephyr and a maroon Stutz with a driver
in matching livery. Jack had the Stutz built to specification so that he
could enter the rear door without removing his hat.

In the first years of their marriage, being seen while looking handsome
was the thing: in Manhattan the couple frequented nightclubs on upper
Broadway and listened to Benny Goodman and the Chick Webb Band.
They ate at French restaurants—Longchamps, for example, and La
Rue's, which they considered a neighborhood restaurant. Once in a while
they'd travel up to Harlem to catch Duke Ellington's band at the Cotton
Club, or they'd go west to the huge Paramount Theater on Times Square
at Forty-third Street.

Janet enjoyed her life as much as Jack did. Who wouldn't? Money
was multiplying exponentially; their social group was the tops; they had
no obligations to anyone but themselves. Janet's chief occupation, besides hostessing, became riding. She was given more opportunity to ride
seriously because the Bouviers maintained a fine stable in East Hampton.
Yes, occasionally Jack's flirtations peeved Janet and there would be
arguments; and, yes, occasionally their parents' interference could be
maddening; but all in all, life was fun.

Just a few months after their marriage, Janet and Jack were elated
by the news of her first pregnancy. Janet had maintained her youthful
figure through regular riding and swimming; besides, she surely would
not complain of any first trimester nausea to her glamorous husband.

They had no reason to think that the good life would end.

It was well that Janet and Jack could rejoice in the birth of Jacqueline
Lee Bouvier on July 28, 1929, one year and three weeks after their
wedding, for there would be little to celebrate in the following months.
Their joy didn't mean that there weren't also great strains, however,

especially since this twenty-two-year-old mother and thirty-eight-year-old father were determined to keep focused on adult interests.

Jackie's birth, for example, should have occurred in a Manhattan hospital rather than one out in the country. But even though the baby was overdue by the end of June, Jack insisted that Janet travel to East Hampton, a trip that must have been extremely uncomfortable for a heavily pregnant woman.

At Lasata, Janet began to feel contractions and was taken to Southampton Hospital. To call the 1913 structure a hospital is generous; with twenty beds, it looked scarcely larger than today's health clinics. Luckily, the eight-pound baby and her mother remained in wonderful health, and no advanced medical care was needed. But the trip to the country was another of Jack's unnecessary gambles, this time for both his baby and his wife — a selfish choice that might have had serious health implications. At least the physician was not a country doctor: their own physician was just as social as the Bouviers and was in East Hampton when the call from Lasata came.

An English nanny saw to the baby's basic needs, and Janet's slim figure quickly returned, helped by resuming her riding. In an era when a new mother would typically be confined to the hospital for a week or ten days, and instructed not to use stairs for another few weeks, Janet entered the annual East Hampton riding competitions a mere twenty days after giving birth. And she won a third-place ribbon.

The baby was immediately called Jackie because, as Janet said, "You couldn't call a little girl Jacqueline." Her baptism took place in Manhattan at the Church of St. Ignatius Loyola. Janet insisted on naming Jim Lee godfather, but Jack always had more than one man's share of family pride — all the Bouviers were chauvinistic about their heritage — and feared that "Old Man Lee" might play too important a role in the life of his *own* firstborn angel.

The morning of the christening, Jim became extraordinarily busy at the office and left only the minimum margin to get to the church. Business came first, after all. He hadn't anticipated a traffic jam. So with the ceremony about to begin and Jim nowhere in sight, Jack was vehement that the ceremony start anyway, according to Kathleen Bouvier.

The monsignor began the short ritual. Janet was nervous about beginning without her father and kept looking back over her shoulder whenever she heard footsteps on the stone floor. Before long, the chaplain asked for the baby's godfather to step forward. There was a confused silence. Then Jack stepped into the void and pushed his nine-year-old nephew Miche, Bud's son, forward.

By the time a discomposed Jim Lee arrived a few minutes later, out of breath and embarrassed, there was no turning back. A mere few minutes' tardiness had cut him out of his important role. Jack must have felt triumphant; Jim, resentful.

This may have been the only time Jack bested a member of the Lee family. He ignored advice from everyone. Jack would ride the Cannonball out to East Hampton on Friday afternoons with his brother-in-law John Ryan, who had married Janet's sister Marion. "I'm getting out of the market," Ryan would tell him. "It's too good to be true. You really should get out, too."

Jack would agree with his brother-in-law but add, "I'll give it a few more months first." Then he gave it a few more months. And a few more.

In early October the heart of the Bouvier family was ripped out by the death of thirty-six-year-old Bud from acute alcohol poisoning. He left a young son, Miche, and the wife who had divorced him, the former Emma Stone.

A few weeks after the shock of Bud's death, the nation's boom years abruptly ended with the crash of the stock market. By mid-November no citizen remained immune from its effect. A few lucky investors, including Jack's great-uncle Michel, had invested heavily in municipal bonds and therefore lost only half their fortune. Others in the Bouvier family, including Jack, were not so lucky.

In that time, particularly in Janet and Jack's group, you never talked about feeling pinched, even if all your friends were in the same situation. The couple was eaten by worry, but Janet was the partner more skilled at plastering over fissures. For her, it was stiff-upper-lip time. Jack reacted by escalating his drinking—this, after Bud's death!—and escaping the house whenever possible.

Jack's mother, devastated by the loss of her youngest son, was incapable of providing her remaining son with good advice. In fact, she indulged Jack more than ever. Her husband, J.V., had hoped that the baby's birth would mature Jack. Now J.V. was truly disgusted by his surviving son's failure to face reality. They argued over money, and Jack resented his father's running tally of how much he had spent on each of his children and grandchildren, including the fatherless Miche.

Jim Lee was busy cutting his own losses and those of the Central Savings Bank. He immediately made a U-turn by putting out stop orders on new buildings, realizing that cooperative houses were going into

bankruptcy because tenants couldn't maintain the fees. Anxious land-
lords were breaking grand rental apartments into smaller units. With
construction halted all over the city, and a local workforce that was
nearly 30 percent immigrant and dependent on blue-collar jobs, everyone
was afraid of the future.

Janet was frightened by the economic havoc but still felt entitled to
the only life she had ever known. Like many women, she had been taught
to rely on men for support and felt that it was up to Jack to pull his
family out of the crisis. Of course, this was unfair: even the financial
wizard Bernard Baruch couldn't have performed this miracle. As a result,
the couple's fights over money were vicious. And they didn't mind holding them in front of other family members.

As the slump deepened, John Davis remembered, Janet literally
shrieked at Jack to get more money. "You have to," she commanded
him. Jack, of course, could have no more performed this magic trick
than turn back time to the heyday of the 1920s.

Janet panicked; in reaction, Jack choked. Unable to adapt to a new
and ugly world, he hoped to maintain his old lifestyle by having others
fund it. First he turned to his great-uncle Michel, who had been relatively
unaffected by what was now a full-blown depression. Jack asked for
$100,000 ($1 million today); Michel lent him $25,000. Although this sum
would have brought tears of gratitude to the eyes of the average man,
who earned about $2,000 annually—if he was lucky enough still to have
a job by 1930—Jack found it almost insulting. His attitude did not ingratiate him to anyone.

Fortunately, the family's housing was taken care of by both sets of
parents. Certainly, there was no way that the family could use Central
Park as a bucolic escape, as its grass was now dotted with hundreds of
cardboard and scrap-metal shacks—dubbed Hoovervilles, after the President who was blamed for the Depression. Still, while others were living
in the street, Janet and Jack expected to continue to season in East
Hampton. His parents capitulated and in 1930 paid the lease for Jack
and Janet's Rowdy Hall at 111 Egypt Lane, a three-bay saltbox cottage,
renovated after its use as a former boardinghouse for young artists.
(Later, Jack's parents allowed the couple to summer in a house they
owned on Appaquogue Road called Wildmoor.)

New Yorkers knew things had hit bottom when the Depression
reached Park Avenue. Jim Lee was faced with tenants rich the day
before but now reneging on their rents. No matter how he tried to re-

structure leases, he still had empty chambers in the best of his buildings. To a developer, a building with empty apartments looks like a tiara with missing diamonds.

The long-anticipated 740 Park Avenue had just opened—to many vacancies. Jim was initially elated when John D. Rockefeller Jr., the son of the world's richest businessman, took a triplex. Yet the very presence of the Rockefeller family had the unanticipated consequence of deterring others who might be able to afford the building. No one, they figured, was as rich as Rockefeller. So, as realty expert Carter Horsley puts it, "740 took a bath."

Jim decided to help his daughter and his building simultaneously. In 1932 he offered Janet and Jack a free duplex in 740 Park Avenue. The following year, with still too much empty space in the new building, Jim acknowledged that he and Margaret had been miserable for years and saw the empty apartments as an excuse finally to separate. After all, their daughter Winnie, although still at home, was twenty years old and could adapt to his absence. So he moved his wife and daughter from the duplex at 750 Park into the new building at 740. He himself escaped to a vacant apartment more than twenty blocks away, at his Shelton Hotel.

Janet and Jack had traded one good address for another that was even better. To their friends, it looked as if the couple was moving up; in actuality, the opposite was true. But accepting the gift of free residence in a luxury apartment didn't mean that Jack was grateful or that Jim was gracious.

Both families had already been "far too involved" in the couple's life, according to Kathleen Bouvier. Janet's mother and younger sister exacerbated the situation when they moved into 740 Park, too. But the worst was that now "Old Man Lee" had the upper hand. And he brought it down hard on Jack's freewheeling habits.

In a four-hour lecture, Jim set out his requirements. First, in exchange for interest-free loans, Jack would have to bring him a detailed monthly accounting of his spending. Jim said he expected to see no charges for club memberships or fancy tailors. Then, until this crisis was over, Jack was not to make any more high-risk investments. Lastly, Jack had to give up three of the family's four cars; the dark blue Mercury convertible was enough.

Jack bitterly resented what he deemed Jim's interference. He appreciated the apartment, but having his father-in-law manage both his personal spending and his business decisions was too much. So, upon moving into the eleven-room duplex that Jim had given the couple, Jack ignored his father-in-law's admonitions and, using the loan from his great-uncle, began an expensive renovation.

He gutted the kitchen, added gold-plated fixtures to the bathrooms, paneled several rooms, and used the extra maid's room for his array of exercise equipment, which emphasized *easy* ways to lose weight. There was an exercise belt to "break up fat" and a portable sauna that allegedly melted off pounds. Kathleen Bouvier remembers a gleaming chrome table dominating the room—so Jack could enjoy his rubdowns without leaving home. To emphasize his perpetually dark skin, Jack sat naked in front of the room's large window and basked in the sun, she said.

As a break from the exhausting supervision of these renovations, the couple left on March 24 for a short cruise to Nassau. They sailed on Cunard's regal *Mauretania*, built in 1909 and a twenty-two-year Blue Riband holder. During the Depression, the ship sailed on weekend "cruises to nowhere," escapist excuses to gamble and drink—some called them booze cruises, as Prohibition was still in effect and the ships sailed to international waters. The voyage to Nassau could be had as cheaply as seventy dollars per person. That low price even appealed to the few wealthy: the Bouviers kept company, for example, with Alfred V. du Pont and his family.

When the couple returned home, they felt the strain of a truncated staff: just a nanny for Jackie, a cook, and two maids. Of course, there were several others who came and went—extra party staff, and the masseuse and trainer for Jack. By 1933 fewer than twenty Americans were considered millionaires. Jack Bouvier was not one, even though he wanted to live as if he still were.

Compared with the experiences of others at the beginning of the Great Depression—which now had its own official title—the couple was living a fantasy life. Or was it a dream world that could turn into a nightmare? Jack's point of view was that there was no real reason to cut back or modify one's style. Things would change. They had to.

Rowdy Hall constituted relatively small quarters. Jack and Janet kept their horses at Lasata, and J.V. picked up those expenses as well as the cost of two grooms for the Bouvier family's seven ponies and hunters. There was an empty stall to board a horse brought by houseguests. (Janet's favorites were Danseuse, Stepaside, and Arnoldean; Jack preferred the aptly named Cock o' the Walk.)

The couple could relax in the Hamptons' casual atmosphere: part of its joy was that it was far less dressy than, for example, Newport. The ladies wore casual frocks during the day, no hats except to shield fair complexions from the sun, and no gloves. Settled as far back as 1648, East Hampton had many elements of a quiet country town. Its riding club, for example, was relatively modest. It had started informally in the 1890s on the village green, then waned, and was formally established in 1924. The clubhouse was no more than a century-old converted farm-house decorated in early American style with loaned furnishings. By 1928 it had added to its grounds and stabling, possessing twenty-nine acres and forty-five box stalls, with plans for seventy-five more. It also held games and activities for children, which members grandly called the "gymkhana."

During the summer Jack would travel out by train on weekends, maintaining the myth that he still had clients. Of course, mostly what he did during the week was chase women, attend to his wardrobe, and work on his tan. "When he got out of his car at the station," remembered his driver, "a lot of heads would turn."

In addition to the "necessary" renovations on the Park Avenue apart-ment, some changes were taking place at the summer home, too. Jack had a small structure on Rowdy Hall's property that had served as a speakeasy for the artsy colony living in the Hamptons during the twen-ties — and whose behavior gave the main house its name — converted into a playhouse for toddler Jackie. Janet landscaped the property and was frustrated when her climbing roses wouldn't climb fast enough. She flared at her gardener when he told her no mature bushes were available locally, "Fly some in!"

In most ways Janet was engaging; for example, she could be an ex-ceptional hostess, with a true ability to ignore even chaos about her. Of course, her allure had a troubling side, too. Prevented, as a woman from a good family, from focusing her energies outside her husband and chil-dren, Janet felt her only socially acceptable outlets were her riding and her social aspirations.

"Janet had an ambition different from my mother and twin sisters," who had no yearnings other than to establish peaceful homes and raise healthy children, remembers John Davis. "Janet wanted to get ahead and make a name for herself socially. She was aggressive and emotionally strong."

Janet's frustration with her husband also fed her need for control. Infuriated by Jack's lack of ambition and appreciation for her father's assistance, she would rail that if it weren't for her father, they would all be on the street.

Jack retaliated by stepping up his affairs with other women. Having recently turned forty, he needed women who would still be impressed by him and his dashing ways. It was easy to carry on his romances, for Janet and baby Jackie could be in only one place at a time. He could use the other home—whether Manhattan or East Hampton—for his assignations.

Jack rationalized his behavior, claiming that his father-in-law had made life miserable for him. "Remember," Jim would warn him, "you're living in my house." Jack saw this as a taunt. *Jim*, not Jack, was the dominant male in the Bouvier household. *Jim* gave Janet and Jack a rent-free home. *Jim* told them what to do and how to do it while Jack had to account for his petty cash and report his expenditures like an adolescent boy with his first allowance. And *Jim* was continually dropping by their home just as if—well, just as if he owned the place.

As Jim's status rose within the household, so did Janet's. Now she was challenging Jack and frankly telling him what to do. Jack felt emasculated; he asked himself who was at fault. He answered his own question: nothing could be laid at his feet. He later told a family member that his wife and father-in-law had castrated him emotionally. He was driven—*forced*, actually—to seek affirmation of his manhood in the arms of other women. Jack would show Jim and his daughter. He would let them know who was in charge of this marriage.

Jack's philandering didn't prevent him from enjoying the benefits of marriage. To provide little Jackie with a playmate, Janet gave birth to Caroline Lee Bouvier on March 3, 1933. The baby was called Lee—the Caroline was after Jack's grandmother Caroline Ewing Bouvier. Jackie was three and a half years old; she was given a bedroom of her own, and Lee inherited the nursery. They shared the nurse.

Jim Lee's influence on his daughters could be seen in the names they chose for their children. Both Jackie and her sister had Lee as their middle names, but Janet decided that the younger child was not to be called Caroline after Jack's grandmother but rather Lee, after her father—Jack's number one enemy. (Janet's sisters were no less impressionable: of Jim Lee's grandchildren, six of eleven had Lee as one of their names; none was called Margaret after their mother. Even some of his great-grandchildren would bear the Lee name.)

Though Jack adored his girls, it was as arm candy for himself and, eventually, their husbands. Still, the man who—unlike his father and forebears—had made no mark on the world saw that his daughters could be canvases for his paintbrush. Jack had never adopted the common belief that daughters were less valuable than sons. In fact, if there was a small space in his heart for anyone but himself, it was occupied by Jackie and Lee. But they weren't enough to keep him at home.

At the beginning of the summer, Janet would drive the girls from Manhattan to East Hampton in the blue convertible, often picking up a speeding ticket on the way. At the halfway point, the threesome would stop for ice cream. The girls knew they were near East Hampton when they started to see potato fields, duck farms, and, of course, horses. Janet had put Jackie on the back of a horse when she was a year old; by age five, Jackie was entering shows on Long Island. Jack carefully clipped and saved the local newspaper stories that mentioned his daughters; he and Janet were pleased to see the family name in such glossies as the *Social Spectator*.

Janet's other athletic activities were also of note. At the Maidstone Club, for example, she captained the ladies' baseball team called the Maidstone Black Ducks. (Jack, too, played ball, naming his team the Wall Street All-Stars.) Janet established a pet dog show for the village fair—and primed the judging committee with her sister Winnie, her mother, and two in-laws. She entered two beagles, an Irish setter, and a Scottish terrier, at which the *East Hampton Star* opined, "Mrs. Bouvier is an expert on the subject of either horses or dogs." In other competitions Janet was disappointed on two counts, though: she lost the prize for best mother to another—although she ran a close second, the newspaper gently noted—and Jackie did not win the Most Beautiful Child contest, either.

While Jack was clipping their first press notices, it was Janet who was earning her reputation as a top-ranked amateur horsewoman. She preferred to enter hunter competitions, in which riders jump over such natural objects as wooden fences and stone walls. Hunter horses have strength and speed and can clear a fence more cleanly than other jumpers.

Ironically, it seemed as if Janet were perfecting her skills and driving herself to excel in direct proportion to the unhappiness of her marriage. Janet had never been a serious rider until her marriage to Jack, whose family belonged to the Riding Club of East Hampton—unlike the Lees, who never joined.

The Hamptons' equestrian pride was the club in East Hampton and the Southampton Riding and Hunt Club, flourishing after a brief cessation during the world war. The events they held attracted such fine riders as Richard Mellon—the industrialist Andrew Mellon's brother—who would bring his horses from Pittsburgh for the competitions. The fancy-dress riding-and-driving-party contest was judged by a group of notables, including artist Childe Hassam and the actress Laurette Taylor.

The level of Janet's horsemanship rose with each year of marriage. In 1928 she entered five events in the East Hampton annual riding show and won a single red ribbon. The following year she was back in the saddle for three events; again, she took third place. By 1930 she was entering a few neighboring events, winning third place in the novice saddle horse competition at the Montauk Horse Show.

In 1931 she rode at the Southampton show, placing fourth with Arnoldean in the ladies' hunter competition, second with Arnoldean in the heavyweight hunter event, and second again with Stout Fellow in the middleweight hunter event. At Montauk Janet rode a saddle gelding, Showman, to second place. Finally, at the Babylon horse show, she won her first blue ribbon with Arnoldean in the hunters-for-sale event. Soon after, at East Hampton, she won two more blue ribbons with Arnoldean as well as a second place in three events, third place on Showman, and fourth place on Show Me.

Janet's competitions were completed by October, so with great pride she attended the opening of the George Washington Bridge, which linked the New Jersey palisades to the city across the Hudson River. She went with the entire Bouvier family to hear two governors—Franklin D. Roosevelt of New York and Morgan F. Larson of New Jersey—speak but, more important, to listen to J. V. Bouvier give an oration on President George Washington at the ceremonies in the center of the bridge.

The next spring, in 1932, three months pregnant with Lee, she rode in both East Hampton and Southampton. She took two firsts, two seconds, two thirds, and one fourth place.

Janet went back to competing a few months after Lee's birth in 1933, and her intensity was startling. At East Hampton's show, she rode in *twelve* events: the first started at 9:50 A.M., when she rode three horses—Danseuse, Arnoldean, and Stepaside—and won one first- and one third-place prize. At 10:10 she began her next event on Arnoldean, winning first. At eleven o'clock she rode Clearandfast; at 11:40 she entered four horses, including her favorite bay mare, Danseuse.

Noon saw Janet entering four horses again, taking first place on Danseuse and winning third and fourth places as well. By 12:35 she was entering Arnoldean to take the blue ribbon in that event. After her win, she took a lunch break and didn't ride until the next event at 2:35, when she failed to place. At the 4:05 event she rode four horses and took a fourth on Arnoldean. At 4:55 she rode *five* horses: she took a first on Danseuse and a second on Stepaside. At 5:10 she was in a team event that took the blue ribbon. At 5:30, in the Ward Challenge Cup, she rode Danseuse to first and Stepaside to second place. Shortly after, in the champion hunter event, she won another first on Danseuse.

Janet enjoyed developing her skills as a rider; she appreciated the Bouviers' horses; she liked to win and seemed to have boundless energy. Then she somehow found time to bathe and change before the evening's dinner dance as she segued from a no-nonsense horsewoman to a faux Southern belle.

Jackie, like her mother, used riding as an anodyne for her unhappy home life. People were noting Jackie's aggressive riding around the same time that she was hiding in the darkened hallway outside her parents' bedroom listening to the fights and arguments. "All they do is scream at each other—scream and yell," Jackie told Davis. He remembers, "The yelling was just overwhelming."

Despite the repeal of Prohibition in December 1933, the year was a difficult one for Jack. Before autumn he had profits of $2 million (nearly $24 million today). He told everyone that he would bank the money and not speculate. But that much money proved too great a temptation; he heard of a promising deal and poured the money into a short-lived auto business. All he had left by the beginning of 1934 was about 10 percent of his profits. Janet was so furious, she could hardly stand to look at her impetuous husband.

As young as Jackie was, she mirrored her parents' acrimony and began showing an angry side. One of Jim Lee's East Hampton maids remembered, "Even as a youngster [Jackie] had a temper. She would carry on something awful until she got her way. Once, I remember, her father refused to allow her to go to a movie with some friends of her own age because he felt that ten-year-olds needed an adult chaperone.

"She jumped up and down, hollered real loud, and twisted her face into a thousand shapes. Her poor dad finally had to give in—she did that with everything."

A staff member of the Maidstone also remembered Jackie's tantrums. "If she was told that she would have to wait to get on the tennis court, or if swimming towels weren't given to her right away, she blew up."

In 1935 Jack's eighty-eight-year-old wealthy bachelor great-uncle Michel Bouvier died. His obituary in *The New York Times* termed him "Wall Street Dean" because of his seniority, dating from 1869, on the Exchange. (John D. Rockefeller, at ninety-six, was third in seniority, having operated a private seat representing his own interests.) The *Times* noted that Michel and another senior man were "the coolest members who left the floor at the close of business" on October 29, 1929, when the entire structure of the financial world was threatened.

Michel Bouvier's estate was valued at $1.65 million dollars ($21 million today). His primary heir, and executor, was his nephew, Jack's father, who received more than $300,000. Other relatives inherited sums ranging from $10,000 to $25,000. Michel also made generous contributions to Catholic charities. Jack received only a small amount, although he gained his great-uncle's brokerage customers, who gravitated to him after Michel's death.

In the fall, after a year in kindergarten, Jackie began the elite Miss Chapin's School. "Jackie's intellectual ambition ran ahead of her chronological age," Janet said. (When Jackie was entering first grade, John F. Kennedy was beginning his freshman year at Princeton University and would soon transfer to Harvard University.) Nancy Tuckerman, Jackie's good friend from childhood, remembered her brightness but also that "Jackie held the distinction of being the naughtiest girl in the class, and this was in the days when good manners and proper behavior were key factors in our education."

Except for the shortcomings in the manners department, Jackie was nearly a mirror image of her mother, in her riding and athleticism, her reserve and her temper. Her dark good looks, though, reflected Jack Bouvier; it was Lee who looked like Janet. The girls began to spend more time with Janet in East Hampton as Janet watched her husband lead a life independent of their marriage. In Long Island, at least, Janet had her horses to ride and a sympathetic family in the Bouviers, for even *they* disdained Jack's womanizing. Maude—for whom he usually could do no wrong—would scold him over his behavior, according to Davis. The Bouviers had already lived through Bud's divorce and death; they had no desire to repeat the sequence. J.V. was by now openly contemptuous of his son. He criticized Jack's spendthrift ways, his obsession with his wardrobe, and his lack of ambition—save for making a quick profit.

Of the next generation, the ten Bouvier cousins formed a tight-knit unit at the obligatory Lasata lunches J.V. held each Sunday. The cousins, including Davis, heard endless praise heaped upon Jackie and Lee by their adoring father as they sat around the table. Jack would insinuate himself into the children's conversation to take his daughters' side, right or wrong, in childish squabbles. No wonder their cousins would respond by getting the girls alone and shoving burrs in their hair or exploding firecrackers when they weren't looking. And no wonder Jackie stuck close to her father, not quite comfortable with the niche her father was carving out for her among her relatives. And as Jack adored Jackie, she, in turn, reflected his love. In that relationship, neither of them made room for Janet, who was more concerned with her young daughters' manners and schoolwork.

Jackie was strongly influenced by the intellectual and artistic life at her grandfather Bouvier's house, where the grandchildren were rewarded for composing poems and drawing pictures. Janet encouraged her daughters' artistic traits, although she admitted, "I can't sketch a line." She also required that they memorize a poem for each holiday. Although Janet claimed that Jackie was reading Shaw and Chekhov at six, the reality was that Jackie hated taking naps and would grab any handy book rather than sleep.

At first Janet held her chin high in the face of her husband's open flirtations and hidden affairs. Her pose hid from their friends the depths to which her marriage had sunk. But even Janet cracked when Jack's behavior with other women *in her very presence* became so humiliating that she refused to go out with him. They would accept an invitation, and then only Jack would attend. The worst happened in 1934, when Janet was still trying to make the marriage work. On June 1 she had entered a two-day competition at New York's Tuxedo Park Riding Academy. Afterward, still in riding togs, she hopped up on a split-rail fence to be photographed with Jack and her friend Virginia Kernochan. When the picture was published in New York's *Daily News*, it clearly showed Jack holding Virginia's hand—out of his wife's view but in her presence. A gossip columnist snidely referred to the threesome's "grand old time."

The *scandale*, as it was delicately referred to by their friends, forced Janet to broach the subject of divorce with her mother and father. (She had to speak to them separately, of course.) However, they were united in their dictum that there had never been a divorce in the family and that one wouldn't happen just because of Jack Bouvier.

So Janet sublimated through riding, especially in her preferred hunter competitions. Her earlier shows were local, ones she could hack to. But this year, for the first time, she entered shows from spring to fall, traveling outside East Hampton to ride in Rumson, New Jersey, and throughout New York: Brooklyn, Tuxedo Park, Westhampton, Brookville, Southampton, Stony Brook, North Shore, Riverhead, and Locust Valley. Her season culminated at the National Horse Show in Madison Square Garden, which was a much larger competition than she had ever entered. Here, Janet's adversary was one of impeccable pedigree: Mrs. John (Liz) Hay Whitney of Upperville, Virginia, took the hunter championship.

Janet's favorite hunter, Danseuse, was no "push button" horse—a horse so wonderfully trained that nearly anyone could ride it to a ribbon. The Bouviers would not have been able to afford this quality of jumper; besides, Janet enjoyed training and grooming her own mount. Then again, riding in the 1930s was less professionalized than it would become; the ability to socialize with friends was a draw for those entering shows and was certainly an attraction for Janet.

This was the first year she entered a competition with Jackie, in the family class at East Hampton. They placed third. Jack was chagrined: he had entered the same competition with his nephew Miche, but they didn't place—and Miche was fourteen years old to Jackie's five. Jackie's first solo competition was at Southampton in the horsemanship for children event; she placed sixth. When Janet entered Jackie in the horsemanship for children under age nine in Suffolk, little Jackie finished fourth.

Janet took time to ingrain in Jackie an intense love of riding that complemented her natural athletic abilities. In retrospect, Lee might have appeared less interested in riding than her sister was; actually, however, she was a fine young rider whose skills were just as strong as Jackie's. When five years old, the same age Jackie began to compete, Lee won third place in the horsemanship entry for children as old as nine years. At age six, she won second place. So perhaps she, like many young girls of the time, simply preferred riding for its own pleasure and the social aura surrounding the sport. Lee finally opted for less dangerous activities the day the family's pony Dancestep fell and nearly rolled over her, leaving a permanent hoofprint on her stomach.

Janet was Jackie's most important instructor through her teenage years, which was unusual. (The same kinds of conflicts generally arise when parents train their own children to ride as when they give them driving lessons.) Children in this group were most often handed over to professionals. But Janet was careful to make sure that Jackie learned to ride the right way: Janet's way. She pushed Jackie to ride "beyond herself," or else she'd never improve. Janet told her that if she found herself in a tricky situation, she should just fall off.

For Janet, 1935 was particularly intense. In her events she rode Danseuse to win five cups and eight blue ribbons, as well as five third and four fourth places. She took Danseuse to eight shows, the chestnut mare Stepaside to four shows, and Arnoldean to one. At the prestigious National Horse Show at the Garden—one of the nation's most important horse shows, held since 1883—Janet took second place on Danseuse in the hunter class. Her ribbon was noted in the sports pages of *The New York Times*. She was also pleased to be named co-chairman of the Riding Club of East Hampton in 1935, a position that reflected its officers' respect for her riding as well as her social position.

Showing well was important to Janet, as her nephew Miche would learn. As his wife, Kathleen Bouvier, told the story, the young Michel was charged with the tasks of saddle-soaping Janet's tack and checking her leather bag for a sandwich, a tradition of actual hunters who carry food for a day in the field. Before one competition, Miche noted that a sandwich was packed, but he didn't realize that it had been prepared for an event some time earlier. Later, when the judges were evaluating Danseuse, one of them absentmindedly took a look inside the waxed paper. A moldy sandwich confronted him and fell apart in his hands. He gave Janet a disgusted look. After the event, she screamed at Miche for embarrassing her and possibly making her lose points.

As she grappled with Jack's incorrigible womanizing and her parents' refusal to let her divorce, riding remained her only outlet. She brought her favorite horse to compete at the Royal Winter Show in Ontario, Canada. She added other locales to her already long list of competitions, traveling to Mineola, Cedar Valley (in Glen Head), Smithtown (in St. James), and 110th Cavalry (in Boston, Massachusetts). Jack was entirely supportive of her events and, at the competitions he attended, would lean down to wipe the dust off her boots with a clean chamois cloth just after she mounted.

Janet interrupted her circuit only briefly, to serve as matron of honor at the wedding of her younger sister, Winnie (now, at age twenty-two, called Win), to Franklin d'Olier of Morristown, New Jersey. The ceremony at the Pierre hotel was lovely, but Janet must have wondered whether the hope of their wedding day, like hers, would be dashed.

After Win's marriage, everyone expected the Lees to divorce. Oddly enough, they did not bother to formalize their estrangement at this time, and stayed married, although always living in separate city and East Hampton residences.

Janet, astride Danseuse or Stepaside, found that she could forget Jack. In 1936 she received two reserves, finishing second. She also won three trophies and another first, three seconds, three thirds, and one fourth. The fact that she had by now broken her nose three times tumbling off her steed didn't stop her.

Janet had a reputation as a sound rider who occasionally beat better riders in the competitive 1930s riding circuit. She was riding hunters — not jumpers — so she was not as aggressive a rider as others were.

Janet, at least, had an escape. On the other hand, Jack felt trapped. The money situation was bad: he owed back taxes, and his great-uncle's estate was demanding repayment of the $25,000 he had borrowed. (One point on which he and his father agreed was the parlous state of the economy. In fact, J.V. gave an address to the town's Women's Republican Club, and the local newspaper reported, "A life-long Democrat, the retired attorney assured the assembled Republicans that, for the first time in three generations, his entire family was going to 'vote Republican.'")

Still, Janet wanted out of the marriage. Mimi Cecil, one of Jim Lee's granddaughters, said, "Finally, despite Granddad's general opposition to divorce, he realized that Jack was an incorrigible womanizer who was incapable of changing." So toward the end of 1936, Janet and Jack separated.

Janet asked her father-in-law to draw up the separation papers — *the betrayal!* Jack thought — which J.V. willingly did. Jack was convinced that everyone was against him, except, of course, his mother. He moved from the duplex into a small suite at the Westbury Hotel, one block west and two south of Janet and the girls. Janet kept the duplex, the daughters, and Danseuse.

Janet was getting out of the marriage at last. Even the Bouviers would not stand against it, although they disapproved and talked against Janet in front of Jackie and Lee. But, as it turned out, the breakup was not yet final.

Two issues conspired against women like Janet who sought divorce in the late thirties: the dogma and norms of the Catholic Church and the divorce law of New York. First, Janet knew that her religion was opposed to divorce. Although Janet's parish priest wasn't able to change her mind, he was able to make her feel guilty.

Then, too, she bumped into New York's restrictive divorce law. From 1787 to 1967 adultery was the only grounds for divorce in that state. But in 1939 Janet hired a capable attorney at Milbank, Tweed and Holt, whose principal Jeremiah Milbank was a friend of Jim Lee's. The attorney told her that the only way to get her divorce was to sue for adultery. Of course, in Jack's case, the charge was a perfect fit.

But Jack didn't want a divorce. Earlier, he had tried to turn the tables on Janet by writing "Old Man Lee" a self-pitying letter libeling Janet, saying that she was involved with another man. He invoked his children's names several times as a reason for Jim to discourage Janet from divorcing him, even writing that "Jacqueline and Lee suggest we forgive and forget." (They were eight and five years old at the time.) Jim ignored the letter and, instead, gave Janet the money for a private detective whose task was to catch Jack with another woman. The detective gathered more than enough evidence — photographs, names, and dates — and turned the material over to Janet.

In the meantime, Jack was preparing his side of the contest by trying to show that Janet was an abusive mother. He took depositions from household help who had seen Janet's temper in action and who were more eager to please the charming Mr. Bouvier than the demanding missus. Housemaids gave statements saying that Janet spanked Jackie for making too much noise and that Janet's mother had tried to slap Jackie on one occasion. Jack even enlisted his daughter Jackie, who went crying to her governess about tales Jack told her of her mother and grandfather's conspiracy against him: "Look at what they're doing to my daddy!"

Janet was enraged at Jack's attacks. She decided to make the detective's scandalous information public. The *New York Daily Mirror* broke the story, which was picked up by the major papers throughout the country. "A blonde" is how the tabloids tagged Jack's current girlfriend.

Janet had what she wanted: good reasons to claim adultery, along with emotional distress, and a public flagellation of Jack Bouvier in the nation's newspapers. But Janet's daughters paid the price for her revenge. Jackie, especially, at nine years old was fair game for schoolmates' teasing. From the children's point of view, the publicity was humiliating. And the girls didn't feel that things had gotten any better. Janet was still unhappy, and both parents tried to get the children to choose sides. Jack kept referring to Janet — in front of his daughters — as "that bitch." Grandfather Lee was peeved at having to help out with Janet's expenses, and their Bouvier relatives had made it clear that Janet was no longer part of the family. Even sisters-in-law and longtime best friends Maude and Michelle dropped her.

But Jackie retreated further into the dream world that she had already established. In role-playing games, she would seize the part of the romantic queen, while Lee would serve as her lady-in-waiting. Given Lee's pragmatism, her edgy personality, and her looks, it's not surprising that Janet would identify Lee as her favorite daughter. If this seems like a dreadful thing to say to children, remember that Janet was only one generation removed from parents who had openly dubbed their own daughters "the pretty one," "the smart one," and so on.

The girls learned to turn to each other for support. Jackie, particularly, did not have a large circle of friends, although she had an active fantasy life with imaginary friends, perhaps to compensate for her lack of real ones. Once, in Manhattan, Lee put on Janet's high heels, walked past the doorman, and was several blocks from the house before being spotted by a family friend. "I'm running away from home," Lee announced as she was scooped up and brought back home to a family who hadn't missed her absence.

Now that Jack was threatening Janet with his own smear tactics, she agreed to drop the New York divorce case. Instead, she took her daughters with her for a six-week "vacation" at the Lazy A Bar Ranch in Nevada. At its end, she entered a courtroom on July 22, 1940, wearing a pure white suit to testify about her marriage and the couple's failure at reconciliation. She stated that "[Jack] used to make very insulting remarks about my father in particular and the rest of my family."

The divorce was granted, but Janet's earlier attempt at embarrassing Jack through publicity boomeranged. Now that the divorce was legitimate news, the newspapers used it as an excuse to retell the scandal; for example, the *Daily News* headlined its story MRS. BOUVIER SHEDS "LOVE COMMUTER."

No wonder Jackie would grow up wary of the media.

After the publicity died down, Janet and Jack went on blaming each other and their respective in-laws. Jim Lee would always despise Jack. The extended Bouvier family would take decades before forgiving Janet for the divorce and its publicity.

And no matter how much Janet did for her eldest daughter throughout her lifetime, Jackie would never forget that Janet had banished her dashing father from her daily life.

Chapter 6

JANET'S ESTATE

Janet was desperate. Here she was, a divorced woman at a time when less than 2 percent of American women were divorced. She had two young daughters, no beau, and no money of her own—her father had not established trust funds for his family, nor had Jack's mother left anything to her grandchildren at her death three months earlier. Jack's support couldn't keep Janet and the girls in their accustomed style. In fact, because the economy brightened and he could find renters, Jim Lee had told Janet that she had to leave the duplex at 740 Park Avenue and move to a less spacious apartment—in another building he owned—at One Gracie Square. Janet took an occasional job as a model for Macy's department store but was paid scarcely more than her transportation costs. She also took a nurse's aide course and volunteered at the Presbyterian Hospital.

Another loss was less tangible but just as real to Janet. To some critical eyes, she had sacrificed her good name for independence from Jack. Her social status had changed, and some people would not introduce her—a divorced woman with children—to their unmarried brothers or sons.

Most of the Bouviers had dropped her, including Maude and Michelle. Her only comfort was the memory of bumping into her former sister-in-law Edie at a party. When Edie saw her, she sat at the piano and sang a song that was then popular, "(I Will Love You) Always." She looked at Janet while she sang. Tears sprang to Janet's eyes as she realized the depth of feeling for her former in-laws—and of one of them, at least, for her.

But the bottom line was that she had sole responsibility for her own bills. With Jack, she had enjoyed a generous allowance; what's more, the couple had never even bothered to try living on his income. There had always been the money Jack would borrow or the free housing to fall back on. Now she was on her own.

With one important exception: Jim Lee was still there to help. But as much as she relied on and appreciated his assistance, she couldn't help but remember that he had urged against her marrying Jack. In addition, she was trying to make a new life for herself and her girls and yet was still dependent on a father who saw no reason not to review her financial accounts just as he had her ex-husband's. No wonder Janet chafed at these constrictions, much as a thoroughbred would fret at being reined in at the gate.

Often she was bitter. "The only good thing from that marriage that I have is Jackie and Lee," she would tell people.

Jack was doing his best to irritate her, and he was succeeding. As if the embarrassment of divorce was not enough, he issued a caustic press release to the New York newspapers stating, "Women are all the victors in my generation."

Janet could forget her troubles on Danseuse. She received Stepaside as part of her settlement but could not keep him—she needed the cash more than a second horse and its expenses. She sold Stepaside to Peggy Kip, who rode on the same circuit. Janet returned to Long Island to chair the East Hampton Horse Show; in her traditional style, she now gave her name as Mrs. Lee Bouvier, placing her maiden name before her former married one. But competitive riding was becoming less important to Janet: she had already proved her abilities, and besides, she had more important things to do—like finding a new husband. It was Jackie who was becoming seriously interested in the sport, winning each event she entered in August's 1940 East Hampton Horse Show.

Despite Janet's declining interest in competitive riding, Jackie was eager to compete in the six-day National Horse Show at the Garden in November 1940 and 1941. The 1940 show was a harbinger of the developing world conflict. It benefited the Red Cross; although the United States was not yet at war, everyone was aware of Europe's desperate straits. The week before the show was tense, as the international situation delayed the acceptance of foreign military teams. National chauvinism played a part in the proceedings; the U.S. Army used its spot on the program not to display fancy dress uniforms, as it had in the past, but to get down to brass tacks. Troopers clad in service khaki, wearing steel helmets and carrying carbines, escorted the foreign teams as ten thousand spectators and the international press watched. Tanks rumbled their way across the Garden floor in an assertive show of iron brawn.

A number of foreign teams could not make the show at all; their countries were embattled. As *The New York Times* noted, missed were "the jolly Canadians, the hard-riding English officers and the effervescent Frenchmen."

Candy Van Alen remembers that show. As the head of the largest American unit of the Red Cross, she was to be given dozens of gorgeous red roses.

During the evening a friend pulled her aside. "Candy," she said, "Janet Bouvier is so blue. It might lift her spirits to receive the roses—would you mind if we gave them to her?" Candy quickly agreed, and Janet's spirits were buoyed, if only briefly.

In 1941 Jackie rode in the junior events along with Ethel Skakel (who would later become her sister-in-law), Edward Albee (the playwright), and William F. Buckley (the conservative writer). Imagine this group meeting again years later, when their separate paths had carried them so far afield. At the time, the young riders were merely friends given free rein by their chaperones to socialize after their time-consuming horse grooming while their mothers or governesses were nominally in attendance somewhere in the arena. Friendship aside, the number of spectators, the importance of the show, and the presence of the press added to the competition and pressure, even in the children's division.

Although the specter of war cast a pall on the show, in that era it "still had vestiges of social prestige," says one of Jackie's fellow riders, Bill Steinkraus. "Earlier in the century, the opening night at the National was like opening night at the opera. It was all dress, and anyone who was anybody in New York showed horses."

Many sporting events were still dominated by amateurs. "At that time," Steinkraus explains, "sport was not to be confused with money-grubbing at any level. In riding, as in tennis and yachting, you dressed and acted appropriately, and the spectators were of the same cloth."

The next summer, the year after the divorce, twelve-year-old Jackie did well at East Hampton, winning second place in horsemanship to young Bill Steinkraus's first. (That Jackie came in second was no disgrace; Steinkraus became a legend in the sport, in 1968 winning the first-ever individual U.S. Olympic gold medal in equestrian sport.) *The New York Times* covered the small but socially important 1941 show on its sports pages, with the head STEINKRAUS CAPTURES TWO TITLES AT THE EAST HAMPTON HORSE SHOW. The story also reported: "Miss Bouvier's Danseuse was a star performer in today's show. Danseuse won blues for her young rider in the horsemanship class for children under 14, the hunter hack event, the riding competition for children under 16 and the ladies' hunter contest for the Hamlin Memorial Challenge Cup."

Jackie rode Danseuse for each of her four blues, leading the *East Hampton Star* to characterize Danseuse as "one of the few famous local horses [with] many championships to her credit." Janet did not ride but, instead, donated a trophy to the show. This would be one of the last shows in East Hampton, for in 1943 the riding club was forced into foreclosure. (Today it operates as the Hampton Classic.)

Janet was still having difficulty coping as a single mother of two independent young girls. She also felt stigmatized as a divorced woman. Moreover, the breakup had not rid her of Jack; he still had generous visitation rights. She knew that celebrating the holidays alone with the girls would be dreary, and she enjoyed socializing with her sisters. Family turmoil had left Jackie and Lee withdrawn. Janet thought these Lee family get-togethers would give them a chance to be more convivial. She cheerfully accepted the invitations extended each year by her elder sister, Marion, and brother-in-law John Ryan for Thanksgiving, Christmas, and Easter. Marion knew that Janet could always be counted on to shine at gatherings and wanted her children to get to know their delightful Tante Janet. (This Irish American family used the French word for *aunt* because they preferred not to grapple with either the nasal midwestern pronunciation or the exaggerated New England articulation.)

Marion and John lived on a wonderful, heavily wooded ten-acre estate in Hewlett, Long Island. One outdoor chore they assigned their five children — John, Joan, Mary-Lee (Mimi), James, and Diana — each autumn was raking leaves. But there was a rule: no jumping in the leaf piles until the Thanksgiving holiday!

One November there was an especially tempting deep pile near the house's walkway. The Ryan children eyed it covetously as they walked past it each day awaiting the Bouvier girls as well as Winnie's children, Ann and Lee-lee. Finally Thanksgiving Day arrived and the first car pulled up, with Janet and the girls. The children went to greet their relatives. Janet's niece Mimi Cecil remembers the smart, bright royal blue suit Janet wore that year and her shiny black patent pumps. As Jackie and Lee piled out, all the children gathered around the ceremonial heap of golden leaves, eager to jump in.

The Ryan kids had learned their manners: "Go ahead, Jackie," and, "You jump in first, Lee."

The Bouvier girls, too, knew what was expected. "No, you start," they demurred.

Finally, nature-loving Janet cried, "Well, if you won't, I will!" slipped off her pumps, and leaped into the crisp pile of leaves until she was buried to the collar of her blue wool outfit. The children followed suit, and the ice was broken; the extended family was laughing together, covered with the surplus of fall.

Excursions out of the house were always exciting for the Bouvier children—the family parties, the girls seeing Jack on weekends, the horse shows—but aside from those special treats, life at home was gloomy. Janet constantly worried about the bills because she refused to live within her reduced circumstances. She spent money nearly as freely as when she had a Bouvier to support her, and she resented her "meager" support payments of $13,000 a year (today, $160,000). Then again, Janet had grown used to living in a certain fashion in both her father's and her husband's houses. She would not accept that things had changed, especially because she felt that *she* was not the one who should be punished for the death of her tumultuous marriage.

But when it came to the children, with other expenses so high, she couldn't—and wouldn't—compete with her ex-husband, who would spoil Jackie and Lee each weekend. The activities Jack planned for them were pure fun. He organized such lighthearted events as attending matinees, shopping at F. A. O. Schwarz, and visiting the nearest pet shop to borrow puppies to walk through Central Park.

Janet, on the other hand, stayed focused on manners and schoolwork. The girls' after-school activities were also for a purpose: ballet lessons from Miss O'Neill, social dancing taught by Miss Hubbell in the Colony Club ballroom, and, of course, riding lessons. Occasionally Jackie would play in Central Park with her girlfriend Kate Roosevelt, the president's granddaughter, but the child's Secret Service guards made the girls feel self-conscious. "It was no fun," Jackie said later to Mary Barelli Gallagher of the eagle-eyed men who watched them play, and the observant young Jackie noted that the guards' presence also made Kate uncomfortable.

There was little frivolity at home with Janet. Even at the table, there were lessons to learn. Dinnertime conversation was conducted in French; if Jackie or Lee could not remember the French *sel* instead of *salt*, Janet would not pass the shaker. Jackie recalled, "Our mother used to make us play a game. We sat at the table, and every child had in front of them ten matches. Each time you said an English word, you'd throw a match away." The person with the last match won the game.

Janet was careful with her girls' recreation, too. Jackie—although a fine amateur rider—was no longer attending shows outside summer months, except for the National. The other children in her circle noticed that she was "more restricted" than they. One fellow noted that although Jackie "adored horses, she was not really a part of the horse-show regulars." It was unthinkable for Janet to take the wheel of a station wagon to drive her daughter to shows around the region, as many other mothers did—how middle class! Nor would she allow another adult—for example, a riding instructor—to supervise Jackie.

The result was that Jackie's ties to the other children who saw one another week after week became tenuous. She was always an outsider, welcomed when she participated but always slightly outside the circle. Jackie was already sensitive to being from a "broken home," as the expression of the times had it, and her isolation from the other young riders only added to her sense of separateness.

Despite the commonality of their interests, Janet bonded as a mother to Lee more strongly than she did to Jackie. Perhaps Jackie's early infatuation with her father tainted the mother-daughter relationship. Although Janet would always be there when Jackie needed her—indeed, Jackie, in turn, was a better daughter to Janet than Lee ever was—she would label photographs in family albums as just plain "Jackie" and as "my Lee."

Believing that her strict control of the girls was the mark of a good parent, Janet resented their father's destructive influence. After all her careful work, she said, he would take them and destroy the values she had worked so hard to instill, so that it would take her weeks to get them to return to good manners. As a consequence, Janet's temper was hair-trigger: an independent Jackie and a smart Lee knew how to set their mother off. Unfortunately, Janet would resort to slaps and spankings, as well as unkind words, when she felt herself at wit's end.

It was becoming clear that her daughters preferred the company of their father—what child wouldn't, given these circumstances? Jackie in particular favored her father over her mother, and when Janet realized this, the fact fed her anger and, possibly, explained her preference for Lee. Her fury overrode her common sense one Sunday night when Jack returned the girls, wearing gifts of inexpensive trinkets, back to their Gracie Square apartment. Janet went on a tear against both the girls and their father. She told her daughters' governess, "If they cry for their father, *spank* them." When the unhappy governess—who herself had been taken by Jack's charm—refused, Janet carried out the task with a vengeance.

Janet found it hard to take comfort in any aspect of her everyday life. She enjoyed dating but had not found a man she could count on. Her religion couldn't help her, as she felt rejected by the Catholic Church. Janet mistakenly thought she had been automatically excommunicated upon her divorce—a common misunderstanding. She was in fact considered still to be a member of the Church, though denied the sacraments. Besides, she was angry with the Church for her clergy's sanctimonious attitude and lack of support for her, a wronged wife. Nevertheless, she continued to take the girls to Church of St. Ignatius Loyola on Park Avenue for mass each Sunday.

Janet stepped up her social drinking; the morning after, she'd sleep until noon. Without riding to keep her sharp, Janet spent too many of her days bleary-eyed. But when she went out at night—her only escape during the dull winter months—her practical sense kept her sights focused on finding a good husband, as remarriage was the only way to ensure her daughters' future.

Jack intuitively knew that the girls were suffering—or was one of Janet's staff tipping him off? Accusations were hurled in both directions. This time, Jack charged her with feeding the girls cold canned food. Janet was furious: it might have been true, but if so, it was Jack's fault. It was the divorce that forced her to reduce her staff, and she was not about to don an apron and whip up dinner on the cook's day off.

Later, her memory of these times took a different spin, and she spoke of them as an intimate interval for the family of three. "Lee loved to prepare meals," Janet said. "When the cook was off, Lee would say, 'Mother, I'll take care of dinner.'"

Perhaps the young Lee preferred her own cooking to the unheated canned food.

While Janet waited out her residency requirement in Nevada, she had met Esther Auchincloss Nash, there to divorce Edmund Witherill Nash (brother to the poet Ogden Nash). Edmund was a heavy drinker and a womanizer like Jack. The women hit it off; as they confided in each other, Esther told Janet about growing up in Newport with her younger brother, Hughdie, and sister, Annie Burr. She mentioned that Hughdie had graduated from Yale University and studied in England, following this with a law degree from Columbia University in 1924, the same degree Janet's father had earned at Columbia twenty-five years earlier.

It seems that while Janet had been learning charm at Sweet Briar, farther north Hughdie Auchincloss had been taking time out from his Manhattan law practice to get married for the first time. In 1925 he married the exotic Maya de Chrapovitsky at the Russian Cathedral of St. Nicholas in New York. She was the descendant of many Russian war heroes, including M. E. de Chrapovitsky, the adjutant general of the Russian military immortalized in a painting by Gesse that hangs in the Winter Palace. Her father, Lieutenant Colonel de Chrapovitsky (often misidentified as an admiral), was killed at Port Arthur in the Russo-Japanese War in 1905 and was posthumously awarded the Cross of St. George. Maya and her mother had escaped the Bolsheviks to come to America.

Hughdie's knowledge of Russia attracted him to Maya. He had traveled there in 1922 as the New York representative of the students' Friendship Fund, formed to assist students in foreign countries. When the couple married, the news appeared in the "Social Circles" column of the *Newport Daily News* following the item "Mrs. Vanderbilt Sr. has opened 'The Breakers' for the season."

In 1927 the couple had a son, named Hugh Dudley Auchincloss III, after his grandfather and father, and nicknamed Yusha—the Russian diminutive for *Hugh*. The family lived in Washington, D.C., because Hughdie was serving in the Commerce Department as a special agent in aeronautics. Then he received a letter from his old Yale friend Henry Luce inviting him to invest in his concept for a weekly newsmagazine to be called *Time*. Luce took care to hold the preferred stock, selling common shares to his college classmates and other investors. Wealthy Hughdie was willing to help out Luce but had no interest in buying stock in his newsmagazine. Instead, he merely lent Luce the money, missing out on an opportunity to make a fortune. (One Yale student's mother who had invested a significant amount later remarked that she lived off her Time-Life dividends for the remainder of her life.)

Just two weeks after Janet had married Jack Bouvier, Maya suffered a terrible accident. The Auchinclosses had thought it would be fun to sightsee over the nation's capital in a two-motored Sikorsky amphibious plane. When the jaunt ended, Maya jumped out and hurried around to the opposite side to thank the pilot. She blundered straight into the sharp, whirling propeller.

A metal blade drove into her head, fracturing and cleaving her skull. Unfortunately, Maya had affixed a brooch on her hat that morning, and the pin was driven into her brain by the force of the propeller. On the other hand, if the brooch hadn't slowed the blade, Maya might have been decapitated on the spot, said her son years later. Her physician announced that the wound "looked as though Mrs. Auchincloss had been struck with an ax wielded at full force." Little hope was held for her recovery.

She did live, but after a lengthy hospital stay she needed to enter the best sanitarium that Hughdie could find. Now he was, in effect, the sole parent of Yusha, only a year old. He changed positions within the government, going into the State Department — where, as a Yale undergraduate, he had anticipated spending his career — again, as an aviation specialist.

Yet he found that government service wasn't enough for him; perhaps he wanted to stay busy enough to forget the accident. So Hughdie organized an investment firm on the side, knowing that the crash had made men in his circle wary of unfamiliar investment houses. He thought he might be able to use his skills — and his name — to profitable advantage, so he borrowed a million dollars (about twelve times that today) from his mother, Emma, for the start-up venture.

Hughdie's decision became more than a personal one, though. A controversy erupted over whether it was proper for a State official to hold outside employment. In fact, the issue was deemed important enough by reporters to raise to Secretary of State Henry L. Stimson at a press conference. The Secretary announced that such decisions were made on an individual basis and were governed by particular circumstances. He did point out, though, that he and the undersecretary had both resigned from their New York law firms when they accepted their posts.

Not surprisingly, given Stimson's comments, in early 1931 Hughdie resigned from State to devote his full efforts to his brokerage firm in Washington — Auchincloss, Parker & Redpath, located at 719 Fifteenth Street, N.W. (The firm also established a New York office.) In order to serve as the company's floor member, in late spring Hughdie bought his own seat on the Exchange for $285,000 ($3.2 million today).

Maya's recovery continued more smoothly than anyone had anticipated. However, in spite of her physical recuperation, her personality had altered. The couple divorced in 1932. Three years later Hughdie married Nina Gore Vidal, daughter of the blind U.S. senator from Oklahoma and the former wife of Eugene L. Vidal, himself an air expert and chief of the U.S. Bureau of Air Commerce (now the Federal Aviation Administration). They were both living in apartments at the Wardman Park Hotel (now the Marriott Wardman Park Hotel), and their marriage took place at the New York Avenue Presbyterian Church.

Nina had a young son, the precocious Gore Vidal, today the well-known author and playwright, who at ten years old would become stepbrother to eight-year-old Yusha.

This marriage brought its own problems. If Maya had been exotic, Nina was quixotic. She was a vivacious woman but also an eccentric and unpredictable wife. Her son Gore would later write that she was an alcoholic and "certifiably insane." It seems that she may have suffered from a bipolar disorder. In any case, everyone agreed that she could be very difficult. For example, she was an alternate delegate to the Democratic National Convention in 1940. However, a few weeks before the event, Nina sent a telegram to Willkie headquarters announcing her support for the dark-horse Republican candidate rather than the incumbent Franklin D. Roosevelt.

One description of her that appeared in the *Washington Herald* several years after their marriage sounds presciently like a description of Janet: "When she enters a room you feel here comes everything that is fresh, healthy and beautiful. Her skin glows warmly and her huge brown eyes are bright. An outdoor woman, she is full of indoor charm. Rides every day of her life. Has two small children of her own."

The two small children referred to were Nina and Hughdie's offspring: Nina (nicknamed Nini) Gore Auchincloss, born in 1937, and Thomas Gore Auchincloss, born in 1939. Nina's manic irrationality was difficult for Hughdie to tolerate, but her affair with an admiral served as a warning shot he heeded. Even this patient man had his limits. They separated in 1941, intending to divorce.

At the same time, Janet took a trip to the Caribbean with friends. She had pulled herself out of her despondency and was determined to remake her life in a way that would ensure security for her daughters. The most logical way to do so would be to forge a successful second marriage. In the Caribbean she met Hughdie Auchincloss, who had gone down with his own friends. She was quick to let him know of her friendship with his sister Esther, who was now remarried to Norman Henry Biltz, a Nevada tycoon. And, as Yusha later wryly notes, "Janet and my father had something in common: they both had unfaithful spouses."

Reserved Hughdie was immediately attracted to the vivacious Janet. Janet had a sweet way of flirting with him: she would glance at him playfully, turn her head to the side, and tease him, "Hughdie, Hughdie, Hughdie." When she took his arm, she'd lean in toward him as if she couldn't bear to be more than a few inches away. You could almost see this man falling in love.

On Janet's part, she was impressed with Hughdie's family tree — studded as it was with Van Rensselaers and Rockefellers, Tiffanys and Vanderbilts — and stressed branches of her history, whether real or imagined, that would lead him to believe that she sprang from similar roots. She most enjoyed the fact that the year's *Social Register* included listings for forty-seven Auchinclosses, compared with forty-two Rockefellers and *only two* Bouviers. She knew that besides his estate Merrywood in Mc-Lean, Virginia — and his mother's two estates in Newport, Rhode Island, and Fairfield, Connecticut — he also had an apartment on Park Avenue. When he was in town, he would take advantage of his memberships in the University Club, the Racquet and Tennis Club, the Grolier Club, and the New York Yacht Club.

She was also genuinely attracted to his quiet demeanor and gentlemanly ways: what a welcome relief from Jack Bouvier! Even his stout figure and tweedy clothes appealed to her, after her ex-husband's cinched waist and silk pajamas. His steady personality complemented the more mercurial Janet, although others found him dull — his stepson, Gore Vidal, later characterized Hughdie as "a magnum of chloroform." Janet and Hughdie had a common goal, however, which was a respectable and well-maintained home life. Certainly, at this point, Hughdie needed a wife to help raise his three children — his two ex-wives were not in the best position to be mothers — and Janet wanted a stable father for hers.

It was wartime in Europe, and matters of the heart were heating up back home. By the end of the year, Hughdie and Janet decided that she should bring the girls down from New York to Washington, D.C., to meet him and his eldest son, Yusha, home from Groton for Christmas break. The bombing of Pearl Harbor on December 7 quickened their desire rather than restrained it. On December 17 Hughdie and Yusha, fourteen years old, met the Bouvier women — Jackie, twelve, and Lee, eight — at Washington's Union Station, which was crowded with servicemen.

Hughdie instructed Yusha to make the girls feel at home and to behave himself, by which Yusha says Hughdie meant "don't tease them." The teenager was impressed with Jackie's "concern for the men in uniform and knowledge of current affairs," especially because of "her French heritage." He didn't see her *at all* as a kid to tease.

At Merrywood, the spectacular estate in McLean that Hughdie had bought with Maya, the new couple drank cocktails while Yusha and Jackie talked about how they could help the war effort. Yusha was determined to join the Marines, even saying that he would drop out of Groton before graduation to do so. Jackie admonished him, saying frankly, "The Marines don't want dumbbells, Yusha."

Yusha remembers, "After supper, and having persuaded Lee to retire, Mrs. Bouvier and my father proceeded to teach Jackie and me how to play gin rummy, which became an evening ritual for the following week." During the day the two families tromped through the woods surrounding Merrywood and poked into the barn. Yusha showed off his polo pony Chief, and Jackie told him about Danseuse, which she now considered her own mare.

Yusha was developing a gentle crush on Jackie and was angry at himself for not having the wherewithal to buy her a Christmas present. Instead, he told her, on her next visit he would share Chief with her.

Jackie quickly retorted, "Which half? Cleaning up and expense?"

They spent mornings visiting the nation's monuments. Hughdie had arranged for the group to have lunch with John Walker, then the chief curator and later the director of the National Gallery of Art, who accompanied them on a tour of the museum. "It was then that I first discovered one of my greatest delights — the deep pleasure experienced in looking at masterpieces of painting and sculpture," Jackie later said.

At Arlington National Cemetery the young people worried that their friends might lose their lives in the war. But if that end was fated, Jackie noted, "What a peaceful place to be."

Jackie and Yusha spent their afternoons hiking through Merrywood's fields — while trying to lose Lee, tracking behind them — and standing on its rocky precipice overlooking the Potomac River. Before the visit ended, Jackie invited Yusha sightseeing in Manhattan with her over their Easter break. (Janet and the girls now rented an apartment at 520 East Eighty-sixth Street.)

When the school year ended, Yusha was back at Merrywood with

Hughdie, who by now had joined the navy and was to serve with British intelligence in Kingston, Jamaica. Despite the stories that later developed about Janet chasing Hughdie because of his wealth, she was actually very reluctant to commit herself. He came with a complicated set of children in tow and could be a little stuffy. It was Hughdie who was doing the pursuing; instead of jumping at the chance, Janet feared making a second mistake.

But her feeling of dread at the prospect of Hughdie's wartime absence clinched her decision. When Janet came down to visit before he shipped out, the couple decided to marry. Hughdie was forty-four years old; Janet, thirty-four.

Hughdie's mother, Emma, couldn't wait to meet Janet, though she had not yet invited her to visit in Connecticut. As she later wrote Janet's mother, Margaret, "I did not want to do *anything until she made up her mind*" (emphasis added). Now that Janet had finally decided to accept Hughdie's proposal, they were free to meet.

Yusha was delighted with the news, except for one concern. He had developed a schoolboy crush on Jackie and guiltily thought that with the impending marriage, his feelings for her were both inappropriate and morally wrong. Hughdie carefully explained to his son that his emotions were allowable; there was no blood relationship with a stepsister. With that off his mind, Yusha was pleased when Jackie later brought him to meet her own beloved father in his new apartment at 125 East Seventy-fourth Street. (Jack would live there for the rest of his life, as the Westbury was too expensive for him even in this accelerated economy.)

In fact, Jackie called Yusha the day before the wedding: "Won't this be fun? I've always wanted a brother, and now I'll get one."

But it was wartime, and the marriage had to be arranged quickly. Janet wore a street-length dress, and Hughdie looked splendid in his white navy lieutenant's uniform. Yusha served as best man: after all, with his typical kindness and consideration for his son, his father had asked him for his approval before proposing to Janet. "I like to think I can claim some credit for having [Janet] as both friend and family," said Yusha years later.

Wartime travel restrictions meant that Jackie and Lee could not go down for the fifteen-minute outdoor ceremony that took place on the morning of June 21, 1942. Hughdie's sister Annie Burr Auchincloss Lewis did attend with her husband, Wilmarth (nicknamed Lefty), as they, too, were living in Washington. Things were so rushed that the bride drove the groom to Union Station — not to depart on a honeymoon with him but rather to see him board a military train for the first leg of his journey to Kingston.

Several days later Hughdie arrived in the eastern Caribbean to trace U-boat action. Yusha escorted Janet up to his grandmother Emma's Dormy House in Fairfield, Connecticut, so that Janet could meet her new mother-in-law, who was too ill to summer at Hammersmith Farm. Janet sent the girls to spend the summer in East Hampton.

Yusha headed west to Nevada. His mother, Maya, amazingly, had recovered from the gruesome accident. Now remarried, with three more sons, she lived in La Jolla, California, although she couldn't leave her young children to visit Yusha at Lake Tahoe, where he was staying with Hughdie's sister Esther and the Biltz family. Nevertheless, Yusha brought photos and proudly showed the Biltzes the new women in his life — Janet, Jackie, and Lee.

Despite her illness, Emma wrote Janet's mother on her blue Dormy House stationery in a letter dated July 3, 1942.

> *It was certainly quite exciting to have Hugh get married and move off to Jamaica — all in a minute — and I feel very sorry for Janet that he had to go. I think he did not realize beforehand, when he asked for foreign service, that he might be getting married the day before and I do hope that he will be able after a while, to get transferred back to this country.*
>
> *It has been such a great pleasure for me to meet Janet and I am sure I am going to like her very much and I feel very grateful to her for accepting my son. He has talked to me a great deal this winter about her . . . but I have not been at all well. . . . Of course, I feel that my son is a pretty nice young man but he has had a great many disappointments. . . . I sometimes feel that he is too good-natured. He hates to hurt anyone's feelings and I have often told him that if he had treated his first two wives a little more severely, they would have more respect for him.*

In a postscript, she added: "My sister's nurse has just called me up to tell me that Janet had been over to see my sister-in-law and they were all perfectly delighted with her."

Later in the month Emma sent her new daughter-in-law diamond jewelry that she had inherited from her Jennings relatives, saying, "This will be from Annie Burr and Esther as well as myself and I hope you will be able to use it. If you want to have it done over in any way, do not hesitate to use the stones."

She also wrote a poignant note, "I am very discouraged about [Hugh-

die] getting back to this country and I feel it is doubtful if I should ever
see him again."

Her premonition was sadly accurate. In less than two months, Emma
was dead.

In the fall Janet and the girls moved into Merrywood. The girls had
spent the summer in East Hampton; unfortunately, Janet was so caught
up in her new life as mistress of Merrywood that she had forgotten to
pack her daughters' clothes. All summer long they were reduced to wearing their cousins' hand-me-downs. On Labor Day Hughdie was still in
the Caribbean and Yusha at Groton. Nini and Tommy were with their
mother, Nina. Janet enrolled the girls in school—Jackie in seventh
grade at Holton-Arms School in Washington, D.C. (now in Bethesda,
Maryland), and Lee in fifth grade at McLean's Potomac School. Lee was
having a difficult time adjusting to losing her life in New York and
turned to her elder sister as her touchstone in this confusing new world.

September brought the death of Emma, at her home in Connecticut.
The War Office sent Hughdie back to Washington to a desk job at the
Pentagon. News of Emma's vast estate became public: she left more than
$5 million (more than ten times that today) to her three children—
Esther, Hughdie, and Annie Burr—and Hammersmith Farm, valued for
the purpose of probate at $177,000 to Hughdie. (The 1942 inheritance's
cash value for the three Auchinclosses would be, today, about $18 million
each.) Hughdie was a very rich man.

He knew it, too. Shortly after his marriage to Janet, one of his friends
at the Metropolitan Club joshed with him: "How is someone old like you
able to attract these beautiful young women?"

Hughdie laughed. "Money, my friend."

Janet set about making herself the mistress of Merrywood and meeting Hughdie's friends. They, too, were interested in Hughdie's new wife.

Janet had been awestruck the first time she had seen Merrywood. It
was a vast estate, far nicer than her former in-laws' Lasata, she sniffed.
Hughdie had bought the house, built in 1919, from the estate of Newbold
Noyes, owner and associate editor of the *Washington Star* newspaper.

Situated on forty-six acres of virgin property atop the Potomac palisades, the two-story Georgian brick mansion was surrounded by ter-
raced gardens. Even from inside the house, a visitor could hear the sound
of the river far below, rippling over boulders heaped askew by glacial
movement eons earlier. A circular driveway, added by Maya, wife num-

ber one, drew visitors to the welcoming white carriage porch, giving the house a soupçon of Southern Colonial style. The house was five bays broad, punctuated by pilasters. A flagstone terrace, edged with boxwood, ran the length of the house. In the back, there were two levels of terraces: an upper stone one and a lower grass one.

Janet had imagined herself mistress of such a great home. The house wasn't only magnificent; it was also pretty. The first floor had an impressive central entrance hall with a grand staircase—again, in the Colonial style. The main floor also included a living room with built-in shelves—perfect for Janet's growing collection of Lowestoft. There was a large circular card room that had been added by Nina, wife number two, but was now marked by a painting above the fireplace of Janet mounted on Danseuse. Several powder rooms, a paneled library, a dining room with a Waterford chandelier and a Cormandel screen, a kitchen with a stove larger than the one in downtown Washington's Mayflower Hotel, a butler's pantry, and a dining room for the five servants completed this level.

The second floor contained two master bedrooms with a sitting room adjoining them; outside, a terrace overlooking the river linked the suites. There were seven other bedrooms and six bathrooms on that floor. The attic level had four bedrooms and two baths.

The basement included a wine cellar, a walk-in refrigerator, the laundry room, and a cold room for game—where Gore Vidal, when his mother was married to Hughdie, first had sex with a girl. His first sex with a boy was on the white tile floor of one of Merrywood's bathrooms. (Later, Vidal would make Merrywood the prototype for the house Laurel Hill in his novel *Washington, D.C.*)

Merrywood's fifty acres formed one of the few remaining untouched preserves in the Potomac palisades. When she learned that George Washington himself had once surveyed the property, Janet felt that she was a custodian of America's legacy.

She would walk the property, much as she had when Hughdie showed it on her first visit. The estate superintendent lived in a six-room tenant house. There was also a four-car garage with a second-floor apartment consisting of five bedrooms, a sitting room, kitchen, and baths. The garage included automatic car-washing equipment, and a level underneath the garage contained an indoor gymnasium, including a badminton court. There was a greenhouse and, nearby, a five-room cottage for the gardener. A shooting range and a tennis court were for leisure hours. The swimming pool, located away from the main house, had both high and low diving boards. And its bathhouse was modeled after a Swiss chalet. Of course, there were stables for the horses. Even the dogs were housed appropriately, in their own kennel.

Janet had moved from being the granddaughter of a woman with an Irish brogue who had started her life in this country in the tenements of the Lower East Side just sixty years earlier to the chatelaine of one of the greatest houses in the nation's capital.

When the girls arrived back from East Hampton, tanned and spoiled, Janet said they could choose the colors for their new rooms and the chintz for their curtains. (For the public rooms, she hired interior designer Elizabeth Draper, who combined Hughdie's family pieces with Oriental rugs and eighteenth-century antiques.) Jackie decided on buttercup yellow; Lee, cornflower blue. Their furniture was painted white, and a border of wild flowers decorated the bedroom walls. Janet was from the genteel school of decorating in which everything was comfortable, flowered, and faded—nothing could appear new. The look evoked images of pedigreed dogs and horses romping outdoors, which, in this case, they actually were.

Janet spotted something she wanted to discard: the Brooks Brothers shirts that sixteen-year-old Gore Vidal had left behind, possibly in his eagerness to flee to his new life, along with the interest he hoped to receive on a $25,000 ($315,000 today) trust fund Hughdie had set up for him. But Jackie wanted to keep his shirts, insisting she could use them for hacking. Jackie's and Lee's bedrooms were on the attic level with the bedrooms of the Auchincloss children—Yusha, Tommy, and Nina—when they visited on holidays.

Of course, Jackie and Lee needed to acclimate to their new stepfather, who was very different from their own father: he was staid, a tad absentminded, and told overly long stories. The greatest surprise was the dinnertime rule of standing by one's chair before meals and reciting the Auchincloss creed almost as if it were a blessing: "Obedience to the unenforceable." This was the price Jackie and Lee paid for living in Auchincloss territory, and if Jackie was heard to mumble it sotto voce, she would have to repeat it *solo* and *con brio*.

Janet was frustrated by wartime restrictions: because of fuel rationing, nearly half of Merrywood had to be shut down. Hughdie did his part by admonishing all to turn off unnecessary lights and by insisting that frozen food should be kept on long tables outdoors. (This actually wasted precious energy whenever the temperature rose above thirty-two degrees, because then the walk-in freezer needed to be quickly turned to its coldest level — but Hughdie was allowed an idiosyncrasy or two.) Fires lit throughout the house helped heat the mansion, but the family still looked forward to spring.

Despite the girls beginning a new year in a totally new school, the couple left them for a trip to Nevada so that Janet could visit Hughdie's sister Esther. While they were there, Hughdie decided to buy his own ranch. A local newspaper claimed that Janet "wants to learn to cook so that they can really live a simple life on the ranch, and Lee is already studying up on the subject of cattle in anticipation!" (The ranch was soon sold.)

Janet's new responsibilities as the mistress of two estates meant cutting back on competitive riding. Besides her demanding schedule, she no longer needed a sport to sublimate her frustration at being stuck in a miserable marriage. When Janet curtailed her own interest in shows, Jackie's opportunity to enter vanished, too. Either Jackie was content to ride at Merrywood and not compete or she was unwilling to force a showdown with her mother. After all, the hunt country of Middleburg, Virginia, was only two hours away, and there were also local riding paths and hunt clubs on either side of the Potomac.

In the meanwhile, Jack Bouvier did not take kindly to the marriage. Despite his cordiality upon first meeting Yusha, he derided Hughdie behind his back. "Take a loss with Auchincloss!" he would snicker to his fellow brokers. According to John Davis, neither was Jack kind to Yusha, despite Jackie's affection for her new stepbrother. Behind Yusha's back, he mocked the shy teenager to others, calling him "Yusha Poosha."

He must not have been happy, either, when he saw a photo of his former father-in-law, James T. Lee, on the front business page of *The New York Times*. The article noted that Lee, by now the president of the Central Savings Bank, was elected to the board of directors of the Chase National Bank. The following year he could read that Jim had bought the old brownstone mansion, with its own pipe organ, at the corner of Fifth Avenue and Forty-seventh Street for $900,000 ($8.8 million today). Its former owner had been Jay Gould, the railroad financier and "the most hated man in America" because of his speculations in gold and in the Erie Railroad, both of which brought ruin to thousands of families. The house was well known in Gould's day because he suffered from insomnia — no wonder — and would pace up and down the block in the middle of the night, guarded by two bodyguards. Gould had died in the massive four-story house in 1892. The article, which referred to Jim as "a large holder of real estate in midtown Manhattan," said he had bought the property as an investment.

By now Jack was using any excuse to drink, and the success of others was certainly making him thirsty. Once the news of "Old Man Lee" set him off, he would segue to Janet's second marriage, Hughdie's incredible inheritance, and his daughters' growing up in another man's (magnificent) house. One martini, two martinis, three martinis, floor.

In 1944 Jack started making periodic check-ins at lavish drying-out clinics, only to check out again and pick up the bottle. He would go on doing so for the rest of his life.

Jackie, though, was clever about what she wanted. She had fallen in love with Merrywood—who wouldn't?—and played this trump card against her father. At Christmas 1942 the girls were visiting Jack in his East Side apartment. By telling him of her luxurious life at Merrywood, she would coax him into buying her another sweater or trinket. Back at Merrywood, she would display her spoils in the hope that Janet or Hughdie would match Jack's gift. The trick worked on occasion; although it was an unbecoming trait of Jackie's, her early victories in manipulation set a pattern.

Jackie and Lee spent the summer of 1943 in McLean, profoundly disappointing their father and also upsetting Lee, who was a beach sprite. But Lee stayed poolside at Merrywood while Jackie rode its fields on Danseuse.

Earlier that year Janet had unexpectedly lost her mother, Margaret, at age sixty-five. Margaret had been visiting Hewlett to see her eldest daughter, Marion Ryan, who was very ill. (The diagnosis was lung cancer—she was a heavy smoker—but the "c" word was never mentioned, according to Marion's daughter Mimi Ryan Cecil, a young teen at the time.) In this somber household, Margaret suffered a stroke during the night. She was buried in the graveyard at St. Philomena Church in East Hampton. Her death was a shock for the Ryan children and one that was repeated a few months later when their own mother died.

Jackie's irrational romanticizing of her father might have been tempered had she known that a married Englishwoman, Anne Plugge, had just given birth to fraternal twins who, although raised as products of the Plugge marriage, were unmistakably the children of Jack Bouvier. He was able to keep their existence secret because they lived in London. Surprisingly, considering the impact he had on his daughters, he never took a role in the twins' lives.

With all the children but Lee in boarding school, Janet could concentrate on adult interests. Jackie had just left for Miss Porter's School in Farmington, Connecticut, a boarding school for young ladies founded in 1843. Long before Jackie left home, Janet had explained menstruation to her in a no-nonsense manner, giving her a special calendar for keeping track of her periods. Janet emphasized to all her daughters that menstruating was a good thing, linking it to their later ability to become mothers.

Janet had refused to allow Jackie to keep Danseuse at Farmington (as the school is called) because she thought it too indulgent. Jackie must have figured that her father would not be able to afford the payment, so she went directly to her grandfather J.V., who agreed to pay for its stabling. Janet was irritated at being countermanded, but gave in.

Jackie and, later, Lee could see their Ryan cousins during the year because they were enrolled at a school in the same town. But Jackie's favorite times were when glamorous Jack visited. The rest of her leisure hours, when she wasn't riding Danseuse, she would spend lying on her dorm bed, reading.

Jackie still made frequent visits to see Jack. When she was expected, Jack would clear his calendar to devote himself to her whims. On one visit Jackie had an appointment with the hairdresser. Kathleen Bouvier, who was visiting Jack with her husband, Miche, remembered Jack's reaction to a phone call from Jackie with the startling news that she was now sporting the new poodle cut.

Jack was beside himself with nervousness. How would she look? Would it suit her? Kathleen tried to soothe him, but he was a "nervous wreck." Of course, when Jackie walked in, they all saw that her thick, wavy hair looked wonderful in that style—and Miche and Kathleen, at least, were a little angry at themselves for being caught up in Jack's obsession with Jackie.

Christmas 1942 was the new family's first time together. Everyone was in a good mood—at Merrywood and elsewhere—since the victories at Midway and Guadalcanal made it look as if the war in the Pacific would soon be won. At home, Jackie and Lee staged their annual Christmas pageant for the group. Jackie played Mary, Lee an angel who sang angelically, and Hughdie a wise man. The lead role—baby Jesus—was played by one of the dogs, admonished to lie quietly in its "swaddling clothes."

Jackie and Lee, now getting used to their new home, called their stepfather Uncle Hughdie or, more whimsically, Unk. (Janet was always Mummy to her children and Aunt Janet to her stepchildren.) Jackie had few friends to the house and would instead spend hours walking alone through Merrywood's forests or talking to the horses in the stable. (A few of Hughdie's Georgetown friends—like Jo Forrestal, wife of the Secretary of the Navy—boarded their horses at Merrywood, and Jackie exercised these mounts.) But with the group of people surrounding her mother's new family, Jackie felt that she didn't belong. The bandleader Peter Duchin remembered her saying, "You know, Peter, we both live and do very well in this world of WASPs and old money and society. It's all supposed to be so safe and continuous. But . . . I [am] not really of it. Maybe because I'm Catholic and because my parents were divorced when I was young—a terribly radical thing at the time—I've always felt an outsider in that world."

Hughdie, of course, was that world's ultimate insider. During the week he would dine each day at Washington's Metropolitan Club across the street from his office. On weekends Hughdie would join his golfing partners at the exclusive men-only Burning Tree Golf and Country Club in Bethesda, Maryland. Janet would join her friends at the Chevy Chase Country Club despite her protests that she played poorly.

On Sundays Janet was careful to continue a custom Hughdie enjoyed, which had been started by his previous wife, Nina. After church, between five to ten friends would gather at Merrywood for a large luncheon. Drinks, good food, and pleasant conversation—Janet shone at hostessing, and Hughdie appreciated her standing Sunday get-togethers. They might play bridge, or if it were late spring, the pool would be open. In that era there were no community pools, most private clubs did not have swimming pools, and private pools were very rare. Janet's giving friends generous access to Merrywood was important to them.

Janet took pride in her luncheons, and Hughdie took satisfaction in having captured her. "Everyone loved Janet right away," remembers her Georgetown friend Ella Burling.

At one luncheon the headmistress of Holton-Arms School was expected. Janet noticed that Jackie and Lee were nervous, understandably, she thought. Then they voiced what was bothering them: "Please, Mummy, take the celery off the table. We'll all be embarrassed. Uncle Hughdie makes so much noise when he chews!" For this particular occasion, Janet agreed.

When Nina had presided over these luncheons, she had invited such journalists as Walter Lippmann, Arthur Krock, and Drew Pearson, as well as U.S. senators, through her father's connections. Since Janet had little interest in politics (although Hughdie liked to be with people in the news—even if he preferred privacy for himself), Janet's luncheon guests tended to be chosen as much for their background as their accomplishments.

Sometimes, Hughdie's cousin Jim Auchincloss, a congressman from Rhode Island, brought over fellow members. On one visit, Uncle Jim helped Jackie and Lee dig a vegetable garden to help supplement rationing. Other frequent visitors would be Henry Luce, whom the children called Uncle Harry, and the Baldriges—he was legal counsel for the U.S. Sugar Refiners Association. Their daughter, Tish, had graduated Miss Porter's a year before Jackie entered. She remembers those Merrywood gatherings well and describes Janet as "the warm and ladylike mistress of a beautiful, well-run house who was terrifically receptive to children."

The Auchincloss friends would return the hospitality, too, by hosting the couple at dinners and parties. Janet and Hughdie could be seen in Washington's exclusive Spring Valley at the home of Perle Mesta, for example, who operated as "the hostess with the mostest" from her house named The Elms (later owned by Lady Bird and Lyndon B. Johnson). Hughdie was more comfortable with people from his own crowd, though, and if he and Janet socialized with a Jewish couple— such as the developer Morris Cafritz and wife, Gwen—it was an exception to the norm.

Janet's life was busy running her two estates. (Hughdie eventually gave up his place in Manhattan.) Stephen Birmingham, the chronicler of the wealthy and well placed, defined a woman like Janet as being "the equivalent of an office manager of a large corporation, whose job it was to see to it that work flowed smoothly."

Of course, Janet had a great deal of help. She engaged her own social secretary, and soon Hughdie would hire Margaret Kearney as his personal secretary at the firm of Auchincloss, Parker & Redpath. Kearney took care of the family bills, saving both Hughdie and Janet the trouble of making sure that, for example, Jackie's bills were sent to Jack and not accidentally paid by Hughdie.

There were charity events that Janet, as the wife of an Auchincloss, was expected to run. She hosted a Red Cross benefit at Merrywood and became a local Community Chest trustee. (Later, Hughdie would become its director.) Janet genuinely cared about the organizations she worked on behalf of—and her organizational skills and energy helped these groups tremendously.

Janet's patriotism ran higher than usual in wartime, and she was determined to do her part for her country. Every week she would put on a blue-and-white nurse's aide uniform and drive across Chain Bridge Road into Washington to volunteer for two full days a week at Columbia Hospital for Women.

Some time after Janet married Hughdie, rumors began spreading that her father was Jewish. Jim Lee had changed his name, the story went—and the rumors persist to this day—to Lee from Levy. That would have meant, of course, that Janet herself was part Jewish, as her daughters would be.

Once spread, the gossip took on a life of its own. "Maybe Jack Bouvier started them to be vicious," Yusha hints. Jack would know that spreading a rumor like this would slow, if not stop, Janet's rise in the new social set she had married into. Hughdie, too, having the limitations of a man raised in an insular group, would not have been pleased if the rumor had been true.

It is doubtful that anyone ever broached this suspicion directly with Janet Lee Auchincloss, who had convinced so many other people that she was a descendant of the Civil War general. She had developed a family genealogy so lengthy that her own family joked that "it went back to 1066 and 'Lancelot' Lee."

The most joyful summer during the war was when Janet, Jackie, and Lee went to Hammersmith Farm for the first time. They were stunned when they saw its beautiful view overlooking the East Passage of Narragansett Bay and the pink, blue, and purple hydrangea bushes everywhere. Although Lee would have preferred to be with friends at the beach in East Hampton, she had lots of opportunities to swim in Newport, too. "We all adored Hammersmith," she remembered. "To arrive there, as a child of eight, was just a fairy tale." Her room was on the third floor, populated only by children and nannies. Again, Lee chose blue, and her view was of front pastures speckled with ponies.

Jackie's cream-colored bedroom was elegantly appointed—two twin beds with white wooden headboards and footboards, with cane insets. She had a chaise longue, an easy chair, a desk, of course, and a dressing table. Her private bath opened off the bedroom. Although the view of the pastures was lovely for the Bouvier girls, it was Hughdie's own offspring—Yusha, Tommy, and Nini—who were given bedrooms with sea views.

Hammersmith Farm was the oldest working farm in Newport. Until the war there were sixteen staff inside the house alone, including two cooks, one for family meals and one for staff meals, as well as a personal maid for Hughdie's wife. By the front door was affixed a plaque of the Auchincloss coat of arms with its motto *Spectemur agenda* (Judge Us by Our Actions). Janet was happy to leave this symbol of Auchincloss pride in place; however, she ordered the house's wood paneling to be painted over to give a lighter look and removed most of the Victorian-style moose heads from its walls, irritating Hughdie's sister Esther, who thought the house should stay as it always had been. Some traditions remained, like the Vulcan stove in the kitchen and the clockman who came every other week to reset first the grandfather clock and then the estate's dozens of other timepieces.

In peacetime Hammersmith Farm had a head gardener and two full-time staff for the rock and flower gardens and the greenhouses. But with the advent of war, the gardens, plants, and driveways of the estate were classified as nonessential. Not only was manpower an issue for such estates, but resources were too scant for seeds and fertilizer to be expended on frivolous luxury plantings.

It seemed to people in Newport that problems came in threes: first, the Depression had actually left nineteenth-century mansions on Bellevue Avenue unoccupied; then the worst hurricane of southern New England hit in 1938, causing both loss of life and property damage; and finally came the war. But each time, Newporters soldiered on.

Throughout Hammersmith Farm, at Hughdie's eager bidding, Farm Bureau experts drew mysterious chalk marks indicating where buildings were to be altered for their wartime uses. (Hughdie had the extensive gardens photographed first so they could be re-created in the future.) The nine thousand square feet of space in the nine greenhouses was perfect for raising broiler chickens, declared the agricultural men, substituting Rhode Island Reds and Plymouth Barred Rocks for fragrant *Lilium henryi* and *Archillea*. When the birds had grown large enough to be trucked out and sold for poultry, the two thousand chicks under electric brooderators in the former gardener's cottage would be shifted to the greenhouse. Tractors, plows, and sprayers were to be moved in with the limousines in the main garage.

Two acres of potatoes, half an acre of sweet corn, and another acre and a half of other vegetables were planted on fields that had never felt a mower. The farm was anticipated to produce more than 34,000 pounds of poultry and 360,000 eggs each year. The *Newport Daily News* summarized in May 1943, "Hammersmith Farm, famed throughout New England, . . . has converted to the war effort with a capital 'E.' "

When the girls arrived for the summer, Janet had to explain that the war meant an alteration in their expectations. Most of the gardeners were in uniform or working in industrial plants, and the girls would have to pick up the slack. In her straightforward way, Janet told her sulking daughters that the war effort involved everyone. Hardship makes people stronger, she would say, emphasizing the value of teamwork to reach a goal. This they understood, and they took pride in their own small contribution to the Allied effort. So if the afternoons were for play — riding horses or enjoying the beach at Bailey's — the mornings were for chores, before the hot sun came straight overhead.

The family's self-sufficiency (if still having a good number in staff can be called self-sufficient) was valuable in wartime. Hammersmith Farm was the closest supplier of fresh food to the Newport naval base, trucking over eggs, chickens, milk, tomatoes, and apples. Two Guernsey cows were named for the girls. Jackie threw feed to the two thousand chicks — which she despised, as they tried to peck her. Also, as Janet remembered, she "was always asking Jackie to come down and weed." Lee worked, too, pruning thorny rosebushes and fruit trees.

It was important for Janet to maintain Hammersmith's rose-and-rock garden, because it had grown legendary under the skillful hand of Emma Auchincloss, who was an officer of the Newport Garden Club. Hammersmith was among the first private gardens in Newport that opened to the public, to raise money for charity. Visitors would ooh and aah at the farm's lily and goldfish ponds, its Italian vases, Egyptian tiling, garden statues, and stonework and walks. The landscaping, after all, had been designed by the firm of Frederick Law Olmsted, also responsible for Central Park. In fact, when Emma was younger, the gardens were photographed and featured in the book *Country Life in America* and in a 1917 popular magazine issue of *The New Country Life*. Hughdie's mother even had various views of the garden painted by A. C. Wyatt, a well-known garden painter whose works had been favorites in the collection of King Edward of England. Eventually, after Janet joined the Newport Garden Club and became an officer, she had many of the town's gardens — including Hammersmith's — hand-painted on glass slides for posterity.

But Emma would have supported the conversion of Hammersmith

for the war effort. After all, during the war Hammersmith's next-door neighbor Fort Adams had jurisdiction of all coastal defenses from the Canadian border to Long Island Sound. In fact, one of Emma's last contributions was to deed a strip of land along the east side of Hammersmith to Fort Adams so the busy base could extend its driveway.

Now the only lawn remaining was a short strip of grass, which Yusha mowed, bare-chested atop a tractor, in circles around the house. Because the farm was reduced to only one operating telephone in the basement, Jackie as the elder sister was often given reception duty. That task she didn't mind; she always brought a book or magazine with her and could enjoy the cool stillness of the lower level.

No matter how much Hammersmith changed after its conversion to food production, the charm of the place remained unmistakable. Its ancillary buildings still looked wonderful: the stables, the 1870s windmill, and the farmhouse dubbed the Castle by one of the many Auchincloss servants who had retired here. ("Come to my castle for milk and cookies," she would say.)

During the summer Janet and Hughdie socialized nearly every evening: guests over, or they at someone's house. Their absences gave both Jackie and Lee a good share of quiet private time; they were too young to drive and hadn't yet made many friends in the area. But the girls loved the outdoors as much as their mother did, and when they heard the honk of Canada geese, they would race each other up the stairs to a west window to catch a glimpse of a flock flying in V formation over the bay toward the land.

Yusha remembered that Jackie liked to walk down Hammersmith's sloping lawn to the bay, in order to sit and watch the ships sail across the water to the naval base. Destroyers, aircraft carriers, and battleships—even submarine nets were set—patrolled the coast against German subs. As the war progressed, Jackie became enamored of military leaders and of all things heroic.

What she couldn't have known was that six months earlier, a young man, a lieutenant junior grade in the U.S. Naval Reserve, was also mesmerized by the view across the bay toward the Newport estates. The youthful officer was a student at the Motor Torpedo Boat Training Center for patrol torpedo (PT) boats. Before he had left Portsmouth to report in February 1943 for active duty in the Solomon Islands, he would sit on a slope in the evening and gaze out over the water to the lights near Hammersmith Farm, wondering what his future held.

Chapter 7

ALL IN
THE FAMILY

The war, at last, was over. Janet was settling into a postwar routine that was interrupted only by the surprising announcement of her pregnancy at age thirty-seven. She had given birth to her third daughter on June 13, 1945, two months before Hughdie's forty-eighth birthday. The couple named the baby Janet Jennings Auchincloss: Jennings in reference to Emma's maiden name and—perhaps—a gesture honoring her having infused the family with a portion of the Standard Oil fortune.

Family friends referred to the baby as Janet Jr. Hughdie, though, was always to call her "baby Janet" even as she grew older. The couple had been married two and a half years; despite the parents' ages, everyone thought the baby was a great idea—she would be the last jigsaw piece to unite the Auchincloss family puzzle.

She was christened in the winter at St. John Episcopal Church, several hours from Merrywood in The Plains, Virginia, but in the middle of hunt country—perhaps to ensure that the baby would be an equestrian. Jackie came down from Farmington, where she had written a poem in the baby's honor. She and Lee, who was attending day school in the area, worked together to compose a scrapbook, "The Red Shoes of Janet Jennings," making reference to a popular movie. (While the girls were working on the scrapbook, John F. Kennedy was planning his first election to the U.S. House of Representatives.)

Late that afternoon Hughdie and Janet had friends out to Merrywood to celebrate the infant's birth. Jackie and Lee, dressed in matching gray dresses, wore corsages of white gardenias. Janet Jr., of course, wore the Lee family christening gown. Unfortunately, the day was cold and drizzly. Merrywood's driveway was so long that it was inconvenient for the guests to park and walk to the house, so Janet arranged for a luxury that was relatively rare at the time: car valets. Janet informed everyone afterward that the baby "behaved in the best social manner."

Two years later, on March 4, 1947, Janet's only son was born and was named after her father: James (Jamie) Lee Auchincloss. The birth meant a twenty-year difference between Jamie and Yusha, Hughdie's youngest and eldest sons.

In addition, Janet was thirty-nine years old: surely an advanced age for a pregnancy in those days. Hughdie was quite nervous about Janet's having the baby so late in life, and he made sure that nothing—including the family's volatile teenagers—would disturb her during the pregnancy. As he had expected, Janet's recovery following Jamie's birth was more prolonged than after her earlier births. Janet, typically, was peeved at herself for not springing back immediately.

Hughdie, of Scottish descent, had a Presbyterian father but was raised as an Episcopalian by his mother. He in turn took his children to Episcopal services, and Janet attended with them. She was still angry at the Catholic Church for considering her marriage to Hughdie invalid and, by implication, Janet and Jamie illegitimate. "This would bother her a great deal," says Kathleen Bouvier.

At church, Yusha noticed that Janet was not taking Communion with the rest of the family and asked her why she held back.

He remembers that she told him, "I've been excommunicated. I can't."

Yusha explained to her that any Christian is welcome to take Communion in the Episcopal Church; her banishment from the sacraments by the Catholic Church did not apply here. Janet was relieved and embraced Episcopalianism as her religion and that of her two youngest children. Religion would be one more difference between the Bouvier girls and their Auchincloss family.

The days went by quietly at Merrywood, each day a repetition of the one before. Hughdie's driver would take him downtown during the workweek. Hughdie shared his office at Auchincloss, Parker & Redpath with his private secretary, Margaret Kearney. She says that he set the tone for the firm: straitlaced, sober, reserved, and proper.

Hughdie looked after a number of accounts for favored clients but never those of the Auchinclosses—those went to the firm's trust department. Hughdie's own investments were handled by the trust staff, headed by James Quinn. The bills of the five Auchincloss children would go for payment to James Quinn, too, while the household bills were looked after by Margaret Kearney.

Often Jackie's or Lee's bills would come to the office by mistake and would be sent straight to Jack Bouvier. Hughdie picked up none of the Bouvier girls' expenses, according to Margaret Kearney, except for the food they ate and the electricity they used while in his home. Janet's own charges went straight to Merrywood; Hughdie would bring them in for his secretary to pay from his personal checking account.

Janet's bills could be extraordinary. She didn't buy in excess, but what she purchased was of top quality: European linens from Manhattan's Léron shop, French soap and Irish crystal. Merrywood's closets bulged with Porthault linens tied with grosgrain ribbons. Sandwiched between the sheet sets were sweet-smelling sachets. Although Hughdie himself was thrifty, he was also the most generous of husbands. Once Kearney asked him about a bill from the luxury Garfinckels department store for one of Janet's charges: an alligator bag that ran $650 (approximately $4,500 today). Hughdie merely raised his eyebrows. "Whatever Mrs. Auchincloss wanted, Mrs. Auchincloss got," Kearney says. "He never questioned her."

Kearney, who prided herself on being error-free, faced a challenging task in sorting out the who's who of the Auchincloss clan. As the person who paid the household accounts, she needed to know the names of the seven children, who their mothers were, and where everyone was living. "When I first went there, I thought to myself, 'Which child belongs to which mother?'"

Hughdie broke from work around noon, when he would walk across the street for a leisurely lunch with one or another of the members of the Metropolitan Club. He did not arrange his lunch engagements; instead, he would sit with whoever happened by. Nevertheless, one of his frequent lunch partners was John M. Harlan, who became associate justice of the Supreme Court in the mid-1950s. After lunch Hughdie would go back to the office for a short time and depart for home in the mid-afternoon.

From Memorial Day through Labor Day, the entire Auchincloss household moved to Hammersmith Farm as Hughdie took a breather from work. He and Kearney spoke every day; she would send envelopes of correspondence up to Newport and receive them back a few days later.

Despite Hughdie's light work schedule, Janet rarely called the office to speak with him. Only occasionally would she visit: if, for example, she were downtown, she might stop in to say hello, especially if she had one of the children with her. But these surprises were rare. Janet was unfailingly polite to Hughdie's secretary and addressed her as "Mrs. Kearney."

Janet, too, was a creature of routine and structure. Each morning she dressed in an outfit appropriate to whatever lay ahead. If she expected to be home for the day, she might wear a beige or white cashmere twin set and a dark skirt. If she was leaving the house, she'd slip on a suit or a wool dress—usually in beige, cream, or taupe. She used brown as the basis of her wardrobe and "never wore tight sheaths—always a soft, full skirt," said her dressmaker, Mini Rhea. "Her necklines were either a deep scoop or square."

Janet donned sheer silk stockings, fastened to garters, and sensible soft-leather pumps with a moderate heel. Finally, she would add a strand of pearls, or if going out, she might also affix a brooch to her collar. Janet never wore casual attire and, unless she was in jodhpurs, never put on trousers. She always had her nails immaculately manicured, although she wore no makeup. Nothing she wore was in the least ostentatious, but all was of the finest quality available.

Bright colors were not for her. Her hairstylist at the downtown Elizabeth Arden salon told another client that he wished Janet would wear more colorful, striking styles. He sniped that Janet—with her beige outfits, pearls, and brown hair and eyes—looked "like a mushroom!" Of course, *not* to stand out was Janet's goal.

Each morning Janet would have the nanny, Maybelle Stratton, bring the children in to say good morning. If she had time, perhaps Janet would chat with one or two girlfriends who would call her on Merrywood's line. When her secretary arrived (starting in the 1950s, this was Mary Barelli Gallagher, who would later work for Jackie), Janet would meet her at the door and escort her upstairs. Janet would work in her sitting room off the bedroom, with her secretary in a separate room on the same floor. Janet would review the day's activities and organize the following day, examine menus and guest lists, and dictate her correspondence. She had copied the robin's-egg blue of the stationery used by Hughdie's late mother for her own writing paper, which was stocked at each of her residences.

Janet often lunched at home; if so, it was a simple repast served to her on a tray in the library. However, the setting included a place mat and napkin of linen, fine china, and sterling silver. Her strongest drink at lunch was a crystal goblet of buttermilk. (She liked daiquiris before dinner.) Usually she ate with her secretary, and unless there was something pressing to discuss, they would chitchat during the meal.

In the afternoon she might drive her Jaguar — a gift from her father — across Chain Bridge into Georgetown to see her girlfriends, to shop, or, when the day was ending, to visit her dressmaker. Mini Rhea, who had one daughter, was impressed at Janet's ability to manage her busy social life, two estates, and seven children. "When she was in for a fitting, she was forever reaching out for my phone to check on how the children were making out at home or arranging to pick up this one here or that one there," she said. "She was completely wrapped up in the young ones and relished their every adventure."

Once a week Janet invited her girlfriends to bring their dogs over so they could go for a nice long walk through Merrywood's wooded acres while catching up on everyone's goings-on. There were always at least four dogs at Merrywood: the ones belonging to the Bouvier girls had French names (Jackie named hers Gaullie, after the general), while the Auchinclosses called theirs by American names.

Evenings, Janet spent with Hughdie. They bathed and dressed before dinner at home; when they went out, five nights a week, their functions usually called for formal wear. Janet's life, like the one she attempted to structure for her family, was well ordered and disciplined. Despite the presence of a baby and a toddler in the house, the estate seemed hushed to visitors and staff. The noisiest presence was the surrounding woods: the birds sang while the crickets and spring peepers added to the melody, but there was little laughter and no loud conversation, even at the pool. On the surface, everything was quiet; everything was quietly perfect.

When Yusha graduated from Groton in 1946, he entered the Marines. Although the war was over and many of his classmates were starting college, he wanted to serve his country and turn his wartime vision into reality.

Jackie was now away from home nine months of the year at Farmington, and soon Lee would be, too. (Jackie and Lee were not at Miss Porter's at the same time; they were three years apart and both entered as sophomores.) Neither Jackie nor Lee was delighted to be at a girls' boarding school, but Jackie at least had been fairly content — she received good grades, her deportment had mellowed radically from her childhood temper tantrums, and she was a natural athlete. Jackie was also an editor of the *Salmagundy*, the school newspaper, for which she wrote and drew a series called "Frenzied Freda." The school's upper-crust philosophy of discipline and character was having its effect on Jackie. She gave a speech there that she titled "Be Kind and Do Your Share." If Jackie was homesick, she never let on to anyone. Yusha remembers, "I never once heard her complain."

Jackie was not an immediate hit with the boys she met at the school's socials; after all, she was tall for her age, large-boned, and slim. Her beauty was not yet fully mature. If Jackie felt lonely — for she did not make girl-friends easily — she could lie on her bed and daydream, or walk to the stable to visit Danseuse, whispering her thoughts to the horse she nicknamed Donny. "Every afternoon," said her Farmington riding instructor Grace O'Connor, "she would ask permission to graze it up by the big ring." Like Janet, Jackie would release frustrations through sports: besides riding, she excelled at tennis and swimming. One young man she dated complained that "she seemed to talk an awful lot about animals."

Jackie's cousin Mimi Cecil would enter interscholastic riding competitions with Jackie, knowing that Jackie had never practiced, and yet see her walk away with the blue ribbon. Her instructor, too, remembered that "she had never jumped the horse assigned to her in ring jumping class. But she went on and won the class." On those occasions when she didn't place, Jackie felt "lower than the proverbial snake," said a classmate at Miss Porter's.

Her assertiveness on horseback was remarkable for a young woman. One time at Hammersmith, Mimi Cecil rode Danseuse, which left no horse for Jackie except a Clydesdale, the farm's workhorse. Jackie rode this Clydesdale bareback — and with bare feet. Cecil warned her to be careful; in response, Jackie jumped the enormous horse over a bale of hay. "She had no fear," Cecil says. "When the Clydesdale bucked, Jackie just laughed."

While Jackie was jumping a Clydesdale as if it were a stallion, Lee was off to the beach or the bay, where she crewed with teenage J. Carter Brown's Wood Pussies.

When Jackie and, later, Lee were away at Miss Porter's, they could visit Hughdie's sister and brother-in-law Annie Burr and Lefty Lewis, who had a house in Farmington. (Lewis was an authority on Horace Walpole and, by this time, had edited twenty-six volumes of Walpole's complete correspondence, to be published by Yale University Press: twenty-four more were to come.)

The couple kept an eye on their nieces and frequently invited them for Saturday tea—although Lee took hers black and turned down the scrumptious rich chocolate layer cake. Jackie enjoyed the treat but found the couple's library nearly as tempting as the desserts. Jackie was bookish—a trait inherited from neither her father nor her mother, although Janet did enjoy fiction and biographies. Jackie eyed her "Uncle" Lefty's collection of rare and antique books, and he took the hint, gifting her at holidays with handsomely bound classics or expensive art books.

Lee arrived at Miss Porter's the year after Jackie graduated. After a short preteen infatuation with Catholicism—Lee even adorned her bedroom with religious icons—at Farmington she turned her interest in dramatics toward school theatrics. She enjoyed being in the spotlight and was extremely attractive—prettier, people thought, than Jackie and with a better figure, too. Lee, of course, resembled Janet in face and figure. Jackie's sister was shorter and more buxom, much to Jackie's chagrin. Lee recognized her advantage and sculpted her curves by dieting with a vengeance.

Although no one minded her taking off the last few pounds of baby fat, it seemed that Lee couldn't stop. Janet was continually fussing over Lee's diminishing weight—with good reason. Schoolmates remember her as terribly skinny, and her face looking tired and drawn. Of course, at the time no one knew what to call this troubling weight loss, but Mimi Cecil remembers how concerned everyone was, and that "Tante Janet talked about sending Lee to a weight-gain clinic in Switzerland" because she was so skinny. That prospect—and Janet's bribe to let her redecorate her room if she would only start eating—at least curbed Lee's zest for starving herself, but she continued to worry Janet.

When Jackie reached her senior year, Janet encouraged her to apply to Vassar College, the school that Janet herself had once planned to attend. Vassar seemed like a good idea to Jackie; certainly many of her schoolmates were going there in the fall. Her acceptance was a sure thing: not only did she have strong grades, but her standardized college entrance results were so high that Janet called everyone to spread the good news. The story zipped around her sisters' families until Jackie's cousins were feeling quite sheepish about their own scores.

Jack Bouvier, who was responsible for the $1,600 tuition, also liked the idea of having his favorite daughter just a short train trip away. Jack preferred the social quality of women's lives to that of the men he worked with on Wall Street. For him, brokering was merely a job, while pursuing women was an art form. For a few years while Jackie was in college, she became infatuated with her father. After all, at home she was competing with toddler Janet Jr. and baby Jamie for attention. When her mother did recognize her, it seemed to the sensitive teenager that it was mostly to criticize. Lee felt the same way. "No matter what Jackie and I did, it was never good enough," she said of her teen years.

One of the few times that Janet did have an honest talk with Jackie, it backfired. Janet started to tell Jackie about how badly Jack had treated her and began to weep. Jackie was stung by the criticism of her father and appalled at her mother's emotionalism. "Jackie wouldn't admit her father had faults," remembers Kathleen Bouvier. Rather than sympathizing with her mother, Jackie made fun of Janet.

Although they were turning into young women, Jackie and Lee were still caught in Janet and Jack's tug-of-war over visitation. The girls always seemed to be packing a bag. There were term vacations and short weekend visits to their father in Manhattan. Thanksgiving, Christmas, and Easter found them at Merrywood, and in June they were at Hammersmith Farm for the season, punctuated by a stay with their father, this time in East Hampton. Both teenagers were leading a life far too peripatetic for their age, and they lacked a permanent place to call home. If Jackie had been asked what one place she considered home, though, it surely would have been Merrywood, just as it was Hammersmith Farm for Hughdie and Janet, and East Hampton for Lee.

Even at East Hampton they were torn between families. While the girls were visiting Jack, Janet expected them to see their grandfather, who still had his house on Lily Pond Lane. Yet Jack told them that "Old Man Lee" had stopped talking to him after Janet divorced him — Jack saw no reason why he should help arrange their visits on *his* time.

Both men behaved foolishly. Jim Lee's other grandchildren remember that when they visited him in East Hampton, if they saw Jack Bouvier at the Maidstone Club, their grandfather would admonish them not to say hello. "He's not your uncle anymore!" Jim Lee would insist. (Their parents told them otherwise.)

Jackie made her social debut shortly before entering Vassar in 1947 in a simple tea dance held at Hammersmith Farm for three hundred friends of Janet and Hughdie's. The couple combined Jackie's introduction with that of baby Jamie, who that morning had been christened at Newport's Trinity Church, the oldest Episcopal church in town. In fact, because Janet was so busy with newborn Jamie, Jackie selected her own gown straight off the rack, avoiding saleswomen in the dressing rooms because of her self-consciousness about her slight figure.

The joint party invitation read: "To meet Miss Jacqueline Lee Bouvier and Master James Lee Auchincloss." The event was understated, just the way Janet wanted it. She had planned another evening event for Jackie at the Clambake Club the next month, which was for young people. Jackie shared her debut dance with Rose Grosvenor, who was the daughter of Hughdie's childhood friend Teddy, the boy he had envied for his bright red bike. Rose was blond and fair; Jackie, brunette and tan. The young ladies looked marvelous next to each other.

The Auchinclosses and the Grosvenors didn't have to order flowers to decorate the party: their own greenhouses supplied enough. By now Janet was an established part of social Newport and was made an officer of the Newport Garden Club (a natural, given the prominence of Hammersmith's gardens). She served with Noreen Drexel, one of the women with whom she would become close friends. The biggest surprise of the evening was when fourteen-year-old Lee appeared in a provocative pink gown that Janet had never seen before. (In fact, the dress was such a success with the young men that Jackie borrowed it to wear — with a padded bra — to another deb party.)

Jackie had two young men she would have felt comfortable asking to be her debut escort but quixotically decided against both. Instead, she turned to her handsome cousin Johnny Ryan — "a ringer" says John's sister Mimi — with the proviso that no one in the family tell the other guests that the mystery man was a relative.

Janet decided that she would invite none of the Bouviers to Jackie's Clambake Club debut. Naturally, Jack and his family were quite hurt. (Hughdie agreed to pay for Jackie's debut because Jack could afford only a modest tea; besides, this was the only way the couple could make sure that Jack was excluded.)

Jack, his sisters, and their children had looked forward to Jackie's debut: they had expected to be at the coming-out, and Newport itself was burning brighter in the social cosmos of the East Coast. The preservation society that opened the Bellevue Avenue cottages to the public was organizing, and Countess Laszlo Szechenyi (Gladys Vanderbilt) had agreed to open The Breakers for charity.

A short time after the debut, Jackie went to East Hampton to visit

Jack. When her cousin John Davis asked her how the party went, Jackie played it down. "Oh . . . it was okay, very nice," he quotes her saying and surmises that the party didn't hold much importance for her. Perhaps, instead, she was purposely avoiding hurting his feelings — and her father's, too. Jack, as usual, focused his anger on Janet: he never seemed to wonder why Jackie didn't stick up for him. Jackie — "the most beautiful daughter a man ever had" — was blameless.

No matter that there had not been any Bouviers present at Jackie's debut, Jack had certainly been there in spirit. He would have been pleased at Jackie's trick in bringing in a handsome mystery man as her date. Her father's training had taken; she had played hard to get.

With its small size and its tucked-away location on the Hudson River, Vassar did not appeal to Jackie. She rarely took part in campus life; despite such visiting lecturers as the poet Stephen Spender or the painter Ben Shahn, Jackie would run each weekend to an event at her date's college or she'd visit Jack Bouvier.

Unlike her other cousins, she rarely stayed with her grandfather Lee when she was in Manhattan. Perhaps Jim Lee was too critical of Jack Bouvier's daughters, or perhaps Jack Bouvier's daughters had learned too much from their father. In any case, Mr. Lee once commented to one of his Chase executives that Jackie was "not an easy girl."

Jackie longed for a future different from Janet and Hughdie's well-regimented life. Even East Hampton was no longer interesting — nor was the silly remark by a New York columnist that she was "Deb of the Year." The columnist had caught a glimpse of Jackie wearing that pink dress of Lee's. Oddly enough, the writer described Jackie's Bouvier swarthiness and strong nose as "classic features and the daintiness of Dresden porcelain."

Jackie insisted to John Davis that she was prouder of making the dean's list than of being named the Deb of the Year. In fact, she disliked the publicity it had generated. Jackie was "different," a puzzled Janet noted, and "difficult." She did not work at making friends. Vassar was a college with no social clubs, secret organizations, or sororities: the only way to honor its most beautiful and popular students was for the seniors to select chosen sophomores for the Daisy Chain. Here, Jackie did not make the list. She was too distant to fit in, and although she dated, she soon became discontent. Janet threw up her hands.

The last month of 1947 brought a shock to Jackie, and to Janet. The jolt was not that Jack's father, J.V., died shortly after Christmas—after all, he was eighty-two years old. Instead, the family was dismayed to learn that he was not as rich as they had thought. Some of the Bouviers were living beyond their means—Jack was $50,000 in debt—and they had expected a lifesaving transfusion from J.V. Instead, they learned that the $1.6 million ($11.4 million today) that J.V. had inherited was gone. Spent. Lasata's lavish lifestyle—one they all had enjoyed—apparently was financed by their future inheritance! All that remained was $800,000, out of which Jack and his three sisters needed to pay taxes before they could take a share.

The Bouviers were stunned. So was Janet—her daughters received a paltry $3,000 each ($21,400 in today's currency). If Jackie and Lee already felt second-class in a first-class Auchincloss household, imagine how they must have seen their position now. After all, it was common knowledge that the stepsiblings Yusha, Tommy, and Nini—and their half siblings Janet Jr. and Jamie—had trusts established for them by family members. The principal of the Auchincloss grandchildren's trusts would generate enough interest to last throughout the lives of those who lived conservatively. The issue was immediately tangible, for the Bouvier girls received only $50, which would now be about $400, from Jack each month.

There were other family dilemmas, too. Janet found out that Hughdie's son Tommy was miserable living with his mother, Nina. Janet had expected it: four years earlier Nina had threatened to send Hughdie's daughter Nini, then nine years old, to a convent school in Tucson. Nini escaped to Merrywood and had been living with Janet and Hughdie ever since. She acknowledged her gratitude when she said, "[Aunt Janet] rescued me."

This particular Christmas, thirteen-year-old Nini was at Merrywood with the entire family except for Tommy, eleven, who was stuck in Georgetown at Nina's house on N Street. There was an awful incident the day after Christmas—Nina was drunk, she was naked, she began screaming and hitting him, and then vomited on him—which convinced Janet that the custody arrangement had to change.

Knowing how difficult Nina was, Janet tried a light hand. "You know, Nina, we have so many children here, one more wouldn't make a difference," she sweetly suggested. "To make it easier for you, why don't we switch the arrangements so that Tommy can be here for holidays and then see you when it's convenient for your schedule?"

Nina recognized this as being in *her* best interest and agreed, although after Tommy moved out, she trashed the clothes, books, and toys he had left. Hughdie was ever grateful to Janet for looking after his children. Now the family was nine, including the seven offspring. There were three of Hughdie's from earlier marriages: Yusha, Nini, Tommy; there were two of Janet's: Jackie and Lee; and the couple together had two more; Janet Jr. and Jamie. Their ages ranged from one-year-old Jamie to twenty-one-year-old Yusha.

Janet's friends marveled at her generosity in handling this many children, especially since all but Janet Jr. and Jamie were either teenagers or poised on either side. Keeping a watchful eye on two toddlers as well as five young people, ages eleven, thirteen, sixteen, nineteen, and twenty-one could not have been easy, especially for a woman who valued a quiet, smoothly run household. One day in Newport at Bailey's Beach, as Janet was rounding everyone up in late afternoon, she remarked to Eileen Slocum that she often felt "like a drill sergeant." Still, Janet's friends marveled at her aplomb.

Yet not everything was as smooth as the surface of Bailey's pool. Nini and Janet had several clashes: one was witnessed by Jackie at Merrywood. Janet felt that Nini had been disrespectful and slapped her, leaving a red mark on the girl's face. But the fight wasn't over—the combatants were glaring and circling around each other like boxers getting ready for the next strike. "Oh, Mummy," sighed Jackie, which broke the tension and ended the confrontation.

Hughdie didn't stand up to Janet, according to Jamie, because he was "shell-shocked by the failure of his first two marriages." Apparently, he wanted this third one to work even if the price was total acquiescence.

Janet tried to control Jackie's smoking, too, a habit that her daughter never would give up. Although both Janet and Hughdie smoked, their doctors had warned them of the health risks, especially given Hughdie's allergies. Jackie would write Yusha—now honorably discharged from the Marines and studying at Yale University—sarcastically referring to Janet's sermon as "Downward Path and Sins of Tobacco." Once, hearing Janet walking upstairs to her bedroom, Jackie tossed her cigarette behind a chair cushion. Clever—until, of course, the smell of burning fabric caught her mother's attention.

Jackie soon became a chain-smoker who once set fire to her car cushion while driving and arrived at her dressmaker's just in time to shout for water. After Jackie threw a few containers of water on the smoldering seat, she ran back into her dressmaker's house: "I think one more pitcher and I won't have to call the fire department."

Jackie's temper could ignite, too, as it did the time when she and Lee had a fierce battle and Jackie kicked in a panel of Lee's bedroom door in frustration. Hearing the goings-on of his largely female family, Hughdie would retreat to the card room, turn off his hearing aid, and concentrate as hard as he could on the next move of his ongoing postal chess game with John Walker, the director of the National Gallery of Art. At most, Hughdie might utter to Janet during her raging storms, "Now, now, Mummy."

Yet Janet's sense of keeping the Auchincloss family together was strong, and the children reflected it. "The children never once spoke of step-this or step-that. They were all brothers and sisters," said Candy Van Alen, whose husband, Jimmy, was one of Hughdie's best friends.

Jackie's European vacation in the summer of 1948, following her freshman year at Vassar, took her away from the family dramas and, more important, gave her a taste of France. "I want to come back and soak it all up," she said afterward. She left Vassar for France again at the end of her sophomore year (at the time, the college did not have a summer abroad program). Janet acceded; after all, the planned trip to Paris for her junior year would not only polish Jackie's French but also put a nice glow on her patina of culture. Jackie spent the summer in a six-week intensive language study before taking off for the Sorbonne.

In August 1949 Jackie left for Paris and proceeded to fall in love with the city, even though her accommodations with an impoverished countess whose house had little heat or hot water came as a shock after life at Merrywood. Janet was naturally nervous if Jackie's letter didn't arrive weekly, but she read aloud those she received with great pride, for Jackie was a descriptive writer. "I have a mania to speak French *perfectly*," Jackie wrote home, and Janet was thrilled.

Jackie was back in Virginia at the end of the academic year to attend Lee's debut in June 1950. Janet and Hughdie gave a dance for Lee at Merrywood, with a dinner preceding it at the F Street Club. As with Jackie, a second party followed for young people—this one in August at Hammersmith Farm, with the Meyer Davis Orchestra: the same ensemble that had needed to increase its volume to mask the shouting at Janet's wedding to Jack twenty-two years earlier.

The family had a scare during the summer when Jackie was visiting Jack Bouvier in East Hampton. She fell off her horse and was unconscious for several days, badly alarming her father. When she recovered, he scraped together enough money to commission society painter Irwin Hoffman for a portrait of Jackie that shows a scar over her right eye.

Having seen Paris, Jackie balked at returning to Vassar. She didn't like its all-women campus and wanted to be in the city. "That goddamn Vassar," she called it. At the time, Georgetown University — Washington's highest-ranked college — did not accept female undergraduates, so Janet paid a visit to George Washington University's admissions dean, showed him Jackie's transcript, and persuaded him that she should transfer with three years' credit, study two semesters at the university, and graduate in May 1951. Janet and Hughdie were pleased that Jackie would live at home and commute to classes across the river. And best of all, she would be farther away from Jack Bouvier's influence.

Jackie's decision to return to Washington did have the negative effect of putting her back under her mother's supervision. Friends who visited Jackie — including her cousin John Davis — felt that they couldn't escape her mother, who followed them from room to room while the young people chatted. More perplexing to them was Jackie's passive acceptance of her mother's interference.

There were frequent disagreements and spats: Jackie, who had taken a college course in child psychology, informed her mother that the excessive number of servants in the household was spoiling Janet Jr. and Jamie. Poor little Jamie seemed dominated by the women in the house; besides all the help and a strong-willed mother, Janet Jr. seemed to enjoy her dominant position as his elder sister and would slap him when he got excited watching *Howdy Doody* on television and shouted back to the screen. Jackie thought this was funny, remembering her treatment of her younger sister. "I really was hard on Lee and riding herd all the time."

Janet was delighted when Jackie received her degree from George Washington University in French literature; as it turned out, she would be Janet's only daughter to graduate from college. Janet worried, though, when Jackie asked to return to France after winning *Vogue*'s Prix de Paris contest in the summer of 1951, even though it was Janet herself who had torn out the contest form for Jackie to enter. But Jackie, who called her year in Paris "the high point of my life," was determined to go back.

Although Janet was initially thrilled at Jackie's interest in all things French, she kept trying to convince her not to take advantage of the prize. Janet did not view the work for *Vogue* as an opportunity; instead, it would keep her sequestered in an all-female office at a fashion magazine. Rather than seeing the importance of Jackie following through on her commitment to the magazine, Janet had a strategic goal for her daughter. The average age for women to marry was then twenty; Jackie was already twenty-one, with no prospects in sight. "You're making the biggest mistake of your life," Janet told her. "You're going to be twenty-two years old in July and you're not engaged yet."

On the other hand, Jack Bouvier was overjoyed at the notion of Jackie living with him in the city for a short training stint before she left for Paris, with Lee nearby at Sarah Lawrence College. According to Kathleen Bouvier, who received his letter full of news about the girls, he was "joyous and optimistic" and talked of nothing else.

Vogue's managing editor, Carol Phillips, took Jackie out to lunch the day she accepted the prize. "She was a sweet, darling girl with not a great deal of confidence," she remembered. Jackie asked her what city would be best for her. "Go to Washington," she advised the ingenue. "That's where all the boys are."

This advice, added to what Janet was saying, made up Jackie's mind. After only a week in training, she forfeited her opportunity at *Vogue* and returned to Merrywood. She wrote the chagrined *Vogue* editors that her mother felt "terrifically strongly about 'keeping me in the home.' " Jackie was beginning to tune out her father's recriminations and follow what she thought was best for her—which, as it turned out, was more likely to be aligned with Janet's opinions.

"It's time I settled down," said the twenty-one-year-old, "and thought about doing something constructive. And I do get lonely for the family when I'm away so long. I've had the experience [of winning] but I don't know about making a career of fashion."

Jackie was afraid of following her heart. "I felt then that if I went back I'd live there forever, I loved Paris so much." But she knew that she needed to be practical. As a consolation prize, Janet and Hughdie sent both girls to Europe for the summer, with Jackie in charge. When the couple themselves went to Europe to join them for a short time, Hughdie counterbalanced Jackie's unquestioning love of anything European by taking the family to the Dachau concentration camp.

Lee was to start college at Sarah Lawrence, but academics did not interest her. She had just been named Deb of the Year, which boosted her self-confidence. Her ascension ratcheted up the competition between her and Jackie, who had been taught by both of their parents, in different ways, that capturing a man's interest was their life's goal. Another woman—even a sister—was just more competition in a crowded field.

So, in college Lee majored in men, balancing several boyfriends at the same time. She followed in Jackie's path and took a semester abroad to study in Florence, Italy. Unlike Jackie, she did not return to college but took a job at *Harper's Bazaar, Vogue*'s competitor. In Lee's case, Janet was more relaxed: was it because Lee was younger than Jackie, or did Janet feel her younger daughter would have less trouble attracting a husband?

Now that Jackie had returned to Washington, she began stopping by Janet's Georgetown dressmaker, Mini Rhea, to ask her to copy some of the French couture looks Jackie had admired in France. Janet had told the dressmaker, "She likes to design her own clothes and I know she would love to work with someone like you who could help her with them."

Jackie told Rhea how much she had disliked being dressed in outfits identical to Lee's when she was a child and, of course, how she detested her school uniforms. (Janet defended herself on the girls' matching dresses: "I wanted to show them I love them equally.") Inspired by the dark-haired gamine Audrey Hepburn, Jackie gave up the full-skirt, cinched-waist look in favor of Hepburn's signature sleeveless sheath. Jackie recognized that the style camouflaged her own wide shoulders, long waist, and small bust. She liked black and white but also chose hot pink and pale yellow. She would order clothes from the large New York department stores, especially Lord & Taylor and Bergdorf's, and the outfits were sent directly to Rhea to fit to the muslin pattern of Jackie's figure.

To encourage Jackie to leave *Vogue*, Hughdie had set up a job for Jackie with a local newspaper, the *Washington Times-Herald*, as their Inquiring Photographer. Janet encouraged her to go to work, although she herself had never held a job before her marriage: "That's why I wanted Jacqueline to do so. It's excellent experience for Jackie." The couple even pledged to pay the rent on a small apartment in Georgetown for her.

Jack Bouvier said he couldn't afford to help her buy a decent automobile. (Or was he angry about her leaving New York?) "She drove a beat-up old car," remembered a fellow worker. "But then the butler would phone and say, 'Please have Miss Bouvier call home.'"

Jackie could get defensive about her job, saying that it proved she could support herself. Yet the position paid $42.50 weekly; her dressmaker's charges started at $35 and went beyond $110. At the same time, she held back from the camaraderie of the newsroom. She refused to date the young men who asked her out and nicknamed them the "fourth floor wolves." Jackie knew that she would find her future husband in a different pool of men.

"I'm going out with a group of friends" would be her first excuse to a would-be suitor. Eventually she needed to be harsher. One suitor said, "She told me quite clearly, if not in so many words, that I was wasting my time."

Jackie started dating John Husted, initially pleasing Janet and Hughdie because his parents were close to the Auchinclosses; John had graduated from Yale, and his three sisters had attended Miss Porter's and knew Jackie from school. Although the young couple didn't seem to feel drawn to each other, Jackie accepted Husted's marriage proposal in December 1951. At their engagement party, "they hardly spoke to each other," Yusha says. Plus, Janet, who usually shone at gatherings, was in a foul mood.

It was all very odd — this dreamy young French literature major being engaged to an investment banker. Everyone who knew them was surprised at the match. "They didn't have the same interests," says Yusha. Janet told him that "Jackie must have fallen off Sagebrush and hit her head."

Perhaps the engagement can be explained by Jackie's growing need for independence from both her parents taking precedence over common sense. In any case, Jackie and Husted didn't have much opportunity to work on the relationship since she was still in McLean and he lived in New York. The couple spent so much time traveling to see each other that Jackie started paying her dressmaker in traveler's checks.

One time while in New York, Jackie brought Husted to meet her father. As prearranged, Jackie left the men alone so Husted could formally ask Jack Bouvier for his daughter's hand. His response was peculiar: "Sure — but it will never work." Husted said, "He never explained, and I certainly didn't push it."

When Janet learned that his income was only $17,000 a year (approximately $100,000 today) and that he would have to rely on this money to support a family, she brought Jackie back to reality. Janet told her that Husted did not have *real* money. When Jackie bridled, Janet reminded her that *Jackie* was the one who answered her high-school yearbook questionnaire by saying that her goal was "not to be a housewife."

Jackie was floundering, and she argued with Janet about dating whomever she wished. "Mummy," she said, "I'm grown up. You can't tell me who I can see and who I can't." Janet responded by slapping the twenty-two-year-old on both cheeks. Later, as angry as Jackie felt, she knew that her feelings for Husted were not genuine. She also recognized that she had more values in common with her mother than she would like to admit. Yes, John Husted's lack of real money would be a problem.

Just as important, Jackie never felt comfortable in the old-money Protestant society the way her mother did. "But Newport — when I was about nineteen, I knew I didn't want the rest of my life to be there. I didn't want to marry any of the young men I grew up with—not because of them but because of their life. I didn't know what I wanted. I was still floundering," she said later. She broke the engagement.

Hughdie, good soul that he was, took time to write the disappointed suitor a note saying that he was sorry the relationship didn't work out. He quoted from Alfred, Lord Tennyson's " 'Tis better to have loved and lost than never to have loved at all." Hughdie added a postscript, "And I ought to know."

Marriage and all it meant was on her mind in June, when Jackie wrote her thoughts to Janet and Hughdie on their wedding anniversary:

It seems so hard to believe that you've been married ten years. I think they must have been the very best decade of your lives. At the start we all had other lives, and were seven people thrown together, so many little separate units that could have stayed that way. Now we are nine—and what you've given us and what we have shared has bound us all to each other for the rest of our lives.

The previous May Jackie had met an intriguing young man named John F. Kennedy, a congressman from Massachusetts. Although she did not hold out great hope for the relationship—he traveled constantly, he was too casual and elusive for her—she was clearly interested. Their twelve-year age difference—Jackie was twenty-two and Jack thirty-four at the time—did not bother her. After all, her father was sixteen years older than her mother when they married. Hughdie, too, was older than Janet by ten years. Jackie also knew that the Kennedy family was very, very rich.

Janet was at first unclear about Jackie's feelings for Jack, noting, "She is the sort of girl who covers her feelings."

If so, Jack Kennedy was her double. He would not show his hand. "It was a very spasmodic courtship, conducted mainly at long distance with a great clanking of coins in dozens of phone booths," Jackie said later. She tried to hurry Jack along when she noticed men falling at the feet of her little sister. Moreover, some of them were serious. Jack teased Jackie, telling her that Lee would marry before she did. And Lee did.

Lee had been dating Michael Canfield since she was fifteen years old and he was twenty-two. When he proposed, Lee assumed and Janet hoped that his trust fund would be enough to augment his publishing income; it was his drinking that made Janet wary. The one thing she liked was his lineage: his father, Cass Canfield, was chairman of Harper & Row publishers, and rumors suggested that Michael, who was adopted, was the illegitimate son of the late Duke of Kent. Considering that Janet had dreamed up a long family genealogy, the possibility that her daughter could be linked to the English royal family was spine-tingling to Janet.

" 'Mummy,' " said Canfield years later in a sarcastic reference to Janet, "could be a mighty charming woman when she set her cap to it." As could Lee, who as the prior year's Deb of the Year had captured a full page in *Life* magazine (owned by "Uncle Harry" Luce) devoted to her beauty. The photos of debs representing such different cities as Baltimore, Philadelphia, and Chicago showed wholesome young women with toothy smiles, chosen for their family lines as much as their looks. New York Lee's portrait was different: she stood with her head tilted and only a hint of a smile — no shiny white teeth showing — as she looked provocatively at the camera and spread her skirt at the hip. She was a very cool Chablis compared with the other debs' fresh whole milk.

Of course, it was a little embarrassing for twenty-three-year-old Jackie; her twenty-year-old sister bumping her out of the bridal sequence. Why not, she suggested in a letter to Nini, now at Miss Porter's, save themselves from spinsterhood by hiring out as maids to meet eligible men at the stunning parties Lee and Canfield would be giving at their Manhattan town house?

Rose Kennedy was perplexed when she saw Lee's engagement announcement. She confused the two sisters and assumed that Jack had let another girl slip through his fingers.

Hughdie, though, saw little levity in the situation and prophesized turmoil ahead for Lee and her future husband. "He will never be able to afford her," he had murmured to several guests at the ushers' dinner.

The wedding was in Georgetown at Holy Trinity Catholic Church on April 18, 1953. Lee wore the bridal veil of Irish lace worn by her grandmother Margaret and by her mother when she married Lee's father. There were two Jacks at this ceremony. One was Jackie's date, Jack Kennedy, who was now the U.S. senator from Massachusetts. The second was Lee's father, Jack Bouvier, who proudly gave her away — but allowed Hughdie to pay for the affair. Janet ensured his sobriety by having his sisters escort him on the train down from New York with instructions to keep a close watch to make sure he didn't drink. They did, and he didn't, and the bride was beautiful.

Moreover, Jack Bouvier, his fatherly role successfully completed, did not drink at the reception afterward. It seemed that seeing Merrywood — this was his first and only visit — sobered him completely as he acknowledged the splendid setting Hughdie had provided Jackie and Lee. By comparison, what did he have to offer them? Nothing better than trundle beds in the guest room of his apartment. Jack wasn't the only man to recognize his own inadequacies: indeed, some guests thought Jack, with his brilliantined hair parted in the middle and his flashy dress, was a figure from a bygone era.

When it was time for the bride to throw her bouquet, Lee aimed it straight at Jackie—as Jack Kennedy watched with a wry smile.

Within a few months both Jackie and Janet had begun to worry about the wedding bouquet's powers. Jack seemed no closer to proposing than he had months earlier. Jackie had a chance to go to London to interview the crowds lining the streets for the coronation of Elizabeth II. She wasn't sure she wanted to go. Jackie was reluctant to leave Jack; she was also fatigued from work and the activities surrounding Lee's wedding. "At that point, she was awfully tired," Janet remembered. When Jackie vacillated, Janet stepped in.

"If you're so much in love with Jack Kennedy that you don't want to leave him, I should think he would be much more likely to find out how he felt about you if you were seeing exciting people and doing exciting things instead of sitting here waiting for the telephone to ring."

Janet sweetened the offer by offering to pick up all her expenses. "Mother gave me the trip," Jackie explained in her self-deprecating way. "My sister, Lee, had just been married, and I guess Mother felt sorry for me." Also, finding accommodations at that late date would have proved impossible, so Janet arranged for Jackie to stay at the home of one of the future queen's ladies-in-waiting.

While in London, the *Times-Herald* published several of Jackie's sketches on the front page. Janet was thinking about Jack and whether he would propose: "I didn't see him while she was [in London], but he must have seen them. I know that because he was always impressed by Jackie's gifts, he must have been impressed by these.

"He called me up from, I think, Cape Cod the day she was flying back from England, and asked me if I knew what flight she was on and what airline.

"He said, 'That plane stops in Boston. I'm going to meet her there.' "

Janet continued, "It was the first time that I felt that this was really a serious romance, at least on his part."

Finally, Jack asked Jackie to marry him.

Chapter 8

JACKIE'S WEDDING,
JANET'S TRIUMPH

No matter how beautiful a wedding appears, there has never been one that was completely harmonious in the making. And when families are as different as the Auchinclosses and the Kennedys — not to mention the Bouviers and Lees — a discordant note or two is sure to be heard prior to playing the wedding march. So it was with the Bouvier-Kennedy ceremony. Although its public appearance at Hammersmith Farm was a perfect tableau of youth, beauty, wealth, and class, the behind-the-scenes events were far from pretty.

It looked to the public — and this was nothing if not a public wedding, unusual in itself, as Jack Kennedy was only a junior U.S. senator from Massachusetts who would not ordinarily attract this much attention — merely as if two wealthy families were being joined in matrimony. "This bride and groom have everything," thought outsiders. "They have no problems."

But tremendous fissures were forming that were to weaken the foundation of the marriage being celebrated on the sloping green lawn of Hammersmith Farm. For one thing, money and wealth were important to all the families involved; yet their comparative bank accounts, appearances to the contrary, varied greatly. The Kennedy family was very rich; the Auchinclosses were rich; and the Bouviers, at this point, had comparatively little money. More important, the Auchinclosses were an established part of social Newport, which was old money and staunchly Republican. The Kennedy wealth was new money; even its vast quantity failed to dazzle the Bellevue Avenue families. Many felt that Jackie's marriage was *not* a step up.

Then there were the families' clashing temperaments. Joe and Rose Kennedy were as ambitious and publicity-seeking a couple as this country has known, while Hughdie and Janet Auchincloss had spent their lives as a private couple. Lastly, Jack Bouvier's pride, lack of discipline, and genetic weakness for alcohol combined to make him a threat to both the Kennedys and the Auchinclosses.

In addition, family unity varied greatly. The Kennedy clan behaved as one. The complicated Auchincloss relatives, steprelatives, and exrelatives acted independently, although they were generally harmonious. Then there were the Bouviers, who did not want their fading fortunes and family squabbles illuminated by press flashbulbs. "The whole Kennedy clan is unperturbed by publicity. We feel differently about it. Their clan is totally united; ours is not," a Bouvier admitted.

So the public saw a carefully scripted, seamless image while disharmony was hidden from view. And in truth, the spin on this wedding could not be blamed entirely on the political Kennedys: the summer engagement announcement that Janet penned for the newspapers perpetuated the false Bouvier claim of descent from French aristocracy. She also said her ex-husband's occupation was "financier." In fact, Jack Bouvier was a stockbroker, and no longer a prosperous one at that. Bouvier had become so irrelevant to New York society that the engagement announcement of Jackie in his summer home paper, the *East Hampton Star*, totally omitted mention of her father. Instead, it described Jackie as "a granddaughter of the late Major and Mrs. John Vernou Bouvier and of James T. Lee of New York and East Hampton." Ironically, when the story appeared, both Jim Lee and Jack Bouvier were summering in East Hampton. Bouvier must have felt humiliated by the oversight and angry at the ascendancy of his former father-in-law. Surely Janet's hand was behind this slight, he fumed.

Once newsrooms got word of the engagement, Janet's announcement was pumped with black ink to become more and more confabulatory.

One story, in farfetched reference to Hughdie's grandfather Oliver Jennings, called Jackie an "heiress to a Standard Oil legacy." Jackie as an heiress was a frequent theme of these fanciful write-ups; Jackie would inherit a great deal in terms of family legacies — some favorable, some problematic — but she knew she would acquire no estate. After all, wasn't that part of the reason for this wedding?

When reporters called to ask where the ceremony would be held, Janet made a telling comment. She answered that the service would be in a Catholic church and added a statement that discounted generations of her own Irish Catholic ancestry. She said of Jackie, "Her father is Catholic, you know."

If Janet's statement was crafty, the formal betrothal date itself was contrived. The couple actually had become engaged in the spring, but Joe Kennedy insisted on embargoing the announcement until an important *Saturday Evening Post* article could be published that introduced Jack as "the Senate's gay young bachelor." (This was well before the adjective *gay* carried today's meaning.) But word leaked out, and Janet was compelled to announce news of the September 12 wedding in late June, a little sooner than planned.

Now that the engagement was public, the Auchinclosses and the Kennedys accelerated their visits to each other. Jackie, for example, left Hammersmith Farm for one of her frequent weekend trips to Hyannis Port. At an evening's entertainment in the small private Kennedy movie theater, she and Jack previewed, presciently, *Gentlemen Prefer Blondes,* starring Marilyn Monroe.

While Jackie was squirming in the newfound attention, Janet was planning. She expected a first visit from Rose Kennedy for the purpose of laying out a preliminary wedding calendar. The ceremony was just three months away. There was no time to be lost in putting together the event. Janet hoped that Rose would be in accord with the small, private gathering that Janet and Hughdie envisioned. She conveniently put the two recent Kennedy weddings — Bobby to Ethel, and Eunice to Sarge Shriver, both of which were large — out of mind.

Even before the engagement was announced, Rose was nervous and excited about meeting the Irish Catholic woman who married into the WASP guild that had kept her own family out of the best social set for several generations. Rather than resenting the Auchinclosses, Rose was elated at her family's upward progress: now, finally, one of her sons was marrying into the clique itself. Gore Vidal pinned the Kennedys to the board when he said, "Of the available Catholic women in the country,

[Jackie] was about the most glamorous and [the Kennedys] regarded it as a big step upwards and an ongoing victory over the WASPs."

The devout Rose did not need to worry about the bride's ancestry, either. Although the Auchinclosses were Scottish Presbyterian, the bride herself identified with the small part—only one-eighth—of her ancestry that was French rather than the less prestigious Irish. Because Jackie's last name was French, she was able to get away with the illusion. Although Jackie's future sisters-in-law teased Jackie whenever they caught a whiff of pretension, Rose encouraged Jackie in her puffery, for to her also, the Bouvier surname had extra cachet.

Rose wanted to make a good impression on Janet at their first meeting. "What should I wear?" is the first question most women ask themselves before an important social occasion. To Rose, who traveled to Paris several times a year to buy the world's most exquisite couture, dressing was an art. But she knew that it was more important for her to fit in at Newport than to show off. Although she loved her day frocks designed by Mainbocher, Dior, and Chanel, actually wearing them might look ostentatious. Rose turned to Hélène Arpels, a wealthy Protestant friend, for help at the critical juncture of meeting Janet. With the assistance of Arpels, she selected an understated blue silk day frock, accessorized with pearls, white gloves, and a cartwheel hat.

Janet did not need to plan a costume ahead of time. She was focusing on September. In fact, she was already irritated at being shortchanged sufficient time to plan a proper wedding. Janet knew she had Joe to blame for the announcement delay. However, she was underestimating herself: her impressive organizational skills and good taste led her friends to feel that she could pull off an important wedding on relatively short notice. Plus, she had just thrown gorgeous nuptials for Lee. Although the location would be different, she assumed the plans would be identical. Janet's peevishness really arose from her disapproval of anyone who would organize his life—much less his son's life—around the press.

Although Jackie was aware of the conflicting social expectations between her mother and her future in-laws, Jack Kennedy was oblivious. Just a short time before Rose's meeting with Janet, he was still telling his secretary, Evelyn Lincoln, that his wedding guests would be "close friends only." Jack also had to ask Lincoln to remind him to make out his list, causing a reaction from another office worker: "See—I told you he'll never make a good husband!"

So shortly before Rose's visit, when Jack pulled into Hammersmith Farm at three in the morning with four more men jammed into a convertible—Jack's feet up on the dashboard, singing loudly and off-key "My Wild Irish Rose"—Janet was steamed. If nothing else, Jack had been taught by his father to gauge other people's reactions to him and respond accordingly, so he advised his buddies, "Let's cut it down. I'm not too solid with the family, and they might throw me out."

When Rose arrived in Newport, her friends the Robert Youngs put her up at their estate, Fairholme, on Ruggles Avenue. At the appointed hour, Rose stepped out of the car in her carefully chosen outfit. A maid escorted her to await Janet in the deck room, which gave her an opportunity to take the measure of its casual decoration and stunning bay view. Janet entered wearing a dress shaded in taupe, and the ladies shook hands. Rose didn't know the customs of social Newport and had assumed she would be offered lunch at Hammersmith Farm. When Janet said they would dine at Bailey's Beach, Rose was taken aback, not understanding that this beach club was more club than beach.

Jackie and Jack joined them on the short journey: Janet at the wheel, Rose in the passenger seat, and the couple in the backseat. If Rose had selected an outfit sure to fit in at Hammersmith Farm, Jack had taken the opposite approach. He was wearing an undershirt, shorts, and bedroom carpet slippers. What Jackie was *not* wearing is important: despite her two-year courtship, her fiancé had not yet given her an engagement ring. Eventually, she received a 2.8-carat emerald-and-diamond ring—selected by Joe.

Arriving at the beach, Jack announced that he would take a short swim before lunch. Jackie joined him. When Jackie came out of the water to change clothes, Jack remained behind, unconcerned about the time. Rose yelled out to her son, commanding him to get out of the water, towel off, and come to lunch. As Jackie remembered, "Rose screamed out, 'Jack! . . . Ja-a-ck!'—and it was just like the little ones who won't come out and pretend not to hear their mothers calling—'Ja-a-ck' but he wouldn't come out of the water." Although Janet was surprised and a little embarrassed at both Jack's and Rose's gauche behavior, she disguised her feelings.

The swimming incident was a mere prelude to the luncheon, which was just as awkward and even more annoying. Rose, who had already seen two daughters and a son married, prattled on with plans for a very large and elaborate wedding, wrongly interpreting Janet's silence as acquiescence. Jack and Jackie said next to nothing, giggling with each other from time to time like "two bad children," as Jackie put it, instead of two adults, thirty-six and twenty-four years old. Janet remained quiet but was downright infuriated at Rose's presumption: *she* was the mother of the bride, and it was *her* place — not Rose's — to make these decisions.

The visit left the issues of the ceremony and the reception unresolved. After a polite handshake, Rose returned to her friends' house for the remainder of the weekend. Janet turned to Jack and told him that she thought an intimate and private wedding would be appropriate. He disagreed and repeated the points Rose had tried to make. Although Jackie herself was of two minds about the plans, she admired Jack's ability to stand up to her mother.

It was Janet's thoughts, however, that Jackie parroted when she received a surprise call from the *Boston Globe:* "I can tell you that I'm planning a small wedding." Then she added, "Things are a little confusing right now."

The next day the same paper quoted her: "Things are a little hard on my mother because the phone just hasn't stopped ringing," and it was "a little frightening" to her. The guests will be "mostly family."

To another newspaper she said, "It will have to be small. Jack and I want it that way." And to one more she commented, "If it were large, it would have to be very large. And we wouldn't want it that way."

When reporters called Jack, they didn't focus on the details of the wedding but rather on his future bride. He responded awkwardly. "I'm quite sure once we're married, she'll become just as interested in Massachusetts and international problems as I am." One columnist added, "Not a romantic quote, perhaps . . ."

And Jackie, asked if she were interested in politics, responded, "Yes." Dead stop. Surprised either by her reticence or by her inability to give an example of her purported fascination, the reporter then asked her political affiliation. To this pivotal question she wanly replied, "I guess I'm a Democrat now."

At the same time, Jack was writing to a friend about the man's attendance at the wedding. "Your special project is the bride's mother — one fine girl — who has a tendency to think I am not good enough for her daughter."

Joe was upset when Rose told him she had failed to talk Janet into a large ceremony, since he viewed Jack's wedding as another political campaign to manage and thought the media could help launch his son onto a national stage. He wasn't about to see Jack miss this chance. Conscious of Janet's stern mettle, Joe set up a visit to Hammersmith Farm.

A few days later Jackie watched Joe Kennedy step off the plane. She recognized the determined look on his face. "Oh, Mummy," she thought, "you don't have a chance."

At Hammersmith Farm, Janet and Joe Kennedy were discussing the wedding, coolly at first and then more heatedly. They disagreed over its size, elaborateness, entertainment, food, expense, and, lastly, the religious ceremony itself. Kennedy even vetoed Jackie's proposed wedding gown, wanting one that was more traditional. The only thing that Janet and Joe agreed on was that Jackie and Jack should marry.

When it became clear to Janet that Joe wanted to use the wedding as a political spectacle, she dug in. She told Joe that she refused to ask Hughdie to bear the expense for Jack's political ambitions. Neither the Auchinclosses nor even the Kennedys knew many of the guests Joe wanted to invite: they were included only because of their position in Boston, Washington, or Hollywood. Hughdie would not pay for this circus: business was not good, and the couple had just paid expenses for Lee's spring wedding at Merrywood. Jack Bouvier could not bear the cost of a simple celebration, much less the kind that Joe wanted. But to Joe Kennedy, price was no object, and he readily agreed to pick up the tab.

Soon more than 750 names made up the list for the wedding ceremony itself. Janet was thankful that St. Mary's Church in Newport could hold no more worshipers than it did. It looked as if the ritual would be as crowded at the altar as it was in the pews: Archbishop Richard J. Cushing of Boston was to officiate, assisted by a monsignor and four priests. In addition, more priests were present on the altar.

The guest list for the reception afterward was taking on a life of its own. Each new version was more bloated than the previous. One July day Janet was particularly indignant when she noticed that Joe was inviting Gloria Swanson, having heard that the actress had been his mistress. Hollywood was one thing; Hollywood tarts were another. Janet's full sympathy went to Rose, when she saw that Joe was willing to flaunt his former mistress in front of his wife.

Janet was soon moaning to her close friend Eileen Slocum, "The wedding will be just awful—quite dreadful. There will be one hundred Irish politicians!"

What Janet didn't know about the Kennedy wedding list—and would never learn, as the complete file was only released decades later—was that Jack Kennedy's office had retyped the guest roll and divided the guests into specific classifications. It reads:

Suggested Lists for Jack's Wedding by Categories

CATEGORY
A. Jack's personal friends
B. Relatives, clergy and newspapers
C. Important city, state and federal officials
D. Important friends of Jack's and members of Jack's office staff in Washington
E. Workers for "Kennedy for U.S. Senator" organization
    a. Teas and receptions
    b. Secretaries
    c. Volunteers
F. Racial groups
G. Labor groups

What's more, the racial groups, according to Jack Kennedy's office, were "Italians, Jews, Lithuanians, Polish, Armenians, Syrians, Portuguese, Negro [there was only one couple listed under this category, apparently accounting for the singular designation], Greek [again, only one couple]." Note that the Kennedy office did not designate "Irish" as a racial group.

Inexplicably, the last race named is "Canadians."

No matter what their "race," the number of guests was growing too large, Janet thought. Correspondence flew back and forth between Hammersmith Farm and Jack's office. One letter from Jack, dated July 26 and addressed to "Dear Mrs. Auchincloss," reads (emphasis added):

I am enclosing a partial list of guests to be invited to the wedding. As you know, many on this list will be unable to attend.

In the next few days I will send you the additional guests, which will not be more than 100.

Of course, a hundred people alone constitutes a good-size normal wedding.

One week later Evelyn Lincoln was sending Janet another letter, explaining, "I am enclosing the *remaining names* on the Senator's wedding list [emphasis added]." Then, at the end of August, Lincoln wrote to Janet's secretary, Kay Donovan, "The Senator would like the following people *to be added* to the invitation list [emphasis added]. . . ." The enclosed list takes up several pages.

No wonder Janet was irate. The Kennedys never stopped. Besides their management of the unending guest list(s), Joe Kennedy had leaned on Jack to pressure Jackie to choose a more "suitable" wedding dress than the design she'd preferred. For several years since coming back from France, Jackie had been sketching her own clothes, which were then executed by Janet's Georgetown dressmaker, Mini Rhea.

Jackie was influenced by the Parisian couture for which she had acquired a taste with Tish Baldrige, and subsequently was the first of Rhea's customers to insist on a slim, clean line with a shorter hemline. Jackie's personal style, as demonstrated by her many sketches, contrasted with the familiar early-fifties mid-calf skirts with wasp waists. Jackie accurately perceived that these styles suited her mother and sister, both of whom were shorter and more rounded than she. But Jackie wanted a distinctive look for her wedding day: one that would stress elegance and flatter her slight bosom rather than compensate for it.

But Joe Kennedy didn't trust his future daughter-in-law's style to appeal to future voters — how wrong he would be — and instead dictated a more traditional gown. He agreed with Janet's selection of a fine dressmaker, Anne Lowe, who had sewn the day dress Janet wore at her wedding to Hughdie eleven years earlier. Joe was particularly satisfied when he learned that Lowe was African American. A Democratic senator's fiancée, he figured, should not be wearing a gown from a Georgetown couturier but rather one by a designer whose race might be used to Jack's advantage.

The call to Lowe from Kennedy's office was no surprise: besides her earlier work for Janet, she had designed gowns for women from such families of quality as the du Ponts, Biddles, and Rockefellers as well as the Massachusetts Lodges, whom Joe both envied and emulated. Lowe's dresses could also be bought at such upscale stores as Saks Fifth Avenue and Neiman Marcus. The dressmaker was the first to admit that she was an "awful snob" and refused clients who were associated with café society. Her mother, a seamstress in Clayton, Alabama, gave Lowe her initial training. When her mother died unexpectedly, leaving four unfinished gowns owed to the wife of the governor, Lowe, at age sixteen, finished the dresses and then left for New York and formal design training. Ultimately, five of her outfits would be included in the Costume Institute of the Metropolitan Museum of Art.

Although Jackie appreciated the exquisite quality of Lowe's work, the dress's design was not to her taste. She wanted a restrained, elegant, and sophisticated gown, with her late grandmother Lee's rose-point Irish lace mantilla as its only accent. What she was talked into instead was a frilly confection, fashioned of fifty yards of silk taffeta, with an excessively full skirt. The most unattractive features were the eleven rows of ruffles stitched on the skirt and the huge concentric circles of ruffles on the bodice, with sprays of embroidered flowers at the bustline and another spray down the side of the skirt. It was a very busy style and one that did not suit the bride. Later she commented that it looked a little like a lampshade. However, Jackie was eager to please Jack and told the press that she was delighted her groom wanted her in a traditional gown.

Besides worrying about Jackie's dress, Joe Kennedy was doing his best to manipulate the upcoming press coverage. In turn, the media were handling the Kennedys. A two-page letter to Jack from an editor at *Look* magazine discussed the competing *Life* magazine cover of the engaged couple that would appear July 20. The editor wrote that the competing story "will not necessarily hurt our cover plans in late September provided, as I told you, that we could be assured of first magazine rights for coverage of your wedding and reception." The Kennedys would not acquiesce.

The turnabout in wedding plans elicited no comments from a friendly media. For example, on June 25 the headline of the *Boston Traveler* read, KENNEDY FIANCÉE PLANS "SIMPLE, SMALL WEDDING." By the middle of August stories mentioned that the invitations to the intimate nuptial had been mailed—fourteen hundred in all.

Something else, in particular, was bothering Janet. Although Congress had adjourned in August, Jack was off sailing in the Caribbean. Having been married to a womanizer herself, Janet sensed trouble ahead. "Why has Jack left on a vacation with George Smathers?" she asked Jackie. "No man in love does something like that," she said, less concerned about her daughter's sensitivities than about making her point.

Janet's comments cut deeply, whittling at Jackie's slender self-esteem. Jackie flared, angry and defensive, showing that she had a few concerns of her own. It didn't help when she received press inquiries about the oddly timed trip. She took only one, from society reporter Betty Beale, a friend of Janet's. "I asked her about the trip because it was so unusual," says Beale. "Why would a man leave his fiancée like that? I had never heard of any behavior like it."

Jack kept in contact with telegrams, although many of them were less than romantic. "Get a hold of Ed Berube. He knows a fellow that's going to make our wedding cake," read one. Janet was appalled when she heard the "fellow's" plans to ice a large sheet cake with blue ocean waves and white doves to represent, as the creator put it, "an ocean of love." With so many guests, the ultimate cake—five feet high with four tiers—had to be delivered in two sections. Even its baker was worthy of a news sound bite: "The biggest, the finest and most important cake of my career."

By early September Jack was back in Newport to apply for the couple's marriage license. Janet innocently called city hall to tell the clerk that her daughter and future son-in-law would be stopping by the office. She never imagined that someone there might tip off the local newspaper. Jack looked surprised when he saw the *Newport Daily News* photographer in wait.

"A photograph, Senator, please," the newsman said.

The East Coast was in the middle of a heat wave, with temperatures reaching 107 degrees. So Jack was dressed comfortably—wearing swimming trunks and a sport shirt—but he didn't want to be snapped looking so casual. "That can be remedied," said the cameraman.

The city clerk lent his jacket, and a law-student bystander gave him his own tie. Kennedy then combed his hair and asked to be pictured only from the waist up, facts that were duly reported in the news story. Jack's attire and his failed attempt to fool the readers received wide attention. When Janet saw the photo, she was dismayed, finally realizing the extent to which Jackie's marriage meant the end of privacy for the family.

As the day approached, Janet's tension wound tighter. Everybody in the family—including Lee, who had arrived with Michael—was doing their best to stay out of her way. Jackie and Lee were trying to take time out for some girl talk, and Hughdie withdrew, as usual, in reaction to Janet's frenzy.

A few days before the wedding, Janet picked up the newspaper and was irked to read that the Roman Catholic Diocese of Providence was announcing a prohibition of "worldly or theatrical" music in church services, including weddings. The banned music included both the traditional processionals, the "Bridal Chorus" from *Lohengrin* march by Wagner, and the traditional recessional, Mendelssohn's "Wedding March" from *Midsummer Night's Dream*. The ban also included "Ave Maria." In addition to what the diocese termed as its "black" list, it also issued an approved "white" list of musical selections.

Janet was alarmed when she saw that most of the music already selected for Jackie's wedding was on the "black" list. Luckily for the family—and oddly coincidental, given Joe Kennedy's influence with the archdiocese—the music ban would not go into effect until October, two weeks after the wedding. Janet sighed and threw down the paper, relieved that she herself had had the gumption to become an Episcopalian.

Everyone at Hammersmith eagerly anticipated the arrival of the bridegroom. He came clad in tattered shorts and sneakers, and the first stop he and his buddies from Hyannis Port made was not his fiancée's home but rather the Newport Country Club to play golf. Jack announced that they wanted to play nine holes, but the club allows only an eighteen-hole game. He gained entrée as a guest of the Auchinclosses, although, of course, the family knew nothing yet of his arrival. Even though the club decided not to stand on form, Janet was furious at Jack's cheekiness. She let him know about it, too.

Jack told one of his golfing partners, "I hope you enjoyed your game, because as a result of it there has been an almost total breakdown of relations between the mother of the bride and her dashing prospective son-in-law. It seems that there is an ironclad rule of the club that nonmembers can only play when there is a member present to sanction the match. Now they know that their worst fears are being realized. They are convinced that one of the last strongholds of America's socially elite is being invaded by mongrels without pedigrees."

On one topic Janet and Joe were agreed. It was their mutual distrust of Jack Bouvier. Bouvier had always scorned Joe Kennedy, telling John Davis that Joe was an "opportunist, a traitor, and a crook." Despite stories that Bouvier had stopped drinking and was sunning and exercising in East Hampton so he could look his best, Janet had reason to be suspicious. As Yusha remembers, "Janet didn't want Bouvier to run into James T. Lee at the wedding events—that's why she cut him out." So Janet, Jim Lee, and Joe Kennedy joined an odd triumvirate that no one could have predicted. All three wanted Bouvier—a complete wild card—dealt out of the deck.

But Jackie wasn't concerned: she thought her father's complaints about having been left out of the wedding plans were just his usual grousing about Janet. She had watched her father give Lee away six months earlier, and if there was ever something Jackie believed in, it was her father's love for her. She was too young at twenty-four to ask herself that if *she* felt stressed by the upcoming nuptial extravaganza, how would her father—with his weak character—react?

Most important, she did not recognize that her mother was conspiring with Joe Kennedy to keep Jack Bouvier out of sight. When Bouvier telephoned Hammersmith Farm, Jackie did not return his calls; perhaps she wasn't told of them. By the time he left New York for Newport, it must have seemed—especially to someone who always overplayed his emotions—that even his beloved Jackie had joined Janet's cabal.

The dominoes were aligned for Bouvier to accomplish his own downfall. For Lee's spring wedding, Janet had arranged for him to be accompanied by an escort of sisters whose sole purpose was to keep their brother from drinking. This time—for the larger and nationally publicized Kennedy wedding—she made no such provision. He was on his own.

While Janet and Joe also colluded to exclude Bouvier from each and every prenuptial event, they extended invitations to his sisters and their families. He was angry at being excluded, and humiliated by the obviousness of his banishment. And he was the bride's own father!

A number of Janet's relatives and friends were being housed at Hammersmith Farm or at friends' houses on Bellevue Avenue or Ocean Drive; Jack Bouvier was left to make his own arrangements. The plans he made included a room at the Viking Hotel with full access to room service. After checking in, he steeled his nerves for a call to Jackie. He wanted to ask her if he could be invited to the next night's dinner for the bridal party and family members to be held at the Clambake Club. But he could not get through. So many calls were coming in to the house that Janet's secretary was marshaling the telephone, with Janet the commanding officer. There was no way to get to talk to his daughter—the daughter he had literally termed "all things holy." He turned both angry and maudlin. The events were taking their toll on a man who knew he fell short in comparison to Hughdie, Jim Lee, and Joe Kennedy; who couldn't let go of a large grudge against his ex-wife; and who possessed a vulnerability to alcohol.

While Bouvier was fuming the day before the wedding, all the Kennedys were in town and delighting in glorious Hammersmith Farm. The oppressive heat wave had just broken, and the farm's huge lawn and bay breezes were the perfect setting for their outdoor games, which they began after breakfast and continued throughout the day. Joe needed to win, whether it was at touch football or delivering the best sentiment to the bride and groom at that night's party. He warned a friend of Jack's who was writing out a toast, "We don't want the Auchincloss side in any way to outshine our boy."

Janet was fussing over the arrangement of Jackie's countless wedding gifts, put out for display and guarded by several off-duty policemen. The quantity was embarrassing, especially when Janet learned that Joe's New York office had two more truckloads on the way. Jack and Jackie were receiving gifts from such close friends as the Chinese Merchants Association of Boston (a porcelain table lamp with red shade) and Van Cleef & Arpels, where Joe had selected Jackie's engagement ring (a jewel-studded house key). As Janet obsessed over the exact position of each gift and the rowdy Kennedys ran and shouted all over the lawn, Jackie needed to retreat from the hubbub.

Across town, on Bellevue Avenue, the doorbell rang at Stonor Lodge. The maid who answered the door recognized Jackie, a frequent visitor to the estate's swimming pool. She asked her inside and told her employer that Miss Bouvier was at the door. Noreen Drexel walked downstairs with a puzzled look on her face.

"Oh, Mrs. Drexel," Jackie implored. "May I stay here for the day? I need to get away from the house. I won't bother you—I brought a book to read." Jackie indicated the volume under her arm.

"Of course, Jackie," said Drexel. "We're always happy to see you."

And so Jackie Bouvier spent the day before her wedding by herself, hiding out at the Drexels' home, curled up in their sunroom reading as she enjoyed the last private moments of her life. Across town the antics of the Kennedys and the frenetic last-minute preparations of Janet swirled about Hammersmith Farm.

Yusha was also headed across town, but toward the Viking Hotel. Janet had tired of Bouvier's constant phone calls and had imposed upon Yusha the unpleasant duty of informing her ex-husband that he would not be receiving a last-minute invitation to that night's nuptial party. Yusha, a kind and sensitive young man who had always gotten along with Bouvier, left the bride's shaken father, got back into his car, and just sobbed. "I told Jackie what I had done," he said later. "She was angry. She thought her mother should have gone over herself. She told me, 'You shouldn't be the scapegoat on this.' "

Jackie's father called room service for a bottle of scotch and a bucket of ice. Once it arrived, he began to fuel his acrimony with liquor. He knew that in a few hours, a bridal party for eighty would be held at the Clambake Club; those present would be the Kennedys, the Auchinclosses, the Lees, and the Bouviers — save for him. Jim Lee had just arrived in Newport to attend the dinner. As Janet's father and a successful man of business, he had been invited despite his earlier refusal to see Jack Kennedy when he made a special trip to East Hampton during the summer to meet him. Janet had smoothed over her father's behavior by telling her prospective son-in-law that it was actually best not to introduce himself to her father until the wedding. Without it being said, Jack knew that Jim Lee's natural animosity toward the Kennedys might queer things, so he let it wait. The bridal dinner would be the first meeting between Jack Kennedy and Jim Lee.

Jim Lee was happy to see Janet but was cool to Joe Kennedy. Rumors about Joe Kennedy beating Jim Lee out of the purchase of Chicago's Merchandise Mart are unfounded; there is no evidence whatsoever that Jim Lee was ever interested in buying the building. In addition, Jim Lee developed buildings from the ground up rather than acquiring them, and he had never built outside metropolitan New York. However, Jim Lee deplored both "sassiety" and social climbers. For this wedding, he had to endure both.

Sometime during the dinner, according to a close family friend, Joe walked up to Jim Lee and asked him if that was *his* Rolls-Royce and driver waiting outside the club. Jim Lee confirmed that it was. "I hope you'll understand that you won't be able to use that car tomorrow," Kennedy said. "It wouldn't look good if the bride's grandfather pulls up in a Rolls-Royce."

Kennedy continued, "There'll be lots of photographers, and we need to think about Jack's future." Jim Lee stood there, dumbfounded, as Joe walked away. His feelings about the man had just been confirmed.

Janet, when told of Joe's dictum, was aghast. Her father had been angry at the groom at her first wedding, and the men had started a shouting match; now, at Jackie's wedding, Janet's father would be furious at Jackie's future father-in-law. Plus he would have to see Jack Bouvier again. The whole situation had gotten out of hand. It was up to her to keep the lid on tightly during the volatile day ahead.

When Jack Bouvier awakened the next morning, several hours before the wedding, his heavy head indicated that he needed another drink. As he began tippling, Janet was calling her former brothers-in-law to go to the Viking Hotel to check up on him. John Davis came, too. The only living witness to the events chronicling Bouvier's behavior that day, Davis observed that, yes, Bouvier had been drinking but that he was also half dressed in preparation for the ceremony. When Bouvier saw his sympathetic relatives, he began railing against the Auchinclosses, but his in-laws knew that such was par for the course. His ability to do his duty by his daughter was duly conveyed to Janet.

According to Davis, Jackie also telephoned—not to her father or uncles but rather to her twin aunts, who were finishing dressing at another hotel while their husbands were at the Viking prepping Bouvier. Jackie asked her aunt Maude, Davis's mother, whether her father was "up to it."

As gently as the aunts could, they suggested to Jackie, and then to Janet, that perhaps Hughdie—just in case—should be prepared to walk Jackie down the aisle. But "just in case" wasn't good enough. Janet had watched her ex-husband move from one drink to falling-down drunk too many times. She could not and would not trust him. The repercussions from the Kennedy family of any incident potentially embarrassing to their scion would be fierce. In her own mind, she had no choice. Bouvier was out of the wedding.

Janet was stern as she informed Jackie. An ugly battle began: Janet on the attack, blaming Bouvier, and Jackie distraught. "I knew he would do this," Janet screamed at her trembling daughter, already dressed in her wedding gown. "Why you wanted him in the first place, I'll never know."

Jackie wept, but she felt pressured, too, by both Janet and Joe Kennedy. She had already begun to substitute her relationship with her father with a warm affinity for Joe. In turn, Joe admired her femininity, courage, and style the same way that her father always had. As she matured, she could also recognize Jack Bouvier's decline. Compared with his continual anger and depression, the Kennedys were so much more glamorous: as she put it, like "carbonated water." She made her choice. Yet, according to Yusha, she would always blame Janet for the heartbreak of her wedding ceremony: "Jackie never forgave her mother for that."

So Janet triumphed. Her only worry was that Jackie's swollen eyes would be noticed. As they approached the church, a crowd of more than three thousand jammed the narrow streets that intersected in front of the brownstone Gothic church. "[Jackie] was quite caught off guard by the number of people watching. As were my father and stepmother," remembers Yusha.

Cars could barely squeeze through, including those of the wedding party, despite police reinforcements holding back sightseers. "Even as a member of the wedding party—you wondered whether you were going to be able to even get into and out of the church. I mean, just masses of crowds outside craning and pushing and crowding in and shoving, just to see the bride," remembered Aileen Train.

Janet was pleased that her father was getting a ride rather than openly defying Joe Kennedy's outrageous request to hide his Rolls-Royce. She was also surprised: this gesture of deference was rare for him. When Jim Lee announced, however, that he would attend the ceremony, and the reception only briefly, Janet had too much on her hands to try to persuade him otherwise.

Janet was already excited by the time an usher walked her to her pew. Everything was going according to schedule; all of the guests had remembered to bring their entrance cards, so there were no unintended slights. Janet sat straight in her pew as friends admired her silk organdie dress and strand of pearls. They compared her with Rose, whose rubies and diamonds were a tad showy for a daytime wedding.

Jackie appeared very nervous but was holding her own. That she had been weeping only served to make her wide brown eyes appear more limpid. Six-year-old Jamie, a page and the youngest of twenty-seven attendants, had balked when he entered the church and saw the crowd, and needed to be prodded to walk nervously up the aisle. The child was so sweet-looking that he was quickly forgiven. The only glitch was a commotion toward the rear when a guest fainted in the overcrowded church. The length of the religious service—a High Mass, which involved a great deal of kneeling—was killing Jack's back. Later, Jack told Yusha that when he needed to stand at the end of the service, he wasn't sure if he could get up without help.

But the wedding guests had no idea of the dramas playing out behind the scenes. They saw only a 2.9-carat diamond set next to a 2.8-carat emerald engagement ring, an archbishop performing the ceremony, and a fifty-yard silk wedding dress.

When the party left the church, traffic backed up more than half a mile as cars inched toward Hammersmith Farm. Sightseers lined the roads and added to the traffic jam by hopping into their own vehicles to join the long line of wedding-guest cars. At the farm twelve valets were busy parking four hundred cars. Janet smiled as she gazed around. Everything that greeted her eye was idyllic. She remembered, "It was a beautiful, clear, bright but very windy day."

They were fortunate that the longest, hottest, and most humid heat wave of late summer had passed. The weather was ideal for the day of the wedding: bridesmaids' skirts were blowing out from the welcome breeze, and the occasional wind gusts kept Janet Jr. busy fixing Jamie's lace jabot and straightening his black velvet shorts. The breeze gracefully lifted hairdos. Janet's two horses were grazing in their pasture, the cows were looking bucolic in the next field, the bay was blue with visible crests of waves due to the wind, and, as if on cue, ships with white sails floated in view of the wedding reception.

Jack stepped out of the receiving line to get a breath of fresh air. He stared out at the harbor and remarked to his Hyannis Port neighbor, "That'd be a helluva place to sail in with the presidential yacht." He also made a prescient comment to Cardinal Cushing during the afternoon. If he should die young, he asked Cushing, would the cardinal be sure to look after Jackie and his family?

Janet would not sit down during the luncheon. She ignored her space at the table as the wedding attendants devoured the pineapple cup, chicken à la king, sliced ham, and potatoes. Rather, she walked around the property with Hughdie, keeping a managing hand on the activities. Even she could not be everywhere at all times, though, and despite her planning, the tent occupied by staff and workers was accidentally served Moët et Chandon champagne while a large proportion of her guests drank the California vintage.

Jackie was hungry, even if Janet wasn't. Jackie had skipped breakfast because of her agitation over her father. Then she had the ceremony to get through and a reception line that lasted for two hours as fourteen hundred guests snaked from the driveway into the house through the living room. Several times Jackie was caught peeking out the window to check on whether the line was receding. When the queue finally vaporized, she and Jack ate lunch at their table and sat for toasts. While

Jack was distracted with his own friends, she took advantage of the chance to walk around the lawn. Her mood turned pensive.

She spotted a family friend, Polly Tunney, wife of the champion boxer Gene Tunney. A grandniece of Andrew Carnegie, Polly had shocked the family with her marriage. Marie Ridder, the Auchinclosses' Merrywood neighbor, was chatting nearby when Jackie approached Mrs. Tunney.

Jackie walked up to her. "Mrs. Tunney, may I ask you a question?"

"Certainly." Polly Tunney smiled.

"How does a married woman cope with an unfaithful husband?" asked the bride.

Marie Ridder gasped in surprise. Mrs. Tunney, too, was taken aback but recovered quickly. "Well, my dear, I always believed in my heart that I was the one he loves."

Jackie murmured a quiet "thank you" as she turned to walk to the banquet table to join Jack.

Chapter 9

TO THE
WHITE HOUSE

Jackie, dressed in her gray Chanel going-away suit, was joking, but Jack did not laugh. The newlyweds were being driven to the Providence airport, where a private plane was waiting to take them to Manhattan for their first night at the Waldorf-Astoria Hotel.

"I bet you're already dreaming of your carefree old bachelor days and whether being married will put a crimp in bachelorhood?" Jackie teased him.

Jack forced a smile.

At Merrywood Janet was relaxing and accepting compliments from her friends about the lovely reception. Thank heavens, Joe Kennedy had agreed to let her make all the arrangements. The food, drink, and decoration were generous but not ostentatious.

To a few close friends, she divulged the awful truth about her ex-husband's failure to escort his favorite daughter down the aisle. Their shock only reinforced Janet's instinct that she had done the right thing, years ago, in divorcing Jack Bouvier. She was proud of Hughdie for stepping in and knew that Jackie appreciated it, too. Despite her weeping before the wedding and then again as she removed her gown, Jackie took the time to speak to Hughdie privately, thanking him before she left on her honeymoon. Now Janet concentrated on getting Hammersmith in order and returning to Merrywood so Janet Jr., eight, and Jamie, six, could get back to school.

In New York, though, feelings ran the opposite way. All the Bouviers knew what had happened; the incident reminded them of Jack's drunkenness at his mother's funeral. Now Jack Bouvier returned to his apartment and went on a binge. "He felt this tremendous need to take those drinks. [His failure to escort Jackie] would be a memory that haunted him his whole life," said his nephew Miche Bouvier.

At the same time, Bouvier enjoyed wallowing in self-pity and dwelling on the subject he should have avoided. The only person allowed in was the day maid. He wouldn't leave the house and wouldn't take calls — not that he had many concerned friends banging down his door to help him through his crisis.

A gracious letter from Jackie forgiving him was the magic gesture that broke the spell. Bouvier brightened: his daughter *was* the most noble goddess in creation. He was so proud of Jackie that he even showed the letter to one of his Wall Street colleagues, forgetting that it highlighted his own inadequacies. Most important, her letter ended the binge drinking.

Jack Bouvier was becoming a caricature of himself. He had always tried to remain on good terms with Janet's sisters, as well as with their husbands and children. That summer Janet's brother-in-law John Ryan, her niece Mimi Ryan, and Bouvier went to a baseball game together. Mimi had graduated from law school at the University of Michigan and was back in Manhattan, working as an attorney. Suddenly, when John Ryan was out of his seat, Bouvier slipped his hand over Mimi's knee. She took his gesture lightly: "Stop it, Uncle Jack. We're related!"

Bouvier replied, "Not any more." Mimi laughed and pushed his hand off.

Bouvier added another hobby to that of flirting and drinking: gambling. Given his precarious financial status, he could not afford to lose wagers — he ran up a debt with his own housemaid. Finally, in 1955 he sold his most valuable asset: his seat on the Stock Exchange. He was bitterly disappointed to receive only $60,000 (about $385,000 today).

Jack Bouvier had further to fall. One night he was an extra man at a large dinner party. A lady of impeccable reputation noticed that he was behaving very oddly. His eyes darted back and forth, not focusing on the guests' faces but rather downward, at the sofa cushions or the floor. The expression on his face was sly. Suddenly, it struck her: Jack Bouvier was checking out the ladies' handbags!

She kept her eye on him throughout the evening. Bouvier was seated next to a friend of hers who had brought an elegant 24-karat gold handbag to the party. When the friend left the table for a minute, the lady saw Bouvier check out the room to see who might be watching. She lowered her own eyes for a moment and then quickly looked up again to see Jack Bouvier reaching down. He grabbed the gold bag and slipped it inside the pocket of his dinner jacket.

The lady was aghast. She had never accused anyone of wrongdoing before—she had never known anyone in her group to steal—but was at a loss what to do. That week she discussed the incident with several friends: Jack Bouvier was a pickpocket of ladies' handbags! Everyone swore not to tell Janet—it would be too humiliating for her—but their affection for the woman was reinforced. How wise she was to leave this man. How foolish her eldest daughter was to worship him.

Jack and Jackie Kennedy returned from their honeymoon in Acapulco. She had wanted to rest and enjoy the Mexican scenery, but Jack wanted to drive to southern California to see some old buddies. She graciously gave in but was perturbed when he thought nothing of leaving her alone while he went out with them for hours on end.

Back in Washington the couple alternated the first few months of marriage between Merrywood during the weekdays, when Congress was in session, and Hyannis Port on the weekends. Many times during the summer Jack would invite his staff to swim at Merrywood. Janet enjoyed having the couple with the family, although sometimes she would forget to let the dogs out of the house and Jack's allergies would kick in. "He would suddenly be unable to breathe," she said. "His eyes would swell and his face would swell."

No matter how many nights the couple stayed with the Auchinclosses, however, Jack addressed his in-laws by their last names. After a few years he might occasionally call Janet "Mummy," although Jackie called Rose and Joe by their first names almost immediately.

Nevertheless, they were constantly staying with the Auchinclosses. For all of Jack's money, the couple had no place to call their own. "No point in having a home of your own until you have children," Jackie remarked. Several friends thought this odd: what did having children have to do with a new couple wanting to establish their own place?

Jackie was trying her best to become more outgoing because Jack liked groups of people around him. It was awkward, however, because she hadn't yet met many of his friends, and once she got to know them, she didn't necessarily like them.

A month after their marriage, they were interviewed by Edward R. Murrow on the popular CBS show *Person to Person*, and the American public was introduced to Jackie's breathless way of speaking. As Murrow preferred to interview his guests at their own residences, Jack and Jackie had to use a borrowed living room in Boston's Back Bay and act "at home."

The couple finally realized they needed a place of their own, especially in Washington. Jack had lived in Georgetown since he had left the navy, renting new houses around the neighborhood every year. Now he rented a row house from a friend in Georgetown at 3321 Dent Place. The couple was given only a six-month lease.

Even though they were in a tiny house for a short time, Jack's boyhood cook, Margaret Ambrose, came down from Boston to the rented house. The couple employed a butler, too. Jackie, sweetly, enrolled in American history classes in order to understand Jack's work better. She attended Georgetown University's School of Foreign Service, the only one open to women.

Jackie kept a low profile—none of her classmates knew that she was married to a U.S. senator. There were a few differences, though, between this graduate student and others: for example, she walked her cocker spaniel to class. When she arrived at her building, she turned the spaniel over to her maid. Both the maid and the dog would wait outside until class ended, when Jackie would come out to walk the dog—and the maid—home.

During her free time, Jackie broke her mother's tradition by wearing slacks when she shopped in Georgetown or relaxed at home. Janet always insisted upon skirts outside the house or at the dinner table. Now Jackie was wearing capri pants in public, with a small scarf tied at the neck of her shirt or sweater.

Jackie was trying to adjust to marriage, particularly marriage to a politician. "The biggest change is . . . you see much older people who are the ages of my mother's friends, or else political jackals who drive me up the wall. We used to go to movies, see young people, young friends; life was informal. Now it's more formal."

To some friends, she added, "They talked about their children and grandchildren, and I talked about [Jamie]." Of course, she did not add what she was telling others, that there was a lot she missed because Jack worked late and she didn't feel she could attend parties without him. When Jack did come home in time for the couple to go out, Jackie observed that "the men have such a wonderful time. They talk together after the dinner." Apparently, she felt that being sequestered with the ladies was not very scintillating.

Jackie gave two formal dinners in the first six months of marriage and invited Janet and Hughdie to one of them. Jackie was very nervous: "That was really terrifying. I think I could entertain a king and queen with less apprehension than my mother, when there are other guests present." Janet, however, complimented her on the lovely party.

After their six-month lease ran out, they moved into a hotel. Jackie was ill at ease dealing with strangers and second-rate furnishings after living in the beautiful homes her mother had run so elegantly. "We were like gypsies living in and out of a suitcase. We spent the [second summer of marriage] off and on in Hyannis Port. I longed for a home of our own. I hoped it would give our lives some roots, stability. My ideal . . . was to have a normal life with my husband coming home from work every day at five."

Despite this, the couple kept on renting houses. At least they were no longer living with relatives, although they continued to vacation either with Janet and Hughdie or with Rose and Joe.

Jackie emulated Janet as she brought order to Jack's life. First, she improved his abysmal diet. Sometimes she made changes he didn't appreciate, like the bottle of wine in the picnic basket she packed for his lunches (the cook prepared the food) rather than the beer he preferred.

To her credit, Jackie was introducing a new dimension into Jack's life: good food and wine, well-run houses, and well-mannered children. Their friend Lord Harlech later said, "She wouldn't go along with the Kennedy atmosphere [at Hyannis]; she had certain standards of her own which she insisted on in her house."

Next came Jack's wardrobe. This, Janet had never needed to tackle: Jack Bouvier was a clotheshorse, as concerned with how he looked as any teenage girl. Hughdie was forty-five years old when she married him and had always dressed like a gentleman. Although Jack Kennedy was a vain man—Jackie used to giggle to her friends that he was always having his "hair done" to keep it full, or she'd jab at him by asking people, "Isn't he vain?"—his clothes were terrible, especially considering how skinny and sickly his chronic illness, Addison's disease, made him look. (Once when Jackie was angry, she told a friend that he had a pumpkin head and a scarecrow body.)

So Jackie improved Jack's wardrobe and, in the process, made him so aware of his clothes that he found himself criticizing a colleague. "Your suit doesn't make a statement," he announced, then howled with laughter when he realized what he had said.

Jackie, the girl who had decried the life of a housewife, seemed to have become just that, albeit with more than her share of household help. During the day she occupied herself with classes, read, or rolled bandages with the other senators' wives. She even took bridge lessons so she could be a better card partner to him.

But at night she was lonely. "Very lonely," she would later say. Jack was gone—where was he?—and she felt awkward going out alone, as a married woman might do today. "I was alone almost every weekend. It was all wrong. Politics was sort of my enemy and we had no home life whatsoever." Although she loved Jack, she took no interest in the details of his office—this was a woman who had not yet registered to vote. In fact, she dedicated herself to being his respite from politics.

Jackie had been mentored by only two men in her life: Jack Bouvier, who had taught her to be courted, and Hughdie, who by his devotion to Janet's every whim gave her a model of a husband. Both these men worked short hours. Yet Jack, even when he was home, paid her little attention.

More disturbing was Jack's confession that he had not been able to wipe out his venereal disease, chlamydia. He took massive amounts of antibiotics to kill the disease and to protect Jackie from getting it—along with the drugs he took to keep his Addison's disease under control—but it was a futile gesture. He had himself tested for a viable sperm count, being unsure of what the disease and the drugs, including the ones that stabilized his Addison's disease, had done to his body.

In addition, Jack's two subsequent spinal surgeries—he came close to death—were a major hurdle for Jackie, one that she cleared cleanly. Not only did she keep him entertained and amused, but in order to take his mind off his pain, she started him on what would be a Pulitzer Prize–winning book, *Profiles in Courage*. The discipline she had learned from Janet in jumping fences with no fear she applied to Jack's recovery as she changed his surgical bandages for months on end until the huge wounds in his back closed.

Jackie did not disclose her problems to anyone at the time. She saw

Janet and Hughdie frequently, just as she tried to avoid her in-laws; Bobby and Ethel lived in Georgetown, too. She bit her nails and chain-smoked.

Although Jack Kennedy was, as Joe Kennedy's son, suspicious of anyone who represented old-line money, he was charmed by Janet. Knowing their reputations, Janet was wary of both men. Janet liked Rose but resented Joe's air of superiority. Still, she knew the Kennedys would maintain the same front that she and Hughdie did by letting people think that Jack Bouvier was rich and Jackie would inherit half of this estate; that her grandfather Jim Lee would leave Jackie a fortune; and that Hughdie had given Jackie a trust fund or would at least share his fortune with his stepdaughters upon his death. Of course, Janet's friends knew otherwise, but to the butcher and the antiques dealer — and to the media — Jackie gave an aura of being heir to several great fortunes.

Joe Kennedy, of course, knew better. After all, the only way he could have assumed that Jackie was rich would have been if he were a fool about money — and about his son's future. He was not.

Everyone, including the Kennedys, knew about Jack Bouvier's finances. He was a broker who held a seat on the Exchange; Joe had been the chairman of the Securities and Exchange Commission. And Kennedy had plenty of friends who could tell him exactly what Bouvier's fortune was (or wasn't).

In addition, a man who had already hired private detectives to follow his son — as Joe did during the war, when Jack was conducting an affair with a pro-Nazi Danish woman — would surely not hesitate to check into his future daughter-in-law's alleged trust funds. In fact, there had never been any talk of Hughdie setting up the Bouvier girls; by the time they were entering college, Hughdie's fortune was starting to decline. Wasn't that the reason the Kennedys had paid for Jackie's wedding?

So the Kennedys had known from the start that Jack was not marrying a rich girl. Only the public had been fooled.

Jackie was jubilant: finally, she was pregnant. It was time to go house hunting at long last. Jackie had loved Merrywood so much — and spent so much time there with her mother while Jack was out of town — that the young Kennedys decided to build a house on Merrywood's property. Hughdie offered them any site they desired. The couple hired an architect who drew up plans following Jackie's initial sketches. "She wanted to have a one-story house with . . . a courtyard, perched up on a cliff over the river," remembered Janet. Unfortunately, Jackie never saw her dream house realized. "It all got rather complicated, bringing in water and heat—and rather expensive."

The couple was unsure of what they wanted to do instead. In the meantime, Janet and Hughdie heard that the nearby Hickory Hill estate was going up for sale. They had been occasional dinner guests of its last owner, former Supreme Court Associate Justice and Mrs. Robert H. Jackson, and sometimes the justice had ridden his horse over to Merrywood.

Jackie "went out and looked at it, Jack looked at it, and I think that what really attracted him about it was the big trees and the fact that [it was once the headquarters of Union Army General George McClellan]," said Janet. The white Georgian-Colonial house, on McLean, Virginia's Chain Bridge Road, had fifteen rooms and ten acres and cost Jack $125,000 in late 1955 ($800,000 in current dollars, although the estate would cost at least $5 million today).

"They bought it and moved in there intending to live there always, and they did quite a lot of remodeling," Janet said. Jackie made a huge effort in Jack's bathroom and dressing room, making sure he could reach the shoe shelves and drawers without bending over and aggravating his back. The public rooms were less practical, though, with delicate Louis XV chairs upholstered in blue-and-white satin fabric.

Now that she was pregnant, Jackie took a break from her studies and began to decorate the estate, with the help of Janet and Janet's decorator, Elizabeth Draper. Hickory Hill, with its swimming pool, gardens, stables, and pastures for riding, had nearly the same ambience as Merrywood and was less than a mile down the road. Jackie wasn't bothered by its isolation; she described McLean of the mid-fifties to a job applicant: "As we live in the country, there are no cinemas nearby, just a small village with a grocery store." With a baby in her arms, her mother nearby, and a horse to ride, she could be happy at Hickory Hill despite Jack's constant absences.

In the fall *Profiles in Courage*, the book that Jackie helped Jack formulate, was published to great acclaim. Jack gave full credit to his wife in the book's acknowledgments. But despite his kind words, their first few years of marriage had been bumpy. And things were not getting easier.

Right before the couple moved into Hickory Hill, Jackie miscarried.

The only people who had been told of the pregnancy were family members; Jack and Jackie told only those same people of the loss. But at night, alone, Jackie could feel the empty rooms of Hickory Hill mocking her.

Jackie's isolation wasn't helping her state of mind. Janet said, "It was a difficult place for Jackie to live. When you're married to a busy senator . . ." Her voice dropped off. "She was alone very much out in the country, because Jack would not get home until very late at night for dinner. When she lived in Georgetown, she could rush down and have dinner with him or he could come home late."

To fill her time while Jack was traveling or late at the office, Jackie began buying couture clothes in the manner she had dreamed of as a junior at the Sorbonne. Jack started complaining about the money. "She's breaking my goddamn ass," he complained to a friend once the Kennedy family's accounting office in New York notified him of the mounting bills. And he began taking potshots at the Auchinclosses, saying of Jackie, "She's got a little too much status and not quite enough quo."

Subtle acts of cruelty were patterning the marriage: Jack would be out late with no call home. By now, Jackie knew the rumors about his women were true, but tried to dismiss them as trivial. "All Kennedys, beginning with their father, have had their fingers in the cookie jar." At the same time, she worshiped Joe Kennedy, saying at one point that she loved him "more than any other man except my husband or my father." Just as Jackie sometimes failed to acknowledge Janet, she also eliminated Hughdie from the mix — her stepfather who had done so much for her — in favor of Joe Kennedy.

The August 1956 Democratic National Convention in Chicago was approaching. Jackie was pregnant again, and she and Janet had beautifully decorated the nursery at Hickory Hill. Jackie did not want to accompany Jack to the convention, as her own obstetrician had told her that the travel and stress might harm her baby. But the Kennedys thought she should go. While Jack stayed in a hotel, Jackie was at the apartment of his sister, Eunice Kennedy Shriver. Jack missed winning the vice presidential nomination by only a few dozen votes.

After the failed convention, Jack flew to Europe to go on a sailing trip with a few buddies (and a complementary number of women). Jackie went home to Hammersmith Farm. During the day she'd go to Bailey's Beach to bask in the sun — Hughdie had been president of the Spouting Rock Beach Association for a year now — and the company of her family. She especially enjoyed playing with Janet Jr., ten, and Jamie, eight, in anticipation of being a mother herself very soon.

Janet was having a difficult summer, though. Jack Bouvier had rented a member's cabana at Bailey's Beach in the "A" section. Janet was forced to walk past him to get to the clubhouse. She was particularly furious at him: Hughdie's firm was not doing well, and her ex-husband was repeating his snide crack "Take a loss with Auchincloss!" Janet borrowed another member's cabana for the season and concentrated on the impending birth of Jackie's baby.

Jackie was napping on the afternoon of August 23 when she was awakened by strong cramps. Then she felt something wet. She bunched her nightgown up to her waist and, to her shock, saw blood coating her inner thighs. She was still bleeding, and barely seven months pregnant.

Nini called the Auchincloss physician, who ordered Jackie to the hospital. Janet helped her into the station wagon and sped her to the Newport Hospital. At seven P.M., the surgeon took a dead baby girl from Jackie by cesarean section. Her baby had separated from the placenta, causing the internal hemorrhaging and the stillbirth.

Janet was, understandably, crazed with anger. As self-centered as Jack Bouvier had been, he had never deserted her while she was pregnant. She called Bobby Kennedy on the Cape, told him to get his brother to Newport _now_, and to come himself _immediately_. All of which Bobby tried to do. However, Jack Kennedy wasn't sure he wanted to break off his sailing to return to Jackie. His reaction was that the baby was dead—what could be gained by his losing vacation time? By now it was August 26.

Janet refused to do Jack's dirty work for him. So Bobby had to tell Jackie that her baby daughter was stillborn. Janet was distraught over Jackie's loss of the baby girl, named Arabella after the tiny ship _Arbella_ that accompanied the _Mayflower_ to the new world. Janet went to the private burial with Bobby standing in for the infant's father. Of course, Arabella would have been Janet's granddaughter, and she mourned for herself as well as for Jackie, who was not allowed to leave the hospital for more than a week. "He should have been there for you," Janet told Jackie.

By the time Jack arrived on the twenty-eighth, his office had told the press that he was sailing offshore in Nice while visiting his parents. Upon his arrival in Boston, Jack was asked if he had talked to his wife. When he confessed that he hadn't, the reporter wrote that "[Jack] said he presumed his wife had not phoned him because she did not want to interrupt his trip."

No one retorted, "Wouldn't your first impulse be to call *her*?" Except for Janet, who had many more questions for her son-in-law. Although Jack always felt that social Newport was a Republican enclave that he could never crack, their disdain was not entirely because he was a Democrat. Social Newport thought his behavior was callous. Regardless of any emotional pain of his own over the loss, as some said, his place was by his wife's side, especially after she had nursed him so carefully through his life-threatening back surgeries. That was the position taken by men educated at Groton and Middlesex, who knew the right thing to do and how a man should act.

Jackie came as close to divorcing Jack as she ever would. She had suspected that he was fooling around in the Mediterranean while she faced the loss of Arabella by herself. She sensed that her Kennedy sisters-in-law saw her inability to bear children as a taint, an inferiority. Perhaps they were using her own image — her emphasis on her French lineage, her love of the arts, and her insistence on being called Jack-LEEN — against her. She might be a lady, but they at least could bear their husbands' children. Rose was no help, either, blaming the stillbirth on Jackie's cigarette smoking.

Janet's conversations with her friends at the time about the state of her daughter's marriage put to rest the myths that Joe Kennedy gave Jackie a million dollars to stay with Jack or that he had established a trust fund that would eventually revert to her. Janet knew the full history of the marriage — after all, Jackie had spent her evenings at Hammersmith while Jack was "working" — and she herself had firsthand familiarity with marriage to a womanizer. Janet feared a dark end to the fairy-tale marriage and said as much to her friends.

She was distraught when she spoke to Eileen Slocum about Jackie and Jack. "What will she do?" Janet asked Slocum: Jackie was married to an ambitious man who philandered. "And if they divorced, what would she have left?" she cried to Slocum.

"She has no children and no estate!" Janet exclaimed — nothing to protect her if the marriage ended. "What will she do?" she asked again, rhetorically. There could be no answer.

Jackie refused to return to Hickory Hill; she wanted to go to Hammersmith instead. She couldn't bear looking at that nursery and, on top of it, being alone again in all those empty rooms. Did she want to break off the marriage? Yes and no. She knew how angry she was at Jack, and how hurt she had been. In the hospital she lashed out at him, blaming the disaster on the strain of her unwanted trip to the Democratic convention. Jack stalked out of her hospital room.

Two days later Pat Lawford gave birth to her daughter Sydney, and two weeks after that Bobby and Ethel had their next baby, Courtney. It made sense for Jack to sell Hickory Hill to Bobby, who had been renting in Georgetown, but it hurt Jackie that Ethel's baby—number five—and not hers, would be in the nursery she had so hopefully decorated.

So Jackie stayed in Newport. She chose to recuperate with her mother, Hughdie, and her younger siblings. The only time she left was to visit Lee in London. Mike Canfield was serving as special assistant to the American ambassador, when he could stand up straight. (Here were two sisters with a father who was a womanizing alcoholic: Jackie ended up with a philandering husband, and Lee with a drunk one.) A bitter Jackie repeatedly told Lee that her marriage to Jack was over. When a drunken Canfield asked Jackie for advice on holding his own marriage together, she responded, "Get more money."

The trip to London was pivotal, although Jackie didn't know it at the time. Lee introduced Jackie to her Euroflash friends; Jackie had never known people so sophisticated, so glamorous, and so intent on living the good life. They were all money and no worries. They shimmered silver; by comparison, Jack's earnest political friends were as brown as Boston beans.

Even Lee's affectation of having her maid dash into the bathroom to drop a gardenia into the toilet after it was flushed struck Jackie as amusing.

Nevertheless, by the end of Jackie's visit, she had decided to give the marriage another try. She knew she had few choices. Janet remembered: "Everybody decided that the best thing would be for her to live in town, where if he couldn't get home, she was in the city with people around her."

She flew to Washington, to another rented house, this time on P Street in Georgetown. During these months she had not gone to Hyannis Port once. She chose Janet over Jack, and Lee over the Kennedy in-laws. Janet was heartsick over Jackie's future: would she ever have the babies she yearned for? What no one knew was that chlamydia, Jack's disease, could be transmitted to a woman's reproductive system and show no symptoms. Untreated in a woman, chlamydia can lead to miscarriages and problem pregnancies.

Janet returned to Merrywood to host her husband's former stepson, Gore Vidal, at lunch. His play *Visit to a Small Planet* was on tour at Washington's National Theatre. Rather than placing him with the adults, she playfully escorted Vidal to the children's table alongside. He claimed he had a "splendid time" talking to the children. No fan of Janet's, he writes, "At least Janet had not the cruelty to put me on her right." After lunch Jackie pulled him away to see his old room, which had become hers.

Hughdie had a frightening attack of asthma, and his family physician insisted that he stop smoking. He missed it badly. Janet said, "I could see that it was painful for him to watch me smoke, so I stopped, even though I was a chain-smoker." Jackie couldn't bring herself to quit but would go outside Merrywood and sit on the upper terrace when she needed a cigarette.

The end of the year brought Janet and Hughdie to Brooklyn for a Long Island University ceremony held on its thirtieth anniversary. Receiving the degree of doctor of laws was James T. Lee, president of Central Savings Bank. Janet, of course, was proud and thrilled for her seventy-nine-year-old father. The write-up in *The New York Times* of his honorary degree must have occasioned a frisson of envy from Jack Bouvier, whose own father had received an honorary LL.D. degree from Columbia University. Later, Janet would confuse the two degrees and say that her father had received honorary law doctorates from both Long Island and Columbia Universities.

The only glitch in the couple's trip to New York came the time they arrived in the city during a cab strike. Hughdie wanted to go downtown to his office and Brooks Brothers. The only way to get there was to take the Madison Avenue bus. "It was crowded," Margaret Kearney says. "He was hanging on to a strap. He felt someone jostle him but he didn't pay any attention. Soon after, he went to look for his solid-gold monogrammed money clip with his folding money, and it was gone. Someone had lifted it out of his pocket." That was Hughdie's first and last experience with public transportation.

In the spring of 1957, Nini Auchincloss, then a student at Bryn Mawr College, became engaged to Newton Steers, a graduate of Yale and its law school. He was twenty years older than Nini and had already founded the Atomic Development Mutual Fund. He was worth $2.5 million ($15.3 million today).

The wedding was held at St. John's Episcopal Church in Washington, with Janet Jr. serving as maid of honor and Jackie as her matron of honor. She had twelve other attendants, and Steers had sixteen. Her three Auchincloss brothers—Yusha, Tommy, and Jamie—and her one Vidal half brother—Gore—were ushers, as was Jack Kennedy. "There were so many in the bridal party that if no one else had showed up, the reception would have still looked like a roaring success," wrote Betty Beale in the *Washington Star*. The reception was at Merrywood and was picture perfect, despite the unusually cold weather that kept everyone from the garden and lawn. The general opinion on Steers was that he might be rich, but he was awfully boring, droning on and on about atomic energy, mutual funds, and their nexus.

The exciting thing was that Jackie had just entered her second trimester of pregnancy. Jackie put tremendous pressure on herself to sustain this pregnancy and cut out anything that might tax her or upset her. She spent her days quietly in her rented house, often whispering, "Three times lucky," and touching wood.

During the spring Jack Bouvier kept calling both his daughters to tell them that he felt ill and was worried. However, he admitted that a workup at Memorial Hospital had pronounced him fine, except for the heavy drinking. Both Jackie and Lee tuned out his laments and ignored his calls, many of which didn't make much sense. Jackie also neglected to tell him of her pregnancy, and he was notably upset when he read of it in *The New York Times*.

Jackie spent much of that summer at Hammersmith Farm. Newport was jammed with reporters because of President Eisenhower's visit to the Naval Training Station. She wrote Janet a thank-you note telling her that she and Jack far preferred Hammersmith to Hyannis—they could relax there, compared with the bedlam of Rose and Joe's house.

In July Jackie saw her father in East Hampton and thought he was depressed and confused. No one knew he had cancer of the liver: his rambling thoughts were a symptom of the disease and not of alcohol. Yusha went to see Jack Bouvier and let Jackie know that he thought her father was seriously ill. Still, Jackie was fighting for her unborn baby and became convinced by Lee that their father was a terrible drain on their energy.

One week after Bouvier was pronounced completely healthy, he collapsed. Miche Bouvier, his late brother Bud's son, got the call and raced to the hospital—this time, Lenox Hill—with his wife, Kathleen. They called Jackie and sent a telegram to Lee in London.

Jack Bouvier was in a coma. The Bouviers were alone with him; Kathleen held his hand during what would be his last minutes. He was incoherent, mumbling different names from his past. Several times he uttered, "Josephine" (for his childhood nurse) and also "Jackie." According to Kathleen Bouvier, the only remaining witness, Jack uttered, "Jackie," as one bead of a long string; it was not an unconscious gesture, as it has been portrayed, of his asking for his favorite daughter. Finally, he let go of Kathleen's hand, gave a slight smile, and sighed for the last time. Kathleen noted that he died with a gentle smile on his face, writing that it was "without the half-mocking quality this time."

Soon after, the Bouviers were aware of someone coming into the room. It was Jackie with her husband, Jack. They stood silently at his bed until a nurse requested that they leave the room.

According to Kathleen, as the foursome stepped into the elevator, Bouvier's physician accompanied them to explain the cause of death. Then, without pausing to offer condolences or to let them begin to come to terms with their loss, he began prattling about Jack Bouvier's unusual skin tone. His pigmentation was extraordinary! said the doctor brightly. He continued: could he have Mrs. Kennedy's permission to dissect her father's skin?

Kathleen says there was only a stony silence in response as the elevator descended to the lobby.

Miche Bouvier and John Davis arranged Jack's service and burial while Jackie wrote a draft obituary for *The New York Times*, insisting that her husband deliver it in person to an editor. Jack Bouvier was buried in East Hampton in the consecrated ground of the church in which he had married his only wife. Those who came out to the grave site noted the ironic low whistle of the Long Island Railroad train as it passed the graveyard to pull into town. How many times had Bouvier been on that train as it pulled into East Hampton on a Friday afternoon. . . .

Jackie had decided she needed a top doctor for her pregnancy, so she and Jack took an apartment in Manhattan. Her efforts paid off on the day before Thanksgiving at New York Lying-In Hospital.

Janet and Hughdie had planned to spend the holiday in Aiken, South Carolina, where ten-year-old Jamie was in fifth grade. Jamie had been sent to boarding school the year before, when he entered fourth grade, and he felt shortchanged by parental inattention. He was angry that Janet, two years older, could go to a private school in the neighborhood until she was in high school. The Aiken boys were not allowed to go home, so the parents came to them. It was important for Janet and Hughdie not to miss this holiday visit. Janet said, "We came rushing up to New York to be there, and Janet [Jr.] came with us so that when the baby had arrived safely, we would take off for Aiken from New York."

They met Jack Kennedy at the hospital at dawn. "I remember how frustrated Janet [Jr.] was," said her mother. "She adored Jackie; she adored Jack; she was terribly excited about the thought of a niece or a nephew—and they wouldn't allow her in the hospital. So the hours that Jack and Hughdie and I sat and waited in the hospital, poor Janet was sitting outside on the curbstone, a very mad little girl." Poor Janet Jr., indeed.

According to Janet, she and Hughdie and Jack chattered in the waiting room—most of it was nervous conversation. Would Jack prefer a daughter or a son? "Anything will be all right with me," he replied.

Finally, the obstetrician came into the waiting room a few minutes after 8:30 A.M. He addressed Jack. "Do you care whether it is a boy or a girl?" This, after Jackie's miscarriage and stillborn daughter.

Jack refused to answer the question. And so the doctor told him that he had a girl and that "Jackie was fine and the baby was fine," Janet remembered. "I will always remember the sweet expression on his face and the way he smiled. And the doctor said, 'She's very pretty.' And I don't remember that Jack said anything. But I just remember his sweet expression and sort of a smile. He just looked radiant when he heard that all was well."

Jackie was still unconscious. Jack arranged to be the one who brought the baby girl in for Jackie to see for the first time, said Joan Braden. Joan and her newsman husband, Tom Braden, were friends with both the Kennedys and the Auchinclosses.

Before Janet and Hughdie left the hospital to collect Janet Jr. from the curb, Janet noticed the forty-year-old new father's ease with newborn Caroline. "He seemed perfectly at home with babies. I don't ever remember his having that stiffness or that being-afraid-to-touch-them that Hughdie seems to have always had." In fact, on the drive back to the Kennedys' New York apartment on Park Avenue, Jack Kennedy took Caroline from her nurse, Maud Shaw, and held the baby close to him.

And Jackie? Jackie would always say that the day Caroline was born was the happiest of her life.

Jackie was ordered to stay in the hospital for several weeks, but she was getting very anxious. Where would the couple live when they returned to Washington? She didn't think it was fair to Janet and Hughdie for them to move to Merrywood with a new baby, but she hated the thought of bringing precious Caroline to yet another rented house. Jackie had looked at "a million" houses, her mother said, nearly all in Georgetown, but couldn't make up her mind.

Jackie had enjoyed Georgetown since she first moved to Merrywood. It was where Janet brought her to shop, the place Jackie and Lee would lunch as soon as Jackie received her driver's license, where Jackie had had an apartment when she was a senior in college, and the neighborhood where Jack Kennedy had lived as a bachelor. Georgetown was the oldest neighborhood in Washington, having been first seen by John Smith in 1607 on his way south to found Jamestown, Virginia. By the early 1700s Georgetown was a bustling area, combining commerce and residences. Its diverse population in the 1800s included third-generation Americans, indentured servants, free blacks, and Europeans.

Because the neighborhood had always been mixed, it was one of the few residential enclaves in Washington that was not "restricted." Anyone with the right amount of money could buy a house. Georgetown became chic in the 1930s when President Franklin D. Roosevelt appointed a number of Jews to his cabinet and in policy roles: neighborhood covenants meant they had nowhere to move except Georgetown. So the area became known for its celebrity politicos and brain trusters, and the natural charm of its Colonial, Federal, and Georgian houses led to its being named a historic neighborhood in 1950.

Jack returned to Georgetown to focus on house hunting. Joan Braden said, "Jackie told me that while she was in the hospital with Caroline, she was so anxious to have a house of her own that the [senator] had gone down to Washington and picked out the N Street house because he liked the door knocker."

Actually, the first thing that appealed to Jack was the house's history: it was built in 1812 for William Marbury, who sued President James Madison for holding up his political appointment. The case, *Marbury* v. *Madison*, decided by the Supreme Court in favor of Marbury, involved the first time an act of Congress had been held unconstitutional and its law void.

The old Federal house at 3307 N Street showed its age, but Jackie was charmed by its history and personality. "It was going to be absolutely marvelous," Janet said of the house. "It was a house with a lot of feeling about it and a lot of charm."

The living room was typical Federal design, double-sized with two fireplaces and punctuated by an arch in the middle. The house was narrow across the front but deep, stretching back to a yard graced by shiny-leafed magnolia trees. With the basement level, it was four stories and larger than it looked. After all, it would have to shelter a butler, maid, cook, and baby nurse. Jack bought it for $82,000, or $500,000 today (because real-estate values have escalated, the house sold for a little over a million dollars in the late 1990s). The cash payment he made was about one-third less than he had spent buying Hickory Hill. "My sweet little house leans slightly to one side and the stairs creak," said Jackie, in sheer delight.

Jackie loved the house and called it "the perfect place." She immediately ordered stationery for her new address: robin's-egg blue with dark blue engraving, just like Janet's. When she arrived in her own house—for Jack had deeded it to her—she had merchants send over their wares for her approval. Needlepoint rugs would come and go. Jackie added new mantels in the high-ceilinged double room and restored the dining-room floor, rubbing it to an antique finish. Books were everywhere, and small drawings were propped up in odd little places, adding a casual touch.

The second floor held the couple's bedrooms, sitting room, and small office. In Jack's dressing room a suitcase was to sit open throughout their years in the house, always ready to be packed. Caroline's room was on the top floor and opened onto her nurse's bedroom. Jackie put white-painted furniture in her daughter's room, much as Janet had for her as a girl. Jackie consulted with her former designer Elizabeth Draper but ended up hiring Mrs. Henry ("Sister") Parish II.

The combination of decor treatments in the public area must have been odd. Here was a city house built in the Federal style, with Sister Parish's cozy chintz-country influence superimposed over Jackie's favorite Louis XVI style. No wonder the look kept changing as Jackie experimented. "There were paint fumes for a year," she admitted.

"[Jackie] did that living room over at least three times within the first four months they were there," Janet said. One week the living-room curtains would be red chintz, and the next week the whole first level would be beige. "Let's see," said Janet, "rugs, curtains, upholstery, a vicuña rug over that sofa, everything, was suddenly turned lovely different shades of beige. I can remember Jack just saying to me, 'Mrs. Auchincloss, do you think we're prisoners of beige?' "

In December Caroline was baptized in the Lee—not the Kennedy—christening gown first used by her great-grandfather James T. Lee, who was now eighty, then by her grandmother Janet and by her mother. Despite the stories that Caroline was named after her aunt Caroline Lee, the truth is that both Lee and Caroline take their names from Jack Bouvier's grandmother Caroline Ewing. Caroline was christened at St. Patrick's Cathedral by Archbishop Richard Cushing of Boston. Her godmother was Lee; her godfather, Bobby Kennedy. Janet was having another busy month: several weeks later Yusha married the daughter of the U.S. ambassador to Chile, Alice Emily Lyon.

Yusha's wedding took place in Washington, D.C.'s historic St. John's Episcopal Church. Janet Jr. was a bridal attendant, and the groomsmen included Jamie and Tommy Auchincloss, Jack Kennedy, and Nini's husband, Newton Steers. When Yusha and his wife returned from their honeymoon, he began work as a partner at Auchincloss, Parker & Redpath.

Jackie, Jack, and the baby were content in their N Street house. Jackie asked Hughdie if Caroline could call him "granddad," as the baby would never know Jackie's father. Several times a week Jack would stop at Merrywood to see the Auchincloss dogs, which he missed—he would pet them and talk to them, then wash his hands and go back to the office or home to Georgetown.

In January 1958 the couple attended an "anti-Inaugural" party held for disgruntled Democrats at the home of Scottie Fitzgerald Lanahan, the daughter of Zelda and F. Scott Fitzgerald. Jackie was now ready to jump into the political fray. With an $80,000 inheritance ($500,000 today) from her father—the first real money of her own—she was pleased to buy Jack a Jaguar like the one Janet drove, which Jack immediately exchanged for an American-made automobile.

Jackie spent the fall campaigning for Jack, who ran for the Senate again as the incumbent. It was her first campaign; Jack had already been a senator when they married. But Jackie preferred motherhood, as long as much of her baby's care was in the hands of the nurse. When Caroline began to toddle and was rambunctious, the noise would carry throughout the compact house; Jackie would insist that Miss Shaw take her outside to play, perhaps in the sandbox in the backyard or at Georgetown's Volta Park on R Street. The house on N Street was as quiet as Merrywood.

Jackie felt that too many demands were being placed on her. What time she had, she wanted to spend alone, curled up with a book or listening to music. Although their N Street house was perfect, it was only four blocks from the Harrimans': great for Jack, since he counted on Averell Harriman's support (as the former Democratic governor of New York) in the 1960 presidential election, but not so wonderful for Jackie, because Janet and Averell's wife, Marie, were friends. Between the baby, the upcoming primary campaigns, and her own need for privacy, Jackie did not relish the frequent suggestions of visits by Janet and Marie to see the baby.

Lee was still in London, but her marriage was cracking wide open. She knew that when she returned to New York after her divorce, she wouldn't get any financial support from Janet, especially in the amount she required. Instead, she approached her grandfather Jim Lee. At the time, her cousin Mimi Ryan was an attorney who lived on her income. She and her grandfather had become great friends over the years, and Jim Lee trusted her judgment. He knew how much she made, and one time he said, "May I ask you a personal question? How do you live on your income?"

Mimi replied that her shared apartment was rent-controlled and that she had a little income from her late mother. "Why?" she asked.

Jim Lee told her, "I have a letter from Lee, who is returning to New York. She wants three thousand dollars a month [$18,000 today] from me—she says she can't live on less." Instead, he put Lee on rations.

The Kennedys' spending was escalating, too, as they decided to purchase a vacation house in Hyannis Port near the homes of Rose and Joe, and Ethel and Bobby. "Just a little house," Jackie said, "it only has five bedrooms."

Lee no longer had to worry about money. On March 19, 1959, shortly after her twenty-sixth birthday, she married Stanislaus "Stas" Radziwill in a civil ceremony in the Fairfax, Virginia, courthouse five miles from McLean, with a dinner given afterward at Merrywood by Janet and Hughdie. Radziwill was a rich man descended from Polish royalty who insisted on being referred to as Prince Radziwill; he was also twice divorced and more than twenty years older than Lee.

In fact, Janet had thought he was divorced just once. Candy Van Alen, who did not trust Radziwill and knew him when he "sat out World War Two in Switzerland," told Janet that Lee would be his third wife. "She wouldn't believe it was true," says Van Alen. "She was furious."

To Lee, Jackie explained, "Why, he is nothing but a European version of your father!" Lee said that her mother's criticism "made me love him all the more."

Some who had known Jack Bouvier thought there was a startling physical resemblance between the two men. Stas offered to campaign for Jack in Polish neighborhoods the next year while Lee was busy at home with their firstborn, Anthony (Tony), who was born five months after the wedding. With Stas, Lee would have two places in England: a town house in London and an estate near Henley-on-Thames.

Jackie's work on Jack's Senate campaign seemed to segue naturally into Jack's run for President. In the Senate Caucus Room on January 2, 1960, Jack declared his candidacy while Jackie, Janet, and Hughdie looked on proudly. One of Jackie's first campaign stops was in New Hampshire, to visit Jim Lee's sister Florence (Mrs. Andrew Anderson).

As Jackie's soft-pitched interviews continued, she stressed what she perceived were her duties as a wife, which included organization and household management. She also added that her husband considered himself "in perfect health."

The camouflage over Jack's health extended to conceal Jackie's background. Campaign press releases never mentioned either Merrywood or Hammersmith Farm—after all, average voters do not give their houses names. The press material minimized her first summers at Newport: "During her fourteenth and fifteenth summers, she helped out at a Rhode Island farm, feeding chickens in the range houses."

The spin continued as Jack's presidential campaign heated up. "I have never had a secretary," Jackie claimed, conveniently forgetting that Janet selflessly had sent her own secretary, Mary Barelli Gallagher, over to N Street, saying, "Jackie needs you more."

Jackie perhaps was not thinking of her three residences (the couple kept an apartment in Boston besides the Cape Cod home) when she said, "We live rather simply." Of course she also claimed, "I don't particularly like to shop."

Jackie would give short talks in French or Italian. Her most important recorded television advertisement—the first to feature the wife of a presidential candidate—was in Spanish. She was decades ahead of her time; the ad, broadcast in cities with large Hispanic populations, marked the beginning of interest-group advertising.

Campaign aides would hold Jackie's cigarette and let her take a puff or two when she was out of sight of the cameras. She gave teas in the double living room of the N Street house, exclaiming to reporters, "Jack gets seventy-five people into this little space."

Crowds were beginning to demonstrate what would be a lifelong interest in Jackie. Her husband noticed that she was drawing more people than he was. Janet, however, thought Jackie should present a more traditional look. Not seeing that the nation was drawn to Jackie's youth, good looks, and sense of style, she actually asked her, "Why can't you look more like Muriel Humphrey or Pat Nixon?"

Still, when questioned about her mother, Jackie couldn't say enough good words. "She is incredible," Jackie said. "She made a great effort to develop our creative instincts. I can't ever remember buying a present when we were little. She encouraged us, instead, to make things.

"I would paint a picture or write a poem — or memorize something. I also wrote some children's books for my little stepbrother. Mother developed our interest in painting and reading."

The Auchinclosses, although traditionally Republican, were getting involved, too, and firmly supported Jack for the Democratic nomination. Janet gave several large teas for Jack at Merrywood. Only Nini, whose husband, Newton Steers, was running for a congressional seat from Maryland as a Republican, openly declared that she and her husband would vote for Richard Nixon. (To the family, this seemed to be a repeat of Nini's mother's declaring for Willkie while serving as a Democratic delegate.)

As the Democratic convention drew closer, a reporter asked whether Jackie was pregnant. (She was, but it was supposed to be kept private for a few more months.) Janet responded neither yes nor no; instead, thinking of the disastrous 1956 trip that preceded Arabella's death, she snapped, "I hope she is. It will give her an excuse not to go to the convention."

But that didn't mean Janet was not pulling her weight for her son-in-law. When Janet was asked to campaign in Kentucky, she said, "I'm no good at this sort of thing." But she did it anyway.

The Auchinclosses felt awkward about being in the public eye because of Jack's candidacy, but they wanted to support Jack and help take pressure off Jackie. Janet described her experience canvassing Kentucky. "I felt about as creepy as I do about making a tape recording, but anyway, I went, feeling like a fool. I did shake a lot of hands and go to a lot of ladies' teas. Anyway, the two counties I campaigned in, if you could call it campaigning, he won."

Although Jack was miffed when Hughdie joked that his contribution to the campaign would be the *absence* of a donation to the Republican Party, Hughdie did finally fork over five hundred dollars. When he was ribbed by his conservative friends, he explained, "I want to live in harmony with Mrs. Auchincloss and the other members of the family." Deep down, he was thrilled and proud that his son-in-law was running for President.

Jackie was pregnant, and this time she would not repeat the tragedy of 1956. She would wait out the results of the Los Angeles convention in Hyannis with Caroline. As it turned out, Jackie literally experienced the brunt of a storm despite her planning: Hurricane Donna blew part of the roof off their house while they were in it. After Jack won the nomination, she appeared at a brief press conference with Janet and Hughdie and Janet Jr., fifteen, and Jamie, thirteen, and then met Jack in New York to campaign for a day before returning to Hyannis. She told reporters that Hyannis would be the couple's vacation home and assured them that there was little chance of Newport's becoming the summer White House.

In an early interview, Jack was asked about the "twenty-year jinx" that began in 1840 and had seen every President die in office at twenty-year intervals (except, much later, for Ronald Reagan). "If I'm nominated and get elected," Jack told writer Stefan Lorant, "I will break the jinx."

More worried about Jackie than about himself, Jack Kennedy called Lyndon and Lady Bird Johnson, who were recuperating from the convention at their Texas ranch. Would Lady Bird carry the load on the women's end of the campaign? Jack asked, mentioning Jackie's pregnancy.

Lady Bird herself had suffered several miscarriages and was completely sympathetic to the Kennedys' plight. "Certainly," she replied.

When the two women met as wives of the candidates, Jackie confessed something to Lady Bird about campaigning. "I don't know how to do anything," she said, minimizing her earlier role in the 1958 Senate election.

Lady Bird, though, took her at her word and was flabbergasted. "If

I were you," she said, "I'd find one or two reporters and have them in and talk about your home. You could do that much." Jackie followed her advice while still in Hyannis and was successful.

Jackie was deeply hurt, though, one day in September when Jack called her from a campaign stop. She returned to the living room and said to everyone, "Today's our wedding anniversary, and Jack never mentioned it."

Although Jackie continued making foreign-language pitches for Jack and began a weekly newsletter called *Campaign Wife* — "One woman is worth ten men," she quotes Jack as telling her — she stopped campaigning for the last trimester of her pregnancy. Her doctor gave her permission to accompany Jack to New York for the third of the "great debates." (For the first two, she threw a "listening party" at her house, with Janet and Hughdie and some close friends.)

On November 2 Jackie and Caroline went to Merrywood to watch the televised broadcast of an interview with Jackie, Caroline, and Jack — and Henry Fonda. The broadcast tied in with a fund-raiser Janet had agreed to hold at Merrywood — its first ever in the house's fifty-year history — for women in the region, and more than a hundred women paid the fifty-dollar admission. Janet held several of these events at Merrywood for Democratic women.

Janet was busy, too, because Tommy was getting married that month in Manhattan to Diana Lippert. Yusha served as best man; Jackie, of course, could not travel to the wedding.

When Jack was elected President in November, Jackie became the third-youngest First Lady in American history. Janet told reporter Betty Beale, who caught her at home the day after the election, that she was "celebrating in my own peculiar way — quietly."

Jackie and Jack had waited for the election returns in Hyannis and then left for Georgetown. Jackie was now in her last month of pregnancy. Jackie and Janet planned to travel to Manhattan after the Thanksgiving holiday and stay there until Jackie's scheduled delivery. (Because Caroline's birth at New York Lying-In Hospital had gone so smoothly, Jackie hoped to have her next cesarean there, too.) Theoretically, Jack would stay in Washington until December 12, the expected day of the surgery, and then fly up to join Jackie and her mother.

With Jackie ordered not to travel — the baby was due in two weeks — Jack was still eager to get to Palm Beach for Thanksgiving weekend. Jackie asked him not to leave — not only was the birth imminent, Caroline's third birthday was on Sunday; still, he insisted. In addition, rather than spending the holiday with his wife, he wanted their dinner to be held a day early. Since Jackie was in no shape to be hostess, the family of three went over to Merrywood, where Thanksgiving was held on a Wednesday. On the holiday itself, the family celebrated Caroline's birthday. A little before eight P.M. the President-elect said good-bye to his family and left for Palm Beach.

At 10:30 P.M., while the airplane *Caroline* was over the east coast of Florida, Jackie called her obstetrician, who sent a private ambulance to her house. A Secret Service agent let the ambulance driver in, and they went upstairs to Jackie's second-floor bedroom, where she was wearing an overcoat over a nightgown. As the men carried the stretcher downstairs, she called out to her doctor, who had just arrived, "Will I lose my baby?"

Jack got word on the plane that an important phone call awaited him in Palm Beach. "I'm never there when she needs me," he said to an aide, as if this early birth was strangely unexpected. On the ground, he learned that his wife was already in surgery.

He switched planes — the chartered American Airlines press plane was faster than his Convair — and after refueling, it turned back to Washington. On the trip home, he heard the good news about his healthy son and wife. Touching back down at National Airport across from the capital, the soon-to-be President was driven at sixty miles an hour the five miles into Georgetown.

Arriving before the new President was an intrepid photographer who nearly got the shot he wanted before being roundly thrown out of the hospital. Crowds also began to gather around the N Street house, filling the sidewalks and spilling off them. The Kennedys' neighbors could get to their house only by walking down the middle of the street. *The Georgetowner* good-naturedly commented, "So this is circus week in Georgetown."

On December 8 John Jr. was baptized — this time, Jack insisted on using a Kennedy christening gown, the one he had worn in 1917. The ceremony took place in the chapel of the Georgetown University Hospital because Jackie had not yet been released. Reporters asked who the baby looked like. Jackie replied, "I don't think he looks like anybody." The Kennedys present told reporters that John Jr. looked like his father. Janet disagreed, saying that little John looked like his mother.

While Jackie was in the hospital, Jack brought Caroline to Merrywood to stay with Janet "for however long Jackie was in the hospital," Janet said. "He had a couple of ducks that somebody had given him, and he brought them out and put them in the little kennel runs at Merrywood." Jamie was home for the holiday and helped Jack. "I remember that Jamie was feeding and watering and cleaning out the runs after these ducks."

When Jackie was released from Georgetown University Hospital, she gave the baby to Maud Shaw while she toured the White House with Mamie Eisenhower, swung by Georgetown to pick up the baby and his nurse, and flew to Palm Beach to recuperate with Caroline and Jack until it was time to move into the White House.

Despite Jackie's reluctance, Jack put her beloved N Street house up for sale. It went quickly, for $110,000. John Jr. was never to spend a night in his mother's favorite home.

$\mathscr{C}$hapter 10

THE PRESIDENT'S
MOTHER-IN-LAW

The morning of January 20, 1961, dawned bright, clear, and cold. The nation's capital had been snowed under the night before, throwing traffic into turmoil and reducing the crowds expected at the pre-Inaugural events to a mere handful of people. "We were snowed in at Merrywood the night before the inauguration," Janet remembered. "Jamie flew down from school. . . . The blizzard began about two-thirty in the afternoon, and Jamie's plane was the last one that got in to National Airport."

Coming back from the airport, the car driven by their butler James Owen skidded into a snow bank on the shoulder of the George Washington Memorial Parkway. "Owen and Jamie tried to persuade Hughdie to stay in the car because with his emphysema he is not supposed to get pneumonia. Anyway, Hughdie did walk [home to Merrywood] something like five miles through the deep snow that afternoon. . . . None of us got out that night because the two government cars that had been assigned to us to take us to the Inaugural

Concert at Constitution Hall could not get up the driveway. I think if we hadn't had the government cars, we might have gotten there. But they blocked the driveway."

The snow continued into the late evening, forcing the soldiers designated as the Auchinclosses' drivers to spend the night at Merrywood. Fortunately, by six A.M. a local man had plowed their long, curved driveway.

Having missed the night's parties, Janet and Hughdie dressed the next morning in eager anticipation of the activities ahead. Jackie's husband was taking the oath of office for the highest position in the nation—even the world. Janet had a good amount of pride at any time, but on this day she could be forgiven for holding her chin high. Gone was her anger at Jack over his treatment of Jackie; erased were the memories of her conversations with friends about her daughter's shaky marriage; obliterated was her dislike of her son-in-law's political and media friends. From this day on, Jack Kennedy would always be "Mr. President" to her.

As the couple glanced at their newspapers, they read front pages filled with statistics: Jack would be the youngest President—following the oldest—and the first Roman Catholic one. Jackie, at thirty-one, would be the third-youngest First Lady and the third Roman Catholic. John Jr. would be the first baby in the White House since 1895. The First Family would be the only Georgetowners to segue into the White House—this, reported solely in *The Georgetowner*. (And, the next day, the fact that Jack Kennedy would achieve the highest approval rating from the American public of any President entering office thus far in the twentieth century—amazing, considering his small margin of victory two months earlier.)

The Auchinclosses finished their last cup of coffee and called out to Janet Jr. and Jamie, who were traveling with them. As they left Merrywood, Janet adjusted her hat, thrilled at the thought of taking her seat near the next President of the United States—her son-in-law—as he took the oath of office. She wondered if she were having a dream. What seemed most incredible was that a mere eight years ago, Jackie had attended the Eisenhower Inauguration as the Inquiring Photographer Girl for the *Washington Times-Herald*. Now Janet had one daughter who would soon be the First Lady and another daughter, a princess (albeit married to a "pretender" prince).

Janet's only disappointment was her father's refusal to attend the Inauguration. At eighty-three, Jim Lee was stepping down from the presidency of the Central Savings Bank to become chairman of its board that very day. Janet was upset that he preferred to attend the functions at the bank rather than the ones in Washington, and she suspected that his dislike of the Kennedy family influenced his decision. However, Janet wasn't going to let anything ruin the day for her.

As Janet left Merrywood for the Capitol, she had no inkling of the plans Jackie had laid.

After the fall election Jackie had agreed to work with the writer Mary Van Rensselaer Thayer on an authorized biography to be published by Harper & Row, and to be serialized beginning in February's issue of *Ladies' Home Journal.* Jackie began the project with great enthusiasm — she was a fine writer herself and a great keeper of scrapbooks — but her pregnancy and the whirl of postelection activities kept her distracted.

To make up for Jackie's unavailability, Thayer called Janet — an old friend — knowing that she often picked up the pieces that her daughter dropped. Janet was eager to help. So Janet met with Thayer and effusively recounted Jackie's life story, giving the author whatever information she sought — and more.

Somehow, Jackie got word of the extent of Janet's assistance. Jackie could never bring herself to confront Janet directly — why should she bother, with so many middlemen at her disposal? — and directed her secretary Mary Barelli Gallagher to call Janet. As Gallagher says, "I was to tell Mrs. Auchincloss that Jackie would prefer that she not show Thayer any more letters 'no matter what she does.'"

Although Janet complied immediately with Jackie's explicit directions, she had already revealed a great deal to Thayer. When Jackie read the advance first magazine article, she was livid, furious. How could her own mother discuss her life in such detail? Janet, of all people, who always emphasized privacy! Jamie heard Jackie rant, but didn't foresee how Jackie would take revenge on their mother.

In the car, Jamie and his parents noticed that their tickets were not numbered consecutively. They shrugged: it was strange that they wouldn't be seated together, but perhaps there weren't enough dignitary seats for the large family. Janet naturally assumed that, as Jackie's mother, she would be placed up front with Hughdie and that the younger Auchinclosses would be farther back. Arriving at the Capitol, Hughdie took Janet by the arm as they walked toward the Inaugural stand. As the elder couple was led to their seats by an usher, they told Jamie and Janet that they would see them later.

When seated, Janet noticed something odd. "All the children were in seats facing [the President]. We could only see the back of Jack's head as he delivered the Inaugural Address but the children were in seats facing him."

Similarly, Jamie—to his great surprise—turned and saw that he was seated next to Eleanor Roosevelt and near Adlai Stevenson. That was quite a thrill for a twelve-year-old boy. Then he looked down to wave at his parents; he was excited and wanted them to see where he was sitting. He scanned the seats close to the podium: no parents. He leaned forward to look right and left: no parents. Then he looked up and down. Finally, by the very top of the stand opposite him, he caught a glimpse of Janet and Hughdie.

"I knew then that Jackie was having the last word and showing her mother that she was angry at her," says Jamie.

"In fact, there's a photograph of the President with his chin raised, looking around. He told me later that he was looking for my parents—he didn't understand why he couldn't see them anywhere!"

Janet, still confused at what she assumed was a mix-up in seating arrangements, arrived at the White House for those post-Inaugural festivities limited to family members. Jackie was upstairs, resting. There was a swarm of people, about 130. Joe Kennedy was still peeved at the bill for the family luncheon he had just hosted.

Hughdie was in a better mood than Joe was. "What am I doing here?" he joked to several Auchincloss family members. "I'm a Republican!"

Nevertheless, the party lacked a focus without the First Lady's presence. There were a lot of questioning looks and aimless chatter as the guests—especially members of the Lee and Bouvier families, who hadn't seen Jackie recently—waited for her to appear. When he arrived, the President affably made the rounds but was visibly perturbed about his wife's absence.

Rose Kennedy was flustered and felt awkward; she never knew how to handle Jackie's independent spirit. Her experience as an ambassador's wife apparently had not made her a smooth hostess. She seemed inept—perhaps she didn't want to assume the part of hostess, thinking that Jackie would be downstairs at any moment.

Joe made his feelings clear. When someone asked him where Jackie was, he snapped, "She's resting, goddammit!"

Janet stepped into the breach. For one thing, she sympathized with Jackie and worried about her. "Jackie was very weak on her pins," remembers Tish Baldrige, the First Lady's social secretary. "Any mother would have welcomed her going upstairs to bed."

Also, Janet was far more polished than Rose: after all, while Rose had spent dinners with her children quizzing them on foreign affairs, Janet had insisted on dressing for dinner and conducting the meal in French. Janet began making the rounds of the room, introducing one group to another and explaining that Jackie was "up in the Queen's Bedroom trying to relax," which seemed to mollify them. Moreover, they were delighted to be introduced by Janet to relatives by blood or marriage—or even by former marriage—whom they had never before met.

Janet herself was never afraid of confrontation with a Bouvier. Now, as the mother of the First Lady, she was operating from a position of strength. Spotting one of the Bouvier twins, her former sister-in-law Maude Bouvier Davis, Janet took her aside and, after the usual congratulatory conversation, spoke candidly.

"Maude, why did you sever our friendship after my divorce from Jack?" she asked. "We had been so close, and then you and Michelle just dropped me."

Maude Davis was taken aback but knew that Janet was right. In the years following the divorce and the death of her mother, she had gained a better perspective. She apologized and explained to Janet how strongly her mother had insisted that all the siblings take Jack's side against Janet.

Janet chided Maude, reminding her why she had been driven to divorce Jack. She also refreshed Maude's memory about her kindnesses to the Bouvier children: Janet never forgot to send a birthday gift, for example, to her godson John, Maude's son.

"Mom," remembers her daughter, also named Maude Davis, "wanted to make amends and reinstate their relationship. They had a heart-to-heart talk." So Janet forgave and forgot. After a twenty-year lapse, Janet and Maude were friends again.

That night at the Inaugural balls, Jackie felt exhausted early on and went back to the White House. She couldn't help being depressed as Jack kept mentioning the name *Arabella,* the flagship that took John Winthrop to New England in 1632. Jack was using that journey as a metaphor for the beginning of his administration, but it reminded her of Arabella, the name of their baby who was born stillborn in 1956.

Jackie had fallen asleep by the time Jack arrived at the White House. The new President was in an odd mood: instead of being ebullient, he felt let down and depressed—was he prescient of how his presidency would end? He wrapped up in warm outerwear and started to trudge through the deep snow toward his old neighborhood, Georgetown.

Soon he allowed his Secret Service agents, who were following behind him in a car, to drive him to his destination. After visiting newsman Joe Alsop and talking until dawn, he finally went back to the White House.

Jackie had spent her first night in the executive mansion alone.

"My pet peeve," said Janet, "is being asked, 'How does it feel to be the mother-in-law of the President?' Literally hundreds of people have asked me that," she said with an end-of-the-rope tone of voice.

"And can you remember one single mother-in-law of one single President, starting with George Washington?" she continued. Then she added with her customary tact, "Except, of course, Mrs. Doud [Mamie Eisenhower's mother]." While the Kennedys—the brothers, their wives, and Rose—were grabbing all the newsprint (here, Jack's father was the only exception; Joe Kennedy knew he needed to stay backstage), Janet tried to stay out of the spotlight and, rather, stood behind Jackie, supporting her when she might otherwise fall.

"Mrs. Auchincloss was a perfect role model for the First Lady," Mary Barelli Gallagher remembers. And a perfect helpmate. Repeatedly, Jackie would fail to show up at official daytime functions, even though they were held in the White House. Janet, who was often invited to the "ladies only" daytime events, would take charge and soothe the guests' ruffled feathers over not seeing the First Lady, just as she had done at the White House reception for the family on Inauguration Day.

Jackie articulated her viewpoint regarding traditional First Lady obligations in a handwritten note on White House stationery to friend Bill Walton:

Just let me tell you what I did—I was tired—& I wanted to see my children—so I just told Tish—who nearly died from the shock—that I would NEVER go out—lunches, teas, degrees, speeches, etc. For 2 months, there was a flap. Now it is a precedent established.

Jackie was not admitting that other people—including Janet, Tish, Rose, her sisters-in-law, and even the President himself—had to pick up the duties she dropped. For example, when she went foxhunting instead of meeting the officers of the National Council of Negro Women, the President stepped in to greet them. In addition, Jackie missed the meeting with the international council of the Museum of Modern Art, because she decided at the last minute to ride with the Orange County Hunt rather than return to the mansion. WHITE HOUSE COOLNESS BOTHERS CLUBWOMEN was the national story when Jackie snubbed the General Federation of Women's Clubs.

Janet also stepped in when a particular group bored Jackie, as did the coffee hour at the White House for the wives of the New York Stock Exchange members or the social for the International Council of Women. Janet joined Jackie again to help her feel more comfortable entertaining, say, Mamie Eisenhower. Janet always knew what to say and do: when informed by society reporters that a congressman's wife, Mrs. Arthur Houghton of the Corning Glass Works Houghtons, was wearing an identical dress to hers, she immediately replied, "Oh, let me see her. I bet she looks divine in hers. She's so pretty." Janet's social skills were tops.

But when Janet stepped in to fill Jackie's absence, the Kennedys made her feel as if she were an interloper: "After all, there was Rose to contend with," says Tish Baldrige. "Rose wanted to be at every [social event], so they had to keep a balance. Janet wanted to see her daughter, have tea with her, take Caroline and do things, and it was hard." Sometimes Jackie would have to instruct her personal secretary to tell Janet she wasn't in, even though "Mrs. Auchincloss was always helping Jackie in any way possible and always tried to be completely loyal to her."

Guests were incredulous when the First Lady gave a tea to honor Janet—and then never appeared. Janet was receiving the guests when Eileen Slocum reached her. "Where's Jackie?" Slocum asked.

"She's out walking the dog," Janet said.

"Out walking the dog?" Slocum said.

Janet shrugged. "She always walks the dog at this hour."

Slocum explains that Janet could have covered up her daughter's behavior but was straightforward and did not want to. "Lots of people said [of Jackie], 'Isn't that awful? Don't you think Jackie should be at the tea given for her mother?'"

Mary Barelli Gallagher makes a similar point. "At times, I would find myself wishing that her daughter could be a bit more considerate of her mother."

In addition to the White House duties, Janet continued her own activities. She was on two boards: the women's board of Washington's
Children's Hospital and the board of its Hearing and Speech Center. As
a kind gesture toward the children, she gave an annual picnic for the
center's patients at Merrywood, offering them a half-day of swimming
and pony riding with a picnic lunch. She was also active in the International Neighbors Club, the Committee of American Field Service, and
the Committee of World Affairs Forum.

Of course, Janet had a responsibility to her two younger children.
Janet's children spanned two generations: the five eldest were adults and
the youngest, Jamie, was about to enter Brooks School. (He confesses
with no sorrow that he was not admitted to Groton, breaking a long
chain of Auchinclosses at the school.) And in the same year, Hughdie
had a grandson christened — Hugh Auchincloss Steers (Nini's son) — and
a daughter debut (Janet Jr.).

All told, Janet and Hughdie had eleven grandchildren during the
White House years as well as their own two school-age children. The
couple was especially eager to see the grandchildren from out of town,
particularly Yusha's twins, who were in their mother's custody after their
parents' four-year marriage ended. Once, Caroline and Tony Radziwill
brought her pony Macaroni into Merrywood's front hall. And it did what
ponies do, to the great merriment of the children. The nannies had it
cleaned up before Janet saw it.

"I'm taking the children over to Mother's for a little while," Jackie
often could be heard saying. Accompanying Caroline and John helped
keep Jackie in touch with her mother's old friends in a setting that was
more relaxed than the White House. But the Auchinclosses enjoyed
having the children by themselves, too, and as the Kennedys became
busier in the White House, Caroline and John would make extended
visits. John, as the baby, was left at Hammersmith Farm during the
summer and fall for weeks at a time without his parents or elder sister.

In fact, Caroline and John visited the Auchinclosses so often that
Merrywood had its own Secret Service moniker: Hamlet. The only other
residences with official appellations were the White House (Crown),
Camp David (Cactus), and the Kennedys' rented country retreat (Cha-
teau). The Hyannis residence of Rose and Joe Kennedy was not on
the list.

After Jackie adjusted to a household staff who were a little more bureaucratic about their duties than she would have liked, she realized she enjoyed being *the* Mrs. Kennedy, as she put it, instead of one of many. Her mother- and sisters-in-law were now, within the White House, called Mrs. Joseph, Mrs. Bobby, and so on. Jackie also took advantage of her large staff — larger still than her mother had at Merrywood! She became fastidious and had the bed linens changed not only each morning but after every afternoon nap as well.

With so much attention being paid to every aspect of her life and her family's, Jackie learned to her embarrassment that the much-vaunted Bouvier forebears were simple craftsmen and that no royal blood flowed through her veins. She lived in terror that news of her late father's illegitimate English twin children would be disclosed.

If Jack Bouvier had not bestowed royal blood upon Jackie, and if he had left her little money, he did leave his antique French Empire desk to her. The White House usher, Mr. J. B. West, noted that the desk was Jackie's "most prized possession. She worried more about scratches-in-transit, or its improper care, than about any other piece of furniture or art in the White House." Jackie still worshiped her father. After she attended the opening of Lincoln Center, she endowed a seat at Lincoln Center's Philharmonic Hall in memory of Jack Bouvier (orchestra seat BB-101). Orchestra seat N-102 had already been endowed in Jackie's name by her classmates, friends, and teachers at Miss Porter's School.

Jackie did not spend many weekends at the White House, preferring to go out to Merrywood or, later, to the couple's country home near Middleburg, Virginia. "She used to leave usually Thursday and come back Monday or Tuesday," said Nancy Tuckerman, a longtime friend.

Janet encouraged Jackie to keep up her riding, emphasizing the sport as an escape from whatever tensions might bother her. At first, Jackie rode at the Kennedys' weekend house, a leased 400-acre Glen Ora estate (at $600 a month, or $3,500 today). Soon she requested permission to ride in the swank Orange County Hunt. (The hunt was named after a county in New York because so many of its members who vacationed in the Middleburg area at the turn of the century actually came from Orange County, New York.) Jackie was not a member, but the hunt allowed her to join the equestrians — because she was a fine rider, not because of her status. (They had said no to the Duchess of Windsor.)

The Secret Service agents made a big commotion over their joining in the hunt—not because of her safety but because they mistakenly assumed they would have to wear "pinks," or red hunting coats, which they apparently thought were sissified. Then, it turned out, none of the detail could ride: the Secret Service would have to send in the troops, in this case, expert army horsemen. As it turned out, the agents solved the problem by merely "hill-topping"—following the hunt from a station wagon to observe from vantage points.

Within a year, though, animal-rights protesters focused Jack's sights on Jackie's foxhunts. He wanted her to stop. Rather than giving up the hunts or confronting Jack directly, Jackie tried to outfox both Jack and the protesters by making her fellow riders swear that they would never divulge when she rode. That was fine with them—their only objection to Jackie was that she was not as good a judge of horseflesh as her mother. After Jackie tumbled headfirst over a horse that balked at a low fence, a member commented, "We have been trying to persuade [Jackie] to buy a better horse, but she will not listen to any of us."

Hammersmith Farm with Janet and Hughdie was Jack's favorite spot as well as Jackie's. Their first visit as First Couple was only two months after Jack took office. Following a short trip to Hyannis, the couple took a yacht to Newport because, as a White House spokesman noted, "Mrs. Kennedy is anxious to spend some weekends at Hammersmith Farm." The Auchinclosses had built a new dock; it was Newport's only private dock to get a safety check from the Coast Guard.

Jackie spent most of the summer of 1961 at Hammersmith, swimming, water-skiing, boating, golfing, and riding, and the children stayed there as well. In 1961 Hammersmith Farm was dubbed "the summer White House" by the press, who had grown accustomed to the town: after all, former President Eisenhower spent his last three summers in office in Newport, residing at Fort Adams, Hammersmith's next-door neighbor.

The beach was a frequent getaway for the Kennedys. Jackie imitated the way Janet would wrap a silk scarf tightly around her head to protect her hairstyle from sea breezes. Dark-framed, oversized sunglasses completed the look. At Bailey's Beach the Auchincloss friends Noreen and John Drexel had made an entryway into their cabana from its parking-lot side. The Kennedys began using their back door to get to the Auchincloss cabana without the fuss of going through the main entrance.

(The Drexels' back door ultimately caused so much envy that such doors were outlawed by the directors of the beach. The Drexels' door, however, was grandfathered in.)

Jack and Jackie also used the heated pool at the Fairholme estate of Mrs. Robert R. Young. The pool was the most elaborate in the summer colony and had cost $250,000 ($1.5 million today) when it was built in 1958. Caroline preferred this pool to the one the beach club had added.

Jack enjoyed those visits as much as Jackie did. Looking out at the bay one afternoon, he said to Hughdie, "This is the most beautiful spot in the world."

Indoors, Jack was not as enthusiastic about Newport. He dictated a letter from Hammersmith Farm. "Dearest Jackie," he wrote, telling her that everyone was in town for the golf weekend and wanted to know why he was there. "I told them I was up visiting [Caroline]. I was taken into the kitchen and introduced to all the help, who are just over from Ireland. I found them more attractive than the guests." He concluded in an ironic tone, "I flew back Monday with your mother, who was in excellent humor."

Some of Jack's newspaper friends saw the Auchinclosses themselves as a little odd. Although they liked the couple, they felt Hughdie verged on the stuffy, and Janet's perfectionism seemed excessive. There was the time that Tom Braden was chatting in the deck room with the Kennedys, and Janet slid off the sofa and began doing sit-ups while everyone was talking. Neither Jack nor Jackie batted an eye. When Jackie saw that Tom Braden couldn't help being distracted by Janet's workout, she just laughed. "Oh, Mummy, stop it."

When the President was at Hammersmith, the Auchinclosses gave him their master bedroom, and they moved into the Castle, a renovated and extended Colonial farmhouse on the estate property that was one of the oldest structures on the island. White House phones were installed in the main house, in Jack's bedroom, and in the den. While the President was there, the Coast Guard checked all boats and ships going past Hammersmith and were especially careful when the President and First Lady received such dignitaries there as Great Britain's minister of defense, the president of Pakistan, and India's Nehru.

The first year Jack was in office, he played golf at the Newport Country Club, receiving a better reception than when he had arrived unannounced before his wedding in 1953. When he was out sailing on the bay, he would invite the Auchinclosses to join him and Jackie. When he was golfing, Jackie would play with Caroline. Once they rode the pony cart along Harrison Avenue with Jackie holding the reins — much as a nanny had held the reins for Hughdie and his sisters half a century earlier. These were relaxed, happy times for both families and for any houseguests lucky enough to be invited. One time when Jack's friends the Bartletts were visiting, Jack told Charlie Bartlett that it "was the best vacation I ever had."

When the Kennedys arrived in Paris in May 1961, Janet was as proud of Jackie as she had ever been. Jackie was the first First Lady to be fluent in a foreign language and to have lived abroad. It was, of course, Janet's emphasis on speaking French that gave Jackie her vaunted skill.

In Paris Jackie made her remarks in French; Pierre Salinger gave his press conference in French — the first White House press secretary in history to give a bilingual press conference; and Jack said in his speech, "I do not think it altogether inappropriate to introduce myself. I am the man who accompanied Jacqueline Kennedy to Paris."

Jack called Janet during the trip to tell her how well Jackie was handling herself. "He was very, very thoughtful about things like that," she said, particularly touched. Their relationship had mellowed to the point where he was regularly addressing her as "Mummy" rather than the more formal "Mrs. Auchincloss."

Charlie Bartlett, too, saw a change in Janet after Jack became President, when she went from one extreme to another. In the rough early days of Jackie's marriage, Janet held Bartlett accountable for having introduced the couple. "She was right cold to me," he says with a twinkle. But when Janet saw Charlie after Jack became President, "her face shone," he says.

There were many things Jack admired about Janet. He certainly envied the language ability of his wife and mother-in-law, sometimes finding his own inadequacy "intolerable," according to Ben Bradlee. He asked Miss Hirsh, Caroline's French teacher, for private lessons, confessing that he wanted to surprise Jackie. Hirsh purchased a French translation of *Profiles in Courage* for him to study. "I can't wait to really surprise the world," he said, although he would ultimately not have enough time to do so.

But not all family relations were smooth, especially between the Auchincloss relatives and the Kennedys. In late fall 1961 Gore Vidal was back in town, and the Kennedys invited him to the White House for a family-and-friends get-together. Vidal thought Janet was a social climber, but he was determined to be polite and conciliatory toward her. When Vidal greeted Janet, he thanked her for raising his half sister Nini. No matter what Janet's faults, he knew that Nini was in better hands with her than with their own mother.

Janet was on edge. For whatever reason, she didn't like Gore Vidal and thought he was being sarcastic — his sardonic manner was his armor. Janet, too, could be at fault: she often misinterpreted the point others were making. Already wary of the clever writer, she berated him instead of thanking him. "How dare you attack your mother?" she said.

"I thought I was praising you!" he replied. It didn't help; Janet was furious.

Gore Vidal realized that he was in a game he had no interest in winning. He walked away. Put in a foul mood by Janet, he flared when Bobby, who was envious of his friendship with Jack, picked a fight. The men quarreled, and Gore left, exasperated with the whole lot.

As Jackie transformed White House parties from stiffly regimented, protocol-burdened dinners to candlelit, sparkling occasions, the hopeful badgered her for invitations. She had evidently gotten over the spleen that led her to snub Janet and Hughdie at the Inauguration. No matter how tightly she and Tish Baldrige squeezed the guest list, Jackie always left room for the pair at her most anticipated parties. "That shows Jackie's kindness to her mother," says Tish Baldrige. When the cellist Pablo Casals played, the Auchinclosses were there. And they were at the glamorous dinner for André Malraux. Tish Baldrige ranks it as "the most important evening Jackie gave. And Jackie cared so much about it."

Jackie was very impressed by Malraux, who was France's Minister of State for Cultural Affairs. As a special gift, she asked Hughdie if she could give Malraux two nineteenth-century illustrated volumes of political caricatures he owned. Hughdie was a noted collector of eighteenth- and nineteenth-century books of art, volumes Jackie had loved looking through when she was a schoolgirl. After presenting the books to Malraux, she learned that they were each worth about $2,000 ($11,000 today) and was embarrassed at having asked Hughdie for them.

Janet was pleased by public admiration for her daughter, even though she thought Lee was the better-looking and agreed with those who criticized Jackie's short skirts and John's long hair. Jackie said, "I feel that I am reasonably turned out when I leave the house, but then my mother will tell me my skirt is too short, my hem uneven, and my top coat button dangling by a thread." But at least she was secure enough to joke about it.

Lee was angrier, saying of Janet, "Every time she comes to the White House, she starts carping at me about how to dress and what to wear."

Tish Baldrige, who is a great admirer of Janet, always found it perplexing that "Jackie and Lee used to criticize her" and thought the reason behind it was that they had been spoiled by their father. "I found Janet absolutely, unbelievably kind and nice" to her daughters, she remembers.

Janet may have irritated them over small issues because she felt she could not talk to Lee about the larger one: Lee's behavior while married to Stas. She was furious at Lee when she accidentally learned of her affair with Ari Onassis by visiting what she thought was Lee's hotel suite. To Hughdie and a few friends, she termed Ari "a moral leper."

Although Jackie was Lee's closest friend, Lee envied the adulation her sister received. After Lee saw the writer Truman Capote in New York, he wrote to a friend of his, "Had lunch with your new friend, Princess Lee. My god, how jealous she is of Jackie. I never knew. Understand her marriage is all but finito."

Janet shouldered a huge task for Jackie in early 1962 when she became area chairman to raise funds for the National Cultural Center. (When the center eventually opened in 1971, it was renamed the John F. Kennedy Center for the Performing Arts.) The selection of Janet, lauded by the *Washington Post* as "a fortunate choice," was critical in getting this first arts center off the ground. *Vogue* called Janet's task "an enormous volunteer job" well suited to "a gentle, disarming woman of both enormous distinction and . . . careful efficiency" and published a full-page formal portrait of Janet celebrating her appointment and promoting the center.

Janet wasn't entirely sure that Jackie would wish her to take such a large role. "Do you really want me to do it?" she asked her daughter. "I do," replied Jackie.

The idea of a cultural center was not a new one. Pierre L'Enfant's plans for the capital city proposed "play houses . . . as may be attractive to the learned and afford diversions to the idle." The thought wasn't acted on until 1948, when the privately run National Theatre on Pennsylvania Avenue closed because of controversy over its racially discriminatory policies. (The National Theatre eventually revamped its operations and reopened.) Citizens pressed for a national arts complex, and in 1950 Congress proposed the first bill in its support. The sponsor of the bill suggested that the center be named after Franklin Delano Roosevelt. For eight years various sponsors argued over — what else? — its location: in the city's Southwest quadrant or in Northwest's Foggy Bottom neighborhood.

In 1958 a bill supporting the center passed Congress, and President Eisenhower — coincidentally, while vacationing in Newport at Fort Adams — signed it into law. Plans for the center faltered, however, when the nationwide fund drive failed. In 1962 Jackie was named honorary chairman of the center and immediately asked Janet for her assistance. The following month Janet became chairman of the pivotal Greater Washington Committee for the National Cultural Center. (Roger L. Stevens was an outstanding appointment as its national chairman because of his experience as a real-estate broker and theatrical producer.)

Janet accepted the nomination modestly at the tea she gave for its trustees at Merrywood. "I have forgotten what I wanted to say. I want to thank you . . ." and she concluded that it was "terribly important" for the building to be of good design. This principle she had learned from her father, and she had taught it to Jackie.

Janet's task was to raise $7 million ($40 million today) in the District of Columbia and environs: not merely for the cash itself but to use as an example to the rest of the nation that support of the arts should be a universal goal. After all, Washington-area residents would benefit most directly from the center; if they couldn't show support, why would the rest of the country?

The following month in Newport, Jackie had Janet at her elbow as she unveiled the architectural model of the arts center. The ceremony was held at the gilded eighty-foot-by-forty-foot ballroom of the historic cottage The Elms. The First Lady sat next to Janet and listened intently when she rose to speak. Janet noted Washington's paucity of arts groups and said, "There should be in our capital a symbol of the growing importance of the arts in American life." She added, "Washington has had almost no national or international influence [in the arts]." The event was covered throughout the world.

Janet set as her goal a dinner for which the group would sell 550 places at $100 each; $25 seats at a larger buffet; and seven events at area universities and a movie theater for which tickets would be sold at $5 or less. Janet chaired a huge gala, An American Pageant of the Arts, a closed-circuit telecast sent live from the National Guard Armory to cities holding local fund-raising dinners for the center from coast to coast. The pageant and dinner were attended by the President and First Lady as well as former President Eisenhower. The three dignitaries sat in the front row for the entertainment, with Janet next to Jackie; Hughdie sat one row behind them. Leonard Bernstein hosted the show, with such artists performing as Marian Anderson, Van Cliburn, Robert Frost, Hal Holbrook, Danny Kaye, Bob Newhart, Jason Robards Jr., Maria Tallchief and child prodigy Yo-Yo Ma. (Janet's menu included Hearts of Pascal Celery — perhaps for Hughdie to chew loudly — and Charcoal Broiled Heart of Filet Mignon sur Canape and Rissolles Potatoes, which she ate while wearing a brown lace bodice over a white-skirted undergown, with a gold medallion indicating her status as chairman pinned to her breast.)

The event raised a million dollars. Then money started to pour in: millions from the Ford Foundation, a million dollars' worth of marble from the Italian government. Gore Vidal, as an ancillary relative, was placed on an advisory council and claims that his advice was "Don't build the center."

The center's success was in large part attributable to Janet's long and hard work for a goal she believed in even while she and Hughdie were having their own financial problems. The *Washington Post* referred to her efforts as "the best send-off possible." At Merrywood, Janet said at one tea she was hostessing, "We cannot fail," and "We feel now that the whole country will pull together to make the Cultural Center possible." She held fund-raisers for business leaders and others at her houses; if anything, Hughdie's business downturn — which made the enormous expense of maintaining two estates so burdensome — kept Janet practical, bringing in, for example, the president of the greater Washington AFL-CIO to obtain labor's support for the center. In the next decade, after the opening of the Kennedy Center, one board member wrote that "it was during her [Janet's] tenure of office that many [people] became very active in the Center and it is due to them that the . . . Kennedy Center exists today."

Someone had to look at costs, after all, and it wasn't Jackie. As an anonymous member of the project commented to Betty Beale, Washington's premier reporter of the West Wing, "[Jackie] has good taste and ideas but no concept of what things cost. I have to tell her all the time to be practical."

The Kennedys returned to Hammersmith Farm again in 1962. Usually their visits coincided with the summer vacations of Janet Jr. and Jamie. This summer Jamie took Jackie, Caroline, and John across the bay to Jamestown in his sixteen-foot boat. They strolled through the town unrecognized until they stopped for ice cream. "No one at first could tell it was the First Lady and her children," said Jamie. "But the man scooping the ice cream could. He broke about four cones for every one he put out," he recalled.

Sometimes the President visited by himself. If Jackie was out of the country—she was traveling for pleasure a great deal, in Italy, for instance—the President would call Janet and ask, as she remembered, "Would it be convenient if I came up to Newport this weekend and stayed with Unk Hugh and you?"

Then, when it was time to leave, Jack would say, "If it wouldn't be too much trouble, I might like to come back next weekend."

Jack and the Auchinclosses established a warm relationship. "I remember that we sat downstairs in the sitting room until about something like one-thirty in the morning just talking about this and that," said Janet.

In August the entire family was at Newport, excited to watch the America's Cup races. In fact, the President made remarks, which would eventually be quoted on a poignant occasion, at a dinner held for the yachtsmen at Hammersmith Farm the night before the race. His brother Ted would repeat his words at a memorial service out at sea thirty-seven years later: "All of us have in our veins the exact same percentage of salt in our blood that exists in the ocean, and, therefore, we have salt in our blood, in our sweat, in our tears. We are tied to the ocean. And when we go back to the sea—we are going back from whence we came."

Jack felt affectionate toward Hughdie, although he did not take him seriously. Jack, after all, admired entrepreneurs like his own father rather than men who inherited wealth. On one weekend day at Hammersmith, Charlie Bartlett was discussing an important foreign policy matter with the President. A crisis was brewing in Yugoslavia, and a gloomy Cold War dispatch from State had just been delivered. The two men were deep in worried discussion when Hughdie—"a charming and sweet man," according to Bartlett—who had been inside watching television, walked up to Jack with his hand outstretched.

"Congratulations, Mr. President!" said Hughdie.

Jack, with his mind still on Yugoslavia, stood up to shake his hand and asked, "Congratulations on what?"

"On Harvard's great victory over Brown!" responded the oblivious Hughdie.

"Good night, Mrs. Kennedy, wherever you are," quipped one wag in reference to Jackie's frequent travels. Jackie was enticed by what she saw as Lee's more glamorous life, and she ran from the White House to escape Jack. She realized that even as President, he was not capable of curtailing his relationships with other women. In fact, she was well aware that his status made gossip even more delicious: now the news in their social circle was not about just a senator but the President!

Jackie did not meet all of Jack's women, but some she knew. One was Mary Meyer, sister to Tony Bradlee, then wife of journalist Ben Bradlee. Meyer (who would be murdered on the towpath of George-town's C & O Canal) was also a friend of Joan and Tom Braden. Once, after the Bradens had moved to California, Tom Braden was visiting in Washington driving down K Street. Suddenly he saw Mary Meyer on the corner. He pulled his car over and jumped out to greet her.

They gave each other a hug, and he asked how she was.

"Oh, Tom," she said. "I've fallen in love with the President."

Jackie worried that Jack would put her in the same position her father had put her mother in. Would she, too, open her newspaper to a photo that proved her husband's infidelity? The difference this time would be the picture's location: on the front page, not buried inside. Sometimes when Lee or another friend visited the private quarters of the White House, Jackie would pull out that old photo of Jack Bouvier holding the hand of another woman with Janet sitting on the split fence, literally looking the other way, and howl with laughter until tears ran down her cheeks.

When Jackie feared being embarrassed by the presence of one — or more — of Jack's women, she declined to accompany him. He attended such functions by himself, just as Jack Bouvier had to go out without Janet. Most notably, Jackie refused to attend the birthday party for Jack where Marilyn Monroe wore a skintight flesh-colored frock and sang birthday greetings to him suggestively. By then Jackie had had enough of her husband's flagrant infidelities.

In some ways Jackie held the upper hand as the aggrieved wife. She let Jack know that she would go only so far in being the First Lady. Sometimes Jack would call Janet to ask her to speak with Jackie about something that bothered him, carefully choosing an issue on which he knew Janet would agree.

One day in Newport Jamie came home excited. He knew that the President had heard criticism of Jackie's relatively casual attire at church, and he had asked her please to dress more formally. Jamie had just seen a glimpse of Jackie walking out of church by herself wearing what looked at first glance like a scarf on her head and flowered gloves. However, Jamie recognized the scarf and gloves: the head covering was actually a decorated dishtowel and the gloves were Janet's cotton gardening gloves!

"Prepare for a storm, Mummy," said Jamie. It wasn't too much later that the White House operator rang—the President wanted to speak to Mrs. Auchincloss.

Jackie, having been raised in two beautiful homes where everything was of the finest design and quality, had moved into a gorgeous mansion filled with second-rate furniture and bric-a-brac. Almost at once she established a committee that included the designer who had helped her with their N Street house, Mrs. Henry Parish II, better known as Sister Parish. (One newspaper headed its story KENNEDYS HIRE NUN TO DECORATE WHITE HOUSE.)

Jackie encouraged her committee to bring fine objects into the mansion; persuaded Congress to pass a bill barring further scavenging of the White House by its various denizens; established a curator and wrote a guidebook (again, remembering that first visit in 1941); and had its library catalogued (perhaps here, she remembered those visits to Lefty and Annie Burr Lewis's house in Farmington). Then, of course, she showed off her efforts in a 1962 televised program.

Her desire to make the nation's house a thing of beauty and comfort derived from her exposure to Janet's caretaking of the Auchincloss homes. Janet looked after Merrywood and Hammersmith Farm meticulously, even putting her daughters to work to maintain them during World War II. Jack, on the other hand, grew up in a house where the staff was charged a dime for every cup of coffee, and the Palm Beach vacation house was painted on the street side only, to save money.

Inspired by the lovely gardens at Hammersmith, Jackie set about improving the White House gardens. Although she took little enjoyment in gardening—perhaps those World War II summers spent weeding and clipping did have their effect! — she knew that a garden could turn a house into a home. The landscape architect Perry Wheeler was responsible for the design improvements, although Jackie fell under the spell of Bunny Mellon, her friend and Janet's, and pulled her into the project.

One day when Mellon was digging in the White House lawn, the mansion's communications officers were thrown into complete consternation and hysteria. Inexplicably, the entire communications system had gone down, isolating the White House from the rest of the world. It turned out that Bunny Mellon's hoe had cut through a buried cable line. Immediately after, the long-awaited modernization took place, and cables were housed in a vault, said Bobby, "secure from any future woman with a hoe."

Jackie's love of beautiful things — especially of well-designed buildings — was deep-rooted, introduced in part by the Bouviers but reinforced by Janet's upbringing. Although Jackie rarely saw her grandfather Jim Lee, her mother's pride in his buildings — some of Manhattan's best-looking and most successful structures — influenced Jackie's efforts.

Jackie had realized that there was not much point in making the White House interior beautiful if the view from its windows was ugly. Lafayette Square, facing the main entrance of the mansion, was lined with historic houses, now fallen into disrepair, and with inappropriately large government buildings.

Jackie proceeded full bore on pulling together a committee to save Lafayette Square, warning a potential committee member that unless he joined, "lovely buildings will be torn down and cheesy skyscrapers go up. Perhaps saving old buildings and having the new ones be right isn't the most important thing in the world — if you are waiting for the bomb — but I think we are always going to be waiting for the bomb and it won't ever come & so to save the old — and to make the new beautiful is terribly important." Under the leadership of architect Jack Warnecke, the tall business buildings were razed and the houses were renovated, bringing the neighborhood surrounding the White House to the grandeur of the mansion itself.

Jack Kennedy supported his wife's efforts. As a Washingtonian for nearly twenty years, he felt deeply about the nation's capital and the influence its beauty could have on government and citizenship. Jackie was strong-minded, but her legacy of renovating the White House, uplifting the quality of entertainment at White House events, and supporting the performing and visual arts could not have taken place if it weren't for the drive for perfection planted in her by Janet.

By limiting her efforts to the White House, Lafayette Square, and the Cultural Center, Jackie was able to carve out some private time for herself as well as demonstrate the importance of the arts. "She would do one thing with superb taste, and it would have a tremendous impact," noted August Heckscher, cultural adviser to the White House. Jack, on the other hand, "certainly in private life would have seemed a little bit like the average husband, sort of being dragged by his wife to do a lot of cultural things which he didn't really enjoy doing very much."

When the White House announced Jackie's pregnancy in April 1963, it marked the first time that a First Lady had been pregnant since Mrs. Grover Cleveland in 1895. (The Cleveland baby was now sixty-eight years old, married to an Englishman and living in Yorkshire, England, where the press industriously located her for interviews.)

When the announcement was made, Jackie was devoting herself to the new country home the Kennedys were building in Virginia's Blue Ridge Mountains, called Wexford after the Kennedy ancestral Irish county. She and Jack had given up their lease on the Glen Ora house and had decided to build one to their own specifications, at a cost of $100,000 ($600,000 today).

A few weeks short of the due date, Jackie, visiting Hyannis in August, began to feel contractions. Jack was at the White House, although not alone, as the White House logs show a visit from Mary Meyer two nights before Jackie went into labor.

Jackie hurried to a nearby military base to give birth to Patrick Bouvier Kennedy. Janet and Janet Jr., dressed in flowered outfits and smiling widely, arrived at the hospital via helicopter from New York, where they were checking the elaborate arrangements for Janet Jr.'s debut the next week at Hammersmith Farm. The public smiles turned to private tears when they learned that the baby had been rushed to Boston and put in intensive care with a respiratory problem.

Janet stayed near Jackie and slept that night in the officers club on the air force base. She visited Jackie again in the morning and, at her request, went to Hyannis to check on Caroline, nearly six, and John, nearly three. Then Janet returned to Jackie, only to leave to meet Jack in Boston, where he was sitting by the baby's incubator. He said to Janet over lunch, "Nothing must happen to Patrick. I just can't bear to think of the effect it might have on Jackie."

When Janet was surrounded by the press, she said to the inquiries about Patrick, "He's doing very well." But reporters noted, "Although maintaining her poise, Mrs. Auchincloss appeared somewhat distressed."

Lee had left Athens, delighted at the initial news and eager to see her sister. Changing planes in London, she learned that the baby was in crisis. By the time she reached the United States on August 9, she had learned that Jackie's baby had died at four A.M. with his father by his side. Jackie was told several hours later by her obstetrician. Jack arrived about five hours after the baby's death. Jackie was never given an opportunity to hold her baby, nor to attend his funeral. She saw him only once.

The Mass for the baby lasted less than half an hour. Janet and Hughdie, Lee, Janet Jr., and Jamie were there, along with Jack and his brothers and most of his sisters. Jamie, the youngest, was particularly affected. "Why did the baby have to die?" he asked his father, who tried to answer as best he could.

Jackie put on a bright face a few days later as she left the hospital. "You've been so wonderful to me that I'm coming back here next year to have another baby," she said to the nurses. "So you better be ready for me."

But she was devastated by the death. "I'm afraid Jackie will have a nervous breakdown," Janet told one houseguest. Jack finally understood how terrible it was to lose a baby: no more questioning why he should break his plans, since the baby was already dead, as he had done with Arabella. This time he grieved deeply. He also put Jackie's feelings ahead of his own. A few times he went to visit Patrick's grave, although he was not known to have ever visited Arabella's. Despite their sadness, the couple both insisted that Janet Jr.'s debut go ahead as scheduled later that week.

After a short rest, Jackie and Jack were to meet at Hammersmith Farm following the debut weekend. Their tenth wedding anniversary was approaching; as Jack boarded the helicopter that would take him to Newport, a political colleague gave him an inexpensive silver-plate bowl. It was clear from Jack's expression that he was unimpressed. Upon arriving at Hammersmith, he presented it to Janet: "Here, Mummy, I brought this especially for you!"

Janet did not understand that he was joking. She accepted it graciously, fussing over its beauty, but was puzzled at such an ordinary gift.

That night Jackie and Jack ate with a few friends and the Auchincloss family—Yusha, Janet Jr., and Jamie were all home—and caught
up on everyone's activities. Jamie, who would start his senior year at
Brooks School, talked to Jack about how he used Jack's political advice
to win the presidency of its Young Democrats chapter. They also wanted
to learn of Janet Jr.'s debut, and she told them how much she had loved
the charming surprise bouquet they had sent.

They listened to the eighteen-year-old, who had graduated from Miss
Porter's School in June, describe the Venetian ball Janet and Hughdie
had thrown for her. The decor was manufactured in New York—that's
where they had been when they heard that Jackie was in the hospital—
and trucked down in two conveyances. Two enormous pink marquees
supported by gondola poles led from the water up to the house. Venetian
lanterns lit the pathways, as did candles set in frosted-glass globes of
different colors. The chandeliers inside the house were festooned with
ribbons and flowers.

The two outdoor dance floors set the mood for more than a thousand
guests, including 260 young acquaintances of Janet Jr., as they danced
to the melodies of the Meyer Davis musicians—all dressed as gondoliers.
Another music trio strolled the grounds, and a pianist provided music
inside the house. Even the help serving dinner was in Venetian costume.
Janet's gown was by Christian Dior.

At dawn, breakfast was served, and the bravest of the partygoers
jumped off the dock into the bay for a brisk swim. Others were thrown
into the water. As the sun rose, some napped in preparation for the
brunch a few hours later at the Slocums' in Janet's honor. That night
Janet was feted at a beach cookout at Nearsea, the Grosvenor estate.
Throughout the gala weekend, Janet Jr. was a lovely young debutante.
Adlai Stevenson sent a note to Jackie afterward, remarking, "I must
confess that I have fallen in love with another member of your family."

The two families had grown comfortable with each other's foibles,
and Jack's presidency had smoothed over Janet's criticism of him. In
fact, Jackie was beginning to think her mother showed a little too much
deference to Jack. Yusha remembers that at one family dinner, Jackie
corrected something Jack had said.

Janet was appalled. "Jackie, how dare you correct the President?
You need to apologize to him."

While Jackie sat dumbfounded, Jack howled with laughter and began teasing his wife. "Yes, Jackie, how dare you correct me? I am the
President!"

In October, at Lee's behest, Ari Onassis invited Jackie to extend her recuperation on his extraordinary yacht *Christina*. Jackie joined him and other guests for only a few weeks—leaving behind a pursed-lipped Janet—but the news ink expended on this two-week ocean voyage could have filled an oil tanker. Despite her acceptance of Ari's invitation and, later, of the expensive necklace he gave her, Jackie warned Lee that her ongoing affair with Ari might hurt Jack's reelection in the fall, although he was expected to be a shoo-in for a second term. Sure enough, the press went wild throughout the entire trip, and the White House feared the impact of its stories on votes. White House staffers joked to one another that Jackie had seceded from the Union. Jack called to suggest that she return early. When Jackie objected, mentioning that arrangements were not made to take her ashore, Jack quipped, "You're a good swimmer, Jackie!"

On one of their last evenings at Hammersmith a month earlier, Jack had thought of a surprise for Jackie. Janet said of that evening, "They'd certainly been through as much as people can go through together in ten years. Tragedy and joy with their children's births and deaths; then Jack's illnesses and Jackie's cesarean operations; mixed in with all the campaigning and finally occupying the highest office in the world. I can't think of two people who had packed more into ten years of marriage than they had.

"And I felt that all their strains and stresses, which any sensitive people have in a marriage, had eased to a point where they were terribly close to each other. They were very, very, very close to each other and understood each other wonderfully. He appreciated her gifts and she worshipped him and appreciated his humor and kindness."

What would be Jack's last gift to Jackie showed his new sensitivity to her wishes. Both Jack and Jackie loved being at Hammersmith Farm—it felt more like home to Jack than the frenetic activity of his parents' house—and the weather was so much better than the Cape's. He thought about making Newport the official summer White House, at least during his presidency. Instead of being perpetual houseguests of the Auchinclosses, he could rent the estate next door. That way, he and Jackie could come and go without putting the senior Auchinclosses out of their bedroom.

Annandale Farm, the place next to Hammersmith Farm, was up for summer rental. It had a large stucco house and twenty-two acres with the same gorgeous view of the bay. The President talked to Senator Claiborne Pell, who thought it a terrific idea. The Pells were friends with both Jack and Jackie and yet knew the Auchinclosses well: before running for office, Pell had worked in Washington for Hughdie at Auchincloss, Parker & Redpath. In fact, that summer Jamie interned at the senator's local and Washington offices. (Once, Jamie entered the floor of the U.S. Senate and sat on the wrong side of the room. Senator Pell spotted him and sent a note over, telling him to move to the other side of the chamber!) The Pells recognized the compatibility of the Kennedys and the Auchinclosses and knew the idea would work.

And so on his September 19 trip to Newport, Jack decided to rent Annandale Farm as a surprise for Jackie. It would be their vacation house for two months during the summer of 1964. Jack asked Pell to help with the negotiations, since his wife's former stepfather owned Annandale Farm.

The senator wrote to the President on October 4, informing him that Annandale's lease papers for the months of August and September were on their way. Jack was eager to surprise Jackie with the lease: he knew how she looked forward to going home to Hammersmith, and, of course, the President himself loved it there. Jack was particularly pleased with the surprise, as he wanted to reward her for agreeing to campaign with him in late fall. He couldn't wait to tell her.

*C*hapter 11

MAYHEM OVER
MERRYWOOD

Merrywood's expenses ballooned in the late fifties at the same time that the recession started to affect the rich as well as those with less money. National unemployment was peaking to a postwar high; a record number of Americans were receiving unemployment benefits. As the country faced an economic downturn, the stock portfolios managed by Auchincloss, Parker & Redpath were shrinking at an alarming rate. It looked as if maintaining two lavish estates was beyond even Hughdie's means, and in late 1957 he asked Janet to economize on the costs of running Merrywood.

She did, first by cutting back on the outdoor workers. But fewer gardeners resulted in an overgrowth of bushes and trees. Janet Jr., then twelve years old, and Jamie, ten, complained that the water in the outdoor pool was too cold because the tangled growth from surrounding trees and shrubbery blocked the sun. Janet was annoyed at their carping: after all, the family was at Hammersmith Farm all summer, and it hardly seemed reasonable for them to complain about the pool when they swam at Merrywood only in May and September.

She was doubly irritated by her children's objections because she felt that she, once again, was being forced into the ogre's position by their father's passivity in the face of trouble. Hughdie found it impossible to be forthright about his financial problems, and he especially didn't want to tell his children that he was having difficulties. So the responsibility for enforcing these new rules of economy fell to Janet, even though she wasn't allowed to give the children the real reason why the family was forced to economize. Nor were the adult children to know. Too often, she took her frustration out on Janet Jr. and Jamie.

At least the temperature of the pool didn't disturb her own swim; in fact, she rather liked its chilliness. Janet was bothered more by her—and her guests'—growing inability to see through the trees down to the Potomac River when she entertained in the living or dining rooms at ground level. Janet reveled in her role as mistress of a beautiful, well-run house, and she resented anything that might interfere with the image she had worked so hard to perfect. Still, she had no choice but to ignore the landscaping at Merrywood; she had to use their dwindling resources to keep Hammersmith Farm from being touched by an ugly financial reality that she and Hughdie hoped would be temporary.

The strain was greatest when the Auchinclosses were with their friends, as neither Janet nor Hugh wanted anyone in their crowd to guess that money was tight. Commented Tish Baldrige, whose parents often socialized with the Auchinclosses, "You don't say you have money troubles when you are in that group. Period."

Someone else familiar with the decade remembers the Auchinclosses' sticky situation. "Hughdie was very upset at the time," said C. Wyatt Dickerson, a Washington real-estate investor, "and he did not want to tell Jackie and Lee."

This was actually the second time Hughdie had thought about the expense of Merrywood's upkeep. Ten years earlier, when he had casually raised the possibility of selling Merrywood, he had caused a family commotion that traveled all the way to France, where Jackie was studying. She had dashed off a quick, concerned note to Yusha, who reassured her that his father was not planning to sell the estate.

There were good reasons for Janet to hold her head high and create the illusion that all was well. In late May 1959 she again hosted her annual Merrywood charity picnic for the Children's Hospital and the Hearing and Speech Center, taking an active role by leading the children, one by one, on her pony. However, the mirage of Merrywood was becoming impossible to maintain, and Hughdie quietly put it on the market for $850,000 ($5 million today) in 1959.

But if Hughdie couldn't afford to keep up such a vast estate, who could? "It was a white elephant," remembers Dickerson. "The Auchinclosses hadn't done anything, because they went to Hammersmith Farm for the summer. It looked very run-down and desolate."

And it didn't sell. The house, with its forty-six acres, remained on the market while the costs of maintenance rose higher and higher. Hughdie and Janet managed to keep the potential sale quiet; no Realtor's sign would be hammered in next to the driveway for all to see. In fact, the impending sale of Merrywood didn't come to the public's attention until shortly after the election of Jack Kennedy to the presidency in November 1960.

Janet's worst fears about public life came true then. She hated being in the limelight, especially receiving unfavorable attention. It wasn't a week after the national election when she was pounced on by a local reporter and asked point-blank why Merrywood was up for sale. Janet coolly responded that she and her husband "would like to take a smaller house in town."

She said that to her friends, too, and claimed that with Jackie soon to be in the White House, it would be more convenient for the Auchinclosses to be closer and not have to commute from McLean. The answer was clearly a pretext; Merrywood was, after all, only a fifteen-minute drive from the White House. And if McLean were such a distance, then why would Bobby Kennedy and his large family be living there when Jack was about to enter the presidential mansion? But the Auchinclosses' friends recognized a face-saver when they saw one, so everyone was kind and closed the circle around Janet and Hughdie. Certainly, for this set, the truly unthinkable would be to have disclosed the truth to the press.

By January 1962, as Jackie was beginning her second year in the White House, the Washington realty developers Sheldon and Ira Magazine made an announcement: their company had optioned Merrywood, with the final sale contingent upon a zoning change. Hughdie would be paid $650,000 ($3.7 million today) but would get the proceeds only after Merrywood's rezoning had been approved.

Magazine Brothers called a press conference to crow that it would construct a luxury development with 1,030 high-rise apartments on the property. They planned to build three brick apartment towers ranging from twelve to seventeen stories, and two rows of town houses. The Merrywood house would become a private club and guest house for residents of the area, and extra swimming pools, tennis courts, and other recreational facilities would be added.

An enormous cry went up from affluent McLean residents who had thus far succeeded in keeping high-density zoning out of their suburb. They were especially angry about the idea of this kind of development on the Merrywood property, which was one of the few intact large estates in the area and remained heavily wooded, despite its bridle paths, tennis courts, pool and pool house, and other outbuildings. In fact, the forty-six acres were much as they had been when George Washington lived twenty miles down the river at his Mount Vernon plantation.

The Magazine brothers retorted that their plan would eliminate only 7 percent of the natural forestation and that the remaining wooded acres would remain as they were. In addition, to keep the area "green," the developers announced that they were literally planning to color the parking-lot pavement green. This infuriated residents still further. "The cars parked there won't all be green, will they?" sarcastically inquired one neighbor.

In addition, the thought of hundreds of, maybe a thousand, residents from this development commuting into Washington on the narrow country Chain Bridge Road was unimaginable. Neighbors were also furious at the unexpectedness of the news: Hughdie had done nothing to prepare them for this sale. Making opponents more suspicious of the project was the fact that the Fairfax County sheriff was a syndicate member of the Magazine Brothers firm.

Opponents' pressure on the county planning commission was successful. Bowing to bitter community objections, the commission refused to approve the rezoning request.

Still, news that the decision would be appealed to the board of supervisors tempered the residents' joy. Everyone showed up at that hearing—everyone, that is, but the Auchinclosses, who were beginning to feel heat from their irate neighbors. "I don't want my own property to be menaced by 1,200 families moving in next to me," said neighbor and nightly radio commentator Edward P. Morgan. The *Washington Post* editorialized against the development, arguing: "No stone should be left unturned [to stop it]."

At the appeal, McLean residents and development representatives alike presented maps, photographs, and slides and printed material that bolstered their position. As might be expected, the two groups disagreed on every issue.

This time, the residents lost. The vote was 5–2 to approve the controversial rezoning. Yet the endorsement had the effect of uniting more people to fight the development, especially when it was noted that only two years earlier an application to build apartments on a seven-acre tract nearby was rejected after citizen objections. That developer, too, had appealed the rejection, but it was upheld by the circuit court only two weeks before the board of supervisors approved the Merrywood project.

Neighbors talked about a private suit. A member of the Virginia House of Delegates asked the state attorney general to investigate criminal action by the board. *Time* magazine called the Auchincloss house, but Janet made it clear that it was not her role to make public statements about the family's finances. Hughdie was then contacted at work and admitted, "It's all very unpleasant."

More disagreeable for Hughdie was his fear that he would not see the $650,000, which he needed badly. In addition, he was shocked at the commotion and sputtered that it was the principle of free enterprise at risk here. Outraged that some people felt he shouldn't be allowed to sell his own property to the highest bidder, he said, "It's extraordinary, their making this fuss."

Janet was miserable every time she heard a new criticism of the sale. She was not only caught between Hughdie and his urgency for fresh capital but was fearful of this brouhaha extending across the river to the White House. Janet's instinct was to protect both Hughdie and Jackie — but to do both would have been contradictory, for helping Hughdie might hurt Jackie's position, and vice versa.

A newly formed group, the Committee for Preserving the Potomac, called on the Auchinclosses to hear them out, asking them to appear at a public meeting to discuss the rezoning. Hughdie told the committee that he thought the development would be "a good thing" for the county and announced that he couldn't do anything even if he wanted to, since he had already signed a contract.

The preservation committee was well aware that Janet was regional chairman of the committee for the proposed National Cultural Center. They took public advantage of this by pointing out to the local press the incongruities and inconsistencies of Janet's planning a national cultural center while exploiting a scenic property that had one border on the edge of the Potomac River and the other only four hundred feet from the National Park Service's George Washington Memorial Parkway.

In fact, Janet's neighbors nearly picketed the tea she planned to hold at Merrywood for the Cultural Center. Janet was terribly upset when she heard of the latest strife and couldn't sleep because of the politicization of the house sale, particularly because so much depended on it. A successful deal would make all the difference in the world to Hughdie's depleted finances. When the citizens called off the confrontation — only because they didn't want their actions misinterpreted as opposition to the Cultural Center — her relief was immense. Still, an ad hoc group of residents did appear from time to time on the street by Merrywood's driveway, carrying signs reading, "Her daughter beautifies the White House and she desecrates our neighborhood."

By March 1962, however, the Auchinclosses were ready to move into the Victorian house they had bought in Georgetown. Janet was delighted she no longer had to swing her car out the driveway past neighborhood women picketing her house or receive cold stares from shoppers when she went into McLean's business district. Although without the money from the sale she couldn't put the problems of Merrywood totally behind her, she could at least avoid the topic now that she was living in Georgetown.

Even there, she wasn't totally free from community commentary. Her extensive renovation of her large corner house with eight bedrooms, fireplaces in every room, a good-size secluded yard, and a swimming pool, along with a three-car garage, evoked criticism. Putting in an elevator seemed a bit grand to her neighbors (Janet protested, saying that Hughdie needed it to help with his breathing), as did the black wrought-iron handrail on the front steps, whose detailing evoked the flag of Rhode Island.

The house, at O and Thirty-first Streets, was built in 1874 and was across the street from historic Christ Church, the Episcopal church where Dolley Madison had worshiped and Francis Scott Key had been a vestryman. Janet immediately added an eighteen-by-twenty-two-foot drawing room, and servants' quarters over the garage. She hired Elizabeth Draper to assist in the decoration.

The Georgetown Preservation Committee squawked when Janet added a bathroom window to the house's garage apartment, claiming a violation of the area's covenant. Nor did the neighbors like the shade of yellow that Janet painted the house's exterior; Janet replied to press inquiries that she thought of the color not as yellow but rather as "buff" and that the newly painted dark green shutters complemented the hue. Worse still were the press reports of one of Janet's workmen striking a neighbor (who had complained about the worker's double-parked car) with a hammer—from behind.

There was another group more powerful than the local preservation committee that was also concerned about Merrywood's development. The National Capital Planning Commission was chaired by Elizabeth Rowe, who was not only a friend of Jackie's but had been appointed to the federal board by President Kennedy. Representing the commission, Rowe sent a letter in April to the chairman of the Fairfax County Board of Supervisors, citing a congressional act of 1930 that provides for "the protection and preservation of the natural scenery of the Gorge and the Great Falls of Potomac." The letter further quoted President Kennedy's recent conservation message to Congress. Finally, it got to the point: "Low density residential development is compatible with this objective [of retaining the skyline and palisades in their natural state]. Tall buildings are not." And it said that any proposed development such as the Merrywood plan should preserve the land "as a continuous natural area."

Rowe, hoping her friendship with Jackie would influence the First Lady, sent a carbon copy of the letter to the White House. She added a cover letter explaining that the National Capital Planning Commission opposed the development of Merrywood. "I thought you might like to know of the action in advance of any press reports," she wrote. Showing her easy familiarity with the Kennedy family, she signed the letter merely "Libby."

Jackie was, by this time, fully aware both of the proposed development and of Hughdie's desperation for the sale to go through. She had raised the topic with Janet at the beginning of the year after the realty company's unwise press conference, which had jump-started all the negative publicity.

Jackie had always appreciated Merrywood just as it was, having written a homesick letter to Yusha when she had studied in France, "I always love it so at Merrywood—so peaceful—with the river and the dogs . . ."

Also, she already had begun her own preservation projects in the White House. If Janet's home was the potential site of angry picketing caused by her involvement with the Cultural Center, what could take place outside the White House fence? Jackie did not want to incur Jack's anger over Hughdie's oblivious actions.

And yet it would seem to have been an easy decision for her. On her own part, she would agree that apartment towers looming over the Potomac were undesirable. But she also saw that her mother was distraught over the family's financial situation. Janet had made it clear that she did not want any more politics involved in the house deal. She thought that the sale was Auchincloss business and was not appropriately one of local, much less national, concern.

So Jackie handwrote a message to her social secretary, Tish Baldrige, on Libby Rowe's cover letter, giving her instructions on how to respond. "Thank her for sending me copy—it was most thoughtful. This is a situation in which I don't want to get involved—but appreciate hearing from her."

As requested, Baldrige answered Rowe and the National Capital Planning Commission, quoting Jackie directly. Baldrige's correspondence referred not to Merrywood directly but rather to "the development of the McLean area."

The next month *Time* published a story that poked fun simultaneously at the Kennedy administration, the Auchinclosses, and the affluent McLean residents. The article ran to an excessive one and a half columns and was embellished with three photographs: an aerial shot of the gorgeous wooded estate and manor house; the architect's model of three high-rises soaring out from the woods and looming over the Potomac River; and a picture of Hughdie, looking stuffy. Now the sale of Merrywood was national news.

Privately and off the record, Jack Kennedy remarked to CBS correspondent Nancy Dickerson that the "one question he hoped never to be asked at his news conference was about Merrywood."

Marie Ridder, a fierce opponent of the Merrywood development, was scheduled to host Robin Lynn's wedding to Angier Biddle Duke, who headed the White House protocol office. The President and the First Lady were to attend, not just because of Duke's position in the administration but also because Jack was an old friend of Walter Ridder (of the Knight-Ridder media company).

Walter Ridder didn't realize that the First Couple was planning to be there until he opened his door to the Secret Service early on the morning of the wedding. As the agents began surveying the house and examining the food being delivered, Ridder called the White House.

Janet snuggles with baby Jackie, unaware of the looming Great Crash.
(*John Fitzgerald Kennedy Library*)

Jackie and Lee with their maternal Ryan cousins: (from left to right) Joan Ryan, Mimi Ryan, John Ryan (who was Jackie's debutante escort ten years later), Jackie, and Lee. (*Courtesy of Mimi Ryan Cecil*)

Janet and five-year-old Jackie win a yellow ribbon in the family-class event at the 1934 East Hampton Horse Show. (*AP/Wide World Photos*)

The end to a marriage: An oblivious Janet doesn't see what the camera
catches—her husband, Jack Bouvier, holding the hand of another woman.
(© *Bettmann/Corbis*)

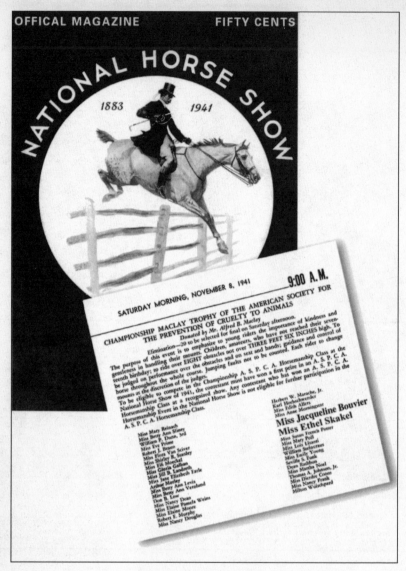

SATURDAY MORNING, NOVEMBER 8, 1941   **9:00 A.M.**

CHAMPIONSHIP MACLAY TROPHY OF THE AMERICAN SOCIETY FOR THE PREVENTION OF CRUELTY TO ANIMALS

Donated by Mr. Alfred B. Maclay

Elimination—20 to be selected for final on Saturday afternoon. The purpose of this event is to emphasize to young riders the importance of kindness and gentleness in handling their mounts. Children, amateurs, who have not reached their seventeenth birthday; to ride over EIGHT obstacles not over THREE FEET SIX INCHES high. To be judged on performance over the obstacles and on seat and hands; guidance and control of horse throughout the whole course. Jumping faults not to be counted. Each rider to change mounts at the discretion of the judges.

To be eligible to compete in the Championship A. S. P. C. A. Horsemanship Class at the National Horse Show of 1941, the contestant must have won a first prize in an A. S. P. C. A. Horsemanship Class as a recognized show. Any contestant who has won an A. S. P. C. A. Horsemanship Event in the National Horse Show is not eligible for further participation in the A. S. P. C. A. Horsemanship Class.

Miss Mary Reinach
Miss Betty Ann Shiney
William F. Thom, 3rd
Miss Eve Prime
Robert J. Braun
Miss Flora Van Sciver
Miss Shirley B. Stanley
Miss Eti Moeckel
Miss Gloria Calhan
Miss Jill B. Lambeth
Miss Jane Elizabeth Earle
Miss Hope Morley
Miss Betty Ann Lewis
Miss Betty Ann Vereuland
Miss B. Low
Don Nancy Dean
Miss Elaine Pamela Weiss
Miss Elaine Moore
Miss Chance Murphy
Robert F. Murphy
Miss Nancy Douglas

Herbert W. Marache, Jr.
Karl Hachschwender
Miss Edith Allers
Miss Anne Morningstar
Miss Jacqueline Bouvier
Miss Ethel Skakel
Miss Susan French Potter
Miss Mary Poll
Miss Lois Hausel
William Swincraus
Miss Emily Young
Seville S. Frank
Dean Rathbun
Miss Martha Noel
Thomas L. Johnson, Jr.
Miss Dierdre Coons
Miss Nancy Frank
Milton Wittschpard

Twelve-year-old Jackie competes against Ethel Skakel, her future sister-in-law, at the 1941 National Horse Show at Madison Square Garden. (*Fishy Design*)

Janet kicks up her heels after marriage to her second husband, Hugh D. (Hughdie) Auchincloss. (*Courtesy of Hugh D. Auchincloss III*)

Merrywood, Hughdie's great estate overlooking the Potomac River — and now Janet's, too. (*Courtesy of Hugh D. Auchincloss III*)

The blended family under the Yule tree: (from left) Lee and Jackie Bouvier, Janet Auchincloss Jr., Nini Auchincloss, Yusha (Hugh D. III) Auchincloss, Jamie Auchincloss, and Tommy Auchincloss. (*Courtesy of Hugh D. Auchincloss III*)

Janet gives a proprietary yet loving touch to her father, the Manhattan developer James T. Lee, at her daughter Lee's debutante party. (*Courtesy of Hugh D. Auchincloss III*)

The bride greets her mother and stepfather at the wedding table. (*Library of Congress, Prints and Photographs Division, Toni Frissell Collection*)

Jackie dances with her stepfather, who had just walked her down the aisle in the absence of her own father. (*Library of Congress, Prints and Photographs Division, Toni Frissell Collection*)

The christening of John F. Kennedy Jr. at the Georgetown University
Hospital chapel: (front row) Jackie with John Jr. and Janet; (middle row) the
President and Mr. and Mrs. Charles Bartlett; (back row) Jean Smith and
Robert Kennedy. (*AP/Wide World Photos*)

A proud Janet poses for a magazine portrait accompanying the story "What Jackie Kennedy Has Learned from Her Mother." (*Courtesy of Hugh D. Auchincloss III*)

The President arrives at Hammersmith Farm and shakes hands with Jamie
Auchincloss while Janet, in sunglasses and head scarf, waits with Janet Jr.
(*John Fitzgerald Kennedy Library*)

Jackie and Jack sail on Narragansett Bay with Janet and Hughdie. (*John Fitzgerald Kennedy Library*)

While John F. Kennedy delivers his 1963 State of the Union address, (from front left) Joan Kennedy, Lee Radziwill, Janet, and Jackie watch attentively; Mrs. Charles Bartlett sits with Hughdie behind them. (© *Bettmann/Corbis*)

After Jackie gives birth to Patrick, an unknowing Janet and Janet Jr. arrive with happy smiles, unaware of the tragedy ahead. (*AP/Wide World Photos*)

A stoic Janet represents the absent Jackie as Lady Bird Johnson dedicates the Jackie Kennedy Rose Garden. (*LBJ Library Photo by Cecil Stoughton*)

On vacation in Marrakech, Janet's Auchincloss family poses for their 1965 Christmas card: (left to right) Jamie, Janet, Hughdie, and Janet Jr. (*Courtesy of Margaret Kearney*)

The wedding party returns to New York City from Skorpios. John Jr. bounces down the stairs first, followed by Jean Smith, Sydney Lawford, Caroline, Pat Lawford, Janet, and Hughdie. (*New York Times Pictures*)

Janet, always wearing a straw hat to protect her complexion, sits outside her beloved Hammersmith Farm, built in 1892. (*AP/Wide World Photos*)

A special gift from Jackie and Lee on Janet's eightieth birthday, including her daughters' reference to her short marriage to their father, Jack Bouvier, rather than her long union with Hughdie. (*Courtesy of Hugh D. Auchincloss III*)

A delighted Jackie claps as Janet blows out her eightieth-birthday candles. (*Courtesy of Hugh D. Auchincloss III*)

"Mr. President, I really don't think you can come," Ridder said. "The newspapers will make hay of your attending a wedding at the house of the people leading the protest against the Merrywood sale!"

"Walter, don't be silly," the President responded. "Everyone knows we're friends. Why can't I attend a wedding at your house?"

Unable to convince the President, Ridder asked him to think about it further. As soon as he put down the phone, Ridder called U.S. Senator Claiborne Pell to explain the situation. Pell agreed with Ridder and called the President, suggesting that he and Jackie skip the ceremony but attend the reception, which he offered to have moved to his Georgetown house. Kennedy was convinced and accepted Pell's offer.

A caravan of Marie Ridder's closest friends was hastily mustered to bring their station wagons around to her house, load up the cars with food for the reception, and drive the refreshments across the river to the Pells' Prospect Street house. There they went out to the garden to help Mrs. Pell and her housekeeper throw tablecloths onto tables set up in the backyard garden stretching along Thirty-fifth Street, a few blocks from Georgetown University. Then the ladies returned to McLean to join their husbands for the Dukes' wedding ceremony. Afterward, the guests motored to the Pell house and were soon joined by the President and First Lady for the reception. Everything went smoothly, but there were half a dozen women, including Marie Ridder, who were exhausted when the day was over.

Ironically, another Merrywood neighbor was none other than Kennedy appointee U.S. Secretary of the Interior Stewart L. Udall, who lived five or six houses down from Merrywood. He, too, was against the sale and cited Teddy Roosevelt's historic "green swath" plan that was to protect the integrity of the national capital area on either side of the Potomac River. Udall intoned to *Time*, "We as a nation have recognized the Potomac Palisades as a great scenic resource, and over the years considerable effort has been expended to preserve its beauty." Years later he remarked ironically on the nearness of his house to the planned development: "I had a personal interest in this, as some people pointed out at the time."

All the same, he believed that Hughdie "was insensitive to what was involved" and that both Janet and Hughdie were trying to distance themselves from the sale. "[Hughdie] got so much money, and his attitude was typical: 'It's my property and I can sell it. It's up to them what they do with it.'"

Within a month of the zoning change, a Fairfax County grand jury was investigating the board of supervisors' approval, and irate citizens asked for a rehearing by the board and also challenged its action in Fairfax circuit court. Not surprisingly, the board refused to rehear the Merrywood project, and in September the circuit court judge declined to overrule the approval.

It seemed the sale and the environmental catastrophe that it would bring was final: nothing stood in the path of the development and, more important, nothing could keep Hughdie from receiving $650,000 from Magazine Brothers. In January 1963 the Fairfax County clerk's office transferred title of the tract from Hugh Auchincloss to the real estate group. Janet and Hughdie finally had the money. The deed was done.

Or was it?

Suddenly, after the Auchinclosses had deposited the check, the White House sprang into action. The Kennedy administration announced that it was shocked to learn that a construction crew had begun clearing land for a high-rise development that would blight Teddy Roosevelt's turn-of-the-century plan to maintain a green sheath up the Potomac River.

"Jackie sparked it," Stewart Udall remembers today. "She was very sensitive to environmental issues.

"I remember talking with Bobby [Kennedy] about it two or three times. You knew if Bobby said something, the President was speaking."

Following Bobby's instructions to Udall, the secretary asked Interior lawyers what could be done to stop the development. They discovered that the Department of the Interior had the authority to slap a "scenic easement acquired by condemnation through a declaration of taking." Interior did so in Alexandria's federal court by seizing control of the right to build from the development company.

Of course, Magazine Brothers, out a hugely profitable development, was crying foul within its own circle: only after payment had cleared the Auchinclosses' account had the Kennedy Interior Department suddenly noticed the Merrywood development and decided it should be stopped. Also, Bobby Kennedy had a McLean property on Chain Bridge Road, and his land would have been affected by the high-rises. The last-minute action by Interior seemed suspicious.

"Both I and the Interior were in a little bit of an embarrassing position," remembers Udall. "Conservation easements were very unusual in the early 1960s. But I wasn't doing it for selfish reasons. First, Bobby was standing in back of me and pushing a little. Second, it was part of the master plan. I was waving the flag of the Potomac plan."

Interior claimed in its 1963 civil action brief that the Merrywood site "has been selected . . . in connection with the administration of the George Washington Memorial Parkway and is required for further use [for] the protection of the natural features . . . for the benefit and enjoyment of the people." Basically, Interior took the right to scenery but not the property itself, which Magazine brothers still owned. Merrywood was worthless to the company, however, unless the land could be developed.

Department of Interior representatives, accompanied by U.S. Park Police, posted signs at Merrywood announcing federal supervision over the property. The signs forbade cutting any tree larger than three inches without specific written permission from Interior Secretary Udall and outlawed subdividing lots into parcels smaller than one acre. The McLean neighbors were jubilant.

In order to take the land, however, the U.S. government had to put down a fair price for the property. The government assessed Merrywood's value at half a million dollars ($2.8 million today). "We had to get $500,000 through the White House, and that kind of money wasn't easy to come by in those days," says Udall.

Of course, this was a full $150,000 less than Magazine Brothers had paid Hughdie and Janet a year before. In explaining the lower price, Udall remarked, "Interior deprived [Magazine Brothers] of the right to build. So that act itself diminished the value of the property," thus excusing the significantly lower value. In addition, the land still belonged to the development company, although Sheldon and Ira Magazine would never have acquired Merrywood if they hadn't thought they'd receive the right to build.

The President himself issued a memorandum on the day of the government's Merrywood seizure, proclaiming, "It shall be the policy of the executive branch to seek to preserve for the benefit of the national capital region strategic open spaces, including existing park, woodland and scenic resources."

Magazine Brothers sought an injunction to prevent the interference of federal authorities with its property, going to court to convince the jury that the government should pay an additional $2 million. The jurors agreed that the company should have received more money from the government but awarded only $244,500. The realty developers ended up with a mere $95,500 more than they had paid Janet and Hughdie.

Magazine Brothers felt that sum barely covered its expenses. The taxes on Merrywood were enormous, and what could be done with forty-six acres that couldn't be developed as planned?

Even then, the Magazine brothers did not publicly comment about the link between the Kennedy administration and Jackie's mother and stepfather. "To their credit," remembers Udall, "they didn't like it but didn't make any accusations."

Of course, the stakeholders in this commercial realty business located in the nation's capital also may have realized that this was one battle they couldn't win. In the end, the property became an albatross to the brothers. They grew "sick of the whole thing" in 1965, said C. Wyatt Dickerson, and sold the entire Merrywood property to him and his wife, Nancy, for $650,000, which was the same amount Magazine Brothers had paid Hughdie. The couple made renovations to the estate house and moved in with their children. They kept the surrounding eight acres for their own family's use, enclosed their property with a white board fence, built two new bridges, pruned every tree, and planted about 150 old English box shrubs, magnolias, and holly trees. All in all, they put an additional $200,000 (one million dollars today) into the estate.

Dickerson, a developer himself, also announced plans to build a cluster of forty-six octagonal and hexagonal manor houses, priced at about $125,000 each ($680,000 today). Because the issue had become a hot potato to Interior, the department was pleased to approve the sale and readily allowed this limited development. Udall announced at the unveiling of the smaller project, "A disaster has become a triumph."

Both Jackie and Lee told Dickerson that they were happy with his proposed buildings, which had left their childhood home unscathed. "It's so special to me," Jackie told him, "and I'm happy now that it is in good hands."

Lee sent him a postcard after she dropped by during Merrywood's renovations. "I'm having a great time looking at my old house," she wrote.

And Janet commented to Dickerson on the development, as well as on the newly spruced-up Merrywood: "It's just so wonderful. I would have liked to have done it myself—if I could have."

Chapter 12

TWO WOMEN IN
CRISIS

Early on the morning of November 22, 1963, Janet awakened
in her Georgetown bedroom. She lay there for a moment,
wondering if she should go back to sleep. She was puzzled
at her lethargy because she usually bounded out of bed once
she opened her eyes. But her strange fatigue made her realize
that she was glad she had no White House duties to take care
of that day, for Jackie was out of town with Jack on a presidential visit to Dallas, papering over cracks in the Democratic Party. And, as awful as the Merrywood sale had been,
at least the worst was behind her. There was only one obligation today, and that was a party: in the evening she and
Hughdie were going to Joan and Ted Kennedy's Georgetown
house for their tenth wedding anniversary party. She had a
few more gifts to pick up for Caroline's and John's upcoming
birthdays but was excited about giving John something she
had already selected for him: a child-size Marine uniform. It
would inspire him to practice his salute, she told her friends.

She dressed quickly, for she was not comfortable going

downstairs in a robe as she had done at her secluded Merrywood estate: here in Georgetown, the house sat at the intersection of two busy streets. Janet slipped on a soft taupe wool dress that fell slightly below the knee and buckled its belt. She brushed her hair, now in a flattering short style, and went downstairs for her usual breakfast of lightly buttered toast, orange juice, and coffee. Soon Hughdie joined her, and he mentioned that he'd heard on the radio that the weather would be unusually pleasant.

After Hughdie left for work, she sat for another few moments, enjoying her coffee yet curious at her odd laziness. The phone rang—to her delight, it was Margaret Walker, a good friend from a titled family in England. Lady Margaret had married John Walker, director of the National Gallery of Art, and the couple lived in Georgetown.

"Let's go and play golf," Margaret suggested.

Janet thought for a second about the papers piled on her desk before rejecting the idea of sacrificing a nice day to desk work. After all, with the crush of White House duties that she had taken over for Jackie and with the amount of official entertaining Margaret needed to do for her husband's job at the museum, there were few chances for the women to see each other.

Janet made up her mind. "That's just what I'd like to do—go out and walk around."

Jackie was in the President's three-room suite at Fort Worth's Hotel Texas, preparing for the day. Sipping coffee, she put on the clothes she had laid out the night before: a pink suit and pillbox hat, with a navy blouse, shoes, and bag. She was still irritated at Mary Barelli Gallagher, her personal secretary, for taking a place in yesterday's motorcade and subsequently not making it to the hotel before Jackie to help with her clothes.

Jackie was running behind schedule, which didn't improve her mood. She had awakened and found that she was menstruating, so it took her a little longer to get ready. Jack had already asked an aide to call upstairs and find out when she would be down. To the crowd he faced at breakfast, he joked, "Mrs. Kennedy is organizing herself. It takes her longer, but, of course, she looks better than we do when she does it." The crowd roared in appreciation.

After dressing, Jackie descended with her Secret Service agents to the hotel's ground floor and was directed toward its largest ballroom.

She arrived twenty minutes late for the day's first event, a spirited chamber of commerce breakfast with two thousand excited Texans in attendance. As she stepped into the room, a roar erupted and she nearly tripped in startled reaction as she walked to the dais.

After Margaret picked up Janet at the house, her car cut over to Connecticut Avenue, traveling north toward the Chevy Chase Country Club. As soon as they entered the tree-lined U-shaped drive, a valet stepped forward to take the car. "Good morning, Mrs. Walker," he greeted her. A second valet opened Janet's door, and the ladies stepped out. They walked directly to the first tee; their clubs would be unloaded and brought to them.

As Janet enjoyed her morning out on the course with Margaret, Jackie was finishing the breakfast event and was heading back up to the hotel suite with Jack. The couple was taking a rare moment of leisure together. Jackie couldn't believe her good luck in having an entire unscheduled hour with her husband. "Oh, Jack, campaigning is so easy when you're President," she said, laughing. Although she had made thirteen trips abroad as First Lady, this was her first political trip since moving into the White House. Then Jackie made a rare offer: "Listen, I can go anywhere with you this year."

As she sat contentedly, her eyes wandered to the art on the wall. Astonished, she realized that the paintings were not reproductions: she was sitting in a small gallery of impressionist and modern paintings and sculpture. She spotted a catalog that referenced the works, which had been borrowed from a Fort Worth art museum just for the presidential visit.

"Look, Jack," she said. "They've just stripped their whole museum of all their treasures to brighten this dingy hotel suite."

He picked up the booklet and suggested they call the woman who had put together the exhibit. They caught her at home with a sick daughter. After Jack expressed his thanks to the nearly speechless museum board member, Jackie came on the phone: "They're going to have a dreadful time getting me out of here with all these wonderful works of art."

The couple's generous phone call was interrupted by the news that the motorcade back to *Air Force One* was ready. From there, they would travel to their next stop, Dallas. Jackie gave the pictures one more look and reluctantly left the suite.

Thirty minutes after boarding the plane, they touched down in Dallas. When Jackie disembarked, the mayor's wife presented her with a bouquet of red roses, which she kept with her. "How odd," Jackie thought. "Why not the yellow roses of Texas, which I've received from everyone else?" The thought quickly left her head.

It was warmer than Jackie had been led to expect, and she regretted wearing the wool suit. A few minutes before noon, Jackie and Jack boarded the presidential car, a specially designed black vehicle whose bubble top had been removed on account of the unexpected sunny weather. The couple sat in the rear seat, with the red roses between them.

The presidential motorcade was nearly half a mile long. Five minutes from the Dallas Trade Mart, the motorcade turned toward an underpass. Jackie saw the tunnel ahead of them. "It will be so cool in that tunnel," she thought to herself.

Nellie Connally, the Texas governor's wife, who was with her husband in the rear jump seats, spoke loudly over the din of the crowd. "You sure can't say Dallas doesn't love you, Mr. President."

Jack smiled and agreed, "No, you can't."

A few sharp noises — did a motorcycle backfire? — and Jackie heard Jack mumble several words. He slumped toward her. Then she heard Governor Connally, from his jump seat, shout out a few words. Jackie asked herself, "Why is he screaming?"

A final shot rang out. Pigeons, alarmed by the report, swarmed up from the trees.

Margaret Walker dropped Janet back at home around noon after a round of golf. Janet began halfheartedly to shuffle the papers on her desk and then decided to freshen up before tackling her work. As she walked up the stairs to her room, the phone rang. Glad for the distraction, Janet picked it up hopefully, thinking it might be another friend with a pleasant suggestion on how to spend the remainder of the day.

"Mrs. Auchincloss, this is Nancy Tuckerman."

Janet had known Nancy since she was a girl at Farmington with Jackie. After Tish Baldrige left the White House, Tuckerman had assumed the role of social secretary.

"What are you doing?" asked Nancy, carefully feeling out whether Janet was with guests.

Janet mentioned that she had just come back from playing golf and courteously started to ask Nancy how she was. But Nancy broke in and said in a tight voice, "I have bad news. The President was shot in Dallas." She explained that it looked as if he was dead.

"Jackie?" Janet choked. "What about Jackie?"

Nancy assured her that her daughter was unharmed but had been with the President when it happened.

"I want to talk to her!" said Janet.

The motorcade by now had arrived at Parkland Memorial Hospital. Jackie remained in the convertible, moaning faintly as she held Jack. "Get up," a Secret Service agent shouted at her. She didn't and she wouldn't. Jackie kept her hand over the terrible wound on her husband's head, wanting to keep the sight of this last moment away from the press she had learned to distrust. Another agent told her that she *had* to move, that the President needed to be taken into the hospital.

"I'm not going to let him go," she said.

The agent realized that she was attempting to preserve this last minute in privacy, that she wanted to keep the fatal, gaping wound in the skull from exposure to public view. He slipped off his suit jacket and put it in her lap. Jackie wrapped it tenderly around Jack's head, and they entered the hospital. As she stepped out of the car, she looked back and saw that its seat was covered with blood—blood and red rose petals.

The President's body—for the Parkland emergency staff had no doubt that he was dead; had the man been anyone besides Jack Kennedy, he would have been declared DOA while still in the car—was rolled onto a gurney. The emergency workers ran with it, Jackie at the stretcher's side with a hand on her husband.

The hospital, well equipped for typical emergencies, was thrown into chaos as hundreds of staff got the word that the President had been shot and was being treated in one of the emergency rooms on the ground level. Dozens of men and women in white uniforms left their stations and began crowding into elevators to try to catch a glimpse of what was going on. One of the first staffers to arrive shouted when he recognized the hospital administrator, *"Jackie's* here? Where?" The administrator had him restrained.

In comparison to the hospital's own workers, the press, which had begun to arrive, was quiet and well behaved.

An agent opened a direct line to the White House, and staff there began to make decisions on whom to patch through. The first caller was

Ethel Kennedy, who handed the phone to her husband, Bobby, who was at Hickory Hill taking a swim after lunch. Bobby's voice so closely resembled Jack's that the agent's knees buckled on hearing it. Ted, now a senator from Massachusetts, was the presiding officer of the Senate and left the Capitol as soon as he was told the news.

Jackie was waiting outside the room where Jack was when she noticed Nellie Connally standing a few feet away. She gently inquired as to how the governor was, and Mrs. Connally replied briefly.

After waiting a few more minutes, Jackie began to circumvent the nurse at the door.

"You can't come in here," the nurse ordered.

"I'm coming in and I'm staying." A pushing match ensued between the nurse and the First Lady. "I'm going to get in that room," Jackie whispered to her.

A physician who witnessed the shoving broke in. "It's her prerogative," he told the nurse, and escorted Jackie into the room where her husband was desperately being attended to by a surgeon.

A few minutes later the surgeon pulled the sheet over Jack's head. The sheet wasn't long enough, though, and the president's feet and ankles were exposed.

The surgeon turned to Jackie: "Your husband has sustained a fatal wound."

Her lips whispered, "I know."

Nancy Tuckerman told Janet that she couldn't be put through to Jackie. She said the plans were for Jackie to return to Washington as soon as possible. She couldn't bring herself to add that Jackie would be returning with "the President," for she knew that Lyndon B. Johnson now held that title. Nancy said that she would let Janet know as soon as *Air Force One* lifted off from Dallas. She mentioned that Lee had called frantically from London, having heard on the radio that the President had been shot, and that Bobby Kennedy had called Lee back to break the news that Jack was dead. The American embassy was already working to find Lee a seat on the next flight back to Washington.

Janet sat there, nearly wringing her hands in anxiety. Her worst fear for Jackie since her marriage to Jack had been a repeat of her own divorce from Jack Bouvier. Although Jack's election to the White House had put off that possibility for at least a few years, she had never imagined that her thirty-four-year-old daughter would end up alone as a *widow*.

Janet called Hughdie at his office, then Jamie at Brooks School. The office brought Jamie to the phone, where he said, nearly in tears, "Mummy, I think he's dead." Janet knew the news would be terrible to him; he had hero-worshiped his charismatic brother-in-law, already declaring himself the first Auchincloss in history to be a Democrat. After telling him that she would have a car pick him up at school and bring him home, she called Farmington to speak to its headmistress so that Janet Jr. would be similarly informed and could make plans to travel back to Washington. Then she called Yusha in New York and asked him to coordinate his travel plans with his stepsister so that she wouldn't have to take a plane by herself. Next, she took a deep breath and asked her butler to call the household staff together.

The Reverend Father Oscar Huber made his way through the crowd outside the hospital. He was pastor of the local Catholic church and had stood outside with the crowd to see President Kennedy's motorcade pass by. When he arrived at Parkland, the Dallas police escorted the priest inside. The police were then relieved by Secret Service agents, who brought him into the operating room. He walked past Jackie and the surgeon to Jack's body. Jack's face was covered by the white sheet, and the priest assumed the President was already dead. He felt it was permissible to give him a last anointing, as this sacrament may be conferred upon a dead person as long as it is within two or three hours of death.

Father Huber opened his black bag and removed the holy oils, the cotton batting, a prayer book, and a stole, which he draped around his neck. He immediately gave him conditional absolution and conditional extreme unction, followed by a last blessing. Dipping his thumb in the holy oil, he traced the sign of the cross on Jack's forehead and ended, *"In nomine patris, et filii, et spiritus sancti. Amen."*

He automatically chose the shorter form of the last anointing because he knew the President had died before he arrived. The surgeon, however, seemed to think the rites were perfunctory.

"Is that *all*?" he asked. "Can't you say some prayers for the dead?"

The priest was surprised. He looked at Jackie for a sign of what she wanted. When he saw her blank stare and the agony on her face, he breathed in deeply and offered, in English, various prayers that are read for someone dying or dead.

He then turned to leave the operating room. "Mrs. Kennedy, my sincerest sympathy goes to you."

Jackie followed Father Huber out of the room. She asked, "Father, do you think the sacraments had effect?"

"Oh, yes," he replied.

"Thank you for taking care of the President," she responded. "Please pray for him."

As the priest retreated, the Secret Service agents were not as gracious as the First Lady had been. One blocked his path and said threateningly, "Father, you don't know anything about this."

He nodded and left for home.

After asking her staff to resume their duties, Janet looked down and started when she saw that she was still dressed in a knit shirt and golf skirt. Of course, the first thing she needed to do was put on some appropriate clothes. Janet didn't even need to think about that; it was instinctive. She went upstairs to her wardrobe and first put her hand back on the taupe dress she'd had on that morning. Her hand hesitated and moved to a black one instead.

As she finished dressing, there was a short knock on her bedroom door.

It was the upstairs maid, with a card on the tray she'd been given by the butler. Janet picked it up and saw that she had a visitor downstairs: the wife of the Peruvian ambassador to the United States. Janet sighed. Of course, the ambassador's wife would be one of the first to arrive. Janet knew from her Washington experience that the lady's husband was the second-highest-ranking member of the diplomatic corps. Janet assumed that the French ambassador's wife, whose husband was highest in rank, was on her way to one of the Kennedy residences, as it was incumbent on that wife to begin the formal rites of diplomacy that lay ahead of them all.

She walked down the stairs to receive the ambassador's wife.

Before leaving the hospital, Jackie decided to place something in Jack's coffin. She remembered the day of Black Jack's funeral when she had purposely worn a favorite bracelet, a graduation gift from him. On impulse, she had unfastened it and slipped it into his hand as he lay in his coffin. And when Patrick died, she had placed a gift she'd given Jack, a St. Christopher medal, in his coffin. Now, she slipped off her unadorned gold wedding ring and worked it all the way to the beginning of one of Jack's knuckles, where she let it remain.

A minute later an eccentric priest arrived, having been let through the phalanx of security. It was the Reverend Father Thomas M. Cain, of the Dominican Fathers at the University of Dallas, a Catholic college. He approached Jackie.

"When did he die?"

Jackie responded, "In the car, I think."

The priest held up a small plastic bag. "I have a relic of the True Cross."

He asked Jackie to "venerate it" and held it out to her. Not sure of what she was supposed to do, she kissed the plastic. Then he announced that he wanted to take it in to the President.

He stepped into the room where Jack's body was lying and waved the bag around in the air and stepped back out into the hallway.

"I have applied a relic of the True Cross to your husband," he told Jackie.

Now Jackie, and the agents around her, were uneasy. But the priest began embracing her, calling her by her first name and promising to write her a letter. The men moved him away from Jackie, but he jerked away from them and lunged toward her again.

"Please, Father. Leave me alone," she told him.

Jackie had been in Parkland more than an hour. "Why can't I get my husband back to Washington?" she asked.

After receiving the ambassador's wife, Janet was at a loss. She wanted to reflect and pray, but the phone was starting to ring and ring.

"Take messages," she told the staff, and left the house, walking across Thirty-first Street to the Gothic Christ Church, the Episcopal church where she and the children worshiped each Sunday. Janet's intentions were to kneel and pray in what she assumed would be an empty church. She was amazed to find it full of Georgetown mourners, with a spontaneous service in progress.

When the service ended, a number of worshipers noted Janet among them and whispered their sorrow at her loss and the nation's. Janet crossed the street again and, entering the house, embraced Hughdie, who had left the office as soon as he could after hearing the awful news.

At the White House, Cordenia Thaxton, the upstairs maid, was in the
sewing room when the news came over the radio. She called Miss Shaw,
the children's very English nanny, who was in John's room. Soon an
agent was on the phone for the nanny, telling her that Caroline and John
were to be taken out of the mansion. Ethel Kennedy telephoned and
offered to have the children over to her house, but Miss Shaw felt the
Auchincloss home would be a better choice. "I racked my brain to think
of a place to take the children that would be away from the turmoil,"
said Miss Shaw later. "Then it came to me. There was only one other
person to turn to—the children's grandmother, Mrs. Janet Auchincloss,
a naturally sympathetic woman with whom I had spoken in other moments of crisis."

She called Janet, who had returned from church. "Oh, yes, yes,"
Janet agreed. "Bring them over to me. This is the place for you all. Come
and stay here . . ."

Miss Shaw quickly packed an overnight bag for the children, for it
was late afternoon by now, and went to get them. She didn't mention to
Nancy Tuckerman that the children would be going to Janet's house,
because she naturally assumed Nancy knew.

Getting home was Jackie's wish, too. She didn't know that the delay in
leaving the hospital was due to a territorial argument between representatives of the state, who wanted to treat Jack's death as if it were solely
a Texas homicide, and representatives of the federal government, who
were protective of their right to investigate a President's assassination.

Finally, when jurisdiction was worked out, the casket was loaded into
the hearse. The bizarre priest with the True Cross relic had somehow
followed them onto the loading dock and was now chanting and waving
his plastic bag in the air again. Secret Service agents were unsure
whether to arrest him or just make sure that he didn't get near the First
Lady, who was standing and chain-smoking near the hearse. They decided on the latter course and watched him closely.

A Dallas policeman opened the passenger door for Jackie, and she
sat down. The undertaker, behind the wheel, called out his window to
the various representatives of local, state, and federal governments,
"Who's going to pay me?"

If Jackie heard, she didn't react.

When the vehicle arrived at Love Field, the coffin was loaded onto the plane, Jackie boarded and chose a seat on the starboard side, as close as she could be to Jack's body. The aircraft's engines were shut down, making it an aluminum oven in the Dallas sun.

As the flight crew prepared to take off for Washington, Jackie decided to compose herself in the plane's bedroom—the area she knew as hers and Jack's. Entering the closed door, she received a shock to see Lyndon Johnson *lying* on the bed—her bed and Jack's!—dictating to a secretary. The man and his secretary, embarrassed, dashed out past her ashen face.

The first engine started up, but the aircraft didn't move. Jackie walked out of her cabin. "It's so hot. Let's leave," she said.

Someone told her that they were waiting for a federal judge to appear. If Jackie understood the judge's significance, she didn't react.

She walked back to her cabin, to be joined by Lady Bird and Lyndon Johnson. After they expressed their condolences, Lyndon said, "Well, about the swearing-in . . ."

He told her that a judge would be arriving within the hour. Jackie nodded, and the couple left. She lit another cigarette and thought, "My God, do I have to wait an hour?"

She continued to sit, alone with her thoughts. She later said, "Three times they gave me the yellow roses of Texas. But in Dallas they gave me red roses. I thought how funny, red roses—so all the seat was full of blood and red roses."

She used the bathroom and noticed, again, that she had her period. She wept once more—Patrick gone, Jack gone—red blood and red roses. She returned to the bedroom and sat alone with her thoughts, not realizing that the judge had already arrived. Everyone was afraid to disturb her, they were waiting for her to emerge from the cabin.

Finally, when Jackie walked out to see how much longer it would be, the ceremony began.

The Bradlees were the first of the family friends to arrive at the White House. *Newsweek*'s Washington bureau chief Ben Bradlee held dear his friendship with Jack Kennedy, and his wife Tony was a friend of Jackie's. Nancy Tuckerman greeted them with the news that the Auchinclosses had already left Hamlet and were on their way to the White House, for the Bradlees also knew Janet and Hugh.

Nancy felt like a schoolgirl around Janet, because she was sure that

Jackie's mother, who had known her since she was at Farmington, always wondered what "Tucky" was doing with a grown-up White House job. Janet was an exacting woman, and Nancy was not sure she always met her high standards. In addition, Nancy had been at the White House only since the summer. Janet, on the other hand, had several years of experience at the White House and was better versed than Nancy in formal hospitality.

Nancy approached Tony Bradlee. "Please send off Jackie's mother." She was afraid that Janet might get too upset when she saw her daughter.

Tony replied half jokingly, "I can't do that with Mums."

Both women realized there was no way to keep the mother of the First Lady from the White House. They would have to cope with Janet and hope for the best.

In the meantime, Ben Bradlee had gotten down on the floor to play games with John. A difficult situation for the adults was made worse by the constant comings and goings of helicopters landing on the South Lawn—the area was abuzz with commotion—since John, who associated the noise with Jack's arrival home, would shout happily, "Daddy's here!"

With so many choppers coming in and going out, John's shouting—now joined by Caroline's—made the sorrow so excruciating for the adults that Ben Bradlee muttered, "I'm going to tell those children."

His wife stopped him. "No, you aren't. You don't have the right."

Jackie was three hundred miles west of the White House, approaching Andrews Air Force Base. The pilot slowed to cruising speed, not wanting to land before the ETA he had given the Secret Service.

Jackie didn't know that hundreds of relatives, cabinet members, and other administration staff had begun arriving at Andrews to greet her and the late President. Bobby was on the airfield, sitting on the tailgate of a truck, determined to be the first to embrace his brother's widow.

Air Force One's pilot was preparing for landing. He wanted to make sure it was a smooth one, for this was the last time he would be transporting President John F. Kennedy.

Miss Shaw, with Caroline, collected an overexcited John from the guests and took him to the car. The Secret Service were on full alert: no one knew yet if the assassination was part of a coordinated conspiracy. The men who were entrusted with Caroline and John were trained to assume the worst. They loaded the Ford with a 12-gauge shotgun and checked their .38-caliber side arms. Miss Shaw and the children sat in a Country Squire station wagon, with the armed car following behind.

Arriving at Hamlet, the agents quickly hustled the children up the black wrought-iron steps into the front door of the yellow house. They closed the curtains on the ground floor and put their shotgun and side arms on a high shelf in the kitchen. The trip safely completed, they sat down to watch the kitchen television, which had been on for hours.

In the living room Miss Shaw tried to help amuse the children. Janet was pale and looked as if she had been crying but acted completely cheerful with the children. She took Miss Shaw upstairs to show her the guest room where she and Caroline would stay, and the women went to the attic to bring down the crib.

The children played until dinner. Caroline was a very bright child and sensitive to other people's behavior. She seemed to intuit that this was not an ordinary day. Certainly, she and her brother had never traveled to their grandmother's house in a two-car caravan. The whole afternoon had been odd, especially the unusual number of helicopters landing and taking off from the lawn.

She wandered, unobserved, into the kitchen and stood there for a few minutes. The agents were engrossed in the news reports and didn't see the little girl taking it all in. They jumped when they finally noticed her and brought her back out to Miss Shaw.

But Caroline became very quiet and refused to play.

Janet wanted to get to the White House, where at least they could help with *something*. Janet decided that Jackie would need her, and Jackie's interests came first. Janet's job was to wait for Jackie. Young children were best left to the staff and the nanny. She and Hughdie would go to the White House to wait for Jackie. Hughdie walked into the kitchen and asked his driver, who was waiting there, to take the couple to the White House.

They were nervous as they drove along Georgetown's M Street and traveled west through Foggy Bottom. The road curved right as it led into Pennsylvania Avenue, and Janet and Hugh could see that the streets near the White House were beginning to become crowded with people who were inexplicably walking toward the First Family's residence.

Many were weeping. Janet was struck by how many shocked Washingtonians had the same impulse that she had: to get to the White House.

At the mansion Janet joined Hughdie, Nancy, and the Bradlees. Waiters arrived with chicken sandwiches and drinks for the guests, for the White House staff, too, wanted to keep busy. The guests only picked at the sandwiches, but they downed the drinks quickly.

After initially trying to keep up the chitchat, the uneasy guests realized that silence was appropriate under the circumstances. Everybody retreated into his or her own thoughts, and only Hughdie stood to greet Jean Kennedy Smith when she entered the room carrying a black mourning dress.

Finally, they learned that *Air Force One* was landing at Andrews Air Force Base and that the First Lady would be accompanying her husband's body to the U.S. Naval Hospital at Bethesda, Maryland, which was only ten minutes from the Auchincloss house, up Wisconsin Avenue.

Although the distance from the White House to Bethesda is short, the cars that carried the Auchinclosses, Jean Smith, Nancy Tuckerman, and the Bradlees squealed through city streets. Ben Bradlee, nervous for their safety, sat up high over the driver to see the speedometer. What he learned didn't assuage his fears: the needle was bouncing at ninety miles an hour.

Finally, they arrived safely. The group ascended the hospital's high tower and entered a drab suite. A navy officer looked at Nancy and, proud of the best suite in the hospital, asked her, "Do you like it?"

She swallowed and replied, "It's nice."

The officer responded eagerly, "This is where Forrestal committed suicide," referring to the death of James Forrestal, the Secretary of Defense under President Truman.

It was such an incredible non sequitur, and such an awful social blunder, that Nancy just stared at him.

Suddenly, Jackie was there, standing in the tower suite.

"There," Ben Bradlee later remembered, "was this totally doomed child, with that god-awful skirt, not saying anything, looking burned alive."

She saw him first and fell in his arms.

"Cry, *cry*," he told her. "Don't be *too* brave." He nodded to his wife to step forward, but Tony realized that Jackie hadn't yet seen Janet standing to the side.

"Here's your mother," Tony said.

Jackie stared into her mother's eyes and tried to smile. They embraced for a good length of time, then Janet, both a pragmatist and truly trying to say words of comfort, pulled back.

"Oh, Jackie, if this had to happen, thank God he wasn't maimed."

Jackie nodded before Bobby pulled her aside, whispering to her that her husband's assassin had been arrested. She stared at him and returned to her mother's side.

Her voice broke. She said to Janet, "He didn't even have the satisfaction of being killed for civil rights. It's—it had to be some silly little Communist."

Janet tried to change the subject. "Will you stay with me tonight?" She added, "You know the children are at O Street now."

That caught Jackie's attention. Her head jerked up. "What are they doing *there*?"

"Jackie," said Janet, confused, "I had a message that you had sent from the plane that you wanted them to come there and to sleep there."

Jackie looked absolutely amazed. "But I never sent such a message."

"You don't want them to be there, then?"

"No," Jackie said. "I think the best thing for them to do would be to stay in their own rooms with their own things so their lives can be as normal as possible."

The Secret Service had been monitoring the room and noted the exchange. By the time Janet got to a phone to call home, Miss Shaw was already getting the confused children ready for the trip back to the White House, and the agents were taking the guns down from the kitchen shelf and putting them into the Ford.

Janet was aware that with the grandchildren gone, her son, Jamie, would be alone at home, except for her staff. In addition, she knew that Janet Jr. and Yusha would be arriving at any time. She was concerned about them and was fatigued from the events of the day. But she had another issue that needed to be addressed.

Janet was concerned about how the children would be told of the tragedy. She had decided that Jackie—who was her first priority now— had been through enough and did not need to take on this additional burden. With all the focus on the enormity of the President's murder, Janet alone centered on the fact that the shooter could just as easily have murdered Jackie. After all, Governor Connally had been wounded.

The thought of her daughter sustaining a head wound like Jack's made her gasp out loud.

Besides, she thought it didn't matter who told Caroline and John, anyway. Janet honestly believed that their youth would protect them from the emotional damage older children might sustain.

So Janet returned to Jackie to raise the question of who should tell the children. Jackie thought for a minute and then responded, "I think Miss Shaw should do exactly what she feels she should do. She will have to judge how much the children have seen or heard or whether they are wondering. She will just have to use her best judgment."

Janet nodded, not arguing, and the women embraced again as Janet announced that it was time for her to get back home. Jackie registered surprise. "Will you stay at the White House, Mummy? Will you sleep in Jack's room?"

"Anywhere you like, Jackie," responded Janet, although she was uncomfortable at the thought of sleeping in the late President's bed. But the request also "touched me very much. I knew she didn't want to be alone," Janet said later.

"Would Uncle Hughdie stay, too?"

"Of course."

She whispered to Hughdie as they left, "We'll stop in Georgetown for toothbrushes."

Janet and Hugh left the naval hospital. Although the trip to the White House would take them through Georgetown, and they could have stopped in to see Jamie and get their toothbrushes on the way, Janet needed to resolve the issue of her grandchildren immediately. A phone call from O Street to Miss Shaw about the children would have sufficed, but Janet decided she needed to speak in person to the nanny. The issue was too important to be misunderstood.

By the time the couple reached the White House, Janet had made up her mind. Once again, she reaffirmed in her own mind that Jackie needed to be protected from an avoidable harsh duty and rationalized that it wouldn't matter to such young children *who* gave them the news.

At the White House, with the children in bed and Hugh having a drink in another room, Janet approached Miss Shaw. Without ceremony, she announced, "Mrs. Kennedy wants you to tell Caroline and John."

Miss Shaw was stunned. She hadn't even thought it was a possibility that the duty would fall to her.

"Please, no. Let this cup pass from me."

Janet was emphatic. "You must. There's no one else."

Miss Shaw argued, "But I can't. I don't have the heart."

Janet was getting irritated. "I know, I know. But you have to."

Thoughts of last August flashed into Miss Shaw's head, of baby Patrick's death, when she had to be the one to tell an excited little girl that the baby she was so happily waiting for had "gone to heaven."

Her thoughts returned to the day's events. "Please, *please*," she begged, "can't someone else do it?"

"No." Janet was emphatic and losing her patience. "Mrs. Kennedy is too upset."

Janet turned on her heel and left Miss Shaw. She rejoined Hugh, and they traveled back to Georgetown for a short and enervating visit with Jamie, Janet, and Yusha.

Jackie was still at the naval hospital, wondering at something her mother had said to her earlier. Ever since she was a young woman, her mother had always feared that she would lose her love of her own country in favor of France. Jackie's triumphant visit to Paris with Jack only augmented her chauvinistic feelings for that beautiful country.

That evening apparently her mother thought that Jackie would be angry at the United States for Jack's murder. She had said to Jackie, "I hope you will never live any place but in this country, because Jack would want that."

Jackie was amazed. "But of course. I'm going to live in Georgetown, where Jack and I were."

The memory of this short conversation ran through her head. Then she turned and spoke out loud to the friends who still surrounded her in the hospital suite. "Where will I live? We sold the N Street house when we moved into the White House."

Bob McNamara, Jack's independently wealthy Secretary of Defense, told her not to worry. *He* would buy a house for her in Georgetown.

After spending a short time at the O Street house and seeing that everything was under control, the Auchinclosses left once again for the White

House. When they arrived, rather than going straight to the family quarters, Janet looked in on the work going on in the East Room, where the President's body would lie. It was already draped in a great deal of black crepe.

Janet's exacting taste was well known and respected by the White House staff. One person asked her, "How do you like it?"

"Shouldn't there be a flag?" she queried back.

"Of course!" was the unanimous response, and people began scurrying to find one.

Then another staffer approached her. "Mrs. Auchincloss, tomorrow a great number of dignitaries are coming into Washington." She added in a tentative voice, "We were hoping that you wouldn't mind hosting the reception for them."

Janet sighed, then nodded her head in agreement and turned to go upstairs. But before she joined Hughdie, she once again tapped on Miss Shaw's door. "As soon as the children wake up in the morning, tell them that we're staying in their father's room tonight." She didn't want them running in expecting to see their dad.

As staff and volunteers worked downstairs throughout the night, she and Hughdie undressed and lay down on Jack's king-size four-poster bed with a stiff horsehair mattress and board.

Janet had fallen asleep when Hugh heard a soft knock on the door. To his surprise, it was Jackie. She was beginning to tire from the drug she had been given to help her rest. "Uncle Hughdie," she said, "I don't want to sleep alone."

He brought her back to the bed and cuddled her until she fell asleep.

Janet had reminded Miss Shaw to tell the children that they were sleeping in their father's bedroom. Caroline and John dashed in at seven in the morning, lugging toys. Janet was already reading the newspaper.

"What's that?" Caroline asked, seeing her father's photograph outlined in black on the front page of the *Washington Post*.

Janet said sadly, "You know that's your daddy."

"He's dead, isn't he? A man shot him, didn't he?"

Janet could not bring herself to reply.

Chapter 13

COMING TO
TERMS

The funeral had ended; the Masses were over; the week's events would be forever burned into the memory of the nation—but the rest of Jackie's life was just beginning. She thought, though, that at age thirty-four her life was over; everything would be anticlimactic after the events in Dallas.

Provi (Providencia Paredes), her personal maid, placed Jackie's blood-splattered pink suit in a cardboard box and brought it to Janet's house in Georgetown. Without opening the container, Janet wrote the date of the assassination on a label she affixed to the box, climbed the stairs to the attic, and stored it next to the box that held her daughter's wedding dress.

Jackie was still in the White House, staying up all night and walking its halls. She had become obsessed with one thought: reuniting her dead children with their father. When her friend and chief of protocol Angier Biddle Duke had given her material on Lincoln's funeral, she read that the President had been buried next to his young child. Jack, she thought, should have his children by him, too. "I'll bring them together now," she said, remembering that Jack had told a friend that he'd "rather be with my family" after death than alone at Arlington National Cemetery.

She called Janet and explained her plan to reinter her dead babies with their father at Arlington. Janet felt it was unnecessary and ghoulish: let the dead rest. Jackie insisted. She wanted it done and wanted it done right. That could mean only one thing: Janet would have to supervise the exhumation of Arabella and Patrick. There was no one else Jackie would trust.

Early one morning a few days later, Janet took a private flight directly to Newport. There she met the director of Newport's best funeral home, the one that had seen to the arrangements for Arabella. They drove together to St. Columba's Cemetery. Janet hadn't been there in seven years—not since Arabella was buried, with Jackie in the hospital and Bobby standing in for Jack.

The gravediggers were there to place the old casket—what little remained—into a new coffin the funeral director had brought with him. Janet was silent during the entire awful interlude. Then she was taken to Hammersmith for the night. She called Jackie, still in the White House, and at her request, told her the terrible details one by one.

Patrick's coffin would be fresh: he had been dead for only three months. Jackie asked Richard Cardinal Cushing to oversee Patrick's disinterment from the Kennedy grave site in Brookline, Massachusetts, the next day.

Cardinal Cushing said he "had the body of Patrick Bouvier Kennedy taken out of the grave at Holyhood [Cemetery] early in the morning to avoid photographers and reporters. On the plane, the *Caroline*, was the tiny body of the child [Arabella] who was buried in Newport." By arrangement, Janet was waiting at Newport's Quonset Naval Air Station with Ted Kennedy. "Thank you," she said when the cardinal greeted her and his driver handed Patrick's casket to the military escort to lay in the plane by the remains of his sister. Ted was ashen. And Janet flew back to Washington with Jackie's dead babies, her task not quite over. The evening of December 5, she joined Jackie, Jamie, Bobby, and Ted at Arlington National Cemetery for an unannounced reinterring of the coffins. "Jackie was single-minded," says Jamie Auchincloss. "She needed to do this and she did—at night, in the dark, by the Eternal Flame."

The next day White House press secretary Pierre Salinger announced the reburial, with no mention of Janet: "[Arabella and Patrick] were brought to Washington today on the family plane and were accompanied by Senator Edward F. Kennedy."

With that accomplished—and the last trip taken by the *Caroline* while Jackie was in the White House—Jackie knew it was time for her to leave the presidential mansion. Even though she had said, "I'm going to live in the places I lived with Jack—in Georgetown and . . . at the Cape," she also realized, "I didn't have anyplace to go." Ethel thought she and the children should move into Hickory Hill, but Jackie knew that would be unworkable. For the short term, Janet's friend Marie Harriman offered the Harrimans' house at 3038 N Street in Georgetown to Jackie and the children.

They moved exactly two weeks after Jack's assassination. Jackie helped Mr. West pack, designating the toys, clothes, and personal mementos she wanted to go to Georgetown; the family's furniture went into storage. Lee, Bobby, and Ethel escorted the three Kennedys to the new house. Marie and Averell moved into the Georgetown Inn on Wisconsin Avenue, where the very tall former governor faced unaccustomed discomfort: the inn's bathtub, he complained, "is too damn short."

Jackie had left the White House without being able to say good-bye to the Johnsons. Embarrassed at her emotions having overcome her manners, she wrote a note of apology. They promptly called to invite her back for a visit. It was an awkward conversation: Lyndon kept insisting that she return to the White House, and Jackie kept saying no. She asked the Johnsons to excuse the commotion they could overhear: John Jr. had just "set off this awful jet plane that's so noisy here in the background." So the children were trying to go about their lives; John, oblivious to the tenor of the household; Caroline, sad and aware. Caroline "just looked ghastly," said her former teacher of that month. "She looked so pale."

Lady Bird wrote Janet, "Never have I wanted more to comfort a person as I have Jackie, or felt so mute and unable to do so. I feel I know Jackie so much better and my admiration and love for her have grown with each passing hour—if Lyndon could, he would take the stars out of the sky and make her a necklace."

A few days later Jackie wept as she signed and wrapped a gift for her mother and stepfather. It was a leather-bound book of presidential Inaugural Addresses. "For Mommy and Uncle Hugh, Jack was going to give you this for Christmas. Please accept it now from me. With all my love, Jackie. December 1963." Jackie thought about Jack's Christmas gift to her—what would have been his new skill in French, intended as a surprise but disclosed to Jackie after his funeral.

Jackie did not want to disappoint Caroline, so she returned to the White House to see her perform in a Christmas play on December 17. The Johnsons were out of town; she again left a note, saying she would visit them after Christmas. Weeping, she was driven back to the Harrimans' house.

Their temporary home was close to the corner of N and Thirty-first Streets, which meant that Jackie was only two short blocks down from Janet and Hughdie. Her mother came to visit often, as did Ethel and Bobby from Hickory Hill. There was never a thought that Jackie would move to Wexford, the new Virginia house that she and Jack had enjoyed for such a brief time—that was just a country home to shelter their five dogs, three ponies, and Jackie's thoroughbred.

Jackie decided that she would stay in Georgetown to raise her children, regretting that she had let Jack talk her into selling the N Street house she had loved so dearly—what comfort it would have brought her. "That first night [after Jack's murder]," Jackie said, "Bob McNamara said he'd buy back our old house in Georgetown. That was the first thing I thought that night—where will I go? I wanted my old house back."

But as she mulled it over, she had second thoughts. "I thought—how can I go back there to that bedroom? I said to myself—you must never forget Jack, but you mustn't be morbid."

At least in addition to her government pension she had inherited around $200,000 in yearly income from trust funds set up by Jack and his family. There were also investments and property worth nearly $2 million ($11.2 million today), which went directly to Jackie. Although she had little cash, coming up with money for a new house was not an issue.

Jackie purchased a house at 3017 N Street for $175,000. In the short time she had been at the Harriman house, she realized she wanted to remain close to Janet and Hughdie, and wanted to have them nearby for the children, too. Jackie knew their pride in her dignity as the nation watched; their good opinion—Janet's, especially—was all-important.

The house Jackie bought was a three-story, twelve-room, mottled-buff-colored brick Colonial, built in 1794, when Philadelphia was the nation's capital, "for lease or sale to a genteel family." Two tall magnolia trees, planted when the house was constructed—"older than the mag-nolias Andrew Jackson planted at the White House," Jackie noted—fronted the steps that led up to a double entrance door.

The rooms were cheery, with a fireplace in almost every one, ample windows that took in the morning sun, and fourteen-foot-high beamed cathedral ceilings. A small elevator was a plus, especially for Maud Shaw, who had grown used to the one in the White House. The best part was the captain's watch in the roof, a tower that permitted a view of the Potomac River, a major shipping port when the house was built.

The house, empty for some time, needed superficial work. Jackie hired interior designer Billy Baldwin to decorate the children's bed-rooms. She gave him photographs of their White House bedrooms, ask-ing him to copy them as closely as possible to give the children a sense of continuity. Jackie wanted to hurry the work so she could vacate the Harrimans' house. Baldwin hired two sets of workers who worked day and night, Sunday through Saturday. Jackie ran back and forth down N Street from the Harriman home to her new house a dozen times a day with swatches and color schemes.

The family moved on February 1, with Jackie carrying such fragile items as a model sailing vessel into the house. Despite the presence of the world's photographers, she dressed much as anyone would on mov-ing day: dark ski pants, black boots, and a knee-length raincoat. Janet Jr. accompanied her, as did Caroline, age six, in a snowsuit. Jackie wanted to keep John Jr., three, out from underfoot and distracted him with a car ride with a Secret Service agent. Both children were restless, having just recovered from the chicken pox.

Lee took up residence with Jackie, bringing her two children, An-thony, five, and Anna Christina (Tina), three. Lee stayed on the second floor with Jackie, while her children slept on the third floor with their cousins. Lee's children were good playmates to Caroline and John, and Janet was delighted to have her two eldest daughters and her grand-children so close by. She visited Jackie every day.

Jackie craved a private life like the one Janet had led. Now that her marriage was over, she naively assumed she could stay out of the public eye. During her "Camelot" interview with Theodore H. White for *Life* magazine, she said, "I'm not going to be the Widow Kennedy. When this is over, I'm going to crawl into the deepest retirement there is."

Jackie was depressed and couldn't imagine a bright future. "I was really in my own shell of grief," she said. Caroline, she was sure, would stay close to her. Of John, she foretold a thought that White never included in his story: "He's so interested in fixing planes; maybe he'll be an astronaut or just plain John Kennedy fixing planes on the ground."

Within weeks of moving into the newly purchased N Street house, Jackie learned that she could not escape being the icon of what the press would obsessively call American "royalty." Crowds of people jammed the street and even set up card tables and spread out their lunches while they waited for a glimpse of America's queen. Binocular-wreathed tourists arrived early each morning in such large numbers that they woke up the household as they tried to sneak ladders onto the front lawn to peek into Jackie's and the children's bedroom windows. They pried the house numerals off the front steps for souvenirs as quickly as Jackie could have them replaced.

Caroline's French teacher took her out one afternoon, and reporters spotted her in the car. "And so the child hid in the car so that she could not be seen," the woman said. Caroline asked, " 'Please tell me when nobody's looking.' "

Billy Baldwin had expressed concern when he first saw the house, and remembered that it "had been chosen for her with the greatest possible bad decision by her sister . . . it was absolutely hopeless . . . [The house was] high up on some steps, and had been designed for publicity. There was no possibility for privacy and in every way it was totally what she should not have had for those children."

Jackie was under constant surveillance, forced to keep the curtains closed at all times. She felt buried alive. "I'm a freak now," she said to Bob McNamara. Janet even heard talk about Jackie drinking excessively.

Other than Lee, she had no real women friends in whom she could confide. Her only other regular visitors were Bobby Kennedy and Bob McNamara. So the reliance she developed on her brother-in-law was understandable. "Bobby is going to teach Johnny. He's a little boy without a father. He'll need a man," she said.

Jackie displayed some symptoms of what would come to be known as post-traumatic shock disorder. She would take circuitous routes to avoid catching a glimpse of her former home. "Even driving around Washington, I'd try to drive a way where I wouldn't see the White House," she said. Yet she couldn't escape: despite her desire for a simple life, her name was thrown up as the next ambassador to France (her brother-in-law Sargent Shriver eventually took the position). President Johnson called again, this time to offer her the ambassadorship to Mexico. No, she said. How about heading the White House cultural program? No, thank you, she responded.

She said she would remain "in seclusion" for a year; she dissolved the four White House committees whose members had advised her as First Lady. Officially, she was devoting herself to the John F. Kennedy Memorial Library, which she hoped would open on the campus of Harvard University. In truth, she was traumatized and deeply depressed, staying up all night and weeping.

Just as the Ancient Mariner of Coleridge's poem spilled out every detail of his ordeal to the Wedding Guest, so did Jackie ask every one of her friends if she could recite the awful incidents of that harrowing day. Tom Braden remembers, "She poured it out. It was a traumatic experience for me and Joan. She poured it out in detail, in shocking detail. Things you wouldn't expect to hear, she told: 'I realized suddenly I had his brains in my hand.'"

She planned for the children's upcoming school years in Washington: John Jr. was to attend a cooperative preschool held on a rotating basis at parents' homes. His teacher would be the Rhode Island woman who had taught the White House school Caroline had attended. Caroline was to enter second grade at the Stoneridge School of the Sacred Heart in Bethesda, Maryland, just north of the naval hospital where Jack's body had been brought. Caroline would have been classmates with her cousin Maria Shriver.

However, word was out as early as March—when Jackie placed shamrocks on Jack's grave on St. Patrick's Day—that Jackie was desperate to leave the gawking tourists behind and was apartment hunting in Manhattan. Finally, in July Jackie's press secretary, Pam Turnure, announced that Jackie was leaving Washington for the relative anonymity of New York. She had purchased the fifteenth-floor apartment of a gray granite Fifth Avenue apartment house and planned to move in mid-September. The arrangements for the apartment at 1040 Fifth were made so quietly that her name did not appear on the contract. The sellers were Mr. and Mrs. Lowell Weicker, who moved upstairs to the penthouse. (Mr. Weicker later became a U.S. Senator from Connecticut.)

Jackie also sold Wexford, although she would often return to the Middleburg area to hunt. At the same time, she moved her office closer to her—from the Old Executive Office Building, west of the White House on Pennsylvania Avenue, to a four-room suite in a small commercial office building at 400 Park Avenue in Manhattan. (Congress had authorized its maintenance and allotted a budget of $50,000 for staff and expenses.)

At the end of June, the three Kennedys left for Hyannis, knowing they would not return to live in Washington. Staff stayed behind to coordinate the move to New York. After a short visit with the senior Kennedy family, Caroline and John were driven to Hammersmith Farm for Jackie's July 28 birthday and a long vacation. Jackie, now thirty-five, cited the trip as an example of the continuity of environments that she wanted for the children. They adored the farm; the only thing they resisted was oyster soup, as Caroline remembered, "which Mummy said we had to eat because it was a delicacy and tasted yummy."

Newport that summer made for a bittersweet memory: next door to Hammersmith Farm was Annandale Farm, which Jack had rented for the family to enjoy this summer, and possibly for Senator Pell and others to buy as a permanent summer White House. A few months after Jack's death, Jackie canceled the rental, but the estate owner, Barclay J. Douglas — who had once been stepfather to Nuala Pell, a Newporter and the senator's wife — refused to return the deposit. Nuala Pell remembers that townspeople were furious at his meanness. The city tax assessor duly reevaluated Annandale's property tax, was *shocked* to find it woefully undervalued, and sent its owner a sky-high new assessment.

Caroline and John stayed with Grandmère and Granddad, as they called Janet and Hughdie, for the rest of the summer. The children loved Hammersmith Farm, and Caroline very seriously signed its guest book every time she visited: "I love it here" or "Hammersmith is beautiful all year round. My favorite house anywhere." While they visited, Jackie left for Europe; this time it was a cruise along the coast of Yugoslavia with friends from Palm Beach. She stopped in Rome to visit Lee, who was renting a summer villa from the Borghese family.

Jackie returned to meet Bobby, who was running for a U.S. Senate seat from New York. He was in Atlantic City, the site of 1964's Democratic National Convention. She shook six thousand hands at a reception to thank everyone who had supported Jack. However, she refused to go inside the huge convention center festooned with giant photos of Lyndon Johnson. (Yusha, who was decorated by the Jordanian government, was jokingly directed by Bobby to do his part for the campaign — dress up in Arab robes, go to Brooklyn, and campaign for incumbent Kenneth Keating.) Jackie returned to Newport and the family until it was time to leave for New York for the children to start school.

While the children were at Hammersmith with their grandparents, Janet suggested that she take Caroline to a Newport shop that carried school uniforms to get her ready for her new school. Caroline was excited about the new gray jumper, white blouse, gray jacket, and red beret and camel coat. "She could hardly bear to put it all away and wait for school to begin," remembered her nanny.

When Jackie and the children returned to New York, they moved to temporary quarters on the eighteenth floor of the Carlyle hotel on Seventy-sixth Street near Madison Avenue, where she and Jack used to stay in the city. This time, though, she specifically asked for another suite with a dissimilar layout from the one she knew.

Maud Shaw would take the children down to the lobby on rainy mornings so they could have a place to play. As the time neared for the family to move into their apartment on Fifth, Jackie dispatched seven workmen, all employees of the Carlyle, to paint the new dwelling.

John kept asking to see the rooms where his daddy stayed, but Jackie could not bear to show him. The day before moving out of the Carlyle, she asked the executive housekeeper to take John to their old suite on the thirty-fourth floor. The boy, nearly four now, stared at the bed and asked, "Did my father sleep there?" and at the desk chair, "Did my father sit there?"

The Kennedys' new apartment was accessible only by a private elevator, which was guarded by two Secret Service agents, and an emergency stairwell. The apartment had five bedrooms. Fourteen windows faced Central Park, with a beautiful view of the reservoir and of the Metropolitan Museum of Art. Nine windows overlooked Eighty-fifth Street. The building, constructed in the 1920s, was located just seven blocks above Lee's eleven-room cooperative at 969 Fifth Avenue and a few blocks below Yusha's apartment on Park Avenue. Lee had been lobbying Jackie to move to the city, promising that Stas would buy a place for the Radziwills, in addition to their house in London. (Jack's sister Jean Smith also lived in New York, as did Pat Kennedy Lawford, who was initially rejected by a number of cooperative boards because she was a Democrat and an actor's wife. Soon Bobby and Ethel would take an apartment at the United Nations Plaza.)

The building entryway's marble floors led to a huge foyer running parallel to Fifth Avenue. The foyer had a fireplace at one end. Jackie paid $200,000 for the apartment, and maintenance fees were estimated at $14,000 yearly.

Jackie's large apartment was originally two, before being joined so its tenants could occupy the entire top floor. Two maids, a cook, and a governess looked after the family and their quarters, which were furnished with French period pieces. Jackie herself placed her father's antique desk. She received some housewarming gifts that never saw the light of day: for example, from Jack's cabinet came a magnificent gold coffee service bearing the men's signatures. The service was never in sight—too many memories, too political, too gold.

Jackie enrolled both Caroline and John in parochial schools. After school she often took the children to Central Park to play, sometimes bringing Caroline's cousin Sydney Lawford. Caroline also rode in the park with her mother, with John reluctantly going along with the females: he preferred helicopters. On one excursion she asked a park patrolman if he would give John a ride on his motor scooter. Alas, it was against policy, he said, but may I have your autograph? Jackie obliged.

Weighing heavy on Jackie's head were the responsibilities connected with her husband's memorial, which was to be named the John F. Kennedy Center for the Performing Arts. Congress, in a close partisan vote—one of the few Republicans to vote for it was Hughdie's cousin, the House's ranking Republican, James C. Auchincloss—funded the center and made it, by law, the only memorial to John F. Kennedy in the nation's capital.

Jackie's mood was dark when she wrote chairman Roger Stevens at the beginning of October:

> *Whatever reservations I may now have about having permitted it to be named after President Kennedy—I think it is only fair to you, and to all the people who have worked so hard, to put them aside for the time being.*
>
> *If, after a fair amount of time, I do not think it is what I wish for him, I will ask Congress to change its name—which they will do. [emphasis added]*
>
> *Last winter, when the decision was made to name it after him, I was not capable of making any decisions....*
>
> *All I care about now is sparing him controversy. He has a right to peace now.*

Jackie was strong-willed. She told Stevens that "the Director must be acceptable to me" and commanded that there be no political patronage when it came to naming trustees. Jackie ran down the list of current trustees and knocked off one after another, calling them "expendable." Of the Seagram heir, she wrote, "Mr. Bronfman—he gave relatively little and he contributes nothing. I assure you—he is expendable." Of Jack's close friend LeMoyne Billings, she said, "But as much as I love him—I think he is expendable."

She continued, "My last and most important point—my representative on the board of the Center. I must have one—Or I wish to pull out of the whole thing right now."

Jackie was irritated because Stevens had initially scheduled its groundbreaking on the first anniversary of John F. Kennedy's assassination. "If I hadn't heard about it, completely by accident, it might have happened. So many things like that—lacking in taste and judgment can happen."

She continued, "If these things cannot be granted—then I will ask in the next session of Congress that the Center's name be changed."

Soon it was November, the dreaded first anniversary of Jack's death. More than forty thousand visitors paid tribute at Arlington National Cemetery. The earliest visitor to the site, arriving at dawn and admitted by the cemetery superintendent, was Janet, sent by Jackie, who remained in Manhattan with Lee because she could not bring herself to go to the grave. Janet laid a cluster of white rosebuds and jasmine in the name of Jacqueline Bouvier Kennedy. Because of the extreme cold, the frail bouquet withered and turned brown before the sun had fully risen.

Even though Jackie felt no obligation to accept any duties that people might expect of a First Lady—voting, for example—Janet still upheld her end of the bargain as the mother of a former First Lady. When the Kennedy Center groundbreaking did take place, Janet was there on Jackie's behalf. Hughdie accompanied her and listened while President Johnson and Senator Ted Kennedy spoke. The gold-bladed shovel, kept in a Park Service vault, had been used to break ground for the Lincoln and Jefferson Memorials by Presidents Taft (in 1914) and Roosevelt (in 1938). Sir John Gielgud recited some Shakespearean speeches.

Jackie was finally starting to come to grips with how her life had changed. Being in New York was helpful: she had always loved New York and everything about it—the museums, the parks, and the people. Jackie was starting to throw parties at her house, mostly for such well-known artists as Leonard Bernstein and Mike Nichols. She invited Bobby to most of her get-togethers.

When it came to Washington events, even those connected with projects she had once championed, Jackie was not interested. A case in point was her flat refusal to participate in a garden project of the new First Lady. The White House was distraught: the Johnsons, certainly, perceived it as a rejection of them, personally and politically. Of course, they were correct. Jackie had learned to dig in her heels: what she wanted to do, she did. And if she didn't want to do it, she wouldn't. Other people — especially Janet — could cover for her.

Jackie actually was never a gardener; it was Jack who had enjoyed the Rose Garden outside the Oval Office, memorizing the roses' Latin names and reciting them to guests. Lady Bird Johnson planted another garden on the east side of the White House; this was the one she wanted to name after Jackie. To make sure the idea wouldn't meet with opposition, Lady Bird checked with Clark Clifford, the Democratic guru, with the head of the National Park Service, and with Bill Walton of the Fine Arts Commission.

As Lady Bird wrote in her journal, "It only remained to call Mrs. Kennedy herself. When I did, she said, 'No.'"

In the spring of 1965 Jackie flew to England to attend Queen Elizabeth's dedication to the late President of a park at Runnymede, the historic Magna Carta site. However, she refused to return to the White House for the East Garden dedication. Instead, she rented a seaside villa in southern Portugal for the month of May.

The Johnsons finally made it clear to Jackie that her opposition would embarrass them. Jackie realized, "That was so generous of Mrs. Johnson to name the garden after me . . . she didn't have to do that." Finally, Jackie agreed but remained modest, telling Lady Bird to "scratch my initials on a tree, or put up a plaque, ever so little, underneath some bench."

Nevertheless, Jackie would not attend the ceremony. "I just couldn't go back to that place," Jackie insisted. Janet begged her — she knew that if Jackie didn't go, she would have be her surrogate. That would be torture: Janet, somehow, was convinced that Lyndon Johnson had arranged for Jack's assassination to put himself in power; she would not be dissuaded from this notion. "She believed that all her life," says Yusha, and Jamie confirms it. "That's what Mother thought, whether or not it makes sense."

In addition, Janet had never understood why Jackie took little interest in the Warren Commission's investigation of the assassination, and tried to convince her to take a more active role. Other than being questioned by its members in her Georgetown house in early 1964, Jackie took no part in its activities.

On the issue of life and death, Jackie was a realist: "What difference does it make?" she would ask. "Will it bring Jack back? No, it won't."

Janet felt physically sick anticipating the White House event. If Lyndon murdered Jack, how could she appear with Lady Bird? It took all her courage to steel herself for the ceremony.

On the day of the dedication, the Jacqueline Bouvier Kennedy Garden was a news-wire story throughout the country. Lady Bird spoke, pointing out her predecessor's mix of "realism and poetry." She termed Jackie a "remarkable young woman who lives the blend with such sensitivity and zest."

Of course, Janet had to acknowledge the dedication to her daughter with some remarks. She kept them short—her voice was badly shaking as she responded, "I know you will understand if I cannot express how I feel about this tribute to my daughter today.

"I cannot think of anything that would mean more to all the people who care about Jacqueline. I cannot think of a more fitting memento of the years she shared with him [President Kennedy] than to have this lovely garden."

The reporters noted Janet's strained voice. *The New York Times* said it was "barely under control," and the *Boston Globe* described it as "emotion-filled" and "almost choked up." The papers attributed it to pride over her daughter and sorrow at the family's loss.

That over, Janet returned to the O Street house. She had carried out another emotionally grueling task as a favor to Jackie, the most difficult thing she had been asked to do since the reburial of her grandchildren Arabella and Patrick.

The following day a messenger brought Jackie a special gift from the White House. It was a signed photograph of the Jacqueline Bouvier Kennedy Garden sent by Lady Bird and Lyndon Johnson. The gift went from Jackie's hands into a pile of material that she was sending to her downtown office. There it rested on a window ledge, surrounded by stacks of mail.

In May 1965 an advertisement appeared in *The Times* of London: "New York—extremely reliable and competent young woman, 25–35, needed to look after girl of 7 and boy 4 in New York City; English or French native language."

Miss Shaw was retiring. "I took Caroline when she was eleven days old. It will be a big wrench leaving her and John," said Shaw. "I've just told them I'm going away for the summer. They'd be too upset if I said I wasn't coming back." She didn't admit that she "did not really like not telling [Caroline] the truth"; it was Jackie who thought it would upset the child too much.

Shaw was not planning to be in contact ever again with the children she'd raised. "When my memory fades in their young minds, it'll be time for me to fade away, too."

Jackie went to London with the children, where she interviewed a number of nannies and hired someone who stayed only a short time. "After Miss Shaw left, she would get only au pair girls," says Marta Sgubin, who was employed by Jackie for the children a few years later. On the return flight from London, Jackie sat by the actress Bette Davis, all the while keeping an eye on her son. "I'm rather worried," she confided. "You see John wants to pilot the plane!"

May was a trying month for Jackie. Now that ground had been broken for the Kennedy Center, she was heavily involved in all its aspects. That month on black-bordered stationery she wrote a lengthy letter to Roger Stevens, saying she wanted to pass on some thoughts. She admonished him curtly: "#1. It should not take three months to get the minutes out."

Then she recounted her recent trip to the studio of Robert Berks, an internationally renowned sculptor who had made a plaster figure of the President for the center for Jackie's approval. No one had communicated to Berks that Jackie wanted the sculpture, which would stand in the center of the intersection where the great halls meet, to be something "abstract that symbolizes his spirit." When she saw the full-length representational figure, she was surprised and displeased, telling Stevens, "I find it extremely offensive and completely unsuitable." And she warned him, "The memorial to President Kennedy must be acceptable to me." And so Berks began to rework the sculpture.

But Jackie and Stevens still had issues over the center, including the sticky question of who would be its artistic director. Jackie wanted a great name from the American performing arts and not merely a professional manager. She and Stevens had asked Leonard Bernstein, the first American to hold the title of conductor and musical director of the New York Philharmonic, who was a friend of both and a colleague of Stevens' (who had produced Bernstein's great popular musical, *West Side Story*).

Under pressure—Jackie told him, "Jack would have wanted it"—Bernstein said yes, then realized he would despise the paper-pushing tasks of an administrator. He cravenly sent his wife, Felicia, to Washington to give Stevens the bad news. Jackie and Stevens were in a quandary.

Then, a month after Jackie's crossness over the proposed sculpture, she wrote Stevens again. This time the mercurial Jackie was floating on air. "I talked to Bernstein Saturday night—it is the most exciting news—he wants to be commissioned for the opening more than anything—

"Roger, this is the best solution. Lennie is so happy—because he is creative—This is what you must do now. Call Lennie—and tell him he is commissioned—he is very *protocolaire* about this."

Jackie gloated when she told Stevens how she assured Bernstein that President Johnson himself would make the announcement. "Lennie loves this idea of course!" Jackie reported that she and Lennie were tearful with joy by the conversation's end.

Yet Jackie's sentimentality went only so far. Apparently, after she and Stevens asked Bernstein to become the center's administrator, they became concerned over the possibility that word of his bisexuality would leak out and taint the center's name. She ended this letter with a postscript mentioning the selection of another man to fill the position, adding, "The man is happily married, so there isn't that problem."

At Newport, May had been a difficult month for Janet and Hughdie, too. First, Yusha's six-year-old son, Cecil, stepped off the median strip on busy Park Avenue right in front of a speeding car. Yusha rushed out to save him, and both were hit. Cecil suffered head injuries and a broken leg, while Yusha's shoulder and leg were punctured.

At home in Newport, the Auchinclosses were upset by their neighbor's plans to sell Annandale Farm to a corporation for a multimillion-dollar apartment venture. When Newport's board of review approved plans for high-rise apartment houses right next to the Auchinclosses' property, Hughdie appealed the decision to the state's supreme court. Imagine: high-rise apartments next to Hammersmith Farm! Shades of the Merrywood tempest—with colors reversed.

When school ended, the three Kennedys were off for a short vacation in Hawaii. Upon their arrival, they were amazed to see five thousand people turn out to greet them. Jackie rented a house in Honolulu, traveled to the different islands, hired a surfing instructor for both children, and enrolled Caroline in hula lessons. Soon she had relaxed enough to exchange her casual linen shifts for brightly colored muumuus, topped by a head scarf, sunglasses, sunscreen, and pink lipstick. Although she didn't hide that she was smoking, she kept the cigarette pack out of view.

Coincidentally, the house Jackie rented was adjacent to the house owned on Diamond Head by Hughdie's nephew (Esther's son from her first marriage) John F. Nash Sr. He conveniently had six children for Caroline and John to play with, ranging from a few years older than Caroline to a few years younger than John. As one of them, John (Jock) F. Nash Jr., remembers, "Caroline and my sisters went off to play while we were with John. One of the girls had gotten hold of a lipstick, and they decorated each other's faces with it, making quite a mess.

"Jackie entered the playroom to tell Caroline and John that it was time to leave. When Caroline ran to her and Jackie saw the lipstick smeared on her face, she ignited. She slapped Caroline repeatedly—first on one cheek and then the other—backing her through the room until they reached the far wall.

" 'Wow,' I thought. I was only a little older than Caroline but I had never seen anything like that before. All the kids stood there stunned."

In Hyannis the Kennedys were expecting Jackie and the children to visit them for a few weeks. When Jackie extended the Hawaiian interlude—at the time, she was dating Jack Warnecke, who had a vacation house there—the Kennedys were inevitably disappointed. Then the family's return was again delayed by an airline strike. Instead of stopping in Hyannis, Caroline and John went immediately to Hammersmith Farm. Jackie joined them for her thirty-sixth birthday celebration a few days later.

They did go to Hyannis for a few days. Jackie watched Caroline participate in the 4-H Stablemates Horse Show in Barnstable, Massachusetts. Caroline, astride Leprechaun, had the pony walk, trot, and canter. Caroline's cousins Kathleen and Courtney, Bobby and Ethel's children, won blues in different events, while Maria Shriver took second in the Pony Pleasure class and the Hunt Seat Trial. Newspapers reported on these events and other horse shows, saying they exemplified "the Kennedy tradition," even though Janet and Jackie were the competitive riders, never Jack and his parents. Oh, well.

Jackie and the children quickly returned to Newport. Janet told Jackie that Rose had called to complain about Jackie's bills. "This cannot go on," Rose said. "Now that Jack isn't here to provide for her, Jackie's going to have to learn to survive on less. My husband's office cannot continue to finance every whim of hers."

The rest of the visit was pleasant, though. John, preferring water activities to horse trials, learned to jump off the Hammersmith pier eight feet above the water. Jackie spent her time painting, picnicking, swimming, boating, and water-skiing. Arriving at Bailey's Beach, Jackie would go through the Drexels' entrance, the same one that Jack had used as President. Some members didn't even recognize her with her hair casually slicked back into a ponytail rather than in its usual bouffant style. Her black pullover was the same shade as the frames of her large sunglasses, and she wore white tapered pants with sandals. She and friends ordered lunch from the beach club's informal self-service counter and returned to the cabana to lounge with Yusha while their children swam under the eye of nursemaids.

John, though, was a handful at that age, throwing buckets of sand on beachgoers. "Watch out," he yelled with glee as the bucket was up-ended on an unsuspecting sunbather. "Wham!" he cried as he threw sand at another. Then he shouted, "Watch me!" as he dashed down to the water.

The evening that Janet and Hughdie threw a black-tie dinner party for forty-three guests, Jackie reverted to her teased hairstyle. John was kept upstairs out of sight. Janet Jr., who was now a young lady at twenty, assisted Janet as hostess. On Labor Day the Auchinclosses gathered on the terrace behind the house to enjoy the bay views and say good-bye to summer.

The two-week visit ended in mid-September with the new school year. Although Jackie rarely breakfasted with her children, she would hug them good-bye as they left for school—John was now in full-day kindergarten—and tried to be back home when they returned. She buckled down to her year, too, which involved serious lunches at the Colony, La Caravelle, Le Pavillon, or Sign of the Dove. She saw most of Broadway's hit plays, as well as ballet, concerts, and movies. Friends were noting that her eyes had stopped filling with tears when she mentioned Jack. At school events with her children, she was as joyful as any other parent. However, she was still cautious with her memories: when a pianist at the Carlyle dining room asked her during dinner if she would mind his playing some selections from *Camelot*, she said, "Yes, I would!"

Jackie had started taking the children for fall outings into New Jersey to the barn-style ranch house she rented in Bernardsville, in the heart of hunt country. She quartered her horses and the children's ponies at a nearby estate, as her place had no stables—although it did have a four-room guest house, where Bobby would stay.

The children were preparing their Halloween costumes to trick or treat within their apartment house, as was customary in Manhattan, when Janet called from Hammersmith. The old windmill had burned down. She and Hughdie had decided to convert it into rental apartments. They thought they could charge more if their tenants could see the bay, which involved moving the windmill closer to the water.

The drill of a workman who was cutting through the steel shaft running through the windmill's center gave off the sparks that started the blaze. The mill burned fast—all was destroyed within an hour. The only thing remaining was a fifteen-foot-high hulk of broken glass and smoldering wood.

This was a difficult month for Jackie: the second anniversary of Jack's death was imminent. She retreated from the children, unable to deal with Caroline's alternating anger and lethargy, and swallowed tranquilizers in large doses. She also worried about John's hyperactivity and asked her Secret Service agents to teach him to box and wrestle.

When the day itself came, Jackie remained secluded, as she had a year earlier. Again, she sent Janet to represent her. Janet—eager to avoid gawking tourists and to ensure that Jackie's bouquet was the first one placed on the grave—arrived before the public mourners were let in. This time she came with no escort and laid white lilies on the President's grave in the chilly gray dawn. That accomplished, she placed smaller bouquets of lilies on the graves of Patrick and Arabella, who was still being called "the unnamed baby" by the world's press. Workmen preparing the President's permanent memorial twenty feet away had ceased their activity in observance of the day.

Jackie didn't get to see the rubble of the windmill until Thanksgiving, when she arrived with the children for their traditional holiday and birthday celebration at Hammersmith Farm. Janet and Hughdie had decided to rebuild the windmill at the site by the water, and Jackie helped them plan the new one: it would be fifty feet high, ten feet higher than its predecessor, with three floors and an observation deck. Jackie was still nervous about five-year-old John's fatherlessness and was continually roping in various men to acquaint him with red-blooded male activities. On this weekend, a Secret Service agent brought John to a parochial high-school football game.

Jackie had always felt great warmth for her younger sister, Janet Jr. In comparison, teenage Jamie was more quixotic and was still devastated over the loss of Jack. Jackie was very excited for her sister when Hughdie and Janet announced Janet Jr.'s engagement to Lewis Rutherfurd, whom Janet Jr. had known since she was thirteen years old. Lewis was a tall, handsome, clean-cut Princeton senior majoring in Oriental studies.

His father was Winthrop Polk Rutherfurd of Park Avenue and New Jersey. Lewis was directly descended from Peter Stuyvesant, New York's last Dutch governor, and was the stepgrandson of Lucy Page Mercer, who had a love affair with Franklin Delano Roosevelt before marrying widower Winthrop Rutherfurd in 1919 and helping raise his six children. (It was Mrs. Rutherfurd, not Eleanor Roosevelt, who was with President Roosevelt at his death in 1945, a fact hidden at the time.)

Janet Jr. was extremely well liked by social Newport. "I was quite envious when Lewis caught her," reminiscences J. Carter Brown. "She was darling, lovely," says Nuala Pell. "So ebullient."

"She's tremendously popular and she has a wingding way of acting; not stuck-up or a biddy or pompous," said a friend of the family, interviewed at the time of the engagement.

Janet had attended Sarah Lawrence College as a music history major and was to start a secretarial job at Parke-Bernet Galleries, which she canceled after her engagement. Janet and Hughdie announced her July 30 wedding in the spring at a small afternoon party at the Auchinclosses' Georgetown residence. Janet Jr. showed off her 100-year-old heirloom engagement ring: a square-cut emerald with a round diamond on each side. She was having her short-sleeved sheer organza wedding dress made by Fontana of Rome.

In May, shortly after the engagement party, three generations of women — Janet, age fifty-eight; Jackie, thirty-six; and Caroline, eight — rode to ribbons at the annual St. Bernard's School horse show. It was to be their only joint competition. The three took second place in the family class competition, in which they paraded their horses, and trotted or cantered.

Individually, Jackie took top honors in a paired jumping event riding Winchester, her bay gelding. Caroline's Macaroni won fourth place in the pony hunter-under-saddle class; in the competition, Caroline did not ride but showed Macaroni for manners and looks. The only member of the family who failed to place in any event was John.

John was not crushed, however, for riding was not his primary interest: flying was. Before he died, Jack had promised that he'd buy the boy a plane when he grew up. Now, on what would have been his forty-ninth birthday, Jackie kept that promise, albeit a little earlier than planned. She bought a 1940 World War II Piper Cub observation plane and placed it in the Kennedys' Hyannis backyard—after it was deactivated, so it could not be flown. The plane had been in private use, but she had it restored to its more exciting—to the children—olive drab with the latest Air Force insignia.

"Jack always said he was going to give John a real plane when he grew up," Jackie said. "It's a little early but now he has it—a real airplane."

With all the upcoming wedding commotion and the many houseguests arriving, Jackie decided to forgo her usual July 28 birthday celebration in Newport and instead have a party in Hyannis. She and the children left for Newport in time for the wedding rehearsal and rehearsal dinner Friday night for a hundred guests at the Clambake Club. (Hughdie and Jamie had just returned from Lewis's bachelor party in New York on Thursday night.)

The rehearsal dinner and the events of the weekend must have brought Jackie back to the day before her wedding, when Jack Bouvier—now dead nine years—was calling her to beg for an invitation.

And on Saturday there would be more memories for Jackie. Since Janet Jr. was marrying a Roman Catholic, the wedding was being held at Newport's St. Mary's Church. It was there that Jackie had married Jack in 1953, with eight-year-old Janet Jr. serving as flower girl. It must have been excruciating for Jackie to put on her sunny yellow silk two-piece dress and go back to the scene that had held so much promise only thirteen years earlier.

Janet, for her part, had been more irritated than nostalgic to learn that she would have to request special permission to hold the ceremony at four P.M. Here was another minor but annoying rule of the Catholic Church: weddings could not be held after noon without a dispensation in those pre–Vatican II days. But permission was granted in this case.

On Janet Jr.'s wedding day, a crowd of three thousand lined the streets and perched in trees surrounding the church. Besides Caroline, the flower girls included Lee's daughter, Christina, and Yusha's daughter, Maya. They wore matching long white organza dresses with blue silk sashes, and wreaths of white and blue flowers. The pages included six nephews of the bride: John, Anthony Radziwill, Cecil Auchincloss (Yusha's son), Thomas Auchincloss (Tommy's son), and Ivan and Hugh Steers, Nini's sons.

Six-year-old John was not as excited to be a page as his sister was to be a flower girl. He was dressed in Edwardian finery for the role—white linen shirt, blue linen shorts, blue satin cummerbund, long socks, and black patent-leather pumps with silver buckles—but stepped out of character when he raised clenched fists to an older boy in the crowd of onlookers who called out, "Sissy!" He was quickly rushed into the church.

Janet and Jackie arrived together, and the throng, mostly women, cried out, "There's Jackie!" Because the wedding was so late in the day, Janet felt sartorially safe adding to her pearl necklace a diamond clip that matched her crescent diamond earrings. Jackie's example of wearing French designers had led Janet to select a gown by Madame Grès. Janet was familiar with the designer through her involvement in Washington's *Alliance Française*, a group sponsored by the French embassy to maintain ties with Americans and others. Janet had promised to co-chair the group's 1968 fashion show, which would highlight the designs of Madame Grès.

The crowds surged forward, trying to touch Jackie while shouting, "There she is! She's beautiful!" but policemen—with the help of news photographers—linked arms and kept them back so that the bride's mother and sister could walk up the steps into the church.

Nuns in the convent across the street were alarmed at the spectacle and knelt in prayer. Janet Jr. arrived with Hughdie—ten minutes late because of the crowds—frightened at what she was seeing. The mob was out of control: some men tried to pick up her limousine, pressing so hard against its windows that the driver couldn't open his door. Trying to leave the car, she was swarmed by well-wishers. "I'm scared," she said to Hughdie, as above her head the awning leading to the church door swayed with the pressure put on its poles by the surging mass.

Ushers and police formed a wedge so she could enter the church. But when she heard the crowd shouting Jackie's name on her own wedding day, she burst into tears and continued crying as she walked up the steps of the church. She lost her equilibrium and was near fainting by the time she came into the shelter of the nave. The commotion delayed the start of the Mass, but as soon as Janet Jr. recovered, the service proceeded without further problems.

Afterward the bride and groom got off safely, but the crowds jammed in again and prevented Janet, Hughdie, and Jackie from leaving for another five minutes, until the police restored order. Finally, when the last guest exited the church and the police relaxed, the spectators rushed the church's entry, plucking white delphinium flowers from vases on the altar and ripping the white canopy and floor runner into bits for souvenirs.

Newport's police chief admitted that he had been unprepared for the behavior of the crowd. Jackie was the most composed of the family. "I'm used to it," she said when asked her reaction.

Five hundred friends came to Hammersmith Farm for the simple reception — not a luncheon, as for Jackie and Jack, or a more formal dinner. It was clear that Hughdie's wealth was showing its limits. Guests showed their invitations to the guard at the driveway checkpoint. More than fifteen hundred others spread out in front of the long drive and lined the low stone wall that failed to serve as a barrier. Those who began walking up the property toward the house were turned away by police.

The legitimate receiving line lasted an hour and a half. The band played Janet Jr.'s favorite songs, "You Fascinate Me So" and "On a Clear Day (You Can See Forever)," the latter melody perhaps in recognition of the concert starring Barbra Streisand that night at Newport's Festival Field. The dance floor got little use as most guests remained in line throughout the reception, which was scheduled to end at seven P.M.

John and the other young boys took full advantage of the smooth empty floor by sliding across it until they collided into one another, to their great merriment. Then they scrimmaged and, after being shooed off the dance floor, ran outside to wrestle on the grass, ending up with green stains and dirt on their linen shorts. Caroline and her little female friends maturely took turns holding a gray-and-white kitten and then stood enraptured by the ponies in the meadow directly off the rear terrace, which was covered with a white-and-green-striped marquee. It was the girls against the boys when John grabbed a stick to herd the ponies through the reception tent.

Later, the Auchinclosses would leave the reception for a black-tie dinner for sixty given by the Drexels at Stonor Lodge; most of the younger guests would proceed to Bailey's Beach for its annual summer dance. The newlyweds were to leave for Hong Kong, where Lewis had a Princeton Fellowship at Chung Chi College of the Chinese University. They would remain there as Lewis entered an import-export business.

But for now, the last of the guests were relaxing on the terrace chairs while the Black Angus steers grazed bucolically and a crisp breeze blew over the bay. The friends scanned past the roses, and beyond the double hollyhocks and blue delphinium climbing up garden arches, toward the water. Just then, as if on cue, into the bay swept the New York Yacht Club Cruise's sailing boats—ninety to a hundred single- and double-masted white sails billowing against the blue sky backdrop, repeating the blue and white colors of the flowers in the garden and of the wedding's theme. The timing made the guests drop their jaws. Janet laughed in delight: she knew the yacht club's schedule and coordinated the wedding date with it in mind.

The summer ended; school started; and soon it was Thanksgiving again at the Auchinclosses' and time to celebrate the birthdays of Caroline, nine, and John, six. Caroline's birthday fell on Sunday, so Janet accompanied Jackie and Caroline to Mass at St. Mary's. Janet began writing her Christmas cards after Jackie and the children departed, thoughtfully including a personal note in each one and enclosing photos of Janet Jr.'s wedding.

Jackie, though, was constantly agitated. She realized that she would never—or at least, not anytime soon—drop off the public's radar. She felt pounded by waves of adulation and attention every time she left the house. In particular, she was worried that her children would never know a normal childhood. She was on the lookout for those who would either exploit or spoil them.

Jackie was becoming known equally for her short skirts and her short temper. In some ways, she was developing Janet's worst controlling manner. "She always has had a funny private me-mine air," said an acquaintance at the time. Concerning the children, she could be a tiger.

Any attempt Jackie might have made to be patient with people who took advantage of her family was challenged when a New York bank auctioned the contents of a safe-deposit box that had belonged to Jack Bouvier's former English lover, the woman with whom he had twins. She, too, was dead—killed in an accident—and the twins had been killed also. Jackie declined to buy the letters that allegedly "dealt with the earthier aspects of love," according to a bank spokesman. They ultimately were sold to a private collector.

Janet was in pain, too, but no longer over Jack Bouvier. Her left arm was in a sling from having broken up a dogfight, necessitating twenty-two stitches, a tetanus shot, and antibiotics. Her niece Mimi Cecil chided her, and Janet snapped, "Well, I wasn't going to take the time to get the hose while the dogs were being injured!" Jackie merely marveled at her sixty-year-old mother when she and the children arrived at Thanksgiving for their seventh and tenth birthdays.

John was excited to see construction started for a big bridge connecting Newport to the mainland, which would end the regular ferry route across the bay. Janet and Hughdie would take its last trip, out of nostalgia. But the boom in Newport construction was what put the Auchinclosses on edge: Hughdie was awaiting word on his bid to develop thirty-three-acre Goat Island, which lay in the bay off Newport's business district.

By the second week of December, Hughdie's economic future received a fatal blow when his proposal to develop Goat Island was rejected by the Newport planners. Instead, Hilton's $8 million, five-year plan—for a convention facility and hotel (now the Doubletree Islander), marina, and a community of apartments and town houses—was accepted over Hughdie's $12.8 million proposal. Hughdie's hopes for a much-needed cash infusion were dashed. What was particularly galling was that the Hilton franchise owner was an out-of-towner, while Hughdie's partners were men whose families had built Newport—in fact, men who were responsible for the economy of Rhode Island. Names such as Nicholas Brown (Carter's father), Wiley T. Buchanan, and Frederick and Howard Cushing stood with Hughdie, although few were as financially needy as he.

Thus, 1968 began with financial worries for Janet and Hughdie. They were still maintaining a huge estate and a good-size house, and they had a large family: in addition to Jackie and Lee, there were five Auchincloss children, most of them with children of their own. The expenses were great. In fact, Hughdie, although seventy years old, still had a son in college: Jamie was an undergraduate at Columbia University.

Jackie was well out of her depression and dating a few men in earnest. She had been linked only with men people wanted to imagine her with: Lord Harlech of London, for example, and the architect Jack Warnecke, who had designed Lafayette Square facing the White House, the Kennedy memorial grave, and the Kennedy Center. Jackie even brought Warnecke back to Hammersmith Farm, in a rare gesture, to meet Janet and Hughdie.

Warnecke was charmed by Janet, and she by him. He told the writer Ed Klein, "I could never understand those people who put down Janet. They described her treating Jackie like a person whipping a horse. I never saw any of that. Janet had real sparkle, and great spirit. She liked me and I adored her."

But the relationship with Warnecke was dying down, to Janet's great disappointment, just as Jackie seemed to be seeing a little more of Ari Onassis. Jackie was spending her usual peripatetic year, traveling to Ireland with the children — John asked for a model of the Aer Lingus plane they flew on, and received it — to Rome to see the Pope, to Montreal, and to Cambodia for the ancient ruins of Angkor Wat. Of course, Newport was sandwiched in between, with visits to Hyannis as well.

For New Year's Eve 1967, however, she chose Ari Onassis. She was with him on January 3 when Janet called to say that her grandfather, Jim Lee, had died at age ninety in his home. Jackie did not cut her vacation short. Jackie and her grandfather had never been close; he had always been one of the few older men whom she could not turn into an absolute admirer.

The service for the retired lawyer, banker, and builder was held at Church of St. Vincent Ferrer in Manhattan. Jim Lee's legacy was his buildings: by the end of his career, he had put up more than two hundred residential and commercial structures throughout Manhattan.

At his death, he was the senior member of East Hampton's Maidstone Club, having been a full member since 1925. Years earlier, when his estranged wife, Margaret, died, she had been buried in the graveyard of Most Holy Trinity Church (formerly St. Philomena Church), where Janet had married Jack Bouvier. In fact, Margaret's final resting place was only a few feet from where Jack was buried.

Preferring not to spend eternity near his estranged wife or former son-in-law, he specifically stated in his will that he wanted to be buried in Westchester County's Gate of Heaven Cemetery, "beside the graves of my mother and father."

Chapter 14

FROM CAMELOT
TO CALIBAN

The spring breezes of 1968 bore no hint of the shipwreck that lay ahead of Janet's plans for Jackie. Janet disapproved of Jackie's passionate romance with Aristotle Onassis. Bobby also spurned the relationship and had asked her to cool it for the sake of his political career until the conclusion of the presidential race. In turn, Jackie promised that she'd be circumspect for Bobby's sake through summer's Democratic National Convention. She additionally agreed that if he won the nomination, she would keep her liaison with Ari undercover until the November election had passed.

Janet was pleased when Kennedy loyalties forced Jackie to abjure Ari's indulgent courting. Janet put her daughter's romance with the shipping magnate out of mind; by November's election, Janet was sure, Jackie would have come to her senses and Ari would be out of the picture. Meanwhile, Janet concentrated on something she had coveted for a long, long time.

Ever since her East Hampton days with Jack Bouvier,

when she had gotten it into her head to claim familial relationship with General in Chief of the Confederate Armies Robert E. Lee, Janet had made this Civil War leader the focus of her own personal research. Janet casually displayed several massive tomes, including *Stratford Hall: The Great House of the Lees* and *Tidewater Dynasty: A Biographical Novel of the Lees of Stratford Hall* on the deck-room coffee table in the hope that the books would evoke queries from guests. The knowledge Janet gained from her reading and research lent credibility to her remarks about her alleged ancestor. When she socialized with, say, Claiborne Pell or John R. Drexel III, who had impressive genealogies themselves, she felt she could hold her own. Luckily for Janet, the weight of their own histories meant that they had little knowledge of Confederate families, and she could successfully carry off the pretense of being "one of the *Maryland* Lees."

Janet had applied ladylike pressure to the board members of Stratford Hall Plantation, the memorial home of Lee and his illustrious ancestors, all of whom had lived at Stratford Hall at some point. Lee's forefathers included Richard Henry Lee and Francis Lightfoot Lee, both signers of the Declaration of Independence. The Confederate general himself was the son of Henry "Light Horse Harry" Lee III, who earned a congressional medal in 1778 when he captured four hundred British soldiers and lost only one of his own in a surprise attack at Paulus Hook, New Jersey.

It was crucial for Janet to establish her alleged bloodline, which, by now, she had convinced herself was genuine. Directorship on the Robert E. Lee Memorial Association board (which the members themselves referred to as the "circle") would authenticate her claim. After all, she already was a committee volunteer and, according to one director, was "a wonderful patron of the Christmas Sale."

In May a Lee memorial director representing Massachusetts corresponded with a fellow director ("fellow," although all the directors have been and currently are women, with each representing her state) and raised the possibility of Janet's nomination to the board. The director began by writing of the most pressing issue: the presence at Stratford Hall of the yellow-bellied sapsucker, an apparent menace to maple and pine trees. Happily, she reported the comforting response of her Massachusetts garden club: not to worry, as Stratford Hall does not contain much boxwood.

She continued:

*I also wanted to write you about several things to do with prospective new
Directors. . . . The immediate need is some material to send to Mrs. Hugh
D. Auchincloss (Janet Lee) with whom I talked for the second time
about serving as Rhode Island Director in Washington on May twelfth.
She seems to be really interested as they intend to be more and more in
Newport, Rhode Island. Hughdie, too, listened intently as his sister Annie
Burr Lewis was regent for Mt. Vernon for many years as was his aunt,
Miss Annie Burr Jennings. I think this tradition in his family means
something. Also, Janet's New York family, I think she feels, goes back
to the same Lee progenitor. [emphasis added]*

By early July Janet's nomination had been seconded and she was
looking forward to a unanimous vote of approval at the annual fall meeting. Her joy at the prospect of being recognized as a genuine Lee — or
so she thought — was mitigated by new worries, ones she could do little
about.

On June 5, 1968, Bobby was shot. He died early the morning of the
sixth. The Auchinclosses were traumatized, fearing that Jack's assassination less than five years earlier had signified the beginning of a trend
rather than a unique tragedy. Janet abhorred violence, and though she
had never felt warmly toward either Bobby or Ethel, she was deeply
saddened for the family — especially for Rose.

Her immediate concern, of course, was reserved for Jackie and the
children. Not only had the murder pushed Jackie into a deep depression,
but it also threw her back to the terrible dark days of her husband's
death. She wept constantly and agonized over the safety of her children,
who were themselves desolate over the sudden loss of their surrogate
father. The cataclysm stressed the already fissured structure of Jackie's
emotional foundation and that of Caroline and John.

Janet had warned Jackie not to rely too deeply on Bobby as a stand-
in for Jack; she had been as worried as the Kennedys about Jackie's
closeness to Bobby, but she had never imagined it would end in his
death. The day before his funeral Mass, Janet sadly accompanied Jackie
and the children to St. Patrick's Cathedral to pray in a pew near Bobby's
coffin.

When they returned to Hammersmith, Janet learned for the first time
that Ari Onassis and his daughter would be visiting the estate. To Janet,

it looked as though the loss of Bobby was sending Jackie back into the arms of Ari as an escape from the cacophony of her personal life, just as had happened after the loss of baby Patrick. In fact, Ari had flown out to Los Angeles to console Jackie and was shocked to find her emotions turbulent and her mind cloudy. Sometimes she talked as if it were Jack, rather than Bobby, who had just been shot. When Jackie asked Ari to visit her at Hammersmith Farm, Janet immediately knew that Jackie was renewing her interest in the Greek. Janet received the news as a personal warning that she needed to prepare herself for the worst.

Nevertheless, Janet and Hughdie welcomed any visit by Jackie and were especially looking forward to seeing John, now seven years old. Caroline, ten, was in Greece visiting the vacationing Radziwills. She had been sent away by Jackie after Bobby's funeral Mass to escape press coverage of the newest Kennedy tragedy, as Caroline was old enough to remember the international media frenzy surrounding her father's assassination. Caroline's visit would also be convenient for Jackie, who planned to spend the summer hopping among Newport, Hyannis Port, and Skorpios and could see Caroline during her trips to Greece.

Jackie and John had no sooner arrived at Hammersmith Farm than he broke out with the measles. Remembering Jackie's devotion to family in a sickroom, as exemplified by the way she had cared for Jack after his spinal surgery early in their marriage, Janet was almost pleased that John had fallen ill. It would give Jackie something other than Bobby — and Ari — to occupy her thoughts.

All of the family were looking forward to an infrequent visit from ebullient Janet Jr. and her husband, Lewis, who were expecting their first child in the winter. The journey taken from Hong Kong by the Rutherfurds sent them west across Russia via the Trans-Siberian Railroad. When the young couple finally arrived in New York, they received word from Janet to remain a few extra days until John's recovery was complete. Janet's older stepgrandchildren — the children of Yusha, Tommy, and Nini — also dashed in and out for visits over the summer. Jamie was there, too; he had just ended his second year at Columbia. He was using his college photography classes to good purpose and was recording everyone's visit with snapshots.

Jackie's despondency lifted when Ari arrived at Hammersmith Farm in late June. Even though Janet in no way approved of this relationship, especially in light of Lee's affair with Ari a decade earlier, she applauded anything that distracted Jackie and buoyed her spirits. She also was confident that Jackie would ultimately break off the romance with Ari.

In the meanwhile, Janet was determined to be polite and cordial to Ari while maintaining a cool distance.

The summer days at Newport passed fairly peaceably, with the grandchildren running off to play on their own. Social Newport is, above all, hospitable and companionable; if the grandchildren tired of one another, they had summer friends in town they could call. Their daily hurdle, though, was Janet's preemption of the telephone. She would pick up the phone after breakfast each morning to call her girlfriends, often staying on the line thirty to forty-five minutes at a time while she chatted about the previous evening's dinner party and plans for the upcoming day. Janet would no sooner end one conversation than begin another. It was impossible for the grandchildren to make dates of their own because Janet was always on the phone.

Hughdie tried to keep peace in the family by installing a separate line in the bedroom solely for Janet's use. But rather than ending the predicament, this only exacerbated it, for Janet ignored her own line in favor of the house phone — all the while forbidding the children to use her personal number! So the youngsters would sit and stew while the precious morning hours went by as they imagined their friends out romping without them. Janet was evidently oblivious to the tension caused by her disregard.

Another contentious issue for the younger generation, who all enjoyed riding, was receiving permission to ride Janet's horse. Janet still rode on a fine mount she kept at Hammersmith Farm. Naturally, all the children wanted to ride it, too.

But when the grandchildren visited, only some of the youngsters had permission to ride: Caroline and John, and Anthony and Tina. These young people were, of course, of Janet's own bloodline. Her stepgrandchildren, Hughdie's grandchildren from his first two marriages, were not allowed to ride her horse. Even the children, as young as they were, clearly saw Janet's pettiness and favoritism, and they resented being given second-rate status in what was an Auchincloss family home. It was curious: Aunt Janet gave them wonderful gifts — she was just as generous to them as to her own grandchildren — but in things that were less tangible, she could be mean-spirited. They wondered why their grandfather Hughdie, if not their own parents, didn't intercede.

The only adult they could count on was Aunt Jackie. When she saw Janet favoring Caroline over, say, Yusha's daughter, Maya, she would admonish Janet for her partiality and reverse Janet's decree. Unfortunately for the children, Aunt Jackie wasn't always around to referee.

By lunchtime, when the family arrived at Bailey's Beach each day, these tempests disappeared as quickly as the children did when they dove off the board and into the seaside pool. The splashing and shouts of other young swimmers, under the watchful eye of the lifeguards as well as the nannies and governesses who hovered on the brink of the pool, distracted everyone from the Hammersmith Farm squabbles.

On a late June weekend, a newly slim Jackie—she had dieted down from her White House size 12 to a size 6—arrived at Bailey's Beach with Ari, his sister Artemis, and daughter, Christina. Lunch was served from a hamper brought from the farm. Noted a beach member, when "everyone else showed up with their ham sandwiches, Jackie was sipping a thermos of bouillon and nibbling raw carrots," still concerned about her weight.

Ari ate heartily, though, and after lunch would march from the Auchincloss cabana down to the beach, heedless of the stares he was receiving from other members. His reputation as a fabulously wealthy fleet owner would have been enough to gain him attention. That he was foreign—and Greek at that (no matter that he had become a citizen of Argentina)—added to his exotic presence among the old-money New Englanders.

But most of the attention focused on the jarring image presented by the ill-matched couple. Jackie was a beautiful thirty-eight-year-old woman, legendary for her golden White House years, widowed from America's most handsome President. Her halo was firmly in place, for the public did not yet know about the unhappy years of the Kennedy marriage. In the glare of the beach's sunlight, next to the remembered dream and unfulfilled promise of Jack Kennedy's Camelot, appeared Ari Onassis: squat, sallow, wrinkled, and sixty-two years old.

Janet's close friend Eileen Slocum spotted Ari from her cabana. "He was the strangest sight. He had long, long arms, with short legs and a chest covered with dark hair," she said. And the oddest swim trunks that anyone on Narragansett Bay had ever seen. While the Newport men wore Bermuda-shorts-length madras trunks, Ari's were minuscule—barely covering his hirsute loins—and were tightly woven of white wool. As he moved jerkily toward the water, Slocum thought to herself, "He resembles a frog."

Ari didn't care that everyone was staring at him; he in turn was trying to figure out Jackie's social circle. "He was looking cunningly around him, as if he were asking himself, 'Who are these people?'" Slocum remembered.

As Ari waded into the water, Jackie shouted out to him, "You Mediterranean types—I hope you don't freeze in the sea!"

Beachgoers chatted about the rumors that Ari was going to purchase Annandale Farm, the Ridge Road estate, with a main house of forty-four rooms, that adjoined Hammersmith Farm. Rather than interpreting the potential purchase as proof of the burgeoning romance between Jackie and Ari, area residents insisted that it demonstrated Ari's devotion not to Jackie but to their lovely Newport. Auchincloss friends remembered that just five years earlier, Jack Kennedy had signed a rental lease on the same estate for the summer of 1964. However, they did not—or could not—bring themselves to tie Ari's interest in Annandale Farm to Jackie, who was once again casting her eye on the property.

On the last day of their visit, Janet gritted her teeth and held a luncheon at the farm for Jackie and Ari and a small group of friends. Shrewd Ari thought it was ultimately in his best interest to pretend he did not notice that Janet's legendary charm seemed forced. Instead, he turned on his own charisma and pronounced Newport "most impressive." Janet's friends were surprised at how gracious he could be. His eighteen-year-old daughter, Christina, however, made her unhappiness with the romantic atmosphere clear. She clung to her father's side and criticized anything American, which strained even Janet's party manners. Jamie was assigned to be Christina's escort, and he thought she was spoiled and completely tiresome.

When the weekend ended, Ari gave Janet a small tape recorder and some Chopin and Tchaikovsky cassettes. This impressed her, since portable recorders were not yet commonplace. Later, he sent elegant jewelry that reproduced ancient Greek designs. When he and his party returned to Greece, Jackie also left Hammersmith Farm with John. Her destination was Hyannis Port, where she joined the Kennedy family for most of the month, occasionally returning to Greece to see Ari and drop in on Caroline and the Radziwills. On July 28 Jackie chose to celebrate her thirty-ninth birthday with Rose, an implicit acknowledgment that Rose's approval of the match to Ari was key.

By the end of the summer, Jackie was off again to see Ari: this time brother-in-law Ted Kennedy also flew from Boston to join Ari on the *Christina*. When the press raised questions, a Kennedy spokesman referred to the trip as "a recuperative cruise" for both Ted and Jackie.

Jackie wanted the threesome to spend time together on the *Christina* so that Ted could get to know Ari and, if she decided to accept his marriage proposal, bless what she sensed would be a controversial union.

Now that she no longer had Bobby to shield her from Kennedy criticism, she needed the good opinions of Rose and Ted. And because her remarriage would mean losing her widow's pension, she also wanted Ted to broker a prenuptial agreement for her.

As far as her friends were concerned, there were no plans for Jackie to marry. Just as in adolescence, she had no inner circle of girlfriends in whom to confide her new romance. The only thing she communicated to them was her desolate, discouraged mood since Bobby's assassination, referring to a possible marriage to Ari by saying, "I don't even want to think about it."

Ted stopped off in London on his way home from Greece to visit the Radziwills, who were back home from their vacation. He wanted to speak with Lee about Jackie's unseemly marriage plans, hoping that Lee's influence, second only to Bobby's since Jack's death, would dissuade her. He knew that Lee had initially been envious of Ari's proposal to Jackie—Lee, after all, had spotted Ari first—and that she was discouraged after her failure as an actress in the lead role in the television drama *Laura* earlier that year. He was relying on long-standing sibling rivalry to make Lee his collaborator against the marriage.

To Ted's surprise, Lee fully supported Jackie. She didn't see why Jackie couldn't marry whomever she wanted and do as she pleased. Besides, she knew from past experience how attractive Ari could be to a woman. Ted left London without the ally he had sought.

Jackie told Janet nothing of her ulterior purpose for Ted's presence on the *Christina*. This time, Janet's opinion of any match would be a secondary consideration for Jackie. She would deal with her mother later.

At the end of September, Janet and Hughdie were back at the Georgetown house and Jackie and the children had returned to New York. By the beginning of October, both Nancy Tuckerman and Ted Kennedy's Senate spokesman were declaring to a clamoring press that no marriage was in the offing. Jackie's acquaintances chimed, "We won't let it happen."

That was Janet's solution, too. When Jackie finally admitted to her mother that she wanted the type of love and security Ari could offer—and could demonstrate in a way that few other men could—Janet was heartbroken. She had hoped that Jackie would marry someone who at least approached Jack's status as President.

Janet then became incensed. She spoke more frankly to Jackie than she had in years. "You don't have to do this, Jackie," she said. "You have a generous income and Secret Service agents to guard the children. The last thing you need to do is bring more change and chaos into John and Caroline's lives. Think of them!"

Janet also ticked off the names of some of the rich *and* attractive men who were interested in her: Lord Harlech (the former David Ormsby-Gore), for example, with whom Jackie had traveled earlier in the year on a trip to Cambodia. Although Janet didn't want to appear superficial, she was repulsed by the physical appearance of Ari Onassis. Jackie's other beaux had both class and money, even if not his staggering wealth. Janet was especially provoked when she realized that Lee was on Jackie's side. How could she have raised two such foolish daughters?

But Jackie had made up her mind. She would marry Ari. Expecting another unpleasant emotional display, Jackie waited until the last minute to let Janet know her final decision.

As the weekend of October 11 began, Janet was sanguine. Naively, Janet thought that an upcoming trip to Hyannis Port by Ari to see the Kennedys might be unsuccessful and put an end to the marriage talk.

So on Friday, Janet jauntily climbed into her Jaguar and drove from Georgetown to Farmington, Connecticut, where she visited her sister-in-law Annie Burr Lewis and her husband, Lefty. Her weekend would be a nice break before she began her first retreat as a new board member at Stratford Hall Plantation. Being elected to the board—at its fortieth annual council meeting—resonated in significance for Janet. And at the end of a busy week, she had a black-tie dinner at the French embassy: she was co-chairman of the benefit for Alliance Française.

On Sunday, October 13, Janet left Farmington and drove back to Georgetown, a good six-hour trip. She spent one night at home with Hughdie and picked up some important notes she wanted to discuss with the board. The next morning she was up early for the two-hour drive down the Potomac River, traveling nearly its full length from the nation's capital southeast to Chesapeake Bay. Janet was excited and a little jittery as she anticipated meeting her fellow board members, who were ladies of impeccable lineage from Virginia and other states, and getting to work on the five-day agenda facing her.

Arriving at Stratford Hall, she settled into one of the simple cottages provided for the retreatants. These directors' cabins were clustered in a secluded wooded area toward the eastern part of the plantation, away from the tourist parking lot, visitor center, and gift shop and a distance from the historic great house. Janet's cabin was comfortable and provided a living room and tiny kitchen, in addition to her bedroom. The dining room and council house were nearby.

Janet spent her first day observing, as she would not be formally elected to the board until Tuesday. Of course, her reputation was not unknown to the members, as she was mother of the former First Lady. Her appearance had been made more dramatic by Bobby's murder only four months earlier. Although few of the directors were Democrats — much less liberals — they had been as horrified as the rest of the nation by the shooting in Los Angeles.

That she was also the wife of Hugh D. Auchincloss carried tremendous weight because the women knew the role of Hughdie's aunt and sister at George Washington's Mount Vernon estate. Another reason for Hughdie's importance was that a significant duty of each director of this all-female board was to make a hefty financial contribution. In fact, its treasurer told Janet to open a separate savings account for her donations and those of her friends to the Lee memorial. Janet should then inform the treasurer of her bank account number so that the woman could withdraw funds as needed by Stratford Hall. Sympathetic endorsement by husbands was mandatory before most married women could take on this financial obligation.

On Tuesday morning, after her welcome to the board as Rhode Island's representative, Janet proudly reported that she had done some research over the summer at Newport's Fort Adams. She learned that Robert E. Lee had served at Fort Adams and that its officers' house was named after him. Janet said that she had found correspondence relating to his stay at Fort Adams in the army's archives and had been promised copies, which she announced she would bring to the board's next meeting in May.

Parts of this story, too, were fanciful. Lee, while a West Point cadet, had spent a summer in the 1820s studying coastal fort construction under Fort Adams's commanding office, Lt. Col. Joseph G. Totten, the foremost American military architect of his day, who became Chief Engineer of the U.S. Army. However, Lee had never been stationed at the fort, nor had it ever named a building after the Confederate general — not surprisingly, as it was still under federal supervision.

These facts were unknown to the directors, though, and in their minds the information Janet brought immediately established her value on the board, for how many of these directors could commandeer army archive documents as readily as the former First Lady's mother?

But Janet's concentration on board matters was shattered on Wednesday by a phone call from Jackie in New York. Ted had just informed her that the *Boston Herald Traveler* would break the story of her engagement to Ari the next day. Because the news was going to become public, Jackie said that she wanted to marry Ari as soon as possible. Janet was distraught. Nothing she could say would dissuade Jackie from her impulsive decision.

Jackie's incoming calls kept increasing throughout the day, interrupting Janet in the council house and the dining room. Janet was embarrassed by these intrusions, both because she was supposed to be concentrating on important committee work and because she hardly wanted to announce to her new circle that her eldest daughter would be marrying this vulgar Greek.

Angrily, she reminded her daughter of her own obligation to the board and told Jackie that she would not shirk her duty merely because Jackie had gotten it in her head that she wanted to marry Ari right away. Janet snapped that Jackie knew how strongly she opposed the marriage; if Jackie wanted to go ahead with it, she could do it alone.

Fatigued from the emotional entanglement, and embarrassed by the questioning looks she was receiving from the other directors each time she was called to the phone—by now, they had heard the marriage rumors—Janet phoned Hughdie in Washington.

"You speak to her," she commanded her husband. "I don't care what it takes, but talk her out of this marriage!"

Hughdie hated to become snared in the mother-daughter argument; in fact, he typically retreated as far away and as fast from emotional scenes and high drama as he could. He had no choice this time, as Janet was insistent. Actually, when it came down to it, Hughdie felt that Jackie was making an awful mistake. The thought of Ari Onassis as Jackie's husband was disconcerting and unseemly.

Jackie's phone rang in her Fifth Avenue apartment on Wednesday night. It was Hughdie.

"You know, Jackie, Mummy and I don't feel that you have really thought this thing with Ari through."

"Oh, Uncle Hughdie," Jackie sighed, "I've made up my mind."

She told him how much his good wishes meant to her and reminded him of his comforting her on that awful night following Jack's murder when he slept next to her on Jack's White House bed. She pointed out that in a month, she would have to bear the fifth anniversary of Jack's assassination. She also brought up the fact that January, two months ahead, would have been the date that Jack ended a two-term presidency. How poignant it was for Hughdie to hear Jackie talk about her dashed plans to return with Jack to private life in Boston to raise their children.

Poor Hughdie felt trapped by her sadness. Out of loyalty to Janet, and because he, too, felt the marriage would be a disaster, he said everything he could to dissuade Jackie. He pointed out the reasons against a marriage by the former First Lady to a womanizing shipowner who was not only a foreign citizen but also once had been under indictment by the U.S. government. He reminded her that she was the widow of a president and said she owed it to Jack to maintain her dignity.

He brought up the twenty-four-year age difference between her and Ari, which made Jackie snicker. She noted that her own father had been sixteen years older than Janet when they married and that Hughdie himself was ten years Janet's senior. "Uncle Hughdie," she said in bemusement, "now I am sure that you are looking for reasons to be against this marriage."

Next, Hughdie brought up the issue of religion, and at this theme, too, Jackie scoffed. Her children would remain Roman Catholic, as would she. When Hughdie raised the topic of children who might be born of the marriage, she sighed exasperatedly. "You and Mummy are different religions; has that been a problem to Janet Jr. or Jamie?"

At that point, Hughdie played his trump card. He brought up her children: Hadn't they gone through enough change and stress in the past five years? Was she going to subject them to a marriage that would bring them into an entirely different culture? And lastly, he reminded her of how badly Ari's adult children, Christina and twenty-year-old Alexander, had turned out, recalling Christina's disagreeable attitude during her weekend at Hammersmith Farm. He added, "Both Mummy and I want you to raise John and Caroline as Americans, with the values you and Jack would want for them, and not as spoiled Greek heirs."

As a matter of fact, in Greece Ari was having his own problems explaining the marriage to his children, neither of whom liked Jackie and who referred to her behind her back as "the widow." In order to coerce Alexander into attending the planned ceremony, Ari struck a bargain. He told his son that he promised to stop his relentless criticism of Alexander's piloting his own plane and would never say another word about it again if only Alexander would show up at the wedding. Alexander agreed to the deal.

Back in the United States, Hughdie, after a full hour and a half of going back and forth with his stepdaughter, was exhausted. His breathing, which was never deep because of his emphysema, was by now extremely fast and shallow. But he had one last duty to perform. He had to call Janet, who was waiting to hear from him in her cabin at Stratford Hall, and break the news: Jackie wouldn't be dissuaded—she was going to marry Ari within a few days.

Janet flushed with anger as Hughdie talked to her: at Jackie, for her rashness, and at Hughdie, for being unable to deter her. She was also irritated at Rose and Ted Kennedy, for Jackie had told Hughdie that they had given tacit approval to the union.

Janet called Jackie. "Fine," she told her. "Go ahead and marry Ari. Since you know how Uncle Hughdie and I feel, you can go to Greece by yourself."

Jackie begged and wheedled. She told Janet that she needed her by her side, recounting how awful things had been for her since June. She also wanted Janet alongside because she could hardly let the Kennedys know that her own mother wouldn't attend the ceremony. Jackie won the argument by standing on propriety: "Mummy, what will people say when they don't see you there?" That shot hit home.

Janet pursed her lips as she hung up the phone and went to tell the board president that she would have to leave Stratford the next morning because of a family emergency. Seeing Janet so shaken, the woman told her not to worry about missing the last two days of the council meeting; the important thing was that the circle members had met Janet and were looking forward to working with her in the years to come.

The next morning, while Janet was zooming down Virginia's country roads toward Georgetown, Hughdie's driver was helping him out of his car and into his office. Hughdie slowly walked up the sidewalk and entered the building, pausing in the company's outer room to grasp a chair while he caught his breath. When he had recovered, and entered his own office beyond, he called to his longtime secretary, "Margaret, do you have my passport?"

"Of course," she said, and gave him a quizzical look. Margaret Kearney went to the company safe and removed it. She handed it to Hughdie.

In response to her puzzled look, he sighed. "We're going to Greece. Jackie has decided to marry Ari Onassis. We spoke for an hour and a half last night, but I couldn't talk her out of it."

Kearney shook her head as Hughdie told her of some of the conversation. Soon after, he let her know that he was returning home to pack for the trip and await Janet's arrival. Before he left the office, he called the house and asked Janet's secretary to respond to press calls by saying that Mrs. Auchincloss knew nothing of Mrs. Kennedy's plans.

Midmorning, Janet pulled onto O Street and parked on the street, leaving the car running for the butler to bring into the garage. First she sat at her desk and wrote a note of apology for missing the Alliance Française benefit at the French embassy that she was to have co-chaired that weekend. Then she ran upstairs to organize her clothes for packing. Janet could not find her passport, so there was more commotion as the couple called Jackie to ask if Nancy Tuckerman could expedite a new one. By now it was past noon, but the combination of Tuckerman know-how and Kennedy power resulted in a two o'clock call from the passport office with the news that Janet's passport was ready. The Auchinclosses' driver went downtown to pick up the passport.

Between packing and fielding calls from friends who hadn't talked to her since she had left for Farmington—could it have been just one week ago?—but had heard the news-wire story, Janet was on the phone with Tuckerman working on the wording of the wedding announcement. Everyone agreed that there had been too many leaks and that it was better to make a statement. The expected date for the wedding was in a week, on Thursday, October 24, but the brief statement made by Tuckerman said only, "Mrs. Hugh D. Auchincloss has asked me to tell you that her daughter, Mrs. John F. Kennedy, is planning to marry Mr. Aristotle Onassis sometime next week. No place or date has been set for the moment."

Privately, Janet was incensed. She called Jamie at Columbia and ranted, "She's finally getting back at me for divorcing her father. That's what she's doing. I just know it."

Nevertheless, by late afternoon Janet and Hughdie had caught a flight to New York from Washington's National Airport. At six P.M. Jackie left her building with the children, four Secret Service agents, two maids, and a lot of luggage.

The doorman told a reporter confidentially, "They won't be back."

Waiting for Jackie at New York's Kennedy International Airport were the Auchinclosses, Jean Smith, Pat Lawford, and her daughter Sydney, who was a close friend of Caroline's. Also at the airport, ninety passengers were dismayed to be bumped from their Olympic Airways jetliner to a later flight. The plane was rescheduled as a charter for the eleven people in Jackie's party. Actually, canny Ari hadn't wanted Jackie to be criticized for taking precedence over everyday passengers.

Upon hearing that Frank Sinatra's jet was sitting at the airport, with no flight planned for the near future, Ari tried unsuccessfully to track him down to borrow the plane. After the Olympic jet had taken off, a newsman found Sinatra and got his reaction.

"The plane had been sitting there for four days," Sinatra said. "He could have had it in a minute."

Jackie had no idea that Ari was trying to find another plane. Her comment, ironically, was that finally she would be married to a man who didn't care about public opinion.

Ari was also busy making plans for the wedding. Because it was to be a Greek Orthodox ceremony, he needed to find a priest. He assigned this delicate task to the chairman of Olympic Airways and told him to find a priest "who understands English and doesn't look like Rasputin."

Just before the plane landed at a military airport in the Peloponnesian peninsula of Greece, the three hundred waiting members of the press received their own Greek welcome: their cameras were confiscated and they were locked in a waiting room while Jackie and her party exited the plane. Jackie stepped into bright sunlight to greet Ari and let the children stretch their legs by dashing around the airfield. Then the wedding party reboarded another plane and flew off with Ari to Préveza, where helicopters ferried them to Skorpios. And the reporters were released.

On Friday and Saturday the wedding party ate and lazed in the sun, occasionally swimming or motorboating. By Saturday night Lee and Stas had arrived from London, as well as a number of Ari's relatives and business friends. Whenever Janet could catch Jackie alone, she would buttonhole her: "Don't go through with this. Tell him you've changed your mind. It's not right for the children." And so on. Jackie would smile enigmatically and walk away.

Sunday became the day of the wedding, which would be held in the forty-seat chapel on Skorpios. Hughdie was to give Jackie in marriage, just as he had done fifteen years earlier, and as he had done for Lee and Nini. He wasn't nervous—this wouldn't involve public speaking, thank heavens—and he thought only briefly about his upcoming duties.

But Janet made plans. As she dressed for the wedding, she knew what she had to do just as surely as she had known before Jackie's first wedding. She was as positive of her actions now as she had been then.

At the same time as the bride's mother and stepfather were dressing for the ceremony, Jackie's Secret Service agent was putting on his suit and tie. This would be the last occasion at which he would guard the former First Lady. He mulled over a thought, then turned back to his luggage to take out a tie clip that was a memento from another year, and he pinned it on. It said *PT 109.*

The bride and wedding party left the *Christina* on a jaunt that headed for Skorpios. Jackie was wearing a Valentino beige-cream chiffon dress with long sleeves and a hem falling just below the knee. Stepping off the boat, she and the rest of her family dashed through a light rain toward the chapel, Jackie holding Caroline's hand as they ran through the mist. John walked alone, with his head down.

Ari's guests, including his daughter, Christina, were already settled in the chapel. Ari scanned the room, looking worried, until he spotted Alexander squeezing through the door, the last of twenty-one guests to enter. Then Ari relaxed.

Just then Jackie walked into the chapel. She dropped Caroline's hand as Hughdie stepped up to join her.

Janet also moved up in front of Caroline and John and advanced as close behind Jackie's back as she could maneuver, according to her later recounting to Eileen Slocum. As Jackie and Hughdie began their march up the nave, Janet stayed practically glued to Jackie's back.

Janet told Slocum that she saw this as her very last opportunity to influence Jackie. Walking so close behind Jackie as she could — so close that her chin was nearly touching Jackie's earlobe — Janet began to whisper in Jackie's ear in an urgent, yet hypnotic tone, "It's not too late. You don't have to do this."

She repeated, over and over, her frantic whispers as Jackie and Hughdie walked toward the altar. "Jackie, you don't have to go through with this. It's not too late to stop. You don't have to do this. You can change your mind. We can leave. It's not too late. . . ."

Jackie ignored Janet completely and never looked back at her mother.

At the front, Jackie separated from Hughdie and turned toward Ari. The couple joined hands. Hughdie gave a wan smile to Janet, and she took his arm as they walked to their pew. Dejected, Janet sat down and watched the priest begin the ceremony. Her worst fears had just been realized.

Chapter 15

LOSING
CONTROL

Vituperation and contempt rained down on Jackie from all over the world. The only exception was the nation of Greece. These citizens — save for Christina and her brother, Alexander, who was caught by the press weeping in his Jeep after the wedding ceremony — thought Jackie's marriage to Ari was a fine idea.

Hughdie was welcomed back to the office by his secretary, who had read in the Washington papers about the ruby-and-diamond jewelry given to Jackie and her mother. He slipped a long red velvet case from an inside pocket. "Margaret, come here. I want to show you something," he said.

Kearney remembers: "I went over to his desk, and it was a beautiful heavy gold chain with a gold medal at the end of it. It was a key ring."

Hughdie explained, "This was a gift from Mr. Onassis to me. But it doesn't fit American keys." They both laughed when Kearney suggested, "Send it back to Mr. Onassis, and tell him it doesn't fit your keys!"

Although Janet was not laughing, she would not publicly join the critics, either. She was very sympathetic to her grandchildren, however, and when reporters asked about them, she replied, "It's been hard on them. Hard and confusing."

She had done her best to dissuade her daughter; her arguments had not worked. Now Janet hoped for the best and presented a unified front to the media, whose scathing criticism of Jackie she thought far too heavy-handed. To friends, she admitted, "Of course, it wasn't the marriage I wanted for my daughter. He's hardly the type of man I hoped she'd remarry, but there wasn't anything I could do about it. Believe me, I tried."

Janet confided in Eileen Slocum, "I wanted Jackie to marry an American hero—a general or a statesman." To Bunny Mellon she complained, "She's finally getting back at me for divorcing her father." Mellon tried to console her: "Dear Janet, you haven't lost a daughter—you've gained a gold mine."

One columnist announced that the only thing that would draw attention away from Jackie's marriage would be President Lyndon B. Johnson's declaring peace in Vietnam.

Not even the clergy were immune from attacks; the elderly Cardinal Cushing had stoked indignation at the religious irregularities of the match by rhetorically asking, "Why can't Mrs. Kennedy marry whomever she wants to marry?" Soon he was announcing his resignation: "I've had it," he said, referring to letters written to him "in the language of the gutter." He educated Catholics and non-Catholics alike by announcing that his sister had married a Jew and that they "lived together in perfect peace and harmony for over 30 years. Her husband went to the synagogue and my sister went to the Catholic Church." The Jackie-Ari-Cushing fracas ended up as the topic for a full day's "Dear Abby" column.

A few reporters sympathized with Jackie's desire to exchange her image—part widow, part martyr, part saint—for the life of a whole woman. Jackie, after all, had decided to get on with her life. She said, perhaps prematurely, "I just couldn't live anymore as the Kennedy widow. It [the marriage] was a release, freedom from the oppressive obsession the world had with me."

Janet did not agree that the marriage freed Caroline and John, no matter how liberating it might feel to Jackie. She thought her grandchildren had too little stability in their lives and that it was wrong for the offspring of a U.S. President to have an imperious Greek tycoon for a stepfather. When she herself had remarried, Janet thought, she provided her daughters with a stepfather of finer character than their own father's, not worse. However, she understood why Jackie craved Ari's wealth to protect Caroline and John after Bobby's murder.

Janet had other reasons to worry about Caroline and John as well. After all, she and Hughdie often sheltered them while Jackie reshaped her life. Ever since Miss Shaw had retired several years earlier, the children had bounced from one young au pair to another. None of them provided the consistency or stability that the children needed, thought Janet, wondering why Jackie didn't notice.

The night the families flew to Greece, for example, Jackie had left Caroline and John at the hotel with their au pair and their Auchincloss grandparents. The Radziwills, down the hall, popped into the Auchincloss suite to say that their children, Tony and Tina, were getting on their nerves. (Tony and John were not so tired from the long trip that they couldn't wrestle in the hallway.) So Lee and Stas, too, left their children with the Auchinclosses at the hotel and went to stay elsewhere. Now the Auchinclosses had four excited children on their hands, and two young nannies. Janet had to take charge once again.

The Auchinclosses handled the situation gracefully. Still, despite Janet's organizational skills and love for her grandchildren, it seemed unfair to ask Hughdie, who was seventy-one and had chronic respiratory problems, and Janet, sixty-one, to fly to Greece on a moment's notice and blithely shoulder the additional burden of four young children.

And yet she was used to it. At Hammersmith the grandchildren visited without their parents and would be accompanied by as many as four sets of nannies. When Nini's son was hospitalized with a mastoid infection, Janet took turns sitting up with the child during the night. In some ways, her children and Hughdie's took advantage of her willingness to do whatever was needed.

After the ceremony, while Jackie was on her honeymoon, the Radziwills returned to London and the Auchinclosses flew back to New York with Caroline and John. The couple made an unusual fuss—for them—when they were seated separately from the children; Janet insisted that she at least be near them for the long trip home. To the press, though, she fully credited the children: "The children were all wonderful. They never fussed. They were such good sports."

While Hughdie and the grandchildren dozed, Janet put together a plan. When Jackie was First Lady, Janet had befriended the governess to a French diplomatic family. Marta Sgubin spoke French as if it were her first language along with Italian, her actual native tongue. As for her English, what it lacked in structure it more than made up for in charm. She also knew some Spanish, Portuguese, and Greek. The woman had more than a decade of child-care experience, a playful personality, and excellent training. She was just what Janet wanted for her grandchildren.

"She adored her grandchildren," Sgubin remembers of Janet. "She was raised by a governess who worked for the family for a lifetime. She gave her own children this stability. After Miss Shaw left, Madame [Jackie] would get only au pair girls. They stayed only a year. It bothered Mrs. Auchincloss. She wanted someone who would stay for years."

Janet and Jackie had been arguing about the nanny situation for several years. Janet knew that her suggestions were unwelcome—she recognized that Jackie thought she was too controlling—but right now, nothing was more important to her than proper care for Caroline and John. Even though Janet couldn't do anything about the decisions Jackie was making for herself, she could try to keep Jackie's benign neglect from affecting Caroline and John. Janet also suspected that the new marriage would leave Jackie more distracted than ever.

Janet and Sgubin had met a few years earlier when they joined La Marotte, a Washington, D.C., group that presented French plays, to polish their French. Janet's admirable American penchant for self-improvement meant that she thought well of those who were similarly motivated. The women hit it off. Janet asked Sgubin to consider working for Jackie, but the governess refused; she was very satisfied with her current position.

Janet wouldn't give up. "She had her eye on me," Sgubin remembers.

Janet again spoke frankly to Jackie, telling her that the children needed someone stable and that she would find the right person. Janet would not let the issue drop; she was steel-willed. Her grandchildren— the President's children—may have been living in a confusing and even cruel world, but they would have all the psychological security Janet could provide.

In Paris, half a year after the Skorpios wedding, Ari Onassis asked to see Marta Sgubin. They talked for two hours and got along well. Jackie realized that Janet's criticism of her revolving-door staff was not going to end until she took measures. So with Ari and Janet decided, Jackie met with Sgubin for an hour and hired her. The decision would prove crucial to the development of the Kennedy offspring America would come to admire so much. Jackie could not know it, but hiring Sgubin was one of the best decisions she would ever make — helped along by Janet.

In fact, the children, who were eleven and eight, were introduced to Sgubin not by Jackie but by the Auchinclosses at Hammersmith Farm. Jackie was in Greece. And Sgubin loved Hammersmith as much as the children did. Janet and Hughdie had everything for the children: carriages with ponies, their own bicycles, even a pet cemetery, with little tombstones, near the windmill. "Hammersmith Farm was very family," Sgubin remembers.

Of course, inside the house, "everything was how Mrs. Auchincloss wanted it. She was very kind but very strict: never rude — that was part of her upbringing."

Before Sgubin arrived at Newport, Jackie had told the children that their new governess spoke only French. Janet went along with the deception; if anyone thought linguistic ability was important, it was she. When John was older, he wrote, "Marta broke down and started speaking English after about 24 hours." So most of the French conversation ended up being among Sgubin, Janet, and Jackie.

Sgubin enjoyed speaking French with Janet. "Mrs. Auchincloss was more fluent, smoother, easier," she remembers. "She spoke it beautifully. Jackie was very good, but Janet Auchincloss was best."

Rose Kennedy? "She didn't know the grammar and needed to look in books." In fact, on one visit Sgubin hid in the closet rather than have to practice French with Rose. "Mrs. Kennedy was very demanding, and I had the children to look after," she explains.

After their weeks at Hammersmith, it was time to start school. Gratuitous remarks from Vatican City calling Jackie "a public sinner" over her marriage to Ari had curdled her relationship with the Church. Now she had a better understanding of Janet's bruised feelings. She transferred John to Collegiate School for Boys, ending his stint in Catholic schools. Sgubin accompanied him on his first day and was introduced to the perils of working for Jackie Onassis when she saw her photograph with John on the front page of the *Daily News*.

It was a glamorous existence for the still-young Sgubin. Games and homework during the week, yachts and sun every weekend. Ari kept his yacht in the Caribbean during the winter; when Friday's half day ended, Jackie, the children, and Sgubin would be on an Olympic flight south to pick up the yacht and spend the weekend in the sun. Then, Sunday night, back to New York, homework, and school.

Yes, it was a dazzling time. But exposure to bright light carries its own risks. Janet spoke to her friends with a resigned sadness, mystified as to why her two eldest children—compared with her two youngest, who led "perfectly normal and quite private lives"—were always in the spotlight. She never recognized that both Jackie and Lee were drawn to the popping flashbulbs they affected to shun.

While her daughters were focusing on their place in the world, Janet's friends gently argued about her expectations. At this point in Jackie's life, they asked, could Janet really expect her to marry a man who wanted someone to make him breakfast every morning?

"But that's just it," Janet said. "Jackie is that kind of person. She loves to do that sort of thing."

A month after Jackie's marriage, Janet attended a fund-raiser for the John F. Kennedy Center for the Performing Arts because she remained committed to the building's construction. Unfortunately, the event chosen was the world premiere of the movie *The Shoes of the Fisherman*. It starred Anthony Quinn, who had also played the lead in *Zorba the Greek*, and was about the papacy. Greeks and Catholics were certainly in the news that season, Janet mused.

She had duties, too, across the river at Arlington National Cemetery. Janet, bundled in tweeds to protect her from the early-morning cold, made her annual trip to the grave site at Jackie's request. She hurried through the back gate and laid her flowers—jasmine, this year—on the President's grave, the babies' graves, and Bobby's grave. So many lost; so much grief, particularly since this was the first anniversary of Jack's death following Bobby's assassination. Ethel couldn't come to the cemetery herself: she was hospitalized, awaiting the birth of her last child.

In Manhattan that day Jackie attended a Mass commemorating what was now the fifth anniversary of Jack's assassination. She did not take Communion—her marriage outside the Church barred her from this sacrament, last rites, and burial in a Catholic cemetery. When Ari arrived from Europe, he joined Jackie and the children in her New Jersey country home, the first time in many years that the family was not at Hammersmith with the Auchinclosses to celebrate Thanksgiving and the children's birthdays. It was also the first time ever that Janet had not seen Caroline and John on their birthdays; uncertain as to how Janet would act around Ari, Jackie decided to celebrate without her.

It was perhaps for the best. Hughdie was ill. The mad dash to Skorpios the month before and its accompanying stress had worn him down. His breathing was becoming more labored, and his bad lungs were weaker with the passage of time.

Janet was there when Jackie needed her; now it was Janet's turn to be supported. Hughdie's physicians had recommended that he undergo treatment at St. Barnabas Medical Center hospital in Livingston, New Jersey. The hospital specialized in lung disorders and had the country's largest hyperbaric oxygen chamber. Just one month earlier Senator Everett Dirksen of Illinois had been treated in the room-size high-pressure unit.

Under the guise of accompanying a friend — tobacco heir Louis Reynolds, who wanted to build a similar chamber near his home in Richmond, Virginia — Jackie and Ari checked out the hospital for Janet. Hospital administrators were thrilled by the celebrity visit and supplied oxygen for Jackie and Ari to quaff like eggnog on Christmas Day. The ruse worked: no one linked Jackie's trip to Hughdie's declining health.

The day before Hughdie was to start treatment, Jackie took an 11:30 A.M. shuttle from New York's La Guardia Airport to Washington's National Airport. The plan was for her to be with her mother and stepfather in case they needed assistance but, at the same time, keep a low profile. Hughdie did not want his illness plastered across the papers. After landing, accompanied by a Pinkerton guard — her marriage automatically ended her Secret Service protection — Jackie went to Georgetown Medical Center to visit Ethel, who had just given birth to her eleventh child, Rory Kennedy, five months after Bobby's assassination. Then she drove to Arlington National Cemetery and stopped briefly for prayers at the graves. She returned to the airport and scanned a newspaper until the one-thirty plane for Newark was announced. When she boarded, Janet and Hughdie had been seated.

When they landed, a car took them to the hospital. Hughdie had a great deal weighing on him: not just Janet's high emotions over Jackie's marriage and the state of the grandchildren but problems of his own besides the health issue. Hughdie had decided to close one of the branch offices of Auchincloss, Parker & Redpath, which was terribly difficult for him — he had never fired staff wholesale before. The company spokesman announced, "The firm has no problems from a capital point of view." But Hughdie knew the truth firsthand.

Jackie was angry at the charges that she married Ari for money. "It's a lie, a complete lie. I don't have any money," she told her friend Truman Capote. "When I married Ari, my income from the Kennedy estate stopped, and so did my widow's pension from the U.S. government. I didn't make any premarital financial agreement with Ari. I couldn't do it. I didn't want to barter myself."

In fact, Jackie did receive a gift of $2 million from Ari ($10 million today) and a $30,000 monthly allowance, which she couldn't live on. People were soon reading about her manic shopping trips: 220 pairs of shoes at a time, for example, or the ninety-seven packages delivered to her apartment building in one day. Ari cut her allowance to a pittance of $20,000 a month.

Then an explosive best-seller written by Mary Barelli Gallagher hit the bookstands. The author divulged the inside story of working at the White House. She wrote of Jackie spending $40,000 a year on her clothes while asking the White House staff to refill old drinks and serve them to guests as fresh. She explained the push-pull relationship between Janet (whom she deeply admired) and Jackie—how sometimes Jackie sought her mother out, other times remaining distant and cool.

Particularly surprising to those who thought the Kennedys were in the forefront of workers' rights was the poor pay their staff received for nonstop long hours. Gallagher described the penurious way they were treated—especially the women—by the men who controlled their salaries. "When I look back on it," Gallagher says, "I know Jackie took advantage of me and then cut me out of her life when it was convenient for her."

What she wrote was true, of course, and could have as easily been written by those who worked for Auchincloss, Parker & Redpath. Margaret Kearney, for example, worked as Hughdie's personal secretary for twenty-two years. Yet, by 1975 she was only making $4,500 annually ($21,000 today). Hughdie took home $100,000 ($500,000 today).

"They never thought to give us a raise," she says. "They forgot that other people have to work for a living. Nor were the household staff paid the going fees. And you never got a Christmas bonus like at the other firms." Kearney assumed that some of the other partners took care of their secretaries privately, but Hughdie never paid her a penny above her salary. She stayed at the firm because of her deep respect for Hughdie, but it was sometimes difficult for her to write out checks for the family's many luxuries when she knew that if it weren't for her engineer husband, she couldn't support herself, much less any dependents, on her income.

The staff saw the Auchinclosses taking care of themselves and not others. Mr. Quinn, who prepared everyone's tax returns, once took Kearney aside and showed her Janet and Hughdie's deductions for charity. She remembers that he asked her, "Can you believe how little these people give?"

Despite the tight purse, Hammersmith had financial problems, too. Neither the personal-property insurance of the Auchinclosses nor the construction company that had set fire to their historic windmill would pay the cost of rebuilding it. The Auchinclosses had no choice but to sue the construction company. Hughdie's lawyers argued that the windmill was part of the Auchincloss family heritage: it was depicted on Hammersmith's gates, mentioned in numerous publications, and replicated in paintings. The windmill also served as a navigational aid to sailors and was even included on their charts.

Janet and Hughdie lost their suit because they were unable to show "acceptable evidence" of the windmill's value, as real-estate agents could not point to any recent sales of historic windmills. The Rhode Island Supreme Court awarded only $1,212 to the Auchinclosses. The amount represented the money already spent preparing the windmill for relocation and cleaning up the burned rubble. The couple had spent $30,000 ($150,000 today) of their own money to construct the new windmill/ guest house that they envisioned.

Then Auchincloss, Parker & Redpath, already on unstable ground, began to feel the tremors of the Nixon recession. By late 1969 it was bleeding red. In addition, "One of [Hughdie's] partner's was rather grand and took a lease on a large building," says Jock Nash, Hughdie's great-nephew. "Hughdie had to bail him out." He used his own personal fortune—what was left of it—to shore up the company, cashed in his insurance policies, and sold his securities one by one. It was a desperate attempt to save the firm and an honorable gesture to protect his employees. "I was very proud of him for doing it, even though I knew it wouldn't work," said Janet, although his actions left her financial future at risk.

But the infusion would not be enough. The company's antiquated record keeping caused tremendous backlogs, which resulted in an SEC citation. The firm was forced to merge with Thomson & McKinnon, Inc. The reconstructed firm operated under the name Thomson & McKinnon,

Auchincloss. Roger Stevens wrote Janet in November 1970, saying op-
timistically, "Give my best to Hughdie and tell him that I hope all his
problems have been solved by now."

Now Hughdie needed to spend more time in the New York offices,
and Janet often went with him. She could visit Yusha and his children
(who were living with their mother), Tommy and his two children, and
Jamie, an undergraduate at Columbia University working for Mayor
John Lindsay. Janet saw Caroline and John primarily at Hammersmith
Farm or at Jackie's apartment. During Jackie and Ari's seven-year marriage, Janet and Hughdie never visited the couple in Greece or traveled
on his yacht, although Ari accepted their invitations to Hammersmith.

Janet's rigidity about certain behavior, and her temper, made relations with relatives bumpy. Yusha, for example, was going to run
Tommy's children home from Newport to New York one Sunday afternoon. In the late morning he went out for a sail with the Grosvenors;
the wind turned, and he didn't get back to Hammersmith until about
five. He called Tommy immediately and told him what happened. "Fine,"
Tommy said. "Take your time, stop for dinner, and I'll see you when
you get here."

But Janet wouldn't be appeased. Yusha was *late*. He tried to explain
what had happened; there was nothing he could have done about the
breeze. "She was furious and yelled at me in front of Manny [Manuel
Faria, the estate superintendent]," Yusha says. Manny, of course, was
embarrassed to witness a family argument.

Yusha was angry. Before leaving for New York, he told Hughdie that
he was going to write Janet a letter. "I wrote her and told her that she
should never treat me that way again on Hammersmith's property. I said
I would not put up with it and that it was not necessary on her part to
behave the way she did."

About a week later Yusha asked Janet if she had received his letter.
"You made a good point," she said.

Yusha remembers, "It was the last time she spoke to me like that."

But it was frustrating because "Jackie and I were the only ones
who would speak up to her" when she lost her temper. "Lee wouldn't,"
he says.

Neither would Hughdie. One time his sister Esther Biltz complained
to Margaret Kearney about his placid temperament: "I wish he would
pick up an inkwell and throw it," said Esther.

Janet resented that several of Hughdie's grandchildren were named
for him but none of them for her. Yusha's daughter, Maya, had the same

name as his mother—Hughdie's first wife—and Janet couldn't tolerate
saying "Maya," for that reason. She referred to young Maya—Hughdie's
own granddaughter—as "that little girl" in a scornful tone. Jackie put
an end to that, speaking sharply to Janet. She had gone too far even for
Hughdie, who agreed with Jackie.

Janet's exacting ways made her everyone's critic. Jamie was a real
free spirit and, as her only son, was usually able to escape her faultfind-
ing. Once, though, he drove eight hours from Washington to Newport,
only to have Janet greet him with "Why do you look like that?" and
yell at him for sloppy attire.

Jamie got back in his car and drove another eight hours right back
home.

Janet didn't understand that her youngest child was bound to be
affected by his baby-boom generation. When he was in college, he let
his hair grow long just like the other young men at Columbia. On a visit
to Georgetown, he stopped by Hughdie's office to say hello.

Margaret Kearney said in a joking tone of voice, "Jamie! Go out and
get a haircut. You're too good-looking to let yourself go." He took her
words good-naturedly—which is how they were meant—and got a trim.
Janet called the next day to thank her.

Soon after the merger with McKinnon, Janet and Hughdie bought
five side acres from Annandale Farm. The estate had new owners, who
were going to tear down the old house and erect a new mansion. The
Auchinclosses thought they should buy land to buffer Hammersmith
from whatever would be built. They paid $50,000 ($220,000 today) for
the land and the stable on it. The new Annandale owners had paid
$25,000 per acre for land fronting the bay, the highest per-acre price for
a large parcel in Newport since the boom years of 1885.

At least it was still possible for the Auchinclosses to purchase the
extra acreage. The merger with McKinnon brought temporary financial
relief, but the more important equity transfusion came from James T.
Lee. His estate was settled for a gross of $11.6 million. Unfortunately,
only $3.2 million went to his heirs—the executor took $770,000; New
York state took $1.6 million; and the federal government, $5.5 million.
Janet complained to Margaret Kearney that her father had not been
wise in setting up his estate to avoid inheritance taxes.

Janet and her surviving sister, Winifred, inherited about $1.6 million
each ($8 million today). In addition, Winnie had summered in East
Hampton, so their father left her his house on Lily Pond Lane as well
as his Maidstone Club cabana.

About $500,000 was funneled to Jim Lee's nieces and grandchildren. He had also made generous donations to charity, especially Catholic schools and cancer foundations, before he died. In fact, his family used to joke that he was "buying his way into heaven."

He had also set up the James T. Lee Foundation, Inc., viable today, funding it with about $1.5 million. In 2000 the foundation had some $7 million in investments, and its board awards grants to New York–area charities, focusing on health care and social welfare. Some of its forty to fifty annual beneficiaries include Ronald McDonald Houses and the Long Island Hospital, Catholic and Jewish charities, and the Clown Care Unit of Big Apple Circus, which visits pediatric hospitals.

What Janet did not mention to Margaret Kearney was the generosity of her father to all the grandchildren but Jackie and Lee. Jim Lee set up trusts for "the children of Janet Lee Auchincloss" and proceeded to name them: Janet Jr. and Jamie Auchincloss. Jackie and Lee were totally ignored. Yet Marion's children received $50,000 each ($250,000 today) and Winnie's children were given smaller amounts. The trusts— rather than outright cash—for Janet Jr. and Jamie made sense because they were by far the youngest grandchildren. Similarly, the significant gifts that went to the Ryan children, and not to Winifred's children, stemmed from their mother having died first; she was not around to inherit an equal share with her sisters.

Jim Lee did put a line in his will saying that not all his grandchildren were included because they had other resources available to them. However, at the time of his death, Jackie was widowed and Lee's husband was far less wealthy than he had once been. Yet their grandfather did not even leave them a token bequest of money or personal property.

Jackie was peeved, and so was Lee. The recession had buffeted them, too. The $2 million Ari had given Jackie was now worth considerably less. Jackie suggested to him that he compensate for the market's drop, but he was not in the least bit interested, pointing out that he gave her bonds and that she alone had decided to invest in the stock market.

At Christmas Jackie did not take the children either to Hammersmith or to Hyannis. Instead, leaving Ari in Greece, she visited Lee at her Berkshire country house. The two women and their children continued their close companionship. Jackie sometimes still went to Hammersmith, especially when she had the children, but to her it was starting to look like one more Kennedy memorial. The presidential flag that had once flown from the lawn was now framed and hanging in the entrance hall. The Auchinclosses had fitted a bronze plaque on the desk used by the

President that listed the bills signed into law at Hammersmith. Jackie wanted her marriage to Ari to take her from these memories; she didn't need to be reminded of them at her own mother's house.

The past had a way of lingering, though. Jackie was obliged to sit for her formal portrait by Aaron Shikler. The question was whether Jackie would return to the White House for its official installation. "I don't know if she will come. And I would never ask her," said Janet. Betty Beale, writing in the *Washington Star,* was a little frustrated at not getting a solid answer, but she accurately described Janet as "always there when Jackie needs her, but never does anything that remotely resembles prying or pinning her daughter down."

Janet entered a more commercial arena by accepting an invitation from Burlington House textile company to judge a home-decorating contest. Tish Baldrige, now the company's public affairs director, had naturally thought of her old friend's mother as a publicity draw. Other judges were women who mixed society with accomplishment, including philanthropist Mary Lasker and Marjorie Merriweather Post's daughter, the actress Dina Merrill.

Janet explained that she preferred an uncluttered, not-too-decorated look. Her own homes, she said, were furnished in traditional style, although she had "a plastic [probably Lucite] little coffee table and a plastic thing by a chair" in her Georgetown house.

Janet judging an interior-design contest made Lee snicker. She was interested in interior design herself and was becoming known for her excellent eye. And she did not think she inherited this talent from her mother, who, she said, "had such classic taste. To me, it was boring to the point of being sterile. Every library, whether it was in New York or East Hampton, had chintz. The same decorator was called in on a bi-annual basis for slipcovers. Very nice but bland."

Janet attributed a high purpose to her involvement with a commercial enterprise. "We will help raise decorating standards," she said, "because when people see pictures of the homes that have won the prizes, they will set higher standards for themselves."

In addition, she mentioned the current recession and the economies it brought. "My husband's company certainly felt it. I think there is a whole new atmosphere everywhere, a different atmosphere."

She added by way of example to the housewives throughout the land, "There were no debutantes at Newport this summer."

Early in 1971 Jackie took the children back to the White House to preview the official portraits of her and their father. She and the children had dinner with the Nixons and their daughters, making it an early night, as Caroline and John, now thirteen and ten, needed to be back for school the next day. The Nixons hung the Shikler portrayal of Jack looking down reflectively, chin on chest, in the Green Room. They put Jackie's portrait in the basement.

But Jackie was tactful about the Nixons. The opening of the Kennedy Center took place without her. From Athens she sent a telegram to Roger Stevens that read, "Deeply regret that unforeseen reasons make it impossible for me to attend opening of Center. That night will really be your night more than anyone's."

Janet participated not as the former First Lady's representative but as one of the center's major fund-raisers. In Janet's opinion, the only thing that tarnished the center was its view north from the roof terrace, where a large office, apartment, and hotel complex had been built. The complex, called the Watergate, was the topic of an angry telegram Jackie had sent Roger Stevens in 1967 in which Jackie asked why name the center after President Kennedy if it is "just a place of entertainment wedged in among commercial buildings."

To Janet's delight, Caroline came up to Newport for its coaching day. "The Newport invitation is like an antique Jaguar jamboree," said Foxy Carter to *Town & Country* magazine. It's an equine sport that has enjoyed a revival since its 1800s heyday, involving great skill — as well as great expense — as the driver must control four horses and a coach.

Janet "had more horse guests than houseguests" as well as a few horse-drawn vehicles. For a short time Caroline even took the four reins of the horses in her left hand ("four in hand"), sitting in a box-seat sporting coach. The young teenager also learned to blow a hunting horn "in no time flat," boasted Janet. "I couldn't get a squeak out of it."

To help maintain Hammersmith, the Auchinclosses decided to turn the old Annandale stable into a carriage house or guest house to rent. More bad luck came when their workmen lit a bonfire of leaves near the stable. Sparks landed on the wooden building and set it aflame. The uninsured building had to be razed.

At least the Auchinclosses were insured for robbery when a professional gang broke in. It had cut a wide swath through social Newport, stealing from the Slocums as well. At Hammersmith a worn path through farmland showed that the thieves had been able to loot the empty house at night over a period of time, even managing to make off with two three-hundred-pound porcelain urns.

Not long after, in early November, Janet and Jackie had a serious discussion over lunch at the Colony Club in New York. Janet filled her daughter in on the financial problems they were having. Hughdie's financial adviser had told them it would be impossible to maintain Hammersmith Farm. Hughdie could not even afford the annual property taxes of $31,000 ($140,000 today). He would have to sell his boyhood estate, the jewel of southern New England.

The Jennings fortune was gone, spent on four generations of Auchinclosses and on a business that lost more money than it made.

Just a few weeks after this shocking news, Jackie returned to Hammersmith for the annual Thanksgiving feast and the birthdays of Caroline and John. The Auchinclosses used the occasion to announce publicly that they were selling Hammersmith Farm. "I don't want you to sell it," Jackie told Janet and Hughdie.

"Hughdie was born in the house, so you can imagine how hard it is for us," Janet told friends. She added that they hoped to keep the new windmill as a family guest house and, for themselves, the Castle—the old farmhouse where the family used to house retired servants.

"Hughdie would like to give [the estate] to the Preservation Society of Newport, but they require an endowment," Janet said. That was out of the question. And attempts by the Auchinclosses and the state to locate the official Kennedy museum at Hammersmith failed.

For years Hughdie had told friends that he was born at Hammersmith and would die at Hammersmith. Now that ending was in doubt. Many of their Newport friends criticized Jackie and Ari for not helping, calling Jackie in particular "selfish."

But Hughdie was the romantic, and his stepdaughter the realist. She and Ari knew that Hammersmith consumed endless quantities of money. Hughdie had already sunk his capital into the place; they were not interested in being next.

At Christmas Janet Jr. and Lewis traveled to Hammersmith Farm from Hong Kong, where Lewis was working for Pan Am. They had one child and were expecting their second in February. The holiday visit was marred by the rumors of fighting between Jackie and Ari, which Janet denied. "Jackie doesn't have violent arguments," she insisted. Nonetheless, Jackie was wafer-thin; Janet hoped that the time Jackie spent with the always-dieting, always-underweight Lee was not affecting her.

After the baby's birth, Janet and Hughdie visited Hong Kong. The younger couple lived luxuriously in a house atop a high hill. Hughdie sent postcards to the New York office, where Tommy was working. "Hope Tom doing well and not getting into trouble with this volume," Hughdie wrote.

In a card to his personal secretary, he joshed, "Have you gone public yet?"

In June 1972 Jackie called Janet to ask if she could stay in Georgetown when she came down for the fourth anniversary family memorial service at Bobby's grave. Janet had a better idea: why not combine the visit with an outing to the second run of Leonard Bernstein's *Mass*? (Bernstein had opened the Kennedy Center the year before with the same program.)

"Jackie thought maybe it would not be appropriate to go see a performance the night before Bobby's memorial Mass," Janet remembered. She thought otherwise, saying, "It couldn't be more appropriate."

Jackie flew down with Caroline, who went immediately to Hickory Hill to be with her cousins, and in fact played hooky from Brearley the next day to spend more time with her favorite of Bobby's daughters, Courtney. Jackie indulged Caroline because the school year was virtually over; she would head to Concord Academy in the fall. Janet reported, "Jackie isn't doing anything particular right now except bringing up her children and being a wife."

The Auchinclosses and Jackie invited Bob McNamara, now president of the World Bank, and his wife over for dinner before the performance. Earlier that week the Kennedy Center director told Janet that Jackie could enter by the side door, the one that was used by the President when he attended.

Janet demurred. "I think she should walk right into the Hall of Nations [the main hall of the Kennedy Center]. She isn't the President, and she should go in the front door." And so Jackie did, escorted by Leonard Bernstein and Roger Stevens.

As she walked to the focal point of the Grand Foyer and viewed the eight-foot-high bronze head of her late husband resting on a slim ten-foot pedestal, she finally understood how its craggy surfaces characterized his energy and personality. "It's beautiful," she said. "It's just beautiful."

The next day she wrote Stevens on Janet's blue O Street stationery:

Dreams take so long to come true — and yours was one of the longest dreams of all and one of the hardest to realize —

The Center is beautiful beyond what anyone could have hoped or imagined —

I am so happy I finally cross the threshold with you . . . and to be there for that first time which was such an emotional one for me. . . .

She signed the note, "Gratefully, Jackie."

That morning a Mass was said at Bobby's grave, with breakfast to follow at Hickory Hill. During the service Jackie went up and received Communion — although she knew that the Church's rules barred her. Perhaps Janet's example of taking Communion at her Episcopal church had influenced her.

Just as Cardinal Cushing had been slammed for apparent favoritism four years earlier, the priest dispensing the sacrament was asked why he allowed Jackie to take the host; after all, it was widely known that she had married a divorced man outside the church. He responded, speaking in the third person: "What people don't seem to realize is that she walked up to the priest. He didn't go to her. No priest would under the circumstances pass her up and not give her Communion. There is no prejudgment here."

Jackie's position focused attention on restrictive Catholic Church rules. Her action encouraged many people throughout the country who had felt excluded to take the sacraments as a matter of conscience. She talked about her decision with Janet back in Georgetown, before leaving for the airport, and Janet applauded her.

In the fall Caroline started boarding at Concord Academy. Jackie in turn rented a house for weekends in the same Massachusetts town. Perhaps she fondly remembered her haven from Miss Porter's at the home of Annie Burr and Lefty Lewis. She and Caroline had grown close. One friend remarked, "They're like one soul."

John, on the other hand, would get on Jackie's nerves just as any twelve-year-old is apt to do. Yet John and Ari were friends, whereas Caroline regarded Ari as an interloper, usurping her father's place. John's needs were simpler: he was grateful for the presence of another male in the family. Ari was fond of John and enjoyed giving him such extravagant toys as a speedboat and a miniature Jeep.

John, too, had become Janet's favorite grandchild, though Caroline was a very close second. "She continually talked about Caroline's brilliance," says Hughdie's granddaughter Maya. "And she *was* brilliant. But the rest of us felt like we came in second."

Janet talked to a reporter about John. "He knows no fear," she boasted. "Even I, who never believed in telling children not to jump a horse over a high fence or dive from a high board, am stopped in my tracks by John."

One friend repeated a remark of Jackie's about her mother. "She's wonderful with the grandchildren until they're a certain age. But as soon as they get minds of their own and she can't control them . . ." John, younger than Caroline and more easygoing, was an obvious choice as Janet's favorite.

Others, too, saw how Janet influenced the third generation. Stephen Birmingham, for example, was a friend of Janet's writing a biography of Jackie. He commented, "Caroline was raised to be exquisite, to be perfect in every way, the way her mother was raised. [Janet] wanted the best of everything for her daughters, and Jackie wants the best for Caroline. Janet Auchincloss had the same perfection drive, and it's a real drive."

If Jackie and Ari's marriage had ever had a chance, it was destroyed on January 21, 1973, by the crash of a Piaggio aircraft piloted by Alexander Onassis: a plane that he himself had begged his father to replace because of mechanical problems. That day, it plummeted 100 feet to the ground, spun, and cartwheeled for 150 yards before crumpling like an accordion. Alexander's head was so badly crushed that he was differentiated from the copilot only by his monogrammed handkerchief. Part of Alexander's brain had exploded out; the rest was pulp in his skull. It was hopeless. At the hospital Ari ordered his life support turned off. Ari reviled Jackie: she had brought into his family "the curse of the Kennedys." She was malevolent, he said, and he cursed the day he married her. Ari began avoiding Jackie.

Caroline was disappointed because Jackie immediately put an end to the flying lessons she'd started at Hanscom Field outside Concord. She student-flew a Cessna two-seater. Jackie was adamant: Ted had suffered a terrible small-plane crash, as had Ethel's parents, who were killed. After Alexander's crash she rued the time she and Janet had spent encouraging John's interest in planes and told Caroline and John she would no longer allow flying lessons.

Spring brought hope to Hammersmith when Paramount Pictures used its dock and exterior carriage house for filming *The Great Gatsby*. The director also used Newport's Rosecliff for the exterior of Gatsby's house. Interiors were shot in England, but the filmmakers preferred Newport's less crowded waters to film the regatta scene.

The venture brought the place prestige as well as income. Robert Redford's family rented the Castle, and the film's director and his wife stayed in the windmill. Hughdie and Janet threw a family picnic for the lead actors and their families, which Jackie and Lee attended.

For a hoot, Nuala Pell and Oatsie (Mrs. Robert) Charles accompanied Mrs. Pell's daughter, who had a part in the movie, to the costume department. As they admired the clothes, the wardrobe mistress asked them if they would be extras. "You are much more like the people we want in this movie. The young don't know how to look arrogant, sophisticated, and rich," she said to their amusement. To participate, they would have to have their hair bobbed, which Mrs. Pell did.

One activity that Janet never missed was Stratford Hall's coaching day, the sport's most prestigious event, even more so than the one at Newport. Hughdie accompanied Janet, and the couple stayed in a guest house on the grounds. On the day itself, Hughdie was stopped from joining a barouche being led by hackney horses. His error was his headgear — he needed to don the appropriate gray topper, which he did with good humor.

Early in 1974 Nini Auchincloss Steers divorced Newton Steers, with whom she had three sons, to marry Michael Straight, deputy chairman of the National Endowment for the Arts. "Nini's going Straight," joked Hughdie.

Straight was from a wealthy and prominent American family; his father was a J. P. Morgan banking partner who had founded the then liberal magazine *The New Republic*. Michael was educated at Cambridge, England, where he became a member of the pre–World War II student communist movement. He kept this secret for several decades before going to the FBI and disclosing his history, in the process exposing Englishman Anthony Blunt, an early Soviet secret agent.

The family attended the New York ceremony and reception. Ironically, it was Michael Straight who had bought Jackie's house on N Street in 1964, where she had lived a short time after Jack's assassination. He had paid $200,000 for the house and was now selling it, ten years later, for $335,000 (approximately $1.2 million today, although Georgetown real estate has escalated faster than inflation). He and Nini

would live in Jackie's former N Street house and then move to Bradley
Boulevard in Bethesda, Maryland, and summer at their place on Martha's Vineyard.

Janet and Hughdie still had not been able to sell Hammersmith Farm
and were strapped for cash. Luckily, that summer they rented it to the
syndicate that formerly owned the yacht *Intrepid*, winner of the 1973
America's Cup. While Janet and Hughdie stayed in the Castle, five executives, their wives, and the eleven-person race crew occupied Hammersmith from June until after the September race.

During the season Janet commented, "I have my children and my
grandchildren with me, so I'm not planning many social events — maybe
a dinner party — but my time is mostly for my family."

Janet was still driving her Jaguar coupe around town; that year she
had perched a French poodle hood ornament on her favorite car. Janet
was perfectly friendly and open as she sped all over Newport and saw
nothing wrong with picking up hitchhikers, so long as it was daytime.
One day her chef was charging the household groceries to the Auchincloss account at a local store. The clerk perked up. "Oh, I know her.
She gave me a ride when I was thumbing. I was sorry I got in the car —
she drives awfully fast!"

A few years earlier Janet had been stopped by a policeman for not
indicating a left turn. "My light is out" was Janet's excuse. When the
officer told her that she should have indicated her turn with an arm
signal, she leaned back in her seat and stretched her right leg out, saying,
"Well, if I put my leg out would you criticize me?"

Meanwhile, Lee and Stas had been living apart for several years. His
real-estate investments were falling in value, and he insisted that Lee cut
down on spending at the same time that Jackie was turning shopping
into a calling. He had lost his money, which had a way of taking the
shine off marriage to a man twenty-one years one's senior.

At the end of 1974 Lee divorced Stas, and Jackie sided with Stas.
Their children, Tony and Tina, were fifteen and fourteen. The couple
couldn't agree on custody, so they made a terrible decision: a boy for
me, a girl for you. Tony would stay in London with Stas, and Tina in
New York with Lee. The teenagers were close, having had largely ab-
sentee parents, and they begged their mother and father to leave them
together. Their pleas were ignored.

Lee had embarked on a new venture, signing a book contract to write
her memoirs. Jackie was as excited about the project as Lee and joined

her at Hammersmith to scour the attic and in Southampton to help her organize. Eventually, an article with photographs appeared in *Ladies' Home Journal*, but the book was never published.

Janet, though, spotted something in her searches through dusty family papers. After Jackie and Lee had gone to Europe together, they wrote and sketched "a kind of thank-you present for our mother" that they called *One Special Summer*. Lee recognized its potential and offered the charming little book to her publisher.

Lee had another project, a television interview show, for which she was interviewed by *The New York Times*. The article noted how much Lee looked like Janet — and was prettier than Jackie — and described Lee in terms that could characterize her mother. "As she spoke, [Lee] seemed shy, nervous — and somewhat impatient. She chain-smoked, calling for her maid to bring her a glass of water, and at one point in the conversation, dashed to the mantel to rearrange some small paintings propped there." Jackie, on the other hand, would give anyone she was speaking to total attention, with the kind of charm her father had.

The constant rooting around for tabloid fodder about the Kennedys finally uncovered Jack Kennedy's womanizing, subjecting Caroline and John to fresh publicity about his sexual escapades. "I would pay a king's ransom to keep this from them," said Jackie. Janet told Jackie to take the high road and refuse to acknowledge the tales. Jackie disagreed and told Caroline and John that their father's affairs never affected his love for them.

In March 1975 Ari died in Paris. Jackie was in New York and not at his side in the Paris hospital, as the world press pointed out. Jackie immediately flew by herself to the service and burial; a saddened Caroline and John, accompanied by Sgubin and Janet, arrived separately. Now that Ari was gone, Janet made her first trip to Skorpios since the marriage seven years earlier. Marta Sgubin remembers, "Mrs. Auchincloss never came except when Mr. Onassis died."

Lee did not attend, at Jackie's request. She told her sister to stay away so the media would not be reminded of Lee's earlier affair with Ari.

Jamie noted, "Now there will be wild speculation about whom Jackie will marry this time, and it's so ridiculous; there's no necessity for her to marry at all." Although Jamie had never reached the easy camaraderie with his half sisters that he had with Jack Kennedy — at this point in their lives, he usually saw them only at Christmas — he hit the mark with this observation.

Ari's death didn't stop the press from floating tales of his having been about to divorce Jackie. Janet denied them emphatically at the same time that she encouraged Jackie to sue Ari's estate for a larger settlement. "There was never any question of divorce," she said. "All marriages have their spots, and they came from very different backgrounds and countries. They had their difficult moments, as you and I have probably had."

All the supposition, Janet said, "just makes me sick. Obviously there was a good difference in ages. She had children in this country. He didn't want to be in this country very much, and they lived a life where they came and went when either one of them wanted to see the other one."

Janet set off a few sparks herself by denying something no one was claiming. "When you say that someone is planning to divorce somebody, it sounds as if his wife had done something dreadful or had a lover or something, which is the very last kind of thing that Jackie would do while married to somebody."

Despite Ari's death, the family celebrated when Caroline graduated from Concord. Everyone was there: Jackie and John, Janet, Rose, Teddy, and Lee. (Caroline seemed to be popping bubble gum during the recessional.)

In 1975 Hughdie's firm finally had to let its Washington staff go. The office manager took Margaret Kearney aside rather than have her hear the news at the all-staff meeting in the crowded conference room. She was angry that Hughdie wasn't capable of telling her the terrible news himself. The next day Janet called Kearney to commiserate. "I thought it was the rock of Gibraltar," she said of her husband's company. Hughdie's associates and employees gave him a citation, which said that they "have had their lives enriched by his high standards, a code of ethics and excellence that included respect for each individual."

In late August Jackie arrived at Hammersmith for the America's Cup races. The Auchinclosses reiterated that they needed to sell Hammersmith Farm, but not to condominium developers. "We have wanted to preserve the shoreline and the open, quiet fields, as well as the house." The state of Rhode Island, which by now owned and operated the adjacent Fort Adams, tried to purchase the estate. The asking price was $1.3 million ($4.2 million today, although, again, real estate has escalated) for fifty-five of Hammersmith's now seventy-two acres, structured so that the state would pay $800,000 for the property and the family would donate the remaining $490,000 and take it as a tax deduction. However, the governor decided that it was still too pricey.

Hughdie would sit in the breakfast room—where the children's table had once been—and look out at the boats sailing past. "He'd get out the glasses and know who everyone was," said Janet's friend Ella Burling. When it stormed, looking from the window, "you felt as if you were on the rolling waves," remembered Marta Sgubin.

Jackie was now forty-five years old and twice widowed. Along with many women of her generation, she had revised her thinking in the past decade. "I have always lived through men. Now I realize I can't do that anymore," she said.

She set about rebuilding the rest of her life by joining the contemporary world of working women, taking a job as an editor at Viking Press, a select publishing house. The timing was right: not only did she no longer have her bicontinental marriage, but Caroline was studying in London for a year before beginning Radcliffe College. To her great disappointment—and Janet's—Caroline said she would not be a debutante. "I guess girls that age just don't want to come out now," Janet admitted.

Lee, too, lost a partner, albeit an ex-husband. Stas Radziwill died unexpectedly of a heart attack in his early sixties. When his estate was settled, it was bankrupt; Stas had secured company loans with his personal fortune, and at his death, all the loans were called in.

Less than a year after Ari died, Hughdie's emphysema worsened. It was the fall of 1976 and he was at Hammersmith Farm, very ill. He was now using a wheelchair to go any distance. He had not been able to sell the estate, and the expenses were eating him alive. He would not have taken money from Jackie, even if she had offered it when she settled with the Onassis estate for what came to, after taxes, a little more than $19 million ($61 million today).

Janet never let anyone see the pain she felt for Hughdie—and herself—as their financial affairs became public. Merrywood's sale had been difficult, but this was worse because gossip focused on the family's straitened circumstances. One tactless remark came from Hughdie's friend and attorney Edward Corcoran, who spoke bluntly: "If you're asking me whether he's selling it because he's broke, the answer is no."

Yet Hughdie still refused to sell Hammersmith to developers. "When you get to be seventy-eight," he said, "you are not too interested in finances. The important thing is having the place preserved."

To help pay costs over the past few years, he had turned to his older sister, Esther Auchincloss Biltz, whose husband was possibly Nevada's richest citizen. No one in Hughdie's family—outside of Janet—knew that she was helping him, which was the way Hughdie wanted it. It was discussed within the Biltz family, though, and in the Nash family of Esther's son by her first marriage. Just as Esther had held the rope for Hughdie when they "practiced" coming down the fire ladder, so now did she step in and help him with Hammersmith's expenses. Hughdie's wish was always to die where he had been born, in his bedroom at Hammersmith Farm, and Esther wanted to ease Hughdie's last journey.

As Hughdie's agonizing long illness worsened, Janet became agitated. She wanted to get back to Washington to vote in the 1976 Ford-Carter race. It was the first time District of Columbia residents could vote in a presidential election, and she was determined to take part—although Hughdie pointed out that she had been voting Democratic since their son-in-law was elected President while, with that one exception, he always voted Republican. So their votes would cancel each other out.

But Janet insisted, and Hughdie always went along with what she wanted. To Yusha, though, he joked about voting being his last act. Despite his failing health, he flew to Washington with Janet and settled in to their Georgetown house to vote the next day. Hughdie wanted to stay a few days to regain his strength before the trip back to Hammersmith Farm. Suddenly he took a turn for the worse.

Margaret Kearney had been keeping apprised of Hughdie's health through Janet. Now Janet called Kearney, who lived nearby in Chevy Chase, and suggested she come see him. There was no nurse for Hughdie: just Janet and the regular staff.

Kearney was shaken when she entered his bedroom, although Hughdie teased, "I must be about to die!"

The light remark was prescient. Hugh D. Auchincloss died that night, November 19, 1976, in his home at Georgetown and not at Hammersmith Farm as he had always wanted. It was a terrible blow to Janet; she had always taken for granted that he would be there for her.

Although some of Hughdie's children were angry that Janet's stubbornness about voting in Washington had kept Hughdie from taking his last breath at Hammersmith, Yusha says, "She had kept him alive for the last five years. She made him go out and stay active. Without her, he probably would have given up."

The memorial service was held at Christ Church across the street from the house: the same Episcopal church where Janet had gone to worship the afternoon she learned of Jack's murder. His widow, children, step-children, and grandchildren attended. Donations were suggested for the charity Hughdie had served as a trustee, the Boys Club of Newport County, and to the Hearing and Speech Center of the Children's Hospital in Washington. There was a second service at Newport's Trinity Church. (Jackie and Lee arrived in separate cars.)

Hughdie had been cremated, and some of his ashes were interred at Island Cemetery. The rest were scattered at Hammersmith Farm — at the dock and in the bedroom where he had been born. Hughdie remains in the place that was his only true home.

Chapter 16

SLIPPING
AWAY

A few years before Hughdie's death, Nini had traveled up from Washington to Newport. Jamie remembers that when she arrived, the family had a good head start on the cocktail hour. Liquor affected Janet more quickly than it did the rest of the Auchincloss tribe; she drank very little water and enjoyed bathing in a very hot, dehydrating tub before dressing for dinner.

That evening they were enjoying their usual strong, frosty daiquiris. When Nini joined them, she casually mentioned something that she had read in the newspaper at the airport.

Janet disagreed. No, that wasn't true.

Nini repeated that she had just read it.

"No, it couldn't be," Jamie remembers Janet saying.

"It happened!" a frustrated Nini insisted. "You're wrong."

On being challenged, Janet flew at her stepdaughter's face with her long nails. "It scared the hell out of us," Jamie says.

Nini grabbed Janet's wrists and pulled her to the floor.

Now Hughdie stepped in—in a rare scolding rage, he dismissed Nini from the house and sent her back to Washington, telling her that she was no longer welcome at Hammersmith Farm.

She did not return in the few years that were left to him but attended his memorial services and joined the family at the Island Cemetery. The service ended; the family began to turn back to their cars.

All but Nini, that is. She remained unmoving. She had never forgiven Hughdie for banishing her from the Auchincloss home. According to Jamie, she made one last gesture and spat on his grave site as Jamie looked on, stunned.

Eventually, though, Nini made her peace with Janet. A few years after Hughdie's death, she published a novel called *Ariabella: The First*, set in suburban Virginia and Newport. Book reviewers tried to guess which character was which Auchincloss family member.

By now, Nini was no longer angry at Janet. During her publicity tour Nini spoke warmly about her stepmother: "I was separated from my mother and raised by Jackie's mother. She is my family. She was all for everybody getting out there trying, working. I was with her from the fourth grade. She raised me; she is my family."

Nini was not the only one to try to mend the small rips in the give-and-take relationship of a large family. The first time Janet lost her temper after Hughdie's death, Yusha warned her, "We're going to need each other now." She realized he was right and curbed her temper. In fact, she sent him a note—"Dearest Yusha," she wrote—thanking him for welcoming her, Jackie, and Lee into the Auchincloss family in 1942. She added, "I feel much nearer to you than if you were my own son—and I wish you were."

Janet was fatigued after years of watching over Hughdie. At one meeting at Stratford Hall, she talked to a director's husband, a pulmonary specialist, about her care of Hughdie. The physician was so impressed that he asked Janet to speak at the annual meeting of the American Lung Association in Atlanta.

Janet was her usual straightforward self, speaking frankly about the everyday life of a pulmonary caregiver. At the end of her talk, the doctors in the auditorium gave her a standing ovation.

Of course, she missed Hughdie terribly. "He was a very great man," she wrote, acknowledging a friend's condolences. "His courage and patience and humor never wavered."

Janet's niece Joan Gaylord remembered when she and Janet were at dinner with their husbands: Janet turned to her and said, "Isn't it wonderful to be married to a man you love?"

With Hughdie gone, Janet was eager to settle the issue of Hammersmith Farm. She pledged not to develop the bay acreage, which she could have done and ensured her fortune. Instead, she kept the estate for sale and in 1977 rented the main house to the Swedish challengers in the America's Cup race.

Discussions about turning the estate into a park began anew. Janet Jr., visiting her mother in the Castle while the main house was occupied, said the family is "interested in any serious offer with the money to back it up." The estate had been unsuccessfully represented by a Newport realty company, and the family thought it was time to try another firm. Jackie told Janet, "The important thing is to get it off your mind—and you need the money." Janet turned to Sotheby Parke Bernet. Sotheby published a glossy booklet and found buyers by the middle of August.

Janet spoke frankly about the sale. "All my children hate it and I hate it, but it is absolutely necessary." The buyers were nine Rhode Island and Massachusetts businessmen who planned to open Hammersmith Farm as a tourist museum, marketing it as the summer White House. Janet was to retain about ten acres, the windmill, and the Castle. The buyers paid $825,000 ($2.3 million today) for the twenty-eight-room main house, eight other buildings, and fifty-four acres. The sale price was $160,000 below the asking price and about $400,000 below the state's appraised valuation. The Auchinclosses agreed to leave the main house furnished, with knickknacks and memorabilia in place.

While Janet's friends knew she would have to sell the estate, they were dismayed at the price she received. Yusha was in Europe and did not participate. According to some, Jackie was "selfish" now that she had settled with the Onassis estate and was busy building her own estate on Martha's Vineyard, where she replicated in her bedroom the Victorian shape and sequence of the windows of her Hammersmith bedroom. People blamed Lee for pushing the sale because she was "afraid her mother wouldn't get another offer," says one of Janet's friends, and pressured her mother into accepting the offer, which she wearily did.

But their friends were shocked by the relatively low selling price and were upset that Janet had not told them she had accepted the bid. "Why did she sell Hammersmith Farm for pennies?" asks John Drexel rhetorically. "It has the best location in Newport." Candy Van Alen agrees: "The price paid was absurd. No one knew she was going to do it." Some blamed Lee's influence. "She had a terrible fear of not having enough money," says one Newporter. And so "Hammersmith Farm was practically given away," says Eileen Slocum.

During an opening party, the mayor of Hammersmith, England, presented the estate with the namesake town's flag. Visitors by the hundreds paid $2.50 on May 1, 1978, to gape at the master suite's blue-and-green flower prints, silk blanket covers, and monogrammed linens; the connecting study used by President Kennedy; Janet's powder-blue dressing room with its trellised ceiling; and of course the deck room, decorated with comfortable, plump blue-and-green linen couches, and tables for chess and backgammon. Visitors learned of the hundred-gallon water heater and saw bookcases filled with hardcover classics as well as paperbacks by Ian Fleming and Dr. Spock. Of course, with more attention focused on Hammersmith, vandalism increased: soon after its opening, the two-by-three-foot aluminum sign with the house's silhouette was stolen from its post at the end of the driveway.

Now Janet was ensconced in the Castle; in season, Yusha traveled up from his New York apartment to live in the windmill. "Living in the windmill makes you feel you're on a ship," he said. "When you wake up in the morning, you can't see any land at all from your bed."

The Drexels were pleased that Janet settled into the drastically smaller house so comfortably. When she entertained her friends for the first time, she never alluded to her reduced circumstances. Janet acted as if she had moved into Marble House rather than the residence where their servants had once lived. (Lee eventually decorated the Castle, which was mentioned in *Architectural Digest*.)

Of course, Janet still had her O Street house in Georgetown. To her horror, *Jackie Oh!*, written by Washingtonian Kitty Kelley, the first book devoted to deconstructing the Jackie myth, was published. The biography included some things that were believable (Jackie participating in psychotherapy) and some that were not substantiated (Jackie undergoing electroshock treatments for depression, Jack Bouvier having sex with the songwriter Cole Porter while they were Yale undergraduates).

In any case, Janet thought the book was trashy. In addition, she worried about the interviews Jamie gave Kelley, hoping that what he divulged wouldn't cause friction between him and Jackie. What dismayed Janet most was that the author took the money she made from her book—it was a best-seller—and bought a house on Dumbarton Avenue in Georgetown behind Janet's own home. When Janet looked through her back windows, she could see Kelley's house.

On one of Jackie's trips to see her mother the following year, she took a private tour of the Hammersmith Farm museum. According to its director, she was "absolutely thrilled. She loved it. She was just so enthusiastic."

The real reason Jackie had come to Newport was not to tour the museum but to meet a special friend of her mother's. They say that a person who has been in a good marriage is eager to re-create the relationship, and Janet had certainly enjoyed being married to Hughdie. So when she learned in 1978 that Bingham Willing Morris, the friend who had filled her dance card at St. Paul's Lincoln Day dance fifty-five years earlier, had lost his wife, she wrote him a note. After all, Janet had first met him when she was thirteen, and his late wife, née Mary Rawlins, had been a bridesmaid at Janet's first wedding, to Jack Bouvier. They had gone their separate ways during the years and hadn't seen each other in decades. He wrote back, and soon Janet and "Booch," a retired investment banker, were talking about marriage.

No one thought it was a good idea—except the couple themselves. "They had no interests in common," says Yusha, except music and dancing. Jackie came up with Caroline at the end of August 1979 and "tried to talk her mother out of the marriage," he says. Jackie encouraged Yusha to use his influence on Janet, which he did to no avail. Lee agreed: it was not a good match. Jamie was in Washington and didn't want to interfere, and Janet Jr. was, of course, in Hong Kong.

Social Newport had never heard of Booch. He lived in Southampton, but "in the woods," said Candy Van Alen, and none of their friends in the Hamptons knew him. Nancy Cavanagh called him "creepy." After the fastidious Hughdie, Booch wore dirty shirts, T-shirts, and undershirts with a towel draped around his neck and floppy cloth hats. "He looked ridiculous," Yusha says. Georgetown disliked Booch, too: Ella Burling characterizes him as "disagreeable, set in his ways, and conceited." He was disliked in social circles up and down the East Coast.

But Janet was lonely and depressed without Hughdie. She wrote a friend, "It will be lovely not to be lonely any more." The Van Alens gave a party in their ballroom at Avalon to celebrate the upcoming wedding. After the guests had toasted the couple, Booch announced that he had "no intention of living in Newport." Candy Van Alen says Janet's friends "considered it a slap." Janet's plans were to live with Booch in Southampton and to return during the season to the Castle.

On October 25, 1979, Janet, seventy-one, and Booch, seventy-three, were married in the Castle in the early afternoon. Jackie was her mother's witness. Lee was present, as were Caroline, Tony, Tina, John, other members of the family, and a few close friends. Janet's dogs were put outside so they wouldn't bother any of the guests. An enterprising reporter for the *National Enquirer* attached himself to a group of friends entering the house but was quickly discovered and ousted before the ceremony.

Janet carried a bouquet of daisies and wore her customary beige. Trinity Church's Episcopal priest married the couple in an "informal and joyous ceremony" with Jackie at her mother's side. The priest remembered, "I finished the ceremony and said, 'The deed is done,' and everybody clapped."

Champagne toasts and brunch followed the wedding. The reception was interrupted once by barking dogs that discovered the *Enquirer* reporter sneaking around the back windows. He was ejected from the property, and soon the couple was off for a thirty-day honeymoon across New England.

They returned to Newport before the month was up, with Janet unhappy and upset. Her very first night with Booch, she realized she had made a mistake. She had knelt down by the bed to say her prayers—a lifelong habit—and while her eyes were closed, Booch, already in bed, stretched out his leg and kicked her. It was a terrible shock to her, although he assured her that it was an accident.

All her wonderful plans were smashed on her honeymoon. She did spend some time in Long Island but preferred to live in Newport, by herself. In addition, Booch talked her into selling her Georgetown house, telling her it was too large.

Lee told Janet that she should not hire professionals to move her belongings from O Street—she herself had just moved three blocks in Manhattan and had been charged $7,000 by the professional movers. Lee recommended that she borrow a truck and hire a driver and another man for the heavy lifting. One of Janet's staff in Newport knew of an organization called the Druids who were available to help.

Chaos reigned on moving day. Crews from two auction houses were tagging valuables for resale because Janet wanted to use the occasion to sell some of the housewares, linens, and furniture that she had accumulated throughout her lifetime.

Ladies who were picking up discards for the Fort Myer, Virginia, thrift shop—with soldiers in tow to lift and carry—argued over whether the doll collector among them could take a few dolls directly from Janet. An argument ensued, and Janet ended up taking all the dolls back and not letting anyone have them.

There were workmen making improvements inside the house and, of course, the Druids moving things out to the truck. An estimated twenty strangers were coming and going for three days.

Janet had some wonderful things. One of the auction houses, Washington's Adam A. Weschler & Son, sold a 266-item lot, including a late-eighteenth-century George III banquet table and a mahogany stool, circa 1750. Other items included silver, glass, paintings, Oriental rugs, tea caddies, and clocks.

After three days of mass confusion, a silver chest holding a set of sterling engraved with the Auchincloss family crest, worth $27,000 ($56,000 today), was missing. Things of lesser value were unaccounted for, too. Everybody who had been in the house, save the generals' wives, were notified that they would be given lie-detector tests. A few days later a green plastic garbage bag with most of the silver was jammed into a mailbox standing in front of Georgetown's post office. Twenty pieces of silver were missing and were never recovered.

And when the incident blew over, the Druids held an auction of their own at a gay bar downtown.

The one thing Janet and Booch had in common was their interest in the Civil War. When they traveled to some Southern battlefields, they stopped at the Asheville, North Carolina, house of Mimi Cecil. (Her husband owns the Biltmore Estate, a Vanderbilt mansion, which he inherited from his mother.) Cecil noticed the discrepancies between Janet's second and third husbands. "Uncle Hughdie waited on Janet as if she were a queen," she remembers. "Booch was a wait-on-me kind of guy."

Janet also recognized the difference. When Booch was out of the room, she turned to Mimi and said, "Hughdie was such a saint!"

It wasn't long before Janet admitted her mistake. She talked to Yusha about ending her marriage to Booch—could it be annulled? she asked, because it had never been consummated. And she very charmingly asked him if he would mind if she went back to using the Auchincloss name. She particularly wanted Hughdie's last name on her headstone. "Of course, you can," Yusha told her. "And if the marriage doesn't work out, I'll help you get a divorce."

At the end of 1981, she separated from Booch and did not return to

Southampton. She confirmed to the *Boston Globe* that she was reverting to her old name of Janet Lee Auchincloss. She wasn't sure that she would seek a divorce, though. "I don't know. I must talk to my lawyers. I'll certainly never marry again."

To help forget Booch, Janet traveled to China with Jamie in 1983. She had broken her ankle and had to travel in a wheelchair with "a very kind son [Jamie] who pushed my wheelchair for hundreds of miles it seemed."

Jamie was good-natured about her injury but irritated at her inflexible food preferences. Although he thought the food was excellent, Janet would eat nothing but American or continental meals. "The food was delicious, and she wouldn't eat anything, subsisting on rice and bread, when she could find it," he says.

After selling the O Street house, Janet bought a condominium at the Watergate apartment building. Then she decided she missed being in Georgetown and quietly sold the apartment in favor of a small Georgetown town house. In June 1983 a gas furnace fire at a neighbor's house caused extensive damage to Janet's home. "The fire was very disorienting to her," remembers Ricky (R. Gaull) Silberman, a former Equal Employment Opportunity Commission commissioner and the wife of U.S. Court of Appeals judge Laurence H. Silberman, who lived two doors down.

Janet never returned to live in Washington. She sold the house and put the proceeds (about $650,000, or $1.1 million today) into a trust for Lee, to be managed by her twenty-four-year-old son, Tony.

Jackie was furious and argued with her mother. Why was she giving one of her children such a large amount of money?

"Lee needs the money," Janet explained.

"So does Jamie!" said Jackie. "You're playing favorites."

The Silbermans were very disappointed when Janet went back to Newport, as she was always so pleasant and "turned out to the teeth" walking her dogs during the day. One of the Silbermans' children was marrying, and Janet would share memories with her: "I remember when Jackie got married—these are wonderful times." They were enchanted with her.

In September 1984 Janet Jr. returned to the Castle with her young children. She had kept busy in Hong Kong: first, teaching French at the Chinese University, then raising her children while being an official of the amateur swimming program and founding the first overseas chapter of the League of Women Voters. When her husband, Lewis, started his venture-capital firm, Inter-Asia Management, she became its adviser.

Arriving in Newport, Janet Jr. complained of a constant backache, and Yusha suggested his chiropractor. At Bailey's Beach she said to the Pells, "I have a cough I can't get rid of." They recommended their doctor in Boston.

The diagnosis was lung cancer. Janet Jr. had never been in strong health as a child. It could be that she had inherited Hughdie's respiratory weaknesses. Janet Jr. never smoked, but Hong Kong, where she had lived for nearly twenty years, was terribly polluted.

During her treatment, Janet Jr. lived in the Castle with her mother, and Yusha volunteered to drive her to Boston for the necessary chemotherapy. As she worsened, and was admitted to the hospital, Jackie "put everything to the side to be there when [her sister] needed her," says Jamie. "Jackie showed her best side then."

During the worst times of treatment, Janet Jr. never complained about her illness. She was stoic, very much in keeping with the Auchincloss tradition. Jackie sat by her bedside, helping her endure. Janet Jr. had achieved remission when she developed acute pneumonia, and on March 13, 1985, her heart gave out with Jackie at her side, holding her hand.

She was only thirty-nine years old and was the mother of Alexandra, Lewis, and Andrew, all young children.

Immediately after her death, Jackie took charge. First she called Yusha and had him tell Janet. Then Yusha told Jamie, who was very upset that he didn't know before Yusha and that he wasn't allowed to be the one to tell his mother. He felt that a controlling Jackie had usurped him.

Jackie organized her half sister's funeral service at Newport's Trinity Church, a few blocks from St. Mary's where Janet Jr. (and Jackie) had married. Although the family was grateful for her planning, Jackie overstepped her role as half sister by being "so controlling," as Jamie put it.

Jackie decided to draw up a guest list on the pretext that the funeral could become a media circus. She then excluded nearly all of Janet Jr.'s friends, including those who considered themselves closest to her. They were terribly hurt, and angry at Jackie.

The day was drizzly, and the pallid mourners looked shocked at the death of such a young woman. Jackie spoke: "Knowing Janet was like having a cardinal in your garden. She was bright and lovely and incredibly alive." She was cremated, and her ashes were buried in Island Cemetery and spread in Hong Kong, New York, and on the sundial at Hammersmith Farm.

Janet did not seem to be herself. Her forgetful behavior had started shortly before her daughter's illness. She would feed one dog and not the other, or, worse, feed one dog several times. Eventually, she was diagnosed with Alzheimer's disease.

Now Jackie became very concerned about Booch and his behavior. She was flabbergasted to learn that he had melted all the wonderful sterling cups Janet had won in hunter competitions to sell for their value as silver.

Jackie especially didn't want him bothering Janet. She saw that her mother, thankfully, seemed to have forgotten that Janet Jr. had died. But when Janet would talk about her daughter as if she were still living, Booch would become angry and correct her, "You know she's dead! She died of cancer last year." Of course, Janet would only get upset. (Some thought his reminders were meant to keep Janet mentally active.)

"Jackie did not want him to be at the Castle at all," Yusha says. "Jackie wanted me to tell Booch to stay off the property.

"Jackie had a temper and was very definite about things like this."

So when Jackie told Yusha to keep Booch away, he reminded her, "They're married!" He suggested that Booch be allowed to visit every other weekend.

"Jackie thought that was too generous," Yusha says. "She said, 'Once a month and not in the house—he can stay in the garage apartment.'"

Yusha continues, "I told Booch what Jackie said and that Jackie had threatened to call the police to keep him out. Booch could have meals at the house, Jackie said, when he visited. If he didn't agree to these terms, I told him that he should call Jackie and talk to her about it.

"He was scared of Jackie and never did."

As her Alzheimer's took hold, Janet mellowed. Yusha and Jackie pulled together a staff headed by Elisa Sullivan, who made sure that Janet was always occupied and comfortable. Sally Ewalt was her nurse, and Michael Dupre was chef for all her meals and those of her guests. Jonathan Topper was her butler. "A very special family feeling" characterized the household, and her staff recognized those years as special for all of them.

To them, she was Mrs. Auchincloss "unless Mr. Morris was around," remembers Michael Dupre.

When her niece questioned her about why she took notes when they talked, Janet candidly admitted that she was afraid she was losing her mind.

At the Castle her day began when Michael Dupre would arrive to serve her breakfast in bed at about 7:30 A.M. She ate lightly, sometimes only having a piece of fruit. After breakfast she would do some easy stretching exercises with a masseuse who came in for an hour or so each day, and have a rubdown. If she ate lunch alone, she would have a fruit salad with cottage cheese, or soup. Sometimes she had lunch guests of up to twelve people and would make sure a lovely dessert was served. She preferred to bring together co-volunteers of such Newport organizations she supported as the Historical Society of Newport County or the Redwood Library.

After lunch she'd take a good walk with her dogs and return home for tea and cookies, followed by a nap. Then it would be time to bathe and dress for dinner. Yusha, living in the windmill, would usually join her at dinner. Janet was still fastidious in her dress and a perfectionist in her house. Walking the dogs, she'd always put on a hat and gloves. "Even with Alzheimer's, you would never see her without hat and gloves, stockings," says Marta Sgubin, who by then was Jackie's cook. Then, after the disease made her very confused, Janet would come back home and insist on replacing her walking shoes in the exact same spot on her shoe rack. She couldn't remember her past, but she knew where everything went in her house.

She had a few breaks from her organized schedule when she would read. During the season she would be driven to the beach and sit outside her cabana, enjoying the summer weather. When she was no longer able to comprehend what she read, she would still carry a book with her—most often it was *Tidewater Dynasty*, about the Lee family, or *Stratford Hall*.

Sometimes when her mind would wander, she would go next door to her old estate, thinking it was still hers, sometimes stacking and restacking the coffee-table books that she could never align to her satisfaction.

All of her care was made possible by Jackie's financial support. She set up a million-dollar trust for her mother and made sure that Janet continued the activities she used to like, even if she didn't comprehend everything going on. Jackie would not let her mother lie idle or feel useless; she cared enough about Janet to realize that she would have

hated the thought of vegetating. And despite Jackie's now being a working woman, first as an editor at Viking and then at Doubleday, she took
a generous amount of time from her schedule to spend with her mother.

Not that Janet always appreciated it. Jamie remembers a time when
Jackie arrived for a visit wearing red, which flattered her but was a
color that Janet, whose most daring color was brown, couldn't stand in
clothing. "Mummy wouldn't want to say anything; she was trying not to
notice for about two hours. It was driving her crazy," Jamie remembers.

In addition to the money, Jackie put care into selecting a devoted
staff. They took her out to whatever might be interesting: a play in town,
a moviefest at Salve Regina College, a Christmas concert or an Easter
service, and, of course, the annual Newport Music Festival. Yusha or
Jamie would even accompany her to Stratford Hall, where she was now
an honorary director, having served as a member of the board for sixteen
years. In fact, coaching day at Stratford Hall in July 1987 was dedicated
to Janet. The proclamation reads, "Mrs. Auchincloss was the person
most responsible for the initiation of Coaching Days at Stratford beginning in 1973."

One time at Stratford, Janet pulled Yusha over to a genealogical tree
of the Lee family that hung in the visitors' center. Janet was upset.
"Where's my father, Yusha? I can't find my family on here." Of course,
her family was not there, but rather than perturb Janet, Yusha — who is
tall — pointed to one of the top branches. "Here it is. I can see your family
up here!"

Elisa Sullivan was struck by Janet's ability to communicate with animals, and their apparent recognition of her love for them. She was with
Janet at a stable in Virginia; Janet knew that she could no longer ride,
but she wanted to see the horse anyway. As soon as she exited her car,
the farm dogs gathered around her, tails wagging for the caresses she
gave them.

The oddest thing happened when they walked into the barn, Elisa
remembers. "All the horses looked up and started to shuffle. They raised
their heads; a few whinnied softly, and the others made gentle noises. It
was as if they sensed a friend had joined them."

Jackie came to visit Janet often and stayed in an upstairs guest room.
When she learned that Janet's sister Win had also been diagnosed with
Alzheimer's, she was terrified. Back in New York, she tossed out all her
aluminum pans because aluminum cookware had erroneously been
linked to the disease.

Just as Jackie was generous with her mother, she was supportive of

Lee, too. She knew that her father had been an alcoholic and perhaps, looking at Lee, she thought, "There but for the grace of God . . ." Earlier in the decade Lee faced her alcoholism (after her second serious car accident in one year) and decided to change the way she had been living. Previously her daughter, Tina, had escaped her by moving in with Jackie—and Lee blamed her sister for appropriating her daughter's affections. Lee, however, rarely visited Janet and was criticized in town for her inattention.

Jackie made sure to include her mother in all public family occasions, even though there was the possibility that she might say something embarrassing. Yusha drove Janet up to Boston for the dedication of Harvard's John F. Kennedy School of Government. She wouldn't have been able to attend if not for him: Booch refused to drive her.

"Booch hated the Kennedys," says Yusha, "and he wouldn't drive Janet, even though he was a Harvard graduate."

"I argued with him. 'I went to Yale. You're the Harvard man!'

"His response was, 'I can't stand the Kennedys.'"

So Yusha had to drive Janet up to Cambridge the day after he had a root-canal operation. To make matters worse, Janet kept asking him questions the entire way: "Where are we going? Why are we going? When will we get there?"

He remembers, "I explained everything to her once. Finally, I stopped the car and told her my tooth hurt and I'd turn the car around if she didn't let me listen to the radio."

"But it started up again, and continued all the way to Cambridge." (And he never made good on his threat, either.)

Once at Harvard, she asked Jackie who John F. Kennedy was. Jackie turned to Yusha, "Is she always like this?"

On another trip, with Jackie in the backseat, Janet held a lengthy conversation with Yusha as if he were his father, addressing him as Hughdie. "Now, Hughdie, don't drive so fast," and so on. The best was when she started complaining to him that "Yusha is turning into a beach bum."

Jackie was flabbergasted as Yusha talked to Janet about himself in the third person, as if he were Hughdie.

As Janet's grandchildren grew older, they made fewer trips to Hammersmith. Caroline returned from England and graduated from Radcliffe, then Columbia Law; John graduated from Brown University in nearby Providence and earned a law degree—to Jackie's great relief—from New York University. Once Janet lost her ability to recognize them, Jackie saw no real reason to encourage Caroline and John to visit. She made up the difference.

When Janet still had her Georgetown house, her companion Elisa would accompany her south. They would go to the Kennedy Center, shop, visit Jamie (who then lived in Washington), take tea at Ella Burling's house on R Street, go to the Smithsonian museums or lectures at the National Geographic Society.

Yusha needed all his diplomatic skills to handle his unpredictable stepmother. When Caroline married Edwin Schlossberg, Jackie and Yusha agreed not to volunteer the information that the Schlossbergs were Jewish. "She didn't know it," says Yusha.

When he told her that Caroline was marrying Edward Schlossberg, Janet asked, "What kind of name is that?" Yusha quickly responded, "It's German. It means 'castle.'" He says, "That seemed to appease her."

Making it stickier was the fact that Jackie, since 1980, had been dating Maurice Tempelsman, who was Jewish and, under civil law, still married to his wife, Lily. (She had obtained a religious divorce.) He and Jackie were an excellent match: Jackie sometimes spoke of her gratitude at escaping her old social world, which would not have accepted a Tempelsman—or a Schlossberg.

So when the arrangements for Caroline's wedding were being made, Jackie thought that she would put Leon Tempelsman (Maurice's son, who headed Lazare Kaplan Diamonds), the Schlossbergs, Janet, and Yusha in one car, with Yusha riding up front with the driver. Then she thought better of it.

Yusha faced the situation directly. When he met the groom's parents on Caroline's wedding day, he cautioned them, "Caroline's grandmother has Alzheimer's disease—don't pay any attention to anything she might say; just go along with it." As it turned out, Janet was so confused that she only kept asking whose wedding it was.

Some friends remembered to invite Janet to their functions even when her conversation had grown circular. The Drexels supported her, and John Drexel remembers, "Even with Alzheimer's, she looked marvelous. Up to the end, her voice was perfectly lovely; her beauty came from within. No one could touch her charm."

At their dinner parties, Janet wouldn't always remember who everyone was but was perfectly enchanting nevertheless. Unfortunately, some people were uncomfortable with her changed personality and avoided her.

Janet's granddaughter Maya—whom Janet had treated so badly when Maya was a girl—had moved to a house in Newport, and she would stop by the Castle every day to help Janet walk the dogs. With Alzheimer's, Janet's need for control and her harshness had melted away. Those whom she had offended found that she was now pleasant company; some were as generous as Maya and as eager to forgive.

"Janet did not seem to acknowledge how she had acted before," Yusha said. "Perhaps she regretted some of the things she had done."

Everyone in social Newport praised Yusha for his daily attention and care for his stepmother.

There were still a few sharp edges to her personality, though. Janet's doctors forbade her to drink wine because of her medications. So Yusha purchased ersatz, nonalcoholic wine drinks. His plan didn't work; although Janet may not have remembered her best friend's name, she recognized that she wasn't drinking the real thing. "What's this? It's not wine!" she'd exclaim.

For Janet's eightieth birthday in 1987, the family gathered: Jackie, of course, Jamie, Yusha and Maya, and friends. Although Maurice Tempelsman accompanied Jackie occasionally, he did not visit often and was not present at Janet's birthday party.

Janet had always encouraged her children to give gifts that they had created. For this important birthday, her family and staff gathered written memories and sentiments from her family and friends, as well as photos. Jackie and Lee had a mock newspaper drawn up, headed, JANET AUCHINCLOSS—BEAUTY STILL A CHAMPION AT 80—HAPPY BIRTHDAY, MUMMY. The album was presented to her that night.

Caroline reminded her that she was Janet's first grandchild and that she had followed in "Grumpy Lee's" footsteps in being named a Harlan Fiske Stone scholar. (This was a misunderstanding; James T. Lee was not a Stone scholar—Stone and Lee were *classmates* at Columbia Law in 1898. Columbia did not initiate this honor until the 1920s.)

John wrote on his page that books on World War II were his favorites and that his favorite music was "some stuff you probably haven't danced to, Grandma." He went on, "I won a mock-trial at law school, so I'm happy about that. I'm going skiing at Christmas and fox-hunting with my mother and Caroline."

Most people sent snapshots of themselves to be pasted on the same album page as their recollections—Nini's showed her chugging beer—but Lee sent a full-page black-and-white photo of her looking very smart in a black-and-white herringbone-patterned shirt.

Her relatives through marriage to Hughdie, too, were represented. The author Louis Auchincloss and his wife, Adele, wrote, "You have been the star of the Auchinclosses!" One friend said, "We of the French Group miss you every Tuesday." Another one remembered, "I think of the time we all met in Rome and you asked me (age 20) to chaperone Lee (age 18) in Paris!" A friend teased her, "I recall you won money while attending the Kentucky Derby with me in 1984."

Janet had always loved her dogs and horses, and the outdoors. Walking along the bay, picking buttercups, and chatting to the dogs was her pleasure. She wouldn't mind when Sunshine, her chef Michael Dupre's golden retriever, hopped in bed with her during breakfast, joining Janet's own Jack Russells Victoria and Taffy. Once Dupre saw that she had tears in her eyes as she looked out at the Angus steers grazing on the land. "I'm fearing for their future," she exclaimed.

When she became very ill and housebound, Eileen Slocum would stop by and talk with her about their family's weddings and good days gone by. She believed that the death of Janet Jr. accelerated Janet's illness. "It certainly took a toll."

Janet told Eileen Slocum that every night after her prayers she would recite the children's names to herself so she would not forget anyone. Then she recited them for Slocum in order of birth: "Yusha, Nini, Tommy, Jackie, Lee, Janet Jr., and Jamie." She seemed satisfied that she could still remember.

Toward the end, her children and stepchildren wanted to appoint a guardian for Janet because they were unwilling to give that power to Booch. Jackie did not want to have the responsibility, even though she was faithfully visiting her mother nearly every weekend, flying up from Manhattan or down from the Vineyard. Yusha agreed to make the necessary decisions, although he would always check with Jackie before making a judgment on anything important.

In July 1988 Caroline had her first baby and named her Rose, at Jackie's insistence. "It was a slap in the face to Janet," Yusha says, remembering how much Janet had wanted a grandchild named after her. When Caroline arrived with daughter Rose and Jackie in August, Janet at first didn't recognize Caroline or understand whose baby it was. Then the fog lifted, and she told Caroline, "She's lovely."

In mid-March 1989 Janet was admitted to a hospital in Providence after a fall at the Castle caused a hairline fracture of her hip. Although it was not a serious injury, it spelled the beginning of the end.

By July Janet had begun to fail. Yusha called Jackie, who was headed for Hyannis to help the Kennedy family celebrate Rose's birthday; Rose would be ninety-nine. Instead, Jackie went immediately to Newport and stayed beside the hospital bed that had been set up for Janet on the Castle's main level. Jackie held Janet's hand and spoke to her as twilight set in.

Booch was in the house, upstairs, the radio blaring. Jackie and Yusha were irritated at his lack of respect and consideration. Yusha told him to turn it off.

Although Janet considered herself an Episcopalian, the staff working in her house knew she had been baptized a Catholic, so a priest from Salve Regina College, a friend of Yusha's from his graduate studies there, stopped by the Castle and gave her last rites.

Later that Saturday night Janet, eighty-one, died. She was in the Castle at Hammersmith Farm with her daughter Jackie and her stepson Yusha at her side. She had raised four children and three stepchildren, had fourteen grandchildren and stepgrandchildren, and one great-grandchild. But perhaps as she released her hold on life, she was thinking of the time she and Elisa slipped into the barn, with the dogs happy around her and the horses lifting their heads to neigh softly in greeting.

A thousand spectators lined the streets before the service for Janet at Trinity Church. But they weren't there for her. As Jackie stepped out of her silver limousine, a blizzard of cameras went off, also capturing images of John, Caroline and Ed, and Lee. No one but the press seemed to notice her: she walked through the crowd of mourners and stood by herself at the top of the stairs. "For one nanosecond, she looked terribly lost. And then, out of nowhere, Ted Kennedy came up and took her arm. She gave him a big smile." Ted and his son Patrick, with Ethel and several of her children, represented the Kennedy family. Sargent Shriver, Eunice's husband, attended for his family members. Altogether, three hundred friends and relatives were there.

By arrangement, Jackie sat with Yusha. Lee and Jamie sat in the same pew, and the grandchildren were several pews back. Booch sat farther to the rear of the church. They heard a bagpiper play the Scottish hymn "Amazing Grace." In addition to the traditional readings were three excerpts from Janet's eightieth-birthday album. Tears ran down Lee's face; only once, during the Lord's Prayer, was a single droplet visible on Jackie's.

The family attended the private burial at Island Cemetery on Newport's Farewell Road. A wooden box containing some of Janet's ashes and covered with one of her favorite scarves was buried. The family retired to the Castle.

Later they would take her remaining ashes and scatter them off the dock and throughout the garden at Hammersmith Farm and at the bottom of the sundial. Yusha reminded Jackie that they had sprinkled Janet Jr.'s ashes across the sundial itself.

"Janet Jr. on top of Mummy," Jackie exclaimed to Yusha. "She'd like that!"

Epilogue

Janet's will was written five years before her death. In it, she left Booch $25,000 and a gold watch. Her grandchildren and stepgrandchildren each inherited $3,000. The longtime estate manager of Hammersmith Farm, Manuel Faria, received $30,000 for himself and $60,000 for the college education of his two children. The butler, Jonathan Topper, got $8,000.

Unknown to the family was that in Washington, D.C., Adam A. Weschler & Son auctioned off safety-deposit-box items that had never been retrieved. Among the lots were Janet's engagement and wedding rings from Jack Bouvier, long forgotten.

Janet's real estate, including the Castle and the windmill, was divided into sevenths: six shares to her six living children and stepchildren—Yusha, Nini, Tommy, Jackie, Lee, and Jamie—and the remaining seventh divided among Janet Jr.'s three children.

Janet's stated hope was that they would use the residences and not sell them. Janet's friends questioned whether Jackie and Lee should have received a share of the property; it was the Auchincloss estate, and they were not Auchinclosses. Certainly, they thought, Jackie—with her *real money*—didn't need a one-seventh share of the Castle and windmill.

Yusha now lives in the Castle year-round, renting his siblings' share from them. Tommy lives with his wife Diana outside Albany, New York, on a farm. Jamie lives in Oregon. Lee never liked Newport anyway, so she sold her share to Nini, who now owns two-sevenths. Nini, who divorced Michael Straight, lives in Washington, D.C., and traditionally goes back to Newport at the end of the season, for the America's Cup races.

Lee's life is still full of drama. Shortly before Janet's death, she had married movie director Herbert Ross. She caused a commotion at the London premiere of his film *Steel Magnolias* because she was assigned a seat in the second row. It was a royal command performance, and—perhaps because she had been a princess of sorts herself—she wanted to sit with the royals in the front row. She jockeyed up to the first row and planted herself next to Prince Charles, throwing the entire seating scheme off kilter. When she was asked to move to her assigned seat, she refused. The royal family heard people whispering, "Wrong seat! Wrong seat!" They thought it was *their* error, so they stood up and moved down. The arrangements fell into total disarray; the palace, and Herbert's studio, were furious at Lee.

In early 1999 Lee separated from Ross. She spends most of the year in Paris and intends on continuing to use the last name of Radziwill.

As for Jackie, she had entered the best period of her life. She maintained a low profile as a book editor and a slightly higher one as a preservationist of New York's skyline. She was instrumental in stopping the destruction of New York's best buildings—Grand Central Terminal, for example—and blocking the construction of tall buildings that stole the sky, as she put it. Perhaps these actions were an acknowledgment of respect for her grandfather Jim Lee's buildings.

Caroline became an accomplished author of two books, happily married and the mother of another daughter and a son. Caroline and her brother remained close.

John, finally, passed the New York bar exam but incurred his mother's displeasure by dating Madonna. She laid down the law, just as Janet had to her. Next Jackie objected to the actress Daryl Hannah, who according to Jackie looked like an unmade bed—an uncanny imitation of Janet's early criticism of her.

Maurice Tempelsman, a self-effacing, sophisticated man, was more than happy to provide a quiet setting for Jackie to sparkle in. He had been living with her since 1988 and had largely escaped notice by the press.

Jackie, of course, loved being outdoors and continued to ride. In late winter 1993 she startled everyone when she unaccountably fell from her horse. By January she was diagnosed with lymphoma. Although she knew she had the fast-killing variety, she remained optimistic until May. She made a special trip to the Prints and Photographs Division of the Library of Congress. When she arrived, unescorted, she ensconced herself at a back table to gaze, unobserved, at the Toni Frissell photographs of her wedding to Jack. Even when the end was near and she had requested to die at home as her mother had done, she took small pleasure in the fact that she would not live to see her mind reduced by Alzheimer's disease.

With hundreds of people keeping vigil on the street below, she died at her Manhattan home on May 19, with her children, now thirty-six and thirty-three years old, by her side. She had planned her funeral and designated Lee's son, Tony, as a pallbearer—he himself was receiving chemotherapy and would die five years later at age forty—and her daughter, Tina, as a reader. Lee played no part in the ceremony. Jackie was buried with great ceremony next to Jack Kennedy and near her two babies, Arabella and Patrick.

Jackie's half brother Jamie did not receive an invitation to Jackie's memorial service. He called Yusha and asked him to tell Nancy Tuckerman, still acting as Jackie's assistant, "People know me. I'm not there, it would look bad," as he remembers. He raised the possibility of standing outside the church even if he wasn't allowed inside. And so, using this leverage, Jamie was allowed to pay his last respects to his sister.

Maude Davis, Jackie's aunt, had no such bargaining power (and wouldn't have used it if she had). She was the only living sibling of Jack Bouvier—in her eighties, she was the oldest remaining member of the Bouvier family—and very much wanted to say good-bye to Jack's eldest daughter. In fact, Mrs. Davis was even a member of the church where Jackie's service was held. But Jackie was angry at John Davis, Maude's son, for having written a friendly biography of Jackie and a critical book on the Kennedy family. Jackie's hypersensitive anger extended to his mother, who, of course, was not even involved.

Mrs. Davis even went to her parish priest, who was embarrassed to have to deny her admission to her own niece's service in her own church. In the end, he ran off an extra memorial program for her, and she said a quiet prayer for Jackie. "She was really hurt" by Jackie's exclusion of her, says her son.

And so the grudges lived beyond the grave.

But one person who was allowed to be there sat unrecognized in a back pew. She was Lily Tempelsman, Maurice's legal wife, come to pay her respects to Maurice's virtual wife. The peculiarity of the situation underscored this lack of resolution in Jackie's story: she seemed destined never to achieve full contentment.

And five years later, when John's plane plummeted from the sky, taking with him his wife and sister-in-law, we knew why Jackie had to die before her time.

In a public rebuke, Jackie's will left money to both of Lee's children but none to Lee. Jackie left her one-seventh share of the Hammersmith Farm property to Yusha, so he, like Nini, now owns two-sevenths of the property. As usual, the press stepped over Janet as if she never existed and reported that Jackie "willed the remaining Hammersmith Farm property" to Yusha. Of course, it was not hers to give.

Her apartment on Fifth Avenue sold for $9.5 million; as its contents were being removed for auction, John sat on the curb across from the building, unnoticed, and watched silently as the furnishings of his childhood were carefully loaded in movers' trucks.

Jackie had told her children to sell her items at auction for all they could get—and they did. The grand total was $34.5 million, but what shocked people were the escalated prices paid by the buyers. The auction had been expected to bring in about $5 million—and that estimate took Jackiemania into account. The simple book of Inaugural speeches that Jackie inscribed to Janet and Hughdie for Christmas after Jack's assassination sold for $110,000. The engagement diamond Ari gave to Jackie was appraised at $660,000; it sold for $2.4 million.

Jackie may have loved Jack Bouvier beyond all reason, but apparently his grandchildren, who never knew him, felt less sentimental. The prized French Empire desk that Jackie placed lovingly in the White House's West Sitting Room and in every other dwelling she lived in went for $68,000 (the appraised value was $2,000).

The auction catalog itself sold 104,000 copies at $90 for the hardcover and $45 for the softcover editions. Of the entire proceeds, only a few million dollars went to charity; the remainder, more than $30 million, was funneled to the two young Kennedys. Caroline felt the unfamiliar sting of public criticism.

A few years later Janet's heirs sold the furnishings and decorative objects of Hammersmith Farm's main house, which was going to be converted back into a private home. They put the items on the block at Christie's. The high-end estimate of the proceeds was $177,000; the auction brought a third more, or $234,000.

The Auchincloss family could have realized much more, but Caroline specifically requested that the Kennedy name not be used in connection with the auction—even though Hammersmith Farm is where her parents' wedding reception was held—and so the Auchinclosses lost out on hundreds of thousands of dollars. Janet certainly would have disapproved of the official Kennedy auction and would have preferred the quiet, dignified Auchincloss affair.

Now in private hands, Hammersmith Farm is no longer open to tourists.

Merrywood, too, has been in the hands of various owners throughout the years. In 1999 a renovated and expanded seven-acre Merrywood was sold for a staggering $15 million.

The Georgetown O Street house coincidentally was put up for sale in late 2000 for $4.4 million. In an odd turn of events, it became the house of choice for Senator Hillary Rodham Clinton and her husband, Bill, as they sought a home in Washington, D.C.—a choice vetoed for security reasons by the Secret Service because it sits right against the sidewalk.

The homes and belongings Janet prized are all dispersed. And in all the talk over the years about Jackie, and in all the eulogies she received at her death and then again when her son was so shockingly killed, those mentioned were her children; her past husbands, Jack and Ari; her father, Jack Bouvier; and her in-laws Rose and Joe Kennedy. Not one reference is made to the woman, Janet Lee Auchincloss, who purposely and sometimes unwittingly shaped Jackie into the icon of an era.

*N*otes

PROLOGUE

Boller, Paul F. Jr. *Presidential Wives: An Anecdotal History*. New York: Oxford University Press, 1988.

Caroli, Betty Boyd. *First Ladies*. New York: Oxford University Press, 1987.

Foreman, Norma Ruth Holly. "The First Lady as a Leader of Public Opinion," Ph.D. dissertation, University of Texas at Austin, May 1971.

CHAPTER 1: AMERICAN DREAMS

Note: All current (2000) dollar equivalencies throughout the text are calculated from the Web site of the Federal Reserve Bank of Minneapolis, www.mpls.frb.org.

American Irish Historical Society. *That the World May Know*. New York: American Irish Historical Society, 1998.

Auchincloss, Joanna Russell, and Caroline Auchincloss Fowler. *Auchincloss Family Tree, 1957*. Salem, Mass.: Higginson Book Co., 1957.

Columbia University. Alumni cards, 1987–1968. "Mr. James Thomas Aloysius Lee."

Columbia University Alumni Register 1932. New York: Columbia University, 1932.

Cremin, Lawrence. *The Transformation of the School.* New York: Alfred A. Knopf, 1961.

Davis, John H. *The Bouviers: Portrait of an American Family.* New York: Farrar, Straus & Giroux, 1969.

Downs, Winfield Scott, ed. "Lee, James T.," *Who's Who in New York 1938.* New York: Lewis Historical Publishing Co., 1938.

"James Lee, Ex-Official in City's Schools, Dies," *The New York Times,* May 15, 1928.

"James T. Lee," *National Cyclopedia of American Biography,* vol. 54. Clifton, N.J.: James T. White & Co., 1973.

"James T. Lee," *Who's Who in New York 1938.* New York: Lewis Historical Publishing Co., 1938.

La Salle University. *Mission and Goals.* Philadelphia: 1999.

———. *De La Salle Brothers.* Philadelphia: 1999.

Peters, Brooks. "Auchincloss," *Quest,* June 1990.

Pierce, R. Andrew. "Northern Irish Ancestry of Rose Anna Cox Fitzgerald, Great-Grandmother of a President," *Nexus: The Magazine of the New England Historic Genealogical Society,* October/November 1994.

Ravitch, Diane. *The Great School Wars.* New York: Basic Books, 1974.

Thompson, Lloyd, and Winfield Scott Downs, eds. "James Lee," *Who's Who in American Medicine.* New York: Who's Publications, 1925.

Genealogical Research

R. Andrew Pierce, P.O. Box 6101, Boston, MA 02114, supervised and conducted genealogical work on the family of Janet Lee (Auchincloss). He was assisted in New York City by Joseph M. Silinonte.

Selective sources used:

Ardolina, Rosemary Muscarella. *Old Calvary Cemetery: New Yorkers Carved in Stone.* Bowie, Md.: Heritage Books, Inc., 1996.

Emigrant Savings Bank records of Thomas Merritt, New York City.

Headstone #2797, Maria Curry Merritt, 1928, Old Calvary Cemetery, New York City.

Index to Civil War pensioners, 1890

Marriage certificate, New York City, of Thomas Merritt and Maria Curry, June 6, 1875

Newark, New Jersey, census: 1860, 1870, 1880

Newark, New Jersey, city directories, 1855–56, 1870, 1874m, 1878m, 1879–80

New York census: 1880, 1900, 1920

New York City cemetery compilations

New York City directories, 1860–1940

New York City Enumeration District Guide, 1900

Soundex Index, 1900

St. Patrick Pro-Cathedral, Newark, New Jersey, baptismal records for James
   Lee, b. December 23, 1852; baptism, January 1, 1853
U.S. census for New York City: 1880, 1900, 1920

Research Collections
Columbia University, Alumni Records, New York City
La Salle University, Archives, Philadelphia, Pennsylvania
Local History and Genealogy Room, New York City Public Library, New York
   City
Museum of the City of New York, New York City
Newport Historical Society, Newport, Rhode Island
New-York Historical Society, New York City
Yale University, Alumni Records, New Haven, Connecticut

Private Collections
Courtesy of Hugh D. Auchincloss III:
   Auchincloss family Bible, family records from 1730 to present time in-
      scribed therein
   Auchincloss genealogy wall chart, the Castle, Hammersmith Farm

Interviews
Hugh D. Auchincloss III, Newport, Rhode Island
Nancy M. Miller (Mrs. Edward F. Jr.) Cavanagh, Newport, Rhode Island

CHAPTER 2: NEWPORT SUMMERS
Amory, Cleveland. "Newport: There She Sits," *Harper's*, February 1948.
———. *The Last Resorts*. New York: Grosset & Dunlap, 1952.
———. *Who Killed Society?* New York: Harper & Brothers, 1960.
Auchincloss and Fowler. *Auchincloss*. Op. cit.
"Auchincloss Left $7,500 to Hospital," *The New York Times*, May 14, 1913.
Auchincloss, Louis. *A Writer's Capital*. Minneapolis: University of Minnesota
   Press, 1974.
Baughman, James L. *Henry R. Luce and the Rise of the American News Media*.
   Boston: Twayne Publishers, 1987.
Biltz, Esther Auchincloss. "I Remember . . . Reminiscences of Hammersmith
   Farm," *Newport History* (bulletin of the Newport Historical Society), spring
   1994.
Birmingham, Stephen. *America's Secret Aristocracy*. Boston: Little, Brown and Co.,
   1987.
———. *The Grandes Dames*. New York: Simon & Schuster, 1982.
———. *The Right People: A Portrait of the American Social Establishment*. Boston:
   Little, Brown and Co., 1968.
Cable, Mary. *Top Drawer: American High Society from the Gilded Age to the Roaring
   Twenties*. New York: Atheneum, 1984.
Chernow, Ron. *Titan: The Life of John D. Rockefeller, Sr.* New York: Random
   House, 1998.

De Ros, Robert. "New England's 'Lively Experiment,' Rhode Island," *National Geographic,* September 1968.

Gelderman, Carol. *Louis Auchincloss: A Writer's Life.* New York: Crown Publishers, 1993.

Heminway, C. Stuart, ed. *Four Years Out, A Record of Yale 1920.* Waterbury, Conn.: Heminway Press, 1924.

Hopf, John T. *Hammersmith Farm.* Newport, R.I.: Camelot Gardens, Inc., 1979.

"Hugh D. Auchincloss Dies," *The New York Times,* April 22, 1913.

"In Town & Country," *Town & Country,* March 15, 1913.

Long, George W. "Rhode Island, Modern City-State," *National Geographic,* August 1948.

Martin, Ralph G. *Henry and Clare: An Intimate Portrait of the Luces.* New York: G.P. Putnam's Sons, 1991.

Newport: Season of 1875: With Map, List of Summer Residents and Tide Table. Newport, R.I.: Davis & Pitman, 1875.

"Newport Summer Residents." *The Newport Directory, 1885.* Newport, R.I.: Sampson, Murdock & Co., 1885.

Panaggio, Leonard J. *Portrait of Newport.* Providence, R.I.: The Savings Bank of Newport, 1969.

————. *Portrait of Newport II.* Providence, R.I.: The Savings Bank of Newport, 1994.

Patterson, Morehead. *History of the Class of Nineteen Hundred Twenty* (Yale University). New Haven, Conn.: Tuttle, Morehouse and Taylor Company, 1920.

Peters. "Auchincloss," op. cit.

Preservation Society of Newport, County. *Newport Mansions, Year Round 2000.* Newport, R.I., 2000.

"Summer Residents." *Newport & How to See It, with Summer Residents, 1871.* Newport, R.I.: Davis & Pitman, 1871.

Swanberg, W. A. *Luce and His Empire.* New York: Charles Scribner's Sons, 1972.

Warburton, Eileen. *In Living Memory: A Chronicle of Newport, Rhode Island, 1888–1988.* Newport, R.I.: Newport Savings and Loan Association, 1988.

Research Collections
Newport Historical Society, Newport, Rhode Island
Newport Room, Newport Public Library, Newport, Rhode Island
Redwood Library and Athenaeum, Newport, Rhode Island
Yale University, Alumni Records, New Haven, Connecticut

Private Collections
Courtesy of Hugh D. Auchincloss III:
    Auchincloss family Bible
    Auchincloss genealogy chart
    "Chart drawn up for the purpose of showing Colonial Ancestry of the descendants of John A. Auchincloss and Elizabeth Buck"

Emma Jennings Auchincloss letter to Mrs. James T. Lee, East Hampton, July 3, 1942

Original manuscript of Esther Auchincloss Biltz, memories of Hammersmith Farm

Interviews

Hugh D. Auchincloss III, Newport, Rhode Island

Frank Hale, president, Fort Adams Trust, Newport, Rhode Island

Margaret (Mrs. Robert L.) Kearney, Chevy Chase, Maryland

Dick Masse, superintendent, Fort Adams State Park, Newport, Rhode Island

John (Jock) F. Nash Jr. (grandson of Esther Auchincloss Biltz), Bethesda, Maryland

CHAPTER 3: BUILDING THE FACADE

Alpern, Andrew. *Historic Manhattan Apartment Houses*. New York: Dover Publications, 1996.

————. *Luxury Apartment Houses of Manhattan*. New York: Dover Publications, 1992.

Andrews, Suzanna. "Vanished Opulence," *Vanity Fair*, January 2001.

"Apartments," *Encyclopedia of New York City*. New Haven, Conn.: Yale University Press, 1995.

Berkman, Johanna. "The Fall of the House of Steinberg," *New York*, June 19, 2000.

Burns, Ric, and James Sanders. *New York: An Illustrated History*. New York: Alfred A. Knopf, 1999.

"Central Savings Bank Elects Chief Executive," *The New York Times*, January 20, 1961.

Davis. *The Bouviers*. Op. cit.

"Deaths: Lee," *New York Evening Post*, May 15, 1928.

"Died: Lee," *New York Sun*, May 15, 1928.

"Dr. James Lee Dies at 75," *New York Herald Tribune*, May 15, 1928.

"Elected to Directorate of Chase National Bank," *The New York Times*, April 29, 1943.

"Fence May Get Life Under Baumes Law," *The New York Times*, May 7, 1927.

"Fifth Avenue Mansion of Jay Gould Sold," *The New York Times*, April 29, 1944.

Goldberger, Paul. *The City Observed: New York, A Guide to the Architecture of Manhattan*. New York: Random House, 1979.

Gray, Christopher. "Quality Developer with a Legacy," *The New York Times*, March 12, 1995.

Hawes, Elizabeth. *New York, New York: How the Apartment House Transformed the Life of the City, 1869–1930*. New York: Henry Holt and Co., 1993.

Homberger, Eric. *The Historical Atlas of New York City: A Visual Celebration of Nearly 400 Years of New York City's History*. New York: Henry Holt and Co., 1994.

"Hospital Site Sold in $7,000,000 Deal," *The New York Times*, April 9, 1927.

"James Lee, Ex-Official in City's Schools, Dies," *The New York Times,* May 15, 1928.

"James T. Lee," *National Cyclopedia of American Biography.* Op. cit.

"James T. Lee Buys East 48th St. Site," *The New York Times,* January 22, 1928.

"James T. Lee, 90, Summer Resident," *East Hampton Star,* January 11, 1968.

Klemesrud, Judy. "8 Holdout Tenants at Closed Shelton Towers Win 5-Year Fight," *The New York Times,* July 30, 1976.

Landau, Sarah Bradford and Carl W. Condit. *Rise of the New York Skyscraper, 1865–1913.* New Haven, Conn.: Yale University Press, 1996.

"L.I.U. Ceremony Held," *The New York Times,* November 28, 1956.

New York City Directory (Polk directory), 1933–34. New York.

New York City Directory (Trow directory). New York: Trow Publishing, published yearly, publication volumes consulted from 1870 to 1925.

"New York's Changing Scene," *New York News,* November 25, 1956.

"New York's Changing Scene," *New York News,* July 12, 1959.

"Old New York in Pictures," *New York Tribune,* June 8, 1929.

"One of Selling Syndicate Repurchases Nurses' Home," *The New York Times,* April 12, 1927.

"Open New Subway Lines to Traffic: Called a Triumph," *The New York Times,* August 2, 1918.

Oser, Alan S. "About Real Estate," *The New York Times,* April 7, 1976.

"Park Avenue Corner Sold to Builder," *The New York Times,* January 17, 1923.

"Park Avenue Deal Involves $2,500,000," *The New York Times,* October 20, 1922.

Patterson, Jerry E. *Fifth Avenue: The Best Address.* New York: Rizzoli, 1998.

"Record Listing," *The New York Times,* April 5, 1981.

Reed, Henry Hope Jr. "998 Fifth: Classical New York Apartment House," *New York Herald Tribune,* April 8, 1962.

"Renaissance in Gracie Square Offers Apartments for Affluent," *The New York Times,* November 22, 1964.

Stern, A. M., Gregory Gilmartin, and Thomas Mellins. *Architecture and Urbanism Between the Two World Wars.* New York: Rizzoli, 1987.

Swanson, Carl, ed. "Real Estate: Eastern Standards," *New York,* January 29, 2001.

"30-Year Transition Completed in Area on the Upper East Side," *The New York Times,* October 22, 1961.

Trager, James, ed. *The People's Chronology.* New York: Holt, Rinehart and Winston, 1979.

White, Norval, and Elliot Willensky, eds. *American Institute of Architects Guide to New York City.* New York: American Institute of Architects, 1978.

Research Collections

Columbia University, University Archives and Columbiana Library, Lowe Memorial Library, New York City

Local History and Genealogy Room, New York Public Library, New York City

Museum of the City of New York, New York City

New-York Historical Society, New York City

Interviews

Verne Atwater, former chairman and president, Central Savings Bank, New Jersey

Hugh D. Auchincloss III, Newport, Rhode Island

James Lee Auchincloss, Ashland, Oregon

Florence (Mrs. James) Bloor, Hilton Head, North Carolina

Mary-Lee "Mimi" Ryan (Mrs. William A. V.) Cecil, Asheville, North Carolina

John H. Davis, New York City

Carter B. Horsley, New York City

Raymond T. O'Keefe, James T. Lee Foundation, Inc., New York City

Lewis Rutherfurd, Hong Kong

CHAPTER 4: THE BLACK SHEIK

Amory. *Last Resorts*. op. cit.

Bookbinder, Bernie. *Long Island: People and Places, Past and Present*. New York: Harry N. Abrams, 1983.

"Bouvier Estate Goes to Widow," *The New York Times*, January 19, 1926.

"Bouvier, John Vernou," *National Cyclopedia of American Biography*, vol. 47. Clifton, N.J.: James T. White & Co., 1947.

Bouvier, Kathleen. *Black Jack Bouvier: The Life and Times of Jackie O's Father*. New York: Kensington Publishing Corp., 1974.

Class History, 1914, Sheffield Scientific School, Yale University, New Haven, Connecticut, 1914.

Class of 1914S, Yale University. Twenty-five Year Record. New Haven, Conn.: Yale University, 1939.

"Cottage List for Season of 1928," *East Hampton Star*, July 20, 1928.

Davis, John H. *Jacqueline Bouvier: An Intimate Memoir*. New York: John Wiley & Sons, 1996.

————. *The Bouviers*. Op. cit.

Davis, Lee. "Living In: East Hampton," *Newsday*, August 13, 1988.

Fearon, Peter. *Hamptons Babylon: Life Among the Super-Rich on America's Riviera*. Secaucus, N.J.: Birch Lane Press, 1998.

Gaines, Steven. *Philistines at the Hedgerow: Passion and Property in the Hamptons*. Boston: Little, Brown and Co., 1998.

Hefner, Robert J., ed. *East Hampton's Heritage: An Illustrated Architectural Record*. New York: W. W. Norton & Co.

Heymann, C. David. *Poor Little Rich Girl: The Life and Legend of Barbara Hutton*. Secaucus, N.J.: Lyle Stuart, 1984.

"Historic East Hampton" (map). Amagansett, N.Y.: Streetwise Maps Inc., 1998.

"John V. Bouvier, 82, Retired Broker, Dies," *East Hampton Star*, January 8, 1926.

"John V. Bouvier, 82, Retired Broker, Dies," *The New York Times*, January 3, 1926.

"Jubilee Week at Maidstone Club July 5th to 12th," *East Hampton Star*, July 3, 1941.

"Lee Robbery Still a Mystery," *East Hampton Star*, August 6, 1926.

Maidstone Club, The Second Fifty Years, 1941–1991. West Kennebunk, Me.: Phoenix Publishing, 1991.

Maidstone Club Membership Lists: 1915, 1923, 1967. East Hampton, N.Y.

Mansfield, Stephanie. *The Richest Girl in the World.* New York: G. P. Putnam's Sons, 1992.

Markey, Morris. "Summer in the Hamptons," *Holiday,* June 1947.

McBrien, William. *Cole Porter: A Biography.* New York: Alfred A. Knopf, 1998.

"Miss Carter Engaged," *The New York Times,* April 7, 1920.

"Most Holy Trinity Church, 1894–1969," pamphlet, East Hampton, N.Y., 1969.

"Mrs. Caroline E. Bouvier," *East Hampton Star,* January 25, 1929.

"Mrs. J. V. Bouvier Dies," *The New York Times,* January 22, 1929.

Napoli, Michelle. "Lasata to Be Split," *East Hampton Star,* May 25, 1995.

Office of the Town Planner. "Historic and Cultural Features," Town of East Hampton, New York, May 7, 1976.

"$115,000 for 'Change Seat,'" *The New York Times,* January 14, 1920.

"$1,000 Reward," advertisement, *East Hampton Star,* July 30, 1926.

"Ryan-Lee," *East Hampton Star,* January 21, 1927.

1630–1976 Life Styles East Hampton, exhibition program, Guild Hall of East Hampton, N.Y., 1976.

Schwarz, Ted. *Trust No One: The Glamorous Life and Bizarre Death of Doris Duke.* New York: St. Martin's Press, 1997.

Swartz, Charles. *Cole Porter: A Biography.* New York: Dial Press, 1977.

"Summer Colony Notes," *East Hampton Star,* January 21, 1927.

Tanner, Jason. "East Hampton: The Solid Gold Melting Pot," *House Beautiful,* August 1958.

Walls, Jeanette. *Dish: The Inside Story on the World of Gossip.* New York: Avon, 2000.

Who's Who at East Hampton-Southampton. New York: Gutman, 1928.

Woodward, Nancy Hyden. *East Hampton: A Town and Its People, 1648–1994.* East Hampton, N.Y.: Fireplace Press, 1995.

Yale-1914S, Seven-Year Record, New Haven, Conn.: Yale University, 1922.

Research Collections

Pennypacker Long Island Collection, East Hampton Public Library, East Hampton, New York

Sweet Briar College, Archives, Sweet Briar, Virginia

Yale University, Archives, New Haven, Connecticut

Private Collection

Courtesy of Hugh D. Auchincloss III, Newport, Rhode Island:
    Dance card of Janet Lee, St. Paul's School, Lincoln's Birthday, 1924

Interviews

Letitia Baldrige, Washington, D.C.

Kathleen (Mrs. Michel) Bouvier, Remsenburg, New York

Mary-Lee "Mimi" Ryan (Mrs. William A. V.) Cecil, Asheville, North Carolina

John H. Davis, New York City
Maude Davis, New York City (niece of Jack Bouvier)
Candy (Mrs. James H.) Van Alen, Newport, Rhode Island

CHAPTER 5: LIFE WITH JACK BOUVIER

"Annual Benefit Fair Held on Green at East Hampton," *The New York Times,*
    July 30, 1939.
"Baseball Game at Maidstone Club Sunday," *East Hampton Star,* July 14, 1933.
Berke, Allan J. "What Does Love Have to Do with It?" *New York State Bar
    Journal,* January 1997.
Bouvier, John Vernou. *Our Forebears: From the Earliest Times to the First Half of
    the Year 1940.* New York: privately published, 1940.
Bouvier. *Black Jack Bouvier.* Op. cit.
"Cherokee Annexes Jumping Title in Horse Show at Southampton," *The New
    York Times,* August 11, 1935.
"Chileans Take the Jumps," *Newsweek,* November 21, 1938.
"Cottage List for Season of 1929," *East Hampton Star,* May 24, 1929.
"Cottage List — 1935," *East Hampton Star,* July 4, 1935.
"Danseuse, Bouvier Entry, Wins Hunter Championship at Show," *East Hampton
    Star,* August 23, 1934.
Davis. *Jacqueline Bouvier.* Op. cit.
——. *The Bouviers.* Op. cit.
"Devon Yacht Club," *East Hampton Star,* July 3, 1941.
"Dog Shows at Village Fair; Barking Ones, Chinaware," *East Hampton Star,* July
    12, 1934.
"d'Olier-Lee," *East Hampton Star,* April 23, 1934.
"East Hampton Cottage List — 1930," *East Hampton Star,* July 25, 1930.
"East Hampton Cottage List — 1931," *East Hampton Star,* June 19, 1931.
"East Hampton Cottage List — 1932," *East Hampton Star,* July 8, 1932.
"East Hampton Cottage List — 1933," *East Hampton Star,* June 30, 1933.
"East Hampton Cottage List — 1934," *East Hampton Star,* July 12, 1934.
"East Hampton Riding Club's Annual Horse Show August 12," *East Hampton
    Star,* July 20, 1939.
East Hampton Social Guide. East Hampton, N.Y.: 1931, 1938, 1939, 1940, 1941,
    1942, 1943, 1944, 1951.
"E. H. Horse Show at Riding Club Saturday, 15th," *East Hampton Star,* July
    30, 1936.
"E. H. Horse Show Planned Here for Saturday, Aug. 12," *East Hampton Star,*
    July 13, 1939.
"Eleventh Annual Horse Show Saturday Has Fine Entry List," *East Hampton
    Star,* August 15, 1935.
Ennis, Thomas W. "Shopping Center on L. I. Will Make Barns into Boutiques,"
    The New York Times, October 23, 1966.
"Fair at East Hampton," *Social Spectator,* August 14, 1940.
"Fancy Dress Riding and Driving Party Next Saturday at Paddock," *East Hamp-
    ton Star,* July 6, 1928.

Fifty Years of the Maidstone Club 1891–1941. East Hampton, N.Y. 1941.

"Fine Entries in for Horse Show Here August 15," *East Hampton Star*, August 6, 1936.

"First Lady Was First-Class Rider Here," *East Hampton Star*, November 17, 1960.

"Flowing Gold Wins Double Honors at Show," *East Hampton Star*, August 21, 1931.

"Forefathers' Day Attracts Crowds to Academy," *East Hampton Star*, August 15, 1940.

"Franklin d'Olier," *East Hampton Star*, February 23, 2000.

Fuller, Samuel. *New York in the 1930's*. New York: Pocket Archives, 1999.

"Gymkhana at Riding Club Sat. July 18," *East Hampton Star*, July 3, 1931.

Hefner, Robert J., ed. *East Hampton Heritage: An Illustrated Architectural Record*. East Hampton, N.Y.: Ladies' Village Improvement Society, 1996.

"High Hats and Horses," *Newsweek*, November 21, 1938.

"History of the AHSA," American Horse Show Association flier, Lexington, Kentucky.

History of the Hampton Classic. Hampton Classic Horse Show 1999 program, Bridgehampton, N.Y., 1999.

"Horse Show at East Hampton," *Social Spectator*, August 28, 1940.

"Horse Show at E. H. Riding Club Sat., August 14," *East Hampton Star*, July 29, 1937.

"Horse Show Cards Curtailed by War," *The New York Times*, December 24, 1939.

"Horse Show Championships to Exhibitors from Out of Town," *East Hampton Star*, August 22, 1935.

"Horse Show Opens New Social Season," *The New York Times*, November 6, 1938.

"Horse Show Tomorrow," *East Hampton Star*, August 19, 1927.

"Horse Show Year a Brilliant One," *East Hampton Star*, December 27, 1936.

"Horse Show Year Marked by Gains," *The New York Times*, December 26, 1937.

Hunter, Frances. "East Hampton Notes," *Social Spectator*, July 17, 1935.

"Irish Army Riders Reached Heights," *The New York Times*, December 29, 1935.

"Jackie and Ari: The Inside Story," *Boston Herald American*, January 25, 1976.

"James Parrish Lee," *East Hampton Star*, September 18, 1941.

"Jubilee Week at Maidstone Club July 5th to 12th," *East Hampton Star*, July 3, 1941.

"Junior Horse Show Saturday at Riding Club," *East Hampton Star*, August 8, 1940.

"Large Entry List for Dog Show on Sunday, July 5," *East Hampton Star*, July 3, 1941.

"Local Winners at Southampton Horse Show Sat.," *East Hampton Star*, August 4, 1933.

"L.V.I.S. Village Fair Chairmen Meet and Discuss Plans for Event," *East Hampton Star*, July 3, 1931.

Maidstone Club: The Second Fifty Years. Op. cit.

"Maidstone Opens Season with Dinner-Dance," *East Hampton Star*, July 31, 1931.

"Many Entries in Village Fair Dog Show Here," *East Hampton Star*, July 31, 1931.

"Maude B. Davis," *East Hampton Star*, August 26, 1999.

Mauretania, S. S., "Passenger List," Cunard Line, March 24–March 28, 1932.

"M. C. Bouvier Left $100,000 to Public," *The New York Times*, September 4, 1935.

McDonald, John. "A Native of L.I.," *Newsday*, May 21, 1994.

"Mellon Entries Capture Honors at Horse Show," *East Hampton Star*, August 19, 1937.

"Michel C. Bouvier," *East Hampton Star*, August 1, 1935.

"Michel Bouvier 3rd," *East Hampton Star*, July 21, 1994.

"Michel C. Bouvier, Wall St. Dean, Dies," *The New York Times*, July 30, 1935.

Miller, William H. Jr. *The Great Luxury Liners, 1927–1954*. New York: Dover Publications, 1981.

"Montauk Horse Show," *East Hampton Star*, August 15, 1930.

"Montauk Riding Club Now Open for Season," *East Hampton Star*, August 5, 1937.

"Mrs. Bouvier Sheds 'Love Commuter,' " *New York Daily News*, July 23, 1940.

"Mrs. Bouvier Wins 8 Ribbons at Horse Show," *East Hampton Star*, August 20, 1936.

"Mrs. Emma Stone Bouvier Weds Lieut. Allan in New York," *East Hampton Star*, September 9, 1932.

"Mrs. J. Bouvier's Chestnut Mare Takes Honors," *East Hampton Star*, August 25, 1933.

"Mrs. M. S. Bouvier, Prominent Here, Dies in New York," *East Hampton Star*, April 4, 1940.

"Mrs. R. L. Bacon, Major Bouvier Address G.O.P.," *East Hampton Star*, September 3, 1936.

Napoli, Michelle. "Echos of Boarding House Era," *East Hampton Star*, July 4, 1996.

"New Classes Add Interest to 15th E. H. Horse Show," *East Hampton Star*, July 27, 1939.

"1931 Village Fair Receipts Will About Equal Last Year's," *East Hampton Star*, August 7, 1931.

"9th Annual Horse Show at Riding Club August 19," *East Hampton Star*, August 4, 1933.

"Pet Dog Show Committee Meets with Mrs. Bouvier 3rd," *East Hampton Star*, July 24, 1931.

"Pet Dog Show One of Village Fair Features," *East Hampton Star*, July 18, 1935.

Phillips, Cabell. *From the Crash to the Blitz, 1929–1939*. New York: New York Times Company, 1969.

Plateris, A. A. *100 Years of Marriage and Divorce Statistics: United States, 1867–1967*. Hyattsville, Md.: National Center for Health Statistics, Series Reports No. 24, 1973.

"Profits Marked Horse Show Year," *The New York Times,* December 25, 1938.

Radziwill, Lee. "Opening Chapters," *Ladies' Home Journal,* January 1973.

Rattray, Jeanette Edwards. *Up and Down Main Street: An Informal History of East Hampton and Its Old Houses.* East Hampton, N.Y.: East Hampton Star, 1968.

"Rev. Gerald L. K. Smith to Give Address at Bouvier Home Sunday," *East Hampton Star,* August 19, 1937.

Riding Club of East Hampton, Members List, 1915 through 1932.

———. Fourth Annual Horse Show, 1928.

———. Fifth Annual Horse Show, 1929.

———. Ninth Annual Horse Show, August 19, 1933.

———. Tenth Annual Horse Show, August 18, 1934.

———. Eleventh Annual Horse Show, August 17, 1935.

———. Twelfth Annual Horse Show, August 15, 1936.

———. Thirteenth Annual Horse Show, August 14, 1937.

———. Fourteenth Annual Horse Show, August 13, 1938.

"Riding Club's 13th Annual Horse Show August 14," *East Hampton Star,* July 22, 1937.

"Riding Club's 16th Annual Horse Show Saturday, Aug. 23," *East Hampton Star,* July 3, 1941.

"Riding Club to Open," *East Hampton Star,* May 28, 1936.

Rosenbaum, Susan. "Faith and the Country Doctor," *East Hampton Star,* December 30, 1999.

"Rowdy Hall Restored; Filled with Fine Collection of Old Furniture," *East Hampton Star,* June 25, 1926.

"Seal King Is Best at East Hampton," *The New York Times,* August 21, 1927.

"Sons of Revolution Name Bouvier," *The New York Times,* June 14, 1931.

"Stock Exchange Seat for Allen A. Pierce," *The New York Times,* January 10, 1936.

"Successful Year for Horse Shows," *The New York Times,* December 30, 1934.

"Sutherland Rose and Ace o' Hearts Outstanding in Annual Horse Show," *East Hampton Star,* August 23, 1929.

"Sweden's Riders Won Honors Here," *The New York Times,* December 31, 1933.

"The National Horse Show," *Fortune,* November 1932.

"Third Annual East Hampton Horse Show," *Rider and Driver,* September 3, 1927.

"Third Annual Horse Show at Southampton Riding and Hunt Club," *East Hampton Star,* August 7, 1931.

"Two Governors Open Great Hudson Bridge as Throngs Look On," *The New York Times,* October 25, 1931.

"Village Fair a Bright Success," *East Hampton Star,* August 1, 1935.

"Wall Streets-Mugwumps in First of Three Game Series," *East Hampton Star,* July 26, 1934.

Research Collections

American Horse Show Association, Lexington, Kentucky

Local History and Genealogy Room, New York City Public Library, New York City

Museum of the City of New York, New York City
New-York Historical Society, New York City
Pennypacker Long Island Collection, East Hampton Public Library, East
    Hampton, New York

Interviews
Hugh D. Auchincloss III, Newport, Rhode Island
Kathleen (Mrs. Michel) Bouvier, Remsenburg, New York
Mary-Lee "Mimi" Ryan (Mrs. William A. V.) Cecil, Asheville, North Carolina
Sharon Cole, American Horse Show Association, Lexington, Kentucky
John H. Davis, New York City
Maude Davis, New York City
Carter B. Horsley, New York City
William Steinkraus, Norton, Connecticut

CHAPTER 6: JANET'S ESTATE
Books on Riding
American Horse Show Association. *Official Horse Show Record — 1934*. New York:
    American Horse Show Association, 1935.
————. *Official Horse Show Record — 1936*. New York: American Horse Show
    Association, 1937.
————. *Official Horse Show Record — 1938*. New York: American Horse Show
    Association, 1939.
Landon, Alfred M. *Official Horse Show Blue Book: The Equine Hall of Fame*. New
    York: J. W. Waring, Publisher, 1936.
Spector, David A. *A Guide to American Horse Shows*. New York: Arco Publishing
    Company, 1973.
Sprague, Kurth. *The National Horse Show: A Centennial History, 1883–1983*. New
    York: The National Horse Show Foundation, 1985.

General
"At Bailey's Beach, Newport," *Social Spectator*, July 19, 1940.
"Auchincloss Divorce," *Newport Daily News*, May 24, 1932.
"Auchincloss Estate in Excess of $5,000,000," *Newport Daily News*, September
    21, 1942.
Auchincloss, Hugh D. III. "Growing Up with Jackie: My Memories 1941–
    1953," *Groton School Quarterly*, May 1998.
"Auchincloss to Wed Mrs. Nina G. Vidal," *Washington Evening Star*, October 8,
    1935.
Baughman. *Henry R. Luce*. Op. cit.
Blaine, Beth. "By the Way —," *Washington Evening Star*, February 1, 1943.
Birmingham. *Grandes Dames*. Op. cit.
Boss, Judith A. *Newport: A Pictorial History*. Norfolk, Va.: Donning Company,
    Publishers, 1981.
"Changes Among Brokers," *The New York Times*, May 23, 1931.

Coffin, Patricia. "Newport Season," *Social Spectator*, July 31, 1941.

Corbin, Patricia. *Summer Cottages and Castles: Scenes from the Good Life*. New York: E. P. Dutton, 1983.

Dickerson, Nancy. *Among Those Present*. New York: Random House, 1976.

"Elected to Directorate of Chase National Bank." Op. cit.

"Fifth Ave. Mansion of Jay Gould Sold." Op. cit.

Friedlander, Jackie. "Jackie Kennedy's Girlhood Home for Sale," *The Connection* (McLean, Va.), November 6, 1995.

"Gen. Robert Olds Weds," *The New York Times*, June 7, 1942.

"Granted Divorce," *Washington Evening Star*, September 20, 1934.

Greenwald, Marilyn S. *A Woman of the Times: Journalism, Feminism and the Career of Charlotte Curtis*. Athens, Ohio: University Press, 1990.

"Hanes, Here, Plans for Willkie Drive," *The New York Times*, July 24, 1940.

"H. D. Auchincloss Resigns Post," *The New York Times*, January 21, 1931.

"Hears Auchincloss Plans to Hold Post," *The New York Times*, November 28, 1930.

Historical American Buildings Survey Inventory. Fairfax, Va.: Fairfax County Division of Planning, 1970.

"H. M. Iseman Buys Seat," *The New York Times*, January 3, 1936.

"Horse Show at East Hampton," *Social Spectator*, August 30, 1941.

"Horse Show to Aid Soldiers & Sailors Club of New York," *East Hampton Star*, July 31, 1941.

"Hugh Auchincloss Marries in Capital," *The New York Times*, October 9, 1935.

"Hugh D. Auchincloss to Buy Exchange Seat," *The New York Times*, May 8, 1931.

"Hugh D. Auchincloss Weds Mrs. Janet Bouvier at Virginia Estate," *Newport Daily News*, June 23, 1942.

"Hugh Dudley Auchincloss Marries Mrs. Nina Gore Vidal in Washington," *Newport Daily News*, October 8, 1935.

Hunt, Marjorie. "Girlhood Home of Mrs. Kennedy Optioned for Luxury Apartments," *The New York Times*, January 14, 1962.

Ilsley, Henry R. "Preparedness Is Keynote at Opening of Horse Show," *The New York Times*, November 8, 1940.

"Lone Jap Here Works at Rectory," *East Hampton Star*, May 22, 1941.

"Many Entries in for Saturday's Horse Show Here," *East Hampton Star*, August 21, 1941.

Martin, Ralph G. *Henry and Clare*. Op. cit.

"Miss De Chrapovitsky Engaged to Marry," *The New York Times*, April 29, 1925.

"Mrs. Auchincloss Hit by Propeller," *Washington Evening Star*, July 16, 1928.

"Mrs. Auchincloss Is Felled by Plane," *The New York Times*, July 16, 1928.

"Mrs. H. D. Auchincloss Asks Reno Divorce," *The New York Times*, May 24, 1932.

"Mrs. H. D. Auchincloss in Reno for Divorce," *The New York Times*, April 15, 1932.

"Mrs. James T. Lee," *East Hampton Star*, March 4, 1943.

"Mrs. James T. Lee," *The New York Times*, February 27, 1943.

"Mrs. Janet Bouvier Weds Lieut. Hugh Auchincloss," *East Hampton Star,* June 25, 1942.

"Mrs. M. S. Bouvier, Prominent Here, Dies in New York," *East Hampton Star,* April 4, 1940.

"Newport Estate Lease Announced," *Providence Journal-Bulletin,* May 20, 1938.

Newport Social Index — 1941. Newport, R.I.: The Newport Social Index Association, 1941. *Also* 1942, 1944, 1945, 1946.

Patterson. *Fifth Avenue.* Op. cit.

"Peking Chicks Now Roam Auchincloss Rock Garden," *Newport Daily News,* May 9, 1943.

Phelps, Harriet Jackson. *Newport in Flower: A History of Newport's Horticultural Heritage.* Newport, R.I.: Preservation Society of Newport County, 1979.

Randall, Anne, and Robert P. Foley. *Newport: A Tour Guide.* Newport, R.I.: Catboat Press, 1970.

"Red Cross Notes," *Fairfax Herald,* May 26, 1944.

"Riding Club's 16th Annual Show Saturday, August 23," *East Hampton Star,* August 14, 1941.

Stanton, Robert J., ed. *View from a Window: Conversations with Gore Vidal.* Secaucus, N.J.: Lyle Stuart, 1980.

"Steinkraus Captures Two Titles at the East Hampton Horse Show," *The New York Times,* August 24, 1941.

"Steinkraus Wins Double Honors in Horse Show Here," *East Hampton Star,* August 28, 1941.

Tabor, Grace. "A Palate for Garden Making," *New Country Life,* March 1917.

"The Garden of Hammersmith Farm, Newport, Rhode Island," *Country Life in America,* June 1916.

"These Fascinating Ladies!" *Washington Herald,* March 9, 1938.

"Two More Concerns Will Join Exchange," *The New York Times,* May 29, 1931.

"U.S. Army Riders Shone at Garden," *The New York Times,* December 21, 1941.

"U.S. Army Riders Won Show Honors," *The New York Times,* December 22, 1940.

Vidal, Gore. *Palimpsest: A Memoir.* New York: Penguin Books, 1995.

Walsh, Lee. "Two Moves in the Offing," *Washington Evening Star,* November 22, 1960.

"Washington Office Changes Hands," *The New York Times,* June 14, 1931.

"Wed in Cathedral with Russian Rites," *The New York Times,* June 5, 1925.

Research Collections

John F. Kennedy Memorial Library, Boston, Massachusetts:
   Auchincloss, Hugh D. III, "Growing Up with Jackie," Original unedited manuscript, 1997.
Newport Historical Society, Newport, Rhode Island
Newport Room, Newport Public Library, Newport, Rhode Island
Virginia Room, Fairfax County Public Library, Fairfax City, Virginia
Washingtoniana Division, Martin Luther King Memorial Library, District of Columbia Public Library, Washington, D.C.

Private Collection
Courtesy Hugh D. Auchincloss III:
    Emma Jennings Auchincloss, letters to Margaret Merritt Lee, July 3, 1942;
        Janet Lee Auchincloss, July 22, 1942
    Hugh D. Auchincloss III, "Toast to J.L.A.M," December 3, 1987

Interviews
Hugh D. Auchincloss III, Newport, Rhode Island
James Lee Auchincloss, Ashland, Oregon
Letitia Baldrige, Washington, D.C.
Charles L. Bartlett, Washington, D.C.
Ella (Mrs. Poe) Burling, Washington, D.C.
Sharon Cole, American Horse Show Association, Lexington, Kentucky
C. Wyatt Dickerson, Washington, D.C.
Mary Barelli (Mrs. Raymond A.) Gallagher, Alexandria, Virginia
Frank Hale, president, Fort Adams Trust, Newport, Rhode Island
Dick Masse, superintendent, Fort Adams State Park, Newport, Rhode Island
William Steinkraus, Norton, Connecticut
Elisa (Mrs. Joseph J. Sr.) Sullivan, Newport, Rhode Island
Candy (Mrs. James H.) Van Alen, Newport, Rhode Island

CHAPTER 7: ALL IN THE FAMILY
"America's Leading Debutantes," *Life*, December 25, 1950.
"Auchinclosses Give Party Following Christening," *Washington Evening Star*,
    January 8, 1946.
Auchincloss. "Growing Up with Jackie." Op. cit.
Beale, Betty, "Auchinclosses Hold Christening Party," *Washington Evening Star*,
    August 29, 1947.
————. "Exclusively Yours," *Washington Evening Star*, May 25, 1953.
"Biography of Mrs. Hugh D. Auchincloss," file library, Washingtoniana Divi-
    sion, Martin Luther King Memorial Library, Washington, D.C., March 21,
    1962.
Brooks, Katharine M. "Unique Newport Entertainment to Mark Debut and
    Christening," *Washington Evening Star*, July 30, 1947.
Burns, Carole. "At Miss Porter's School, Miss Bouvier Is Just Not for Sale,"
    The New York Times, April 27, 1996.
Callahan, Courtney. "Heads & Tales," *Hamptons*, September 11, 1998.
"Capital Debutantes Presented Yesterday," *Washington Evening Star*, June 17,
    1950.
Ferretti, Fred. "A Novel of Complex Family Ties Sets Off Guessing," *Washington
    Post*, April 17, 1981.
Hatfield, Julie. "Jacqueline Bouvier's Forgotten Essay," *Boston Globe*, March 3,
    1999.
"In Social Circles: Caroline Lee Bouvier Engagement," *Newport Daily News*, De-
    cember 12, 1952.

"In Social Circles: Jacqueline Lee Bouvier Engagement," *Newport Daily News*, January 21, 1952.

"In Social Circles: Miss C. Lee Bouvier Weds," *Newport Daily News*, April 18, 1953.

"Jacqueline Bouvier Makes Bow to Society at Reception," *Providence Journal*, August 2, 1947.

"Jacqueline Good Student to Teach, Says Ex-School Riding Instructor," *Boston Globe*, July 30, 1961.

"John V. Bouvier Is Dead at 82," *East Hampton Star*, January 16, 1948.

"John V. Bouvier, New York Lawyer, Last Rites Here," *East Hampton Star*, January 22, 1948.

Kaplan, Fred. *Gore Vidal: A Biography*. New York: Doubleday, 1991.

"Miss Bouvier Is Wed Here," *Washington Evening Star*, April 19, 1953.

"Miss Caroline L. Bouvier Married to M. Canfield," *East Hampton Star*, April 23, 1953.

Newport Social Index — 1946. Newport, R.I.: The Newport Social Index Association, 1946.

Newport Social Index — 1947. Newport, R.I.: The Newport Social Index Association, 1947.

O'Dell, Frank. "Of Cottages and Kings," *Palm Beach/Newport Illustrated*, September 1983.

Rattray, Jeannette Edwards. "East Hampton," *Social Spectator*, August 15, 1949.

"Senator Kennedy Takes Wife Amid Pomp of Newport," *Boston Globe*, September 12, 1953.

Wooley, Alexander. "The Fall of James Forrestal," *Washington Post*, May 23, 1999.

Research Collections

John F. Kennedy Memorial Library, Boston, Massachusetts:
   Hugh D. Auchincloss III, "Growing Up with Jackie," unedited manuscript, op. cit.

Washingtoniana Division, Martin Luther King Memorial Library, District of Columbia Public Library, Washington, D.C.

Interviews

Hugh D. Auchincloss III, Newport, Rhode Island

James Lee Auchincloss, Ashland, Oregon

Charles L. Bartlett, Washington, D.C.

Kathleen (Mrs. Michel) Bouvier, Remsenburg, New York

J. Carter Brown, Washington, D.C.

Elizabeth Daniels, Vassar College historian and retired professor of English, Poughkeepsie, New York

John H. Davis, New York City

John R. Drexel III, Newport, Rhode Island

Mary Barelli (Mrs. Raymond A.) Gallagher, Alexandria, Virginia

John Hapt, Newport, Rhode Island

Margaret (Mrs. Robert L.) Kearney, Chevy Chase, Maryland

Jane Lingo, assistant director of university relations, George Washington University, Washington, D.C.

Eileen (Mrs. John Jermain) Slocum, Newport, Rhode Island

Candy (Mrs. James H.) Van Alen, Newport, Rhode Island

CHAPTER 8: JACKIE'S WEDDING, JANET'S TRIUMPH

"As the Day Begins," *Indianapolis Star*, September 9, 1953.

Bohlin, Virginia. "Kennedy Fiancée Plans 'Simple, Small Wedding,' " *Boston Traveler*, June 25, 1953.

"Bride Nearly Crushed at Kennedy Wedding," *Atlanta Journal-Constitution*, September 13, 1953.

"Catholic Church Wedding Music Curb Too Late to Affect Kennedy Nuptials," *Newport Daily News*, September 11, 1953.

Feeney, Mark. "More Gore Details," *Boston Globe*, May 19, 1990.

Hopkinson, Natalie. "Fashioning a Show About Extraordinary Designers," *Washington Post*, March 9, 2000.

"In Social Circles," *Newport Daily News*, September 9, 1953.

"Jack Kennedy — The Senate's Gay Young Bachelor," *Saturday Evening Post*, June 18, 1953.

"Jacqueline Bouvier, Senator Kennedy to Wed," *East Hampton Star*, July 16, 1953.

"Kennedy-Bouvier License Issued," *Newport Daily News*, September 4, 1953.

"Kennedy-Bouvier Nuptials Held at St. Mary's Church Before 700 Invited Guests," *Newport Daily News*, September 12, 1953.

"Kennedy-Bouvier Rites Colorful," *Danbury* (Conn.) *News-Times*, September 14, 1953.

Kessler, Ronald. *The Sins of the Father: Joseph P. Kennedy and the Dynasty He Founded*. New York: Warner Books, 1996.

"Life Goes Courting with a U.S. Senator," *Life*, July 20, 1953.

"Miss Bouvier Becomes Bride of Sen. Kennedy at Newport," *Washington Post*, September 13, 1953.

Mulugeta, Samson. "Getting Her Due on Doll's Dress: Designer Deserves Credit," *Newsday*, January 11, 1998.

"Newlywed Kennedys Off by Plane to South of the Border Honeymoon," *Newport Daily News*, September 14, 1953.

"Newport Columnist, Sen. John Kennedy to Be Married Here in September," *Newport Daily News*, September 25, 1952.

Norton, Clem. "Clem Norton Says!" *Lynn* (Mass.) *Telegram-News*, September 13, 1953.

"Notables Attend Senator's Wedding," *The New York Times*, September 13, 1953.

"Notables at Wedding of Kennedy, Miss Bouvier," *Taunton* (Mass.) *Gazette*, September 12, 1953.

Prim, Mary. "Bouvier-Kennedy Wedding Attracts Throng in Newport," *Newport* (Va.) *News*, September 13, 1953.

"R. I. Loses Beautiful Voter," *New Bedford* (Mass.) *Standard Times*.

"Senator Kennedy Marries Jacqueline Lee Bouvier," *Fall River* (Mass.) *Herald News*, September 12, 1953.

"Senator Kennedy Takes Bride Amid Lavish Newport Setting," *Boston Sunday Herald*, September 13, 1953.

"Senator, Newporter Issued Marriage License," *Newport Daily News*, September 4, 1953.

"Senator Weds," *Life*, September 28, 1953.

"Slim Dress in Silk Prints or Black at Newport Wedding," *Women's Wear Daily*, September 14, 1953.

"Throng Sees Senator Take Bride," *Columbus* (Ohio) *Citizen*, September 13, 1953.

"Traffic Curbs Set for Kennedy-Bouvier Wedding," *Newport Daily News*, September 11, 1953.

"27 Attendants for Kennedy Wedding," *Newport Daily News*, September 10, 1953.

Walsh, Rose. "Notables at Wedding of Senator Kennedy," *Boston Sunday Post*, September 13, 1953.

———. "Kennedy Guests Set Smart Style Trends," *Washington Post*, September 16, 1953.

Watts, Elizabeth. "Quiz 'A Little Frightening' Says Kennedy's Fiancée," *Boston Globe*, June 26, 1953.

———. "Senator Kennedy's Fiancée Quits Job," *Boston Globe*, June 25, 1953.

"Wedding Principals Enter St. Mary's Church This Morning," *Newport Daily News*, September 12, 1953.

"What's She Like?" *Brockton* (Mass.) *Enterprise-Times*, June 28, 1953.

Research Collections

Black Fashion Museum, Washington, D.C.

John F. Kennedy Memorial Library, Boston, Massachusetts:

Social Files, Senator's Wedding

Letter to Kay Donovan from Evelyn Lincoln, August 31, 1953

Letter to the Honorable John F. Kennedy from John T. McCullough, July 9, 1953

Letters to Mrs. Hugh Auchincloss:

From John F. Kennedy, July 28, 1953

From Evelyn Lincoln, August 7, 1953, and September 3, 1953

"Suggested Lists for Jack's Wedding by Categories," undated

"Ushers" list forwarded to "Mrs. Auchincloss and Bobby," August 4, 1953

Original notes (III-A) delivered from Theodore H. White to Mrs. Kennedy, December 19, 1963, and edited by her

Oral Histories: Janet Auchincloss, Charles L. Bartlett, Edward Berube

National Museum of American Art, *Threads of Time, Fabric of History: A History of African Americans in Fashion Exhibition*, Smithsonian Institution, Washington, D.C.

Newport Historical Society, Newport, Rhode Island

The Wedding of Jacqueline Lee Bouvier and John Fitzgerald Kennedy, World Wide Web, www.cs.umb.edu/jfklibrary/jbkwed.htm

Interviews

Hugh D. Auchincloss III, Newport, Rhode Island
Charles L. Bartlett, Washington, D.C.
Betty Beale, Washington, D.C.
Kathleen (Mrs. Michel) Bouvier, Remsenburg, New York
John H. Davis, New York City
John R. Drexel III, Newport, Rhode Island
Mary Barelli (Mrs. Raymond A.) Gallagher, Alexandria, Virginia
Rosemary Reed, Toast & Strawberries boutique, Washington, D.C.
Marie (Mrs. Walter T.) Ridder, McLean, Virginia
Eileen (Mrs. John Jermain) Slocum, Newport, Rhode Island

CHAPTER 9: TO THE WHITE HOUSE

"A Healthy, Beautiful Boy Is Born to Jackie," *Washington Daily News*, November 25, 1960.
"Ambulance Men Tell of Alert," *Boston Globe*, November 28, 1960.
"Auchincloss Named to Chest Drive Post," *Newport Daily News*, August 29, 1959.
"Author Says Kennedy Felt He'd Break 20-Year 'Jinx,' " *The New York Times*, November 24, 1963.
"Bailey's Beach Association Elects Dyer President," *Newport Daily News*, September 11, 1960.
Beale, Betty. "Exclusively Yours: Auchincloss Reception Gay," *Washington Evening Star*, June 10, 1957.
———. "Exclusively Yours: More About Jackie Onassis," *Washington Evening Star*, April 13, 1969.
Birmingham, Stephen. "What Jackie Kennedy Has Learned from Her Mother," *Good Housekeeping*, October 15, 1962.
Braden, Joan. *Just Enough Rope*. New York: Villard Books, 1989.
Cheshire, Maxine. "Caroline Chooses Her Wardrobe on Her Own," *Washington Post*, December 18, 1960.
"Christening Held for Kennedy Son," *The New York Times*, December 3, 1960.
Christy, Marian. "The Other Man in Jackie's Life," *Boston Globe*, January 16, 1980.
"Clock Shows Son Born at 12:22," *Boston Globe*, November 25, 1960.
Cremmen, Mary. "Happiness of Children Is Jackie's Main Concern," *Boston Globe*, November 11, 1960.
———. "I'd Be Too Sad to Be of Help If I Couldn't See My Baby," *Boston Globe*, October 29, 1958.
———. "I Shop Once a Week at the Supermarket," *Boston Globe*, August 30, 1960.
Democratic National Committee, Publicity Division. "Biography of Jacqueline Bouvier Kennedy," September 17, 1960.
———. *Campaign Wife*, September 16 and 29, October 6 and 19, and November 1, 1960.
"Diana Lippert Is a Bride at St. James'," *The New York Times*, November 20, 1960.

"Doctor Reading as Call Comes Baby about Due," *Boston Globe,* November 25, 1960.

"First Kennedy Son Baptized," *Providence Journal-Bulletin,* December 9, 1960.

Furman, Bess. "Mrs. Kennedy Will Address Italian Voters," *The New York Times,* September 20, 1960.

Gort, Elizabeth. "The Restoration of Georgetown," *The Georgetowner,* May 16, 1963.

Gros, Diane. "Top 10 Political Advertisements," *George,* February/March 2000.

Hadley, Donald B. "Auchincloss Firm Adds Five Capital Partners," *Washington Evening Star,* February 26, 1958.

Harris, John. "Lovely, Laughing Jacqueline Tells on Senator Jack," *Boston Globe,* February 21, 1954.

"Jackie Gets 'Go Slow' Order from Doctor," *Boston Globe,* November 29, 1960.

"Jackie Kennedy Stops to Visit Aunt Florrie," *Boston Globe,* January 26, 1960.

"Jackie Up, Sees Son for the First Time," *Boston Globe,* November 27, 1960.

"Jacqueline Kennedy," *Boston Globe,* April 17, 1960.

"Jacqueline Tells How Home Is Jack's Refuge," *Boston Globe,* February 18, 1960.

"John Bouvier 3rd, Broker, 66, Dies," *The New York Times,* August 4, 1957.

"John V. Bouvier 3rd," *East Hampton Star,* August 8, 1957.

"John V. Bouvier 3rd," *New York Daily News,* August 4, 1957.

"Kennedy Lands in Boston, Flies to Wife's Side," *Boston Globe,* August 26, 1956.

Klein, Edward. *All Too Human: The Love Story of Jack and Jackie Kennedy.* New York: Pocket Books, 1996.

"L.I.U. Ceremony Held," *The New York Times,* November 28, 1956.

Mackey, Roberta. "Jackie Loves Georgetown Home," *Boston Traveler,* October 14, 1960.

———. "Jackie's Trademark: Elegance and Simplicity," *Boston Traveler,* October 13, 1960.

———. "Woman with Everything," *Boston Traveler,* October 10, 1960.

"Mark Senator John Kennedy," *New Bedford* (Mass.) *Standard Times,* February 28, 1954.

"Miss Alice Lyon to Wed Hugh Auchincloss, Jr.," *Washington Evening Star,* December 15, 1957.

"Miss Auchincloss Engaged to Mr. N. I. Steers, Jr.," *Washington Evening Star,* April 28, 1957.

"Miss Lyon Is Wed at St. John's," *Washington Evening Star,* February 2, 1958.

"Miss Nina Auchincloss Married to Mr. Steers," *Washington Evening Star,* June 9, 1957.

Monroe, Mary Norris. "Would Jackie Kennedy Join the Columnists?" *Newsweek,* November 1, 1960.

"Mother-in-Law for Kennedy," *Boston Globe,* November 3, 1960.

"Mother of the Day: Jacqueline Bouvier Kennedy," *The New York Times,* November 26, 1960.

"Mrs. Kennedy Improving After Loss of Child," *Boston Globe,* August 24, 1956.

"Mrs. Kennedy Learned Politics by 'Osmosis,' " *The New York Times*, July 15, 1960.

"Mrs. Kennedy's Stay in Hospital Extended a Few More Days," *Boston Globe*, August 30, 1956.

Negri, Gloria. "Jackie in White House Would Just Be Herself," *Boston Globe*, July 15, 1960.

"Newlywed Kennedys Off by Plane to South of the Border Honeymoon," op. cit.

Radziwill, Lee. *Happy Times*. New York: Assouline, 2001.

"Random Notes in Washington: How Nixon Lost a Contributor," *The New York Times*, November 14, 1960.

Robertson, Nan. "Mrs. Kennedy Says Criticisms of Her Wardrobe Are Unfair," *The New York Times*, September 15, 1960.

" 'Royal Family' Attracts Crowds to Georgetowner," *The Georgetowner*, December 1, 1960.

Russell, Jan Jarboe. *Lady Bird*. New York: Scribner, 1999.

"Senator Kennedy Flies Here to Be with Ailing Wife," *Newport Daily News*, August 28, 1956.

"Senator Kennedy's Wife Loses Expected Baby," *Boston Globe*, August 24, 1956.

"Senator Kennedy's Wife Under Knife, Loses Her Baby," *Newport Daily News*, August 24, 1986.

"Seven-Pound Girl Born to Kennedy's Wife," *Boston Globe*, November 27, 1957.

"She'll Get a Royal Facial," *Washington Post*, December 20, 1960.

"Spring Outing," *Washington Post*, May 26, 1959.

Steiner, Paul. "When Jackie and JFK Walked Down the Aisle," Women's News Service, September 12, 1969.

Thayer, Mary Van Rensselaer. *Jacqueline Bouvier Kennedy*. Garden City, N.Y.: Doubleday & Co., 1961.

"The John F. Kennedy Family: When Georgetown Knew the Kennedys," *Ladies' Home Companion*, May 1964.

Wescott, Gail. "Remembering Jackie," *People Tribute*, Summer 1994.

"Worried Kennedy Took a Faster Plane Back," *Washington Evening Star*, November 25, 1960.

Research Collections

John F. Kennedy Memorial Library, Boston, Massachusetts:
Oral Histories: Auchincloss, Letitia Baldrige, Bartlett, Lord Harlech (David Ormsby-Gore), Luella Hennessey, Maud Shaw,
The Georgetowner Archives, Washington, D.C.
Washingtoniana Division, Martin Luther King Memorial Library, District of Columbia Public Library, Washington, D.C.

Interviews

Hugh D. Auchincloss III, Newport, Virginia
James Lee Auchincloss, Ashland, Oregon
Charles L. Bartlett, Washington, D.C.
Thomas W. Braden, Woodbridge, Virginia

Benjamin C. Bradlee, Washington, D.C.

Senator and Mrs. Clairborne (Nuala) Pell, Washington, D.C.

Candy (Mrs. James H.) Van Alen, Newport, Rhode Island

CHAPTER 10: THE PRESIDENT'S MOTHER-IN-LAW

Newport Visits

"City, Navy, Prepare for Kennedy Vacation from Sept. 22 to Oct. 4," *Newport Daily News,* September 18, 1961.

Fanta, J. Julius. *Sailing with President Kennedy: The White House Yachtsman.* New York: Sea Lore Publishing Co., 1968.

"Jacqueline, Caroline Fly Home, Meet President in R.I. Today," *Boston Globe,* August 31, 1962.

"Kennedy Goes for Cruise on Yacht; Expects No More Official Visitors," *Newport Daily News,* September 27, 1961.

"Kennedy Is Facing a Busy Weekend Before Leaving Newport on Monday," *Newport Daily News,* September 30, 1961.

"Kennedy Swears in Customs Official at 'Hammersmith Farm' Ceremony," *Newport Daily News,* September 29, 1961.

"Kennedy Visit Here Delayed Until Monday," *Newport Daily News,* September 20, 1961.

"Kennedys Come Here for 10th Anniversary," *Newport Daily News,* September 12, 1963.

"Kennedys Conclude Short Newport Stay; Spend Sunday at Church, Beach, Afloat," *Newport Daily News,* September 23, 1963.

"Kennedys Devoting Time to Rest and Relaxation," *Newport Daily News,* September 28, 1961.

"Kennedys May Go Yachting in Summer," *Newport Daily News,* March 18, 1961.

"Kennedys on Cruise after Visit to Beach," *Newport Daily News,* September 14, 1963.

Kenney, Charles. *John F. Kennedy: The Presidential Portfolio, Recordings from the John F. Kennedy Library and Museum.* New York: Public Affairs, 2000.

"Mrs. Kennedy Drives Children," *Newport Daily News,* October 6, 1961.

"Mrs. Kennedy in Newport with Caroline and John Jr.," *The New York Times,* June 28, 1963.

"President at 'Hammersmith Farm' for Weekend with His Family," *Newport Daily News,* October 9, 1961.

"President Ends Newport Vacation; He May Return Here This Weekend," *Newport Daily News,* October 2, 1961.

"President Ends Visit Here, Flies to See Sam Rayburn," *Newport Daily News,* October 9, 1961.

"President Plans to Return Here for Another Weekend," *Newport Daily News,* September 16, 1963.

"President Rests Here Before Tour," *Newport Daily News,* September 20, 1963.

"President's Plans for Vacation Here Move Ahead at Naval Base, Capital," *Newport Daily News,* September 16, 1961.

"Summer Capital Again," *Newport Daily News,* September 11, 1963.

"The President Greeted by Governors and Family," *Newport Daily News*, September 13, 1963.

National Cultural Center

"A Gift from Italy," *Washington Evening Star*, July 14, 1962.

Bassett, Grace. "Drive Set for Fall for Cultural Center," *Washington Evening Star*, April 19, 1961.

Cheshire, Maxine, and Dorothy McCardle. "5000 Pay Half Million to Put Culture in Capital Letters," *Washington Post*, November 30, 1962.

"Civic Group Seeks to Shift Location of Cultural Center," *Washington Post*, February 15, 1964.

"Clare Luce Joins Culture Center Panel," *Washington Post*, May 9, 1962.

Cleland, Daisy. "College Representatives Feted," *Washington Evening Star*, November 6, 1962.

———. "Mrs. Auchincloss Rallies Cultural Center Interest," *Washington Evening Star*, April 25, 1962.

Coe, Richard L. "Time Is Now on the Center," *Washington Post*, November 18, 1962.

"Cultural Center Campaign Begins 'Arm-Twisting' Phase," *Washington Evening Star*, November 3, 1962.

"Cultural Center Drive Advances on 3 Fronts," *Washington Post*, June 11, 1963.

"Cultural Center Post Goes to J. C. Turner," *Washington Post*, February 19, 1963.

"Cultural Center Site," *Washington Evening Star*, March 13, 1962.

"Dig D.C. Wallets," *Washington Post*, March 22, 1962.

Doolittle, Jerry. "New Arts Commission Dissatisfied with Site Picked for Cultural Center," *Washington Post*, March 11, 1964.

"Downtown Site for Cultural Center, Not Foggy Bottom, Urged by Builders," *Washington Post*, February 22, 1962.

"Drive-in Culture," *Washington Post*, December 9, 1962.

Feeley, Constance. "Cultural Center as Memorial to T. R. Rejected Emphatically by Daughter," *Washington Post*, January 16, 1961.

"First Lady Leads Drive for Center," *Washington Evening Star*, February 25, 1962.

Ford, Elizabeth. "Capital's Culture Gets Lift from Gifts," *Washington Post*, May 6, 1962.

"Franklin Square Urged as Site for Kennedy Cultural Center," *Washington Post*, March 7, 1964.

"Gifts to Cultural Center," *The Georgetowner*, August 22, 1963.

"Groundbreaking Ceremonies Are Held for the Kennedy Cultural Center," *The Georgetowner*, December 10, 1964.

"Ground Breaking Ceremony, December 2, 1964," *Footlight*, December 22, 1964.

Hume, Paul. "Local Groups Given Use of Culture Site," *Washington Post*, November 12, 1962.

———. "Shape of Cultural Center Is Changing," *Washington Post*, January 7, 1962.

Hunter, Marjorie. "Mrs. Eisenhower Visits Redecorated White House," *The New York Times*, June 23, 1962.

Kelly, Orr. "National Geographic Gives Cultural Center $50,000," *Washington Post*, November 27, 1962.

———. "President to Wield Historic Spade," *Washington Evening Star*, November 21, 1964.

Kelly, Tom. "Culture Was Seen but Not Always Heard," *Washington Daily News*, November 30, 1962.

"Kennedy Cultural Center Washington's Home for the Arts," *The Georgetowner*, November 19, 1964.

"Labor Pledges to Aid Culture Center Telecast," *Washington Evening Star*, November 3, 1962.

Landauer, Jerry. "Cultural Center Staff Has Impressive List of Likeliest Donors," *Washington Post*, September 18, 1960.

"Mrs. Auchincloss Aids Cultural Center Drive," *Washington Evening Star*, March 25, 1962.

"Mrs. Auchincloss Heads Cultural Center Drive," *Washington Post*, March 23, 1962.

"Mrs. Hugh D. Auchincloss," *Vogue*, November 15, 1962.

"Mrs. Kennedy Unveils Cultural Center Model," *Newport Daily News*, September 12, 1962.

"Planners Find Flaws in 6 Cultural Center Sites," *Washington Post*, March 12, 1964.

"President Names 3 to Arts Group," *Washington Evening Star*, May 31, 1962.

"Stone Says Center Site Is Close to Social Hub," *Washington Evening Star*, April 30, 1964.

"The John F. Kennedy Center Location Plans Are Defended," *The Georgetowner*, April 16, 1964.

"12 Named to Center's Art Group," *Washington Post*, September 16, 1960.

White House Cultural Activities

Bartlett, Apple Parish, and Susan Bartlett Crater. *Sister: The Life of Legendary American Interior Decorator Mrs. Henry Parish II*. New York: St. Martin's Press, 2000.

"Discussion of 'The Georgetown Waterfront,'" *The Georgetowner*, 1965.

"$409,000 Gift for Beauty," *The Georgetowner*, January 6, 1966.

"Jackie," *Time*, January 20, 1961.

"Jacqueline Again Declines Visit to White House," *Boston Globe*, June 11, 1965.

"John Carl Warnecke, Architect, Models Lafayette Square," *The Georgetowner*, October 1, 1964.

"Kennedy Grave Site Plans Are Unveiled," *The Georgetowner*, November 26, 1964.

Lord, Ruth. *Henry F. du Pont and Winterthur: A Daughter's Portrait*. New Haven, Conn.: Yale University Press, 1998.

Shelton, Isabelle. "Jacqueline Kennedy Garden Once Caused Communication Chaos," *Boston Globe*, May 2, 1965.

Smith, Merriman. "Legend of Kennedy's Taste Was Jacqueline's," *Boston Sunday Globe,* January 6, 1966.

Stewart, Ami. "Children in the White House ... An American Portrait," *The Georgetowner,* July 6, 1967.

Patrick

"Bibs and Bootees Flood White House," *Boston Globe,* July 12, 1963.

Blair, William M. "2d Son Born to Kennedys; Has Lung Illness," *The New York Times,* August 8, 1963.

———. "Funeral Mass Said for Kennedy Baby," *The New York Times,* August 11, 1963.

Brady, Fred. "President at Wife's Bedside," *Boston Herald,* August 10, 1963.

Campbell, Kenneth D. "Onassis Eased Jackie's 3 Tragedies," *Boston Globe,* October 20, 1968.

Falacci, Frank. "JFK Gift to Wife? CIA Not Told," *Boston Globe,* July 29, 1963.

———. "Most Kin on Cape During Blessed Event," *Boston Globe,* August 8, 1963.

"Family Rejoins Mrs. Kennedy," *Boston Globe,* August 10, 1963.

"Happy Days for Jacqueline," *Boston Globe,* May 28, 1963.

Irwin, Don. "3d Baby Due for JFKs," *Boston Globe,* April 16, 1963.

"It Started Out as Cape Outing," *Boston Globe,* August 9, 1963.

"Jackie May Have Her Baby on Cape," *Boston Advertiser,* June 9, 1963.

"Jackie Promises to Visit Ireland," *Boston Herald,* December 20, 1963.

"Jackie Wants Another Baby, and Would Like It at Otis," *Boston Herald,* August 17, 1963.

"Jacqueline Ordered to Curb Activities," *Boston Globe,* August 15, 1963.

"Jacqueline Plans Quiet 34th Birthday Fete Today," *Boston Globe,* July 28, 1963.

"Jacqueline Plans Trip to Greece," *Boston Globe,* September 17, 1963.

"JFK Children Romp in Park with Mother," *Boston Globe,* June 1, 1963.

"Kennedy Baby to Be Born at Otis Hospital," *Boston Herald,* July 24, 1963.

"Love Letter from Camelot," *New York Daily News,* February 27, 1998.

"Mother Cool, Calm in Crisis," *Boston Globe,* August 9, 1963.

"Mrs. Kennedy Awaits News on Discharge," *Boston Globe,* August 13, 1963.

"Mrs. Kennedy 'Fine,' " *Boston Globe,* August 8, 1963.

"Mrs. Kennedy Gets News of Death from Doctor," *Newport Daily News,* August 9, 1963.

"Mrs. Kennedy Given Blood," *Boston Globe,* August 8, 1963.

"Mrs. Kennedy Has Visitors," *Boston Globe,* August 12, 1963.

"Mrs. Kennedy Never Knew Pat Worse 'Til JFK Said He's In ... ," *Boston Globe,* August 9, 1963.

"Mrs. Kennedy's Blunt Answers," *Boston Globe,* January 20, 1963.

"Mrs. Kennedy to Have Baby at Walter Reed," *Boston Globe,* June 5, 1963.

"News Stirs Cleveland Daughter," *Boston Globe,* August 8, 1963.

"Tragic Reunion for Kennedys," *Boston Globe,* August 9, 1963.

". . . Waits in Grief," *Boston Globe*, August 11, 1963.

"Washington's Best-Kept Secret," *Boston Globe*, April 16, 1963.

"Wexford Sends Silver Cup to Baby Kennedy," *Boston Globe*, February 12, 1961.

General

"An Award for the Winner," *The New York Times*, October 28, 1961.

Anderson, Jack. "Jackie Kennedy," *Boston Globe*, August 19, 1962.

———. "Jacqueline Kennedy: How a Year in the White House Has Changed Her," *Boston Globe*, January 14, 1962.

"Auchincloss Divorce," *The New York Times*, March 27, 1962.

Baldrige, Letitia. *In the Kennedy Style: Magical Evenings in the Kennedy White House*. New York: Doubleday, 1998.

———. *Of Diamonds and Diplomats*. Boston: Houghton Mifflin Co., 1968.

Beale, Betty. "Exclusively Yours: Auchinclosses Hold Christening Party," *Washington Evening Star*, August 29, 1962.

———. "Exclusively Yours: Kennedys May Give Up Hunt Country Estate," *Washington Evening Star*, November 12, 1961.

———. "Exclusively Yours: Pony-tailed Jacqueline Passes for Teenager," *Washington Evening Star*, September 5, 1965.

———. *Power at Play: A Memoir of Parties, Politicians and the Presidents in My Bedroom*. Washington, D.C.: Regnery Gateway, 1993.

Braden, Joan. "An Exclusive Chat with Jacqueline Kennedy," *Saturday Evening Post*, May 8, 1962.

Bradlee, Benjamin C. *A Good Life: Newspapering and Other Adventures*. New York: Simon & Schuster, 1996.

———. *Conversations with Kennedy*. New York: Pocket Books, 1976.

———. *That Special Grace*. Philadelphia: J. P. Lippincott Company, 1964.

"Brought in Foxes for Jackie's Club, Is Fined," *New York Herald*, June 24, 1962.

Christmas, Anne. "Mrs. John F. Kennedy 'Accepted' by Exclusive Group," *Boston Globe*, February 26, 1961.

Cooke, Charles. "The Enchantress," *The Georgetowner*, January 20, 1961.

Curtis, Charlotte. "Janet Jennings Auchincloss Presented in Newport," *The New York Times*, August 18, 1963.

———. "Newport Debut Revelry Carries Over to 2d Day," *The New York Times*, August 19, 1963.

Demaitre, Christina. "Mrs. Kennedy Moving to N.Y.," *Boston Globe*, July 7, 1964.

Falacci, Frank. "JFK, Family Enjoy Idyllic Cape Vacation," *Boston Globe*, August 6, 1962.

"French Consul Says Remarks Misinterpreted," *Boston Globe*, July 17, 1962.

Gallagher, Mary Barelli. *My Life with Jacqueline Kennedy*. New York: D. McKay Co., 1969.

Gallup, George. "Gallup Poll Mrs. Kennedy," *Boston Globe*, September 23, 1962.

"Georgetown Album," *The Georgetowner*, May 28, 1964.

Gutin, Myra Greenberg. "The President's Partner: The First Lady as Public Communicator, 1920–1976," Ph.D. dissertation, University of Michigan, 1983.

Hunter, Marjorie. "First Lady, Rider Herself, Attends Horse Show to Present New Trophy," *The New York Times*, October 28, 1961.

"Inaugural Ball May Be Off Limits for Jackie," *Boston Globe*, November 29, 1960.

"Inauguration Day, January 20, 1961," *The Georgetowner*, January 20, 1961.

"Jackie Gets 'Go Slow' Order from Doctor," *Boston Globe*, November 29, 1960.

"Jackie's a Busy Mother," *Boston Globe*, December 10, 1960.

"Jackie Up, Sees Son for the First Time," *Boston Globe*, November 27, 1960.

"Jacqueline Takes Spill; Horse Balks at Jump," *Boston Globe*, November 18, 1961.

"James Bloor," *The New York Times*, January 20, 1961.

Jemahl, Emil E. "Janet Auchincloss Makes Debut at Brilliant Venetian Ball Tonight," *Newport Daily News*, August 17, 1963.

"Kennedys to Live in Historic Home," *Boston Globe*, December 12, 1963.

"Kennedys Watch Show," *Boston Traveler*, October 28, 1961.

King, Mary Sarah. "White House Coolness Bothers Clubwomen," *Boston Globe*, June 26, 1962.

Lewine, Frances. "My Life in the White House," *Boston Advertiser*, July 22, 1962.

Lowe, Jacques. "A Photographer's Portrait of Jacqueline Kennedy," *This Week*, January 8, 1961.

"Mamie Talks Culture with Jacqueline," *Boston Globe*, June 24, 1962.

McArdle, Dorothy. "In '53, Jackie Just Outsider with a Camera," *Boston Globe*, January 20, 1961.

———. "President May Veto Wife's Fox Hunting," *Boston Globe*, March 24, 1961.

"Mrs. Kennedy Celebrates 35th Birthday," *Boston Globe*, July 29, 1964.

"Mrs. Kennedy, Family Move into New House," *Boston Globe*, February 9, 1964.

"Mrs. Kennedy Keeps Memory Green," *Boston Globe*, December 14, 1963.

"Mrs. Kennedy on Board of New Symphony," *New York Herald*, June 26, 1962.

"Mrs. Kennedy on Trail of Fox Near Estate," *Boston Globe*, October 31, 1962.

"Mrs. Kennedy Puts Gift Horse Through Paces," *Boston Globe*, March 23, 1962.

"Mrs. Kennedy Sells Horse That Threw Her," *Boston Globe*, January 29, 1962.

"Mrs. Kennedy Spurs Sales of Curved Sunglasses," *The New York Times*, May 14, 1962.

"Mrs. Kennedy to Pay Duty on Gift Horse," *New York Herald*, April 7, 1962.

"Scotland Apologizes to Mrs. Kennedy for Publicity Stunt," *Boston Globe*, May 21, 1962.

"Seat at Philharmonic Endowed by First Lady," *The New York Times*, October 19, 1962.

Stern, Bert. "Photograph of Mrs. Hugh D. Auchincloss," *Vogue*, November 15, 1962.

Thayer, Mary Van Rensselaer. *Jacqueline Kennedy: The White House Years*. Boston: Little, Brown and Co., 1971.

———. "Jacqueline Kennedy," part 1, *Ladies' Home Journal*, February 1961.

———. "Jacqueline Kennedy," part 2, *Ladies' Home Journal*, March 1961.

———. "Jacqueline Kennedy," part 3, *Ladies' Home Journal*, April 1961.

Thomas, Helen. *Front Row at the White House: My Life and Times*. New York: Scribner, 1999.

Vidal. *Palimpsest*. Op. cit.

———. "Reflections on Capital Glories: A Pentimento of Power Among Washington's Cave Dwellers," *Washington Post*, July 7, 1991.

West, J. B. *Upstairs at the White House: My Life with the First Ladies*. New York: Warner Books, 1974.

White, Theodore H. *In Search of History: A Personal Adventure*. New York: Harper & Row, 1978.

Research Collections

John F. Kennedy Memorial Library, Boston, Massachusetts:
  Oral Histories: Auchincloss, Baldrige, Berube, Bernard Boutin, August Heckscher, Jacqueline Hirsh, Shaw, Nancy Tuckerman, Pamela Turnure, William Walton
  Letters:
    Letitia Baldrige to Stanley Slater, February 1, 1962
    Jacqueline Bouvier Kennedy to Arthur Schlesinger, February 14, 1962
    Kenneth O'Donnell to Hugh D. Auchincloss, December 11, 1961
    Claiborne Pell to President Kennedy, October 3, 1963
    Adlai E. Stevenson to Mrs. John F. Kennedy, October 8, 1962
    Nancy Tuckerman to Arthur Schlesinger, July 15, 1963; Edward Whitty, July 25, 1963; Miss Janet Auchincloss, July 17, 1963
  Audiovisual Archives:
    List of John F. Kennedy visits to Newport
    List of John F. Kennedy visits to Hammersmith Farm, compiled by James B. Hill, February 2000
Lyndon B. Johnson Library, Austin, Texas
  Oral History: Jacqueline Bouvier Onassis
Peabody Room, Georgetown Branch, District of Columbia Public Library, Washington, D.C.
The Georgetowner Archives, Washington, D.C.
Washingtoniana Division, Martin Luther King Memorial Library, District of Columbia Public Library, Washington, D.C.

Interviews

Letitia Baldrige, Washington, D.C.

Charles L. Bartlett, Washington, D.C.

Betty Beale, Washington, D.C.

Benjamin C. Bradlee, Washington, D.C.

J. Carter Brown, Washington, D.C.

Mary Barelli (Mrs. Raymond A.) Gallagher, Alexandria, Virginia

CHAPTER 11: MAYHEM OVER MERRYWOOD

"An Architect's Conception," *Washington Post*, December 9, 1962.

"Apartment Plan Defeated," *Fairfax Herald*, March 23, 1962.

"Auchincloss Estate in Va. May Be Sold," *Washington Evening Star*, January 14, 1962.

"Auchincloss Neighbor Slugged with Hammer," *Washington Evening Star*, May 7, 1963.

"Auchincloss Rejects Plea to Halt McLean High-rise," *Washington Post*, April 25, 1962.

Barron, John. "U.S. Seizes Control of Merrywood," *Washington Evening Star*, November 16, 1963.

Beale, Betty. "Exclusively Yours: Auchinclosses Move; Benefits So Bountiful," *Washington Evening Star*, March 24, 1963.

"Builders Take Option on Auchincloss Estate," *Washington Post*, January 14, 1962.

"Childhood Home of Mrs. JFK Figures in Suit," *Washington Post*, November 19, 1963.

"Controversy Nears End," *Washington Post*, February 12, 1969.

"Decision on Merrywood," *The Georgetowner*, June 24, 1965.

Dickerson. *Among Those Present*. Op. cit.

"Dispute Involves Mrs. Auchincloss," *Washington Star*, January 26, 1963.

"Fairfax Board Approves 17-Story McLean Job," *Washington Post*, April 19, 1962.

"Grand Jury Finds No Irregularities," *Fairfax Herald*, May 25, 1962.

Griffee, Carol. "Manor House Clusters Proposed at Merrywood," *Washington Evening Star*, October 6, 1965.

"Hearing on Merrywood Canceled by Planners," *Washington Evening Star*, June 8, 1962.

"Hugh D. Auchincloss Buys Louis Mackall House on O St.," *The Georgetowner*, June 28, 1962.

Hunter, Marjorie. "Girlhood Home of Mrs. Kennedy Optional for Luxury Apartments," *The New York Times*, January 14, 1962.

Lawson, John. "McLean Girds to Fight Big Apartment Project," *Washington Evening Star*, January 22, 1962.

"Less than Merry at Merrywood," *Time*, May 11, 1962.

"McLean Zoning Stirs Controversy," *Fairfax Herald*, April 27, 1962.

"Merrywood Agreement Sought Prior to Trial," *Washington Post*, November 29, 1963.

"Merrywood Easement Case May Go to Jurors Today," *Washington Evening Star*, September 23, 1964.

"Merrywood Is Their Home Now," *Washington Post*, October 24, 1965.

"Merrywood Jury Calls Eight More Witnesses," *Washington Post*, May 22, 1962.

"Merrywood Sold; 46 Acres Bring $650,000," *Washington Star*, January 11, 1963.

"Merrywood Trial Is Set," *Fairfax City Times*, September 4, 1964.

"Merrywood Zoning Upheld," *Fairfax City Times*, September 21, 1962.

" 'New Merrywood' Plans Termed a 'Triumph' by Secretary Udall," *Baltimore Sun*, October 6, 1965.
"$125,000 Homes to Be Built at Merrywood," *Washington Post*, October 8, 1965.
"Parents of First Lady Buy Home," *Washington Evening Star*, June 8, 1962.
"Sheriff Taylor Is Right," *Fairfax City Times*, December 20, 1963.
Trager. *The People's Chronology*. Op. cit.
"$200,000 Restoration Underway at Merrywood, 'Castle' Plan Dropped," *McLean Journal*, October 28, 1966.
United States of America v. *Magazine Brothers*, civil no. 3134-M, U.S. District Court for the Eastern District of Virginia, November 15, 1963.
"U.S. Acts to Keep Jackie's View," *Washington Evening Star*, November 16, 1963.
Walsh, Lee. "Two Moves in the Offing," *Washington Evening Star*, November 22, 1969.
"Work Stopped at Merrywood," *Fairfax City Times*, November 23, 1963.

Research Collections
John F. Kennedy Memorial Library, Boston, Massachusetts:
  Social Files:
        Letters from Elizabeth Rowe, chairman, National Capital Planning Commission to Fairfax Board of Supervisors, April 10, 1962
        Jacqueline Bouvier Kennedy and Letitia Baldrige, the White House, April 11, 1962
        Letter from Baldrige to Rowe, April 12, 1962, filed November 20, 1962
Peabody Room, Georgetown Branch, District of Columbia Public Library, Washington, D.C.
The Georgetowner Archives, Washington, D.C.
Virginia Room, Fairfax City Regional Library, Fairfax County Public Library, Virginia
Washingtoniana Division, Martin Luther King Memorial Library, District of Columbia Public Library, Washington, D.C.

Interviews
Letitia Baldrige, Washington, D.C.
Charles L. Bartlett, Washington, D.C.
C. Wyatt Dickerson, Washington, D.C.
Senator and Mrs. Claiborne (Nuala) Pell, Washington, D.C.
Marie (Mrs. Walter T.) Ridder, McLean, Virginia
The Honorable Stewart L. Udall, Santa Fe, New Mexico

CHAPTER 12: TWO WOMEN IN CRISIS
"A Family at Rites," *The New York Times*, November 27, 1963.
Arnold, Martin. "Experts Favor Telling Children About Death," *The New York Times*, November 25, 1963.
"A Widow's Courage Catches at the Heart of a Nation as Kennedy Lies in State," *The New York Times*, November 25, 1963.

Baer, Susan. "Jacqueline Kennedy Helped Define the Terms History Uses," *Baltimore Sun,* May 27, 1995.

Beale, Betty. "Exclusively Yours: Jackie Kennedy Set Unusual Record," *Washington Evening Star,* November 24, 1963.

Bell, Jack. "Eyewitnesses Describe Scene of Assassination," *The New York Times,* November 23, 1963.

Bishop, Jim. *The Day Kennedy Was Shot.* New York: Funk & Wagnalls, 1968.

"Capital Is Horrified by Dallas Tragedy," *Washington Evening Star EXTRA,* November 22, 1963.

"Caroline, John Taking Nap, Not Told at Once of Death," *Washington Evening Star EXTRA,* November 22, 1963.

"Caroline Says Farewell in Silence," *Washington Evening Star,* November 25, 1963.

"Chronology of Tragedy," *Washington Post,* November 23, 1963.

Clopton, Willard, and Phil Casey. "200,000 Mourners Visit Grave," *Washington Evening Star,* November 28, 1963.

"Evangelical Bishop Praises Mrs. Kennedy," *The New York Times,* December 5, 1963.

"Family, U.S. Leaders to View Body," *Washington Post,* November 23, 1963.

"Farewell Kiss Given in Dallas Hospital," *Washington Evening Star,* November 24, 1963.

"Federal and District Offices Close, Thousands Throng Capital Streets," *Washington Evening Star EXTRA,* November 22, 1963.

"15,000 Visit Kennedy Grave on Christmas Day," *Washington Evening Star,* December 26, 1963.

"Footnotes to the Assassination: The Kennedy Sense of History," *The New York Times,* December 2, 1963.

Hamblin, D. J. "Mrs. Kennedy's Decisions Shaped All the Solemn Pageantry," *Life,* December 6, 1963.

Hornig, Roberta. "On Way to Chevy Chase Did Caroline Hear News as Car Radio Blared?" *Washington Evening Star,* January 23, 1967.

Hunter, Marjorie. "Kennedy's Wife Kept Composure: Accompanied His Body to Bethesda Naval Hospital," *The New York Times,* November 23, 1963.

———. "Mrs. Kennedy Leads Public Mourning," *The New York Times,* November 25, 1963.

"Jacqueline's Assassination Story," *Boston Globe,* November 23, 1964.

"Kennedy Children Not Told at Once," *Washington Evening Star,* November 23, 1963.

Kinney, Doris G., Marcia Smith, and Penny Ward Moser. "Four Days That Stopped America: The Kennedy Assassination, 20 Years Later," *Life,* November 1983.

Manchester, William. *The Death of a President, November 1963.* New York: Harper & Row, 1967.

McGrory, Mary. "They Were Waiting at the Airport," *Washington Evening Star,* November 23, 1963.

"Mrs. Kennedy Likens the Capital under Her Husband to 'Camelot,' " *The New York Times,* December 5, 1963.

"Mrs. Kennedy Spends Night at Hospital," *Washington Evening Star,* November 23, 1963.

"Mrs. Kennedy's Family at Funeral Rites," *Washington Evening Star,* November 27, 1963.

"Mrs. Kennedy's Sunny Life Is Streaked with Tears," *Washington Evening Star,* November 24, 1963.

Phillips, Cabell. "Senate, Stunned and Confused: Brother in Chair as News Arrives," *The New York Times,* November 23, 1963.

"President's Death Sends Wave of Shock and Sorrow over City," *Washington Post,* November 23, 1963.

"President's Hospital Doctors Used Heart Massage, Oxygen," *Washington Post,* November 23, 1963.

"Princess Radziwill Due in U.S.," *The New York Times,* November 23, 1963.

Raymart, Henry. "Six Cabinet Officers Turn Back After Getting News over Pacific," *The New York Times,* November 23, 1963.

Raymond, Jack. "Kennedy's Body Lies in White House: Rites Tomorrow," *The New York Times,* November 24, 1963.

———. "When the Bullets Struck: President's Body Will Lie in State," *The New York Times,* November 23, 1963.

Reston, James. "Kennedy Babies Reburied with Father in Arlington," *The New York Times,* December 5, 1963.

"Robert Kennedy Hears News During Lunch in McLean," *Washington Evening Star EXTRA,* November 22, 1963.

Roberts, Chalmers. "Disbelief, Then Shock, Shatters Quiet Confidence of Calm City," *Washington Post,* November 23, 1963.

Robertson, Nan. "Children Learn Father Is Dead; Mother Returns to White House," *The New York Times,* November 24, 1963.

———. "Throngs Gather at White House," *The New York Times,* November 23, 1963.

"Scores of Mourners Gather in Churches," *Washington Post,* November 23, 1963.

Shanahan, Eileen. "News Withheld from 2 Children: Mrs. Kennedy Apparently Wishes to Tell Them Herself, They Leave the White House Without Seeing Mother," *The New York Times,* November 23, 1963.

Shaw, Maud. *White House Nannie: My Years with Caroline and John Kennedy, Jr.* New York: New American Library, 1966.

"Shock, Disbelief Numbs Area at News of Kennedy's Death," *Washington Evening Star,* November 23, 1963.

"Shriver Decided Funeral Details," *The New York Times,* November 26, 1963.

"Sniper Kills Kennedy," *Washington Evening Star EXTRA,* November 22, 1963.

"Sorrowing Kennedy Family Gathers at White House to Console Widow," *Washington Evening Star,* November 23, 1963.

Sullivan, Ronald. "Priest Describes How He Administered Last Rites after the President's Death: Mrs. Kennedy Takes Part in 15-Minute Ceremony but Appears to Be in Shock," *The New York Times,* November 23, 1963.

"Ted Kennedy Gets News in Senate Chair," *Washington Evening Star EXTRA,* November 22, 1963.

"The Final Hours of Kennedy's Life," *The New York Times,* November 23, 1963.

"The President's Death: The Scene, Return to Washington," *The New York Times,* November 23, 1963.

"Throngs Stand All Night to See Return of Body," *Washington Evening Star,* November 23, 1963.

UPI and American Heritage. *Four Days: The Historical Record of the Death of President Kennedy.* Washington, D.C.: American Heritage Publishing Company and United Press International, 1964.

Walsh, Pamela M. "A Glimpse Between the Lines: JFK Library Opens Notes," *Boston Globe,* May 27, 1995.

"White House Gets Word via Newsmen," *Washington Post,* November 23, 1963.

White, Theodore H. "Camelot," *Life,* December 6, 1963.

Wicker, Tom. "Kennedy Is Killed by Sniper as He Rides in Car to Dallas; Mrs. Kennedy Safe," *The New York Times,* November 23, 1963.

"Wife's Kiss on Deathbed Described," *Washington Evening Star,* November 24, 1963.

Research Collections

John F. Kennedy Memorial Library, Boston, Massachusetts:
   Oral Histories: Auchincloss, Bartlett, Cardinal Cushing, Reverend Father Oscar Huber, Jacqueline Hirsh, Shaw, Cordenia Thaxton, Tuckerman, Walton, J. B. West
   Unedited manuscript, Theodore H. White, "Original delivered to Mrs. Kennedy, December 19, 1963," III-A.
Lyndon B. Johnson Library, Austin, Texas:
   Oral History: Jacqueline Bouvier Onassis
Washingtoniana Division, Martin Luther King Memorial Library, District of Columbia Public Library, Washington, D.C.

Interviews

Hugh D. Auchincloss III, Newport, Rhode Island
James Lee Auchincloss, Ashland, Oregon
Thomas W. Braden, Woodbridge, Virginia
Benjamin C. Bradlee, Washington, D.C.
Mary Barelli (Mrs. Raymond A.) Gallagher, Alexandria, Virginia
The Honorable Stewart L. Udall, Sante Fe, New Mexico

CHAPTER 13: COMING TO TERMS

"Annandale Property Sold in Newport," *Washington Evening Star,* May 13, 1965.

"A Solemn but Happy Occasion," *New York Daily News,* August 1, 1966.

"Auchinclosses Hosts at Daughter's Dinner," *Washington Evening Star,* July 30, 1966.

"Auchinclosses Hosts at Daughter's Dinner," *Newport Daily News,* July 30, 1966.

"Auchincloss, Mrs. Hugh," *Celebrity Register,* 1966.

Baldwin, Billy with Michael Gardine. *An Autobiography*. Boston: Little, Brown and Co., 1985.

Becker, Ralph E. *Miracle on the Potomac: The Kennedy Center from the Beginning*. Silver Spring, Md.: Bartleby Press, 1990.

"Beneficial Change: Move to New York," *Newsweek*, July 20, 1964.

Berguist, Laura. "Jacqueline Kennedy Goes Public," *Look*, March 22, 1966.

————. "Lonely Summer for Jacqueline Kennedy," *Look*, November 17, 1964.

Bigart, Homer. "Mrs. Kennedy Will Move Here to Escape Memories in Capital," *The New York Times*, July 7, 1964.

Bill, Brendan. *John F. Kennedy Center for the Performing Arts*. New York: Harry N. Abrams, 1981.

Birmingham, Stephen. "How the Remarkable Auchincloss Family Shaped the Jacqueline Kennedy Style," *Ladies' Home Journal*, March 1967.

"Blaze Ruins Windmill in Newport," *Providence Journal-Bulletin*, October 28, 1965.

Brady, Frank. *Onassis: An Extravagant Life*. New York: Jove/Harcourt Brace Jovanovich, 1977.

Burton, Humphrey. *Leonard Bernstein*. New York: Doubleday, 1994.

Cafarakis, Christian. *The Fabulous Onassis*. New York: Pocket Books, 1973.

"Caroline Is Nine," *Washington Evening Star*, November 28, 1966.

"Caroline May Still Go to White House School," *Boston Globe*, November 26, 1963.

"Caroline Stars on Horse," *Boston Globe*, July 26, 1965.

Carpozi, George Jr. *The Hidden Side of Jacqueline Kennedy*. New York: Pyramid Books, 1967.

"Change of Address," *Time*, December 20, 1963.

Cheshire, Maxine. "Wedding Bells Ring for Janet This Summer," *Washington Post*, April 3, 1966.

Christy, Marian. "Fur Fashions Follow Jacqueline's Cue," *Boston Globe*, July 18, 1965.

————. "Jackie and the Children Conquer Hawaii," *Boston Globe*, June 22, 1966.

————. "Jacqueline Switches to Splashy Mini-Muus," *Boston Globe*, June 29, 1966.

Conroy, Sarah Booth. "Lady of the Manor," *Washington Post*, May 22, 1994.

Cremmen, Mary. "Speaking of People, New Home on N St.," *Washington Post*, February 23, 1963.

"Engaged," *New York Post*, May 11, 1966.

Evans, Peter. *Ari: The Life and Times of Aristotle Onassis*. New York: Charter Books, 1988.

"15 Rooms in Home Bought by Jacqueline," *Boston Globe*, July 29, 1984.

Forbes, T. Curtis. "Unruly Mob Jams Street for Nuptials," *Newport Daily News*, August 1, 1966.

Fraser, Nicholas. *Aristotle Onassis*. Philadelphia: J. P. Lippincott Co., 1977.

Freidin, Seymour. "Jacqueline Kennedy Boosted as Next Ambassador to Paris," *New York Post*, September 2, 1964.

Gilmore, Eddy. "Mrs. Kennedy Starts Vacation in Ireland," *Washington Evening Star*, June 15, 1967.

Hackett, Walter. "Mrs. Kennedy's Quiet Time," *Washington Evening Star*, September 9, 1966.

———. "Newport Bride Mobbed by Crowds," *Washington Evening Star*, August 1, 1966.

"Hammersmith Farm Is Lively," *Washington Post*, August 1, 1966.

"Hammersmith Farm Newport: A Summer White House 1961–1963," Brochure, Camelot Corp., Newport, Rhode Island, 1996.

"Heading for Quiet of Home," *New York Daily News*, July 30, 1966.

Healy, Robert. "She Gave the American People Majesty," *Boston Globe*, November 26, 1963.

"Hugh Auchincloss Jr., Son Hit by Auto on Park Ave.," *The York Times*, May 2, 1965.

Hunter, Marjorie. "Thousands Visit Kennedy's Grave," *The New York Times*, November 23, 1965.

"Jacqueline Busy on 35th Birthday," *Boston Globe*, July 28, 1964.

"Jacqueline Declines to Buy Granddad's Love Letters," *Boston Globe*, September 28, 1967.

"Jacqueline Kennedy 36 Today," *Boston Globe*, July 28, 1965.

"Jacqueline Rents Villa in Portugal," *Boston Globe*, April 18, 1965.

"Jacqueline's Birthday," *Boston Globe*, July 28, 1964.

"Jacqueline to Leave Cape for Rhode Island," *Boston Globe*, July 25, 1964.

"Jacqueline Turned Down Posts Offered by LBJ," *Boston Globe*, September 14, 1964.

"James T. Lee, 90, Grandfather of Mrs. J. F. Kennedy," *Providence Journal-Bulletin*, January 4, 1968.

"James T. Lee, 90, Summer Resident," *East Hampton Star*, January 11, 1968.

"Janet Auchincloss Is Married in Newport," *The New York Times*, July 31, 1966.

"Janet Auchincloss Rutherfurd, 39, half-sister of Jacqueline Onassis," *Boston Globe*, March 14, 1985.

"Janet Jennings Auchincloss Betrothed," *The New York Times*, May 9, 1966.

"Janet Jennings Auchincloss Wed to Lewis P. Rutherfurd," *The New York Times*, July 31, 1966.

"John Better, Burns on the Mend," *Providence Journal-Bulletin*, July 5, 1966.

"John F. Kennedy Jr. Has Minor Surgery," *Washington Evening Star*, July 4, 1966.

"John-John to Attend a Co-operative School," *Providence Journal-Bulletin*, May 20, 1964.

"John Jr. Eats Cake, Sees Game," *Boston Globe*, November 26, 1965.

"John Kennedy Jr. is 7," *The New York Times*, November 26, 1967.

"John Kennedy Jr. Suffers Arm, Back Burns," *Providence Journal-Bulletin*, July 22, 1966.

"John Kennedy Jr. Suffers Minor Burns in Campfire," *Washington Evening Star*, July 2, 1966.

"John Kennedy Jr. to Mark Sixth Birthday Today," *Providence Journal-Bulletin,*
    November 25, 1966.

Johnson, Lady Bird. *A White House Diary.* New York: Holt, Rinehart and Win-
    ston, 1964.

Jones, Brian C. "Goat Island Project Contracted," *Newport Daily News,* December
    1, 1965.

Kaplan, Fred. "Grand Total," *Boston Globe,* April 27, 1996.

Kaull, James T. "He's a Swinger Now," *Providence Journal-Bulletin,* February 5,
    1968.

"Kennedys Coming Home Tomorrow," *Providence Journal-Bulletin,* July 23, 1966.

"Kennedys Land in Boston," *Washington Evening Star,* July 21, 1967.

"Kennedys Return with Brogue," *Washington Evening Star,* July 20, 1967.

Klein, Edward. *All Too Human.* Op. cit.

———. *Just Jackie: Her Private Years.* New York: Ballantine Books, 1998.

Kober, Barbara. "His Son's Education Is Just a Picture Now," *Washington Eve-
    ning Star,* June 12, 1966.

Lee, James Thomas. Last Will and Testament, stamp-dated January 1978, New
    York City.

"Miss Janet Auchincloss Becomes Bride," *Providence Journal-Bulletin,* July 31,
    1966.

"Miss Janet Auchincloss Engaged," *Washington Evening Star,* May 9, 1966.

"Miss Janet Auchincloss Weds Mr. Lewis Rutherfurd," *Providence Journal-
    Bulletin,* July 30, 1966.

Morris, Barbara Bradlyn. *The Kennedy Center: An Insider's Guide to Washington's
    Liveliest Memorial.* McLean, Va.: EPI Publications, 1994.

"Mrs. Hugh D. Auchincloss," *Washington Evening Star,* November 26, 1967.

"Mrs. JFK, Children Back Home," *Boston Globe,* July 25, 1966.

"Mrs. JFK Marks Her 38th Birthday," *Boston Globe,* July 28, 1967.

"Mrs. Kennedy Accepts Invitation to Cambodia," *Boston Globe,* October 2, 1967.

"Mrs. Kennedy and Caroline Win Horse Show Prizes," *The New York Times,*
    May 16, 1966.

"Mrs. Kennedy and Son Begin 2-Week Visit in Newport," *The New York Times,*
    August 29, 1965.

"Mrs. Kennedy Buys Historic Georgetown Home," *Boston Globe,* December 14,
    1963.

"Mrs. Kennedy Flies Here with Children After Hawaii Trip," *The New York
    Times,* July 26, 1966.

"Mrs. Kennedy Hopes to Fly to R.I. Nuptials," *Providence Journal-Bulletin,* July
    16, 1966.

"Mrs. Kennedy in Newport," *The New York Times,* August 21, 1964.

"Mrs. Kennedy in Newport," *The New York Times,* November 23, 1967.

"Mrs. Kennedy Marks Birthday," *Boston Globe,* July 28, 1966.

"Mrs. Kennedy Off Today for Adriatic Yacht Cruise," *The New York Times,*
    August 5, 1964.

"Mrs. Kennedy Rejects $3000 Gift to Library," *Boston Globe,* November 13, 1967.

"Mrs. Kennedy Remains at Her Apartment Here," *The New York Times*, November 23, 1965.

"Mrs. Kennedy's Office Moved to New York," *The New York Times*, September 24, 1964.

"Mrs. Kennedy Takes Son on a Carousel," *The New York Times*, September 17, 1964.

"Mrs. Kennedy to New York: A Search for Privacy," *U.S. News & World Report*, July 20, 1964.

"Mrs. Kennedy to Vacation at Mother's Newport Home," *The New York Times*, July 23, 1964.

"New Home for Jacqueline Kennedy and Children," *U.S. News & World Report*, December 9, 1963.

"Newport Promised Big Hotel Under Urban Renewal Plan," *Newport Daily News*, December 2, 1967.

"Nursemaid Wanted by Mrs. Kennedy," *Washington Evening Star*, May 19, 1965.

"Other Woman in FDR's Life Disclosed," *Providence Journal-Bulletin*, August 12, 1966.

"Papal Consolement Whispered to Jackie," *Boston Herald*, October 15, 1965.

"Permit Issued for Hammersmith Farm Windmill," *Providence Journal-Bulletin*, March 28, 1966.

Peyser, Joan. *Bernstein: A Biography*. New York: Beech Tree Books, 1987.

"Pope Receives Jacqueline Warmly," *Boston Globe*, October 5, 1965.

"Q.," *Boston Globe*, October 11, 1964.

"Queen Expected to Greet Mrs. JFK," *Boston Globe*, March 20, 1965.

Radziwill, Lee, and Jacqueline Onassis. *One Special Summer*. New York: Delacorte Press, 1974.

Reeves, Richard. "Jacqueline Leases Fox-Hunting Place," *Boston Globe*, October 21, 1965.

"R. I. Teacher for John-John," *Providence Journal-Bulletin*, May 21, 1961.

Robertson, Nan. "A White House Garden Is Named for Mrs. Kennedy," *The New York Times*, April 23, 1965.

———. "The Nation Remembers Its Slain President," *The New York Times*, November 23, 1964.

"Roman Holiday Begins for Jacqueline Kennedy," *Washington Evening Star*, July 10, 1967.

Sakler, Ernest. "Jackie Visits Old Friends," *Washington Evening Star*, July 11, 1967.

"Senator Regrets Mrs. Kennedy Leaving Capital," *Washington Evening Star*, July 10, 1964.

Sgubin, Marta, and Nancy Nicholas. *Cooking for Madam: Recipes and Reminiscences from the Home of Jacqueline Kennedy Onassis*. New York: Scribner, 1998.

Shannon, W. V. "Future of a Noble Lady," *Good Housekeeping*, April 1964.

Shearer, Lloyd. "Will She Marry Again?" *Boston Globe*, December 4, 1966.

Sherman, Marjorie W. "Janet's Wedding Mobbed," *Boston Globe*, July 31, 1966.

Smith, Kelly. "Jackie's Half-Sister Wed in Mob Scene," *Boston Sunday Herald*, July 31, 1966.

————. "John's Favorite Shell Among Wedding Gifts," *Washington Evening Star*, August 1, 1966.

Smith, Liz. "Jackie Comes Off Her Pedestal," *Boston Globe*, January 12, 1967.

"Society: A Tiny Party on Fifth Avenue," *Time*, April 30, 1965.

"Society: Graceful Entrance," *Time*, October 1, 1965.

Stanfill, Francesca. "People Are Talking About: The Long Good Buy," *Vogue*, November 2000.

Steiner, Paul. "John Kennedy Jr. Is Six Today," *Washington Evening Star*, November 25, 1966.

Sullivan, Lorana O. "Busy Weekend," *Providence Journal-Bulletin*, July 29, 1966.

"Swank Apartments at Annandale," *Providence Journal-Bulletin*, December 16, 1964.

Thayer, Mary Van Rensselaer. "To Center in Historic Home," *Boston Traveler*, January 9, 1964.

"The Kennedy Children Get a New Toy," *The New York Times*, May 28, 1966.

"The Kennedys: Dancing at the Dove," *Newsweek*, October 4, 1964.

Thomas, Helen. "Kennedys Leave the White House," *Boston Globe*, December 7, 1963.

"Two Kennedys Move," *Boston Globe*, July 10, 1964.

"Washington Hairdresser Newport-Bound," *Washington Post*, July 6, 1966.

White, Theodore H. "For One Brief Shining Moment," *Time*, July 6, 1966.

"Widow Kennedy Wasn't for Jackie," *Newsday*, May 27, 1995.

Winship, Frederick M. "Jacqueline Kennedy in Seclusion," *Boston Herald*, November 21, 1964.

"Year of Mourning Set by Mrs. Kennedy," *U.S. News & World Report*, December 23, 1963.

Research Collections

John F. Kennedy Memorial Library, Boston, Massachusetts:
    Oral Histories: Janet Lee Auchincloss, Cardinal Cushing, Hirsh, Lady Bird Johnson, Robert McNamara
    Unedited manuscript, Theodore H. White, "Original delivered to Mrs. Kennedy, December 19th, 1963," III-A
Library of Congress, Roger L. Stevens Collection
Correspondence from James C. Auchincloss, October 20, 1965; Jacqueline Bouvier Kennedy, October 8, 1964, and May 16, 1966
Lyndon B. Johnson Memorial Library, Austin, Texas
    Oral History: Jacqueline Bouvier Onassis
Washingtoniana Division, Martin Luther King Memorial Public Library, District of Columbia Public Library, Washington, D.C.

Private Collections

Courtesy Hugh D. Auchincloss III, Newport, Rhode Island:
    Janet L. Auchincloss Morris, Scrapbook given on her eightieth birthday

Interviews
Hugh D. Auchincloss III, Newport, Rhode Island
James Auchincloss, Ashland, Oregon
Thomas W. Braden, Oakton, Virginia
Mary Barelli (Mrs. Raymond A.) Gallagher, Alexandria, Virginia
John (Jock) F. Nash Jr., Bethesda, Maryland
Senator and Mrs. Claiborne (Nuala) Pell, Washington, D.C.
Marta Sgubin, New York, New York
Eileen (Mrs. John Jermain) Slocum, Newport, Rhode Island

CHAPTER 14: FROM CAMELOT TO CALIBAN
"Ari Sought Sinatra Jet," *Boston Globe,* October 20, 1968.
Armes, Ethel. *Stratford Hall: The Great House of the Lees.* Richmond, Va.: Garrett
    and Massie, 1936.
Beale, Betty. "Jackie Upstages the Candidates," *Washington Evening Star,* Oc-
    tober 20, 1968.
———. *Power at Play.* Op. cit.
Cheshire, Maxine. "Jacqueline Flies to Onassis," *Washington Post,* October 18,
    1968.
Eleni. "Fashion Notebook: Couture Designs by Madame Grès," *Washington Eve-
    ning Star,* October 19, 1968.
"From Camelot to Elysium (Via Olympic Airways)," *Time,* October 25, 1968.
Gallup, George. "Mrs. JFK 'Most Admired' Again," *Boston Globe,* December 28,
    1966.
"Guard with JFK Tie Pin," *Boston Globe,* October 21, 1968.
"Jackie, Ted Cruise with Onassis," *Boston Globe,* August 7, 1968.
"Jacqueline, Children Lose Privilege of Burial Near JFK at Arlington," *Boston
    Globe,* October 25, 1968.
"Jacqueline Gets Down to Size 7–9," *Washington Post,* January 23, 1968.
"Jacqueline Kennedy," *Boston Globe,* October 25, 1968.
"Mother Announces Jacqueline to Wed Onassis in Week," *Boston Globe,* October
    17, 1968.
"Mother to Escort Bride," *Boston Globe,* October 19, 1968.
"Mrs. JFK Flies to Athens to Wed," *Boston Globe,* October 19, 1968.
"Onassis Guest of Jackie," *Boston Globe,* July 17, 1968.
"Onassis Spent Weekend Here, Swam at Bailey's Beach in July," *Newport Mer-
    cury,* October 18, 1968.
"Plan Event," *Washington Post,* September 25, 1968.
Roberts, Carey, and Rebecca Seely. *Tidewater Dynasty: A Biographical Novel of the
    Lees of Stratford Hall.* New York: Harcourt Brace Jovanovich, 1981.
Sgubin. *Cooking for Madam.* Op. cit.
"Rose 'Not Surprised,' " *Boston Sunday Globe,* October 20, 1968.
"Ship Owner, 62, May Marry Mrs. JFK," *Washington Post,* October 17, 1968.
Sparks, Fred. *The $20,000,000 Honeymoon: Jackie and Ari's First Year.* New York:
    Bernard Geiss Associates, 1970.
Walls. *Dish.* Op. cit.

"Wedding Bells for Jackie Kennedy," *U.S. News & World Report,* October 28, 1968.

Research Collections
John F. Kennedy Memorial Library, Boston, Massachusetts
Library of Congress, Roger L. Stevens Collection:
    Correspondence from Jacqueline Bouvier Kennedy, September 27, 1967
Robert E. Lee Memorial Foundation, Stanton, Virginia:
    Fortieth Annual Council Minutes, October 13–17, 1968, including Board of Directors Roster and Appendix 28, "Report of the Records and Research Committee"
    Letter from Mrs. Randolph C. (Mary H.) Harrison to Mrs. John B. (Florence) Hollister, July 6, 1968
    Letter from Mrs. John B. (Florence) Hollister to (Dottie), May 28, 1968
    Letter from Mrs. Austin Leland to Mrs. Hugh D. (Janet) Auchincloss, November 4, 1968
    Letter from Mrs. Lloyd P. (Florence B.) Shippen to Mrs. John B. (Florence) Hollister, July 6, 1968
Washingtoniana Division, Martin Luther King Memorial Library, District of Columbia Public Library, Washington, D.C.

Interviews
Hugh D. Auchincloss III, Newport, Rhode Island
James Lee Auchincloss, Ashland, Oregon
Maya Auchincloss, Newport, Rhode Island
Mary Barelli (Mrs. Raymond A.) Gallagher, Alexandria, Virginia
Frank Hale, president, Fort Adams Trust, Newport, Rhode Island
Judy Hinson, Stratford Hall Plantation, Robert E. Lee Memorial Association, Inc., Stratford, Virginia
Dick Masse, superintendent, Fort Adams State Park, Newport, Rhode Island
Marta Sgubin, New York City
Eileen (Mrs. John Jermain) Slocum, Newport, Rhode Island

CHAPTER 15: LOSING CONTROL
"A Day in Jackie's Life," *Washington Evening Star,* June 7, 1972.
"A Gathering of the Greek," *Washington Evening Star,* December 16, 1970.
Anderson, Jack. "A Reply to Critics of Jackie Onassis Stories," *Boston Globe,* May 9, 1975.
———. "Both JFK, Ari Upset by Jackie's Spending," *Boston Globe,* April 15, 1975.
"A Storybook Ending," *Newsday,* September 9, 1972.
"At Home with Jackie," *Parade,* September 13, 1970.
"Attend Funeral," *The New York Times,* November 23, 1976.
"Auchincloss Farm to Be Sold?" *Providence Journal-Bulletin,* June 24, 1975.
"Auchincloss Firm Expands," *The New York Times,* December 28, 1966.

"Auchincloss Says He Isn't Surprised on Farm Rejection," *Providence Journal-Bulletin*, May 8, 1976.

"Auchincloss Tells of Wish to Save Family Estate," *Newport Daily News*, April 23, 1976.

Axler, Judith. "In a Way, Actors Put On a Show Before Movie Opened," *The New York Times*, November 16, 1968.

Baskin, Claudia. "Whirlwind Day for Jackie," *Washington Evening Star*, December 18, 1968.

Beale, Betty. "Exclusively Yours: Historic Hammersmith," *Washington Evening Star*, November 28, 1971.

———. "Exclusively Yours: Jackie, Husband Due in U.S. About Nov. 15," *Washington Evening Star*, October 22, 1968.

Birmingham, Stephen. "Is a New Jackie Emerging Again?" *Boston Herald*, June 20, 1976.

Bohlin, Virginia. "JFK, Jackie Engaged 20 Years Ago Today," *Boston Herald*, June 25, 1973.

"Buyer Plans Homes, Museum on Jacqueline's R.I. Home," *East Hampton Star*, August 17, 1977.

"Cardinal in Plea to Public; Be Charitable to Jacqueline," *Boston Globe*, October 23, 1968.

Caroli. *First Ladies*. Op. cit.

"Catholic Cloud Over the Marriage," *U.S. News & World Report*, November 4, 1968.

Cheshire, Maxine. "Jackie's '2d Family' Just a Tycoon Away," *Washington Post*, November 27, 1968.

Christmas, Anne. "Bouvier Heirlooms," *Washington Evening Star*, October 14, 1970.

"Church Reforms Lessen Jackie's Penalty," *Boston Globe*, November 10, 1968.

Columbia, David Patrick. "Cooking for Madam," *Avenue*, November 1998.

"Committee Endorses Plan," *Providence Journal-Bulletin*, March 27, 1977.

"Cultural Center Proposed for Hammersmith Farm," *Providence Journal-Bulletin*, August 10, 1977.

Curtis, Charlotte. "A Princess Writes a Story, and That Makes It a Party," *The New York Times*, December 20, 1972.

Dobson, Gwen. "Luncheon with Jamie Auchincloss," *Washington Evening Star*, December 22, 1972.

Dolan, Mary Anne. "Kennedy Center Bows to Jackie Onassis," *Washington Evening Star*, June 6, 1972.

Fitzgerald, John F. "Hammersmith Farm Sold," *Providence Journal-Bulletin*, August 17, 1977.

"$5 Million Birthday Gift," *Boston Globe*, October 25, 1970.

Flynn, Barry M. "Rhode Island Delegation," *Providence Journal-Bulletin*, April 9, 1975.

———. "State Eyes Longshot to Get JFK Museum," *Providence Journal-Bulletin*, April 6, 1975.

Frederiksen, Robert C. "Bay Island Park," *Providence Journal-Bulletin*, August 29, 1976.

———. "Fort Adams Budget Eyes Grand Plan," *Providence Journal-Bulletin*, January 4, 1976.

———. "R.I. Moves to Buy Part of Hammersmith Farm," *Providence Journal-Bulletin*, December 23, 1975.

"Grey Gardens: A Haunting Story," *East Hampton Star*, October 22, 1998.

"Hammersmith Farm Sale," *Providence Journal-Bulletin*, October 30, 1975.

"Hammersmith Owner Visited by Garrahy," *Providence Journal-Bulletin*, August 3, 1977.

"Harsch: Rumor Wrong," *Providence Journal-Bulletin*, July 28, 1977.

"H. D. Auchincloss Death Notice, Thomson & McKinnon Auchincloss Kohlmeyer Inc.," *Wall Street Journal*, November 24, 1976.

"Hear Him Run," *Washington Evening Star*, April 19, 1974.

Heymann, C. David. *A Woman Named Jackie*. New York: Carol Communications, 1989.

"Historic Hammersmith Farm Up for Sale," *Washington Sunday Evening Star*, November 28, 1971.

"How Onassis Got His Riches," *U.S. News & World Report*, November 4, 1968.

"Hugh Auchincloss Dies, Prominent D.C. Banker," *Washington Evening Star*, November 22, 1976.

"Hugh Auchincloss of Newport Dies," *Providence Journal-Bulletin*, November 22, 1976.

"Hugh Auchincloss Sr., Stockbroker, Dead," The New York Times Biographical Service, November, 1976.

Insinger, Wendy. "First-Class Coaching," *Town & Country*, December 1987.

"In the Cardinal's Own Words," *Boston Globe*, October 26, 1968.

"Jackie and Ari: The Real Story: All the Elements of Greek Tragedy," *Boston Herald*, January 31, 1976.

"Jackie a Ray of Hope for Excluded Catholics," *Boston Globe*, July 30, 1972.

"Jackie, Ari Visit Oxygen Chamber," *Boston Globe*, December 6, 1968.

"Jackie at the Kennedy Center: 'It's Beautiful, It's Just Beautiful,'" *Washington Post*, June 6, 1972.

"Jackie, Kin Come to Rescue of Beales," *Newsday*, June 22, 1972.

"Jackie Kin Ordered Out," *Newsday*, December 11, 1971.

"Jackie Onassis Continues Cruise," *Boston Globe*, November 11, 1968.

"Jackie's Anniversary Quiet," *Boston Globe*, October 21, 1969.

"Jackie's Letters Reported Found in a Wastebasket," *Boston Globe*, February 13, 1970.

"Jackie's Note for Refund Brings More than JFK Gave," *Boston Globe*, November 7, 1969.

"Jackie's Party Lasts Until Dawn," *Boston Globe*, August 1, 1969.

"Jackie's 'Removal' of Onassis Antiques Probed," *Boston Herald*, January 16, 1976.

"Jackie's World Tranquil at 40," *Boston Globe*, July 28, 1969.

"Jackie Thrifty—to Extreme!" *Boston Globe*, July 28, 1969.

"Jackie to Keep Name of Onassis," *Boston Herald*, May 15, 1975.

"Jacqueline Kennedy Onassis," *Boston Globe*, July 28, 1969.

"Jacqueline Marks 41st Birthday," *Boston Globe*, July 28, 1970.

"Jacqueline Meets Ted, JFK Institute Board," *Boston Globe*, April 27, 1970.

"Jacqueline Phones Hub, Talks with Cardinal," *Boston Globe*, October 24, 1968.

"Kennedy In-Law Backs Museum," *Providence Journal-Bulletin*, April 1, 1975.

Klemesrud, Judy. "For Lee Radziwill, Budding Careers and New Life in New York," *The New York Times*, September 1, 1974.

Koch, Fritz. "Hammersmith Opening Day Is a Success," *Providence Journal-Bulletin*, May 2, 1978.

Lee, James T. Last Will and Testament, State of New York, Surrogate's Court, County of New York, file no. P-357-1968, January 22, 1968.

———. *In the Matter of the Application to Determine the Estate Tax under Article 26 of the Tax Law upon the Estate of James T. Lee, Deceased*, File no. P357-1968, January 11, 1972.

Lehew, Dudley. "Jacqueline Must Wear Black Once Again," *Boston Herald*, March 16, 1975.

Lennon, Peter D. "High Society and Common Folk Rub Elbows at Music Festival," *Providence Journal-Bulletin*, July 22, 1973.

"Like Dining in Museum," *Washington Evening Star*, May 10, 1971.

Mancusi, Peter. "Hammersmith Farm Is Put on Market for $5 Million," *Providence Journal-Bulletin*, August 17, 1979.

Miller, Gerald. " 'Jackie Fever' Hits Greece," *Boston Globe*, October 22, 1968.

"Mother of Jackie: Divorce Story False," *Boston Herald*, April 19, 1975.

"Mother to Escort Bride," *Boston Globe*, October 19, 1968.

"Mrs. JFK Big on Memos," *Boston Globe*, April 8, 1971.

"Mrs. Onassis, Caroline Visit Quincy Market," *Boston Herald*, September 19, 1976.

"Mrs. Onassis in 1st White House Visit," *Boston Globe*, February 4, 1971.

"Mrs. Onassis to Help Pell in R.I.," *Boston Globe*, October 17, 1972.

"Mrs. Steers Wed to Michael Straight," *The New York Times*, May 2, 1974.

"New Book Blurs Fairy Tale Image of Jacqueline," *Boston Globe*, June 27, 1969.

"Newport Officials, Garrahy," *Providence Journal-Bulletin*, August 18, 1977.

"Newport, Where 'Inflation Stings a Little, but It Doesn't Really Hurt,' " *The New York Times*, July 19, 1974.

"Nixon–Mrs. Onassis Visit 'Relaxed,' " *Boston Globe*, February 5, 1971.

Norwich, William. "A New Balance: Lee Radziwill Finds Serenity in Paris," *The New York Times*, October 22, 2000.

"Onassis Gives Jackie Ruby 'Almost Too Large to Lift,' " *Boston Globe*, October 24, 1968.

Onassis, Jacqueline. "A Dream Realized," *Ladies' Home Journal*, September 1971.

"Onassis: Memories of an Insomniac," *Washington Evening Star*, March 17, 1975.

"Onassis Mother-in-Law Denies Divorce Claim," *Boston Globe*, April 19, 1975.

"Onassis Next Envoy, Greek Paper Says," *Boston Globe*, November 8, 1976.

"Onassis to Entertain Astronauts on Skorpios," *Boston Globe*, May 28, 1970.

O'Neil, Paul. "For the Beautiful Green Jacqueline, Goodby Camelot," *Boston Globe*, October 24, 1968.

Ramaker, Robert. "Tourist Potential at Hammersmith," *Providence Journal-Bulletin*, December 31, 1975.

"Red Roses Galore for Jackie's 40th," *Boston Globe*, July 29, 1969.

Robertson, Nan. "John F. Kennedy Remembered Five Years after Death," *The New York Times*, November 21, 1968.

"Sadness Over Grey Gardens," *Newsday*, March 10, 1972.

Schwadron, Terry. "Backing Needed for Farm Appraisal," *Providence Journal*, November 19, 1975.

————. "First All-American Music Festival Readies Newport Opening," *Providence Journal-Bulletin*, July 23, 1975.

————. "Hammersmith Farm Plans Not Tied to JFK Library," *Providence Journal-Bulletin*, October 31, 1975.

————. "Negotiations on for Estate," *Providence Journal-Bulletin*, June 25, 1975.

Sgubin. *Cooking for Madam*. Op. cit.

Sheehy, Gail. "The Secret of Grey Gardens," *New York*, July 23, 1975.

"Shikler on Portraits," *Washington Evening Star*, March 26, 1971.

"Skorpios," *Life*, November 1, 1968.

Sparks, Fred. "Jackie and Ari: The First Five Years," *Boston Herald*, November 25, 1973.

Stack, James. "Change Denied in Rome's View," *Boston Globe*, May 29, 1969.

"Stanislas Radziwill Dies; Brother-in-Law of JFK," *Washington Evening Star*, June 29, 1976.

Steinem, Gloria. "Why Women Work: Gloria Steinem on Jacqueline Onassis," *Ms.*, March 1979.

Straight, Michael. *After Long Silence*. New York: W. W. Norton & Co., 1983.

"The Ear," *Washington Evening Star*, May 29, 1976.

"The Kennedys: Identity Crisis," *Newsweek*, November 11, 1968.

"The Last to Know," *Newsday*, February 29, 1972.

"2 Brooklyn Banks Plan Merger; Thomson & McKinnon Sets Link," *Wall Street Journal*, December 16, 1969.

"Vatican Still Has Reservations," *Boston Globe*, October 21, 1968.

"Walled Swiss Village Opens Gate for Newport Music Festival," *Providence Journal-Bulletin*, July 15, 1973.

"Wedding at Skorpios," *Time*, November 1, 1968.

"Wife Must Promise to Obey, Fear," *Boston Globe*, October 21, 1968.

Wilber, Helen A. "Davodet Plots an Alpine Buffet for a Newport Music Benefit," *Providence Journal-Bulletin*, July 31, 1973.

Winslow, Ron. "Group to Urge Fish Program Restoration," *Providence Journal*, March 1, 1976.

"Wire Services Ditter on Cardinal's Comment on Jacqueline Wedding," *Boston Globe*, October 23, 1968.

"Yacht Even Has Gold Plumbing," *Boston Globe*, October 21, 1968.

Research Collections

John F. Kennedy Memorial Library, Boston, Massachusetts:
    Oral History: Cardinal Cushing
Library of Congress, John L. Stevens Collection:
    Correspondence to Janet Auchincloss, November 20, 1970; from Jacqueline Onassis, August 24, 1971, and June 5, 1972
Newport Room, Newport Public Library, Newport, Rhode Island
Stratford Hall Plantation, Stratford, Virginia
Washingtoniana Division, Martin Luther King Memorial Library, District of Columbia Public Library, Washington, D.C.

Interviews

Verne Atwater, New Jersey
Hugh D. Auchincloss III, Newport, Rhode Island
James Lee Auchincloss, Ashland, Oregon
Maya Auchincloss, Newport, Rhode Island
Betty Beale, Washington, D.C.
Ella (Mrs. Poe) Burling, Washington, D.C.
Mary-Lee "Mimi" Ryan (Mrs. William A. V.) Cecil, Asheville, North Carolina
Michael Dupre, Newport, Rhode Island
Mary Barelli (Mrs. Raymond A.) Gallagher, Alexandria, Virginia
Charles Higham, Los Angeles, California
Judith Hinson, Stratford Hall Plantation, Robert E. Lee Memorial Association, Inc., Stratford, Virginia
Margaret (Mrs. Robert L.) Kearney, Chevy Chase, Maryland
John (Jock) F. Nash Jr., Bethesda, Maryland
Raymond T. O'Keefe, president, James T. Lee Foundation, Inc., New York City
Nuala (Mrs. Claiborne) Pell, Washington, D.C.
Marta Sgubin, New York City
Eileen (Mrs. John Jermain) Slocum, Newport, Rhode Island
Elisa (Mrs. Joseph J. Sr.) Sullivan, Newport, Rhode Island

CHAPTER 16: SLIPPING AWAY

"Ask the Globe," *Boston Globe*, August 16, 1989.
"Auchincloss Auction Close?" *New York*, November 1, 1999.
Auchincloss, Janet Lee. Codicil to the Last Will and Testament of Janet Lee Auchincloss, Newport, Rhode Island, June 29, 1984.
———. Last Will and Testament of Janet Lee Auchincloss, Newport, Rhode Island, March 9, 1984.
Baker, John F. "Editors at Work: Star Behind the Scenes," *Publishers Weekly*, April 19, 1993.
Baroody, Elizabeth. "Stately Stratford," *Country*, April 1983.
Beale, Betty. "Wealth on Wheels, on the Hoof at Stratford," *Washington Evening Star*, April 10, 1977.
Berman, Avis. "Historic Houses: Hammersmith Farm," *Architectural Digest*, August 1991.

Calta, Marialisa. "Her Famous Family Gathers at Wedding of Mrs. Auchincloss," *Providence Journal-Bulletin,* October 26, 1979.

Cheshire, Maxine. "VIP — The Auchincloss Family's Missing Silver," *Washington Post,* April 7, 1980.

"C. of C. Favors Auchincloss Farm Purchase," *Providence Journal-Bulletin,* February 17, 1976.

Conroy, Sarah Booth. "Of Coaches and the Team Spirit," *Washington Post,* April 26, 1987.

Croft, George L. "Of Coaches and the Team Spirit," *Boston Globe,* June 5, 1980.

Fireman, Ken. "Janet Auchincloss Dies, Wealthy Mom of Jackie O.," *Newsday,* July 24, 1989.

Fitzgerald, John F. "Hammersmith Farm Owner's Death Clouds State Acquisition Plans," *Providence Journal-Bulletin,* April 15, 1977.

————. "Hammersmith Farm Sold to Consortium, Will Become Museum," *Providence Journal-Bulletin,* August 17, 1977.

————. "Hammersmith Farm to Be Sold," *Providence Journal-Bulletin,* August 16, 1977.

Fleming, Michael. "Inside New York," *Newsday,* July 31, 1989.

Frederiksen, Robert C. "Brenton Village Acquisition Moves Closer to Approval," *Providence Journal-Bulletin,* May 25, 1977.

————. "Hammersmith Farm," *Providence Journal-Bulletin,* June 7, 1977.

————. "Hammersmith Purchase Is Aired Anew," *Providence Journal-Bulletin,* February 16, 1977.

Gaines, Judith. "Newport Pays Its Last Respects," *Boston Globe,* July 28, 1989.

————. "Wampanoag Dispute Goes Beyond Land," *Boston Globe,* January 28, 1989.

Haberman, Clyde, and Alvin Krebs. "A Visit to Newport," *The New York Times,* August 28, 1979.

Hanafin, Teresa M. "A Kennedy Is Wed, an Era Remembered," *Boston Globe,* July 20, 1986.

Heymann. *Jackie.* Op. cit.

Higham, Charles. *Rose: The Life and Times of Rose Kennedy.* New York: Pocket Books, 1995.

"Jackie Quits over Book on Ted Kennedy," *Boston Herald,* October 15, 1977.

"Jackie Wedding — Sort Of," *Washington Post,* August 21, 1979.

"Janet Lee Auchincloss Morris, 81," *The New York Times,* July 24, 1989.

"Janet Lee Auchincloss Morris, 81," *The New York Times,* July 25, 1989.

"Janet Lee Auchincloss, Mother of Jacqueline Onassis, Dies," *Washington Post,* July 24, 1989.

"Janet Rutherfurd Active in Women's Group," *Boston Globe,* March 19, 1985.

Jones, Brian C. "Hammersmith Farm Will Open to the Public Starting May 1," *Providence Journal-Bulletin,* January 28, 1978.

————. "Tourists Flock to the Green," *Providence Journal-Bulletin,* November 19, 1978.

Klein. *Just Jackie.* Op. cit.

Koch, Fritz. "Tour Provides Closeup of 'The Way We Were' at Hammersmith Farm," *Providence Journal-Bulletin*, July 14, 1977.

Lawford, Valentine. "Seasons in the Sun: Mrs. Hugh D. Auchincloss's Historic Newport Home," *Architectural Digest*, July 1985.

"Lee Radziwill Weds Director Herb Ross, and Hollywood Throws Rice at Jackie's Place," *People Weekly*, October 10, 1988.

"Local Auctions," *Washington Post*, May 10, 1990.

McCabe, Carol. "Hammersmith Farm Becomes a Tourist Attraction," *Providence Journal-Bulletin*, May 1, 1978.

McVicar, D. Morgan. "Janet Auchincloss Morris, 81, Mother of Jacqueline Onassis, Dies in Newport," *Providence Journal-Bulletin*, July 24, 1989.

"Mrs. Auchincloss to Marry for the Third Time," *The New York Times*, August 21, 1979.

"Mrs. Onassis Is the Witness at Her Mother's Wedding," *The New York Times*, October 26, 1979.

Negri, Gloria. "The Kennedys Gathered for Ceremony," *Boston Globe*, September 20, 1980.

"New England Briefs Onassis Work Resumes," *Boston Globe*, February 4, 1982.

"Notes on People," *The New York Times*, August 18, 1977.

"Onassis, Indians Near Settlement," *Boston Globe*, December 21, 1989.

Panciera, Andrea. "Spectators Flock to See Celebrities at Funeral," *Providence Journal-Bulletin*, July 28, 1989.

"People," *Boston Globe*, December 6, 1981.

"Remembering Jackie . . . The People Whose Lives She Touched Talk to Us," *Town & Country*, July 1994.

Riggs, Doug. "Newport Society Bids Farewell to a Lady," *Providence Journal-Bulletin*, July 28, 1989.

Scanlan, Christopher. "Party Given to Celebrate Auchincloss Betrothal," *Providence Journal*, August 26, 1979.

Schwadron, Terry. "Fort Continues to Generate Tourism Ideas," *Providence Sunday Journal*, January 11, 1976.

Seavor, Jim. "Jackie Onassis's Mother, 81, Injures Hip," *Providence Journal-Bulletin*, March 20, 1989.

Smith, Robert L. "Hammersmith Will Tax Owner's Pocketbook," *Providence Journal-Bulletin*, July 6, 2000.

Stevenson, Douglas. "Blaze Damages 3 Georgetown Town Houses," *Washington Post*, December 3, 1986.

"The Bride Wore Beige," *The New York Times*, October 26, 1979.

White, Laura. "Jackie O. Flings a Flower," *Boston Herald*, September 1, 1978.

"Winifred d'Olier," *East Hampton Star*, November 28, 1991.

Private Collection
Courtesy Margaret Kearney, Chevy Chase, Maryland:
    Auchincloss, Janet Lee, Christmas card to Margaret (Mrs. Robert L.) Kearney, undated, circa 1970s

———. Letter to Margaret Kearney, January 24, 1977
———. Letter to Margaret Kearney, October 1, 1979

Interviews

Michael Dupre, Newport, Rhode Island

Charles Higham, Los Angeles

Judy Hinson, Stratford Hall Plantation, Robert E. Lee Memorial Association, Inc., Stratford, Virginia

Senator and Mrs. Claiborne (Nuala) Pell, Newport, Rhode Island

R. Gaull "Ricky" (Mrs. Lawrence H.) Silberman, Washington, D.C.

Elisa (Mrs. Joseph J. Sr.) Sullivan, Newport, Rhode Island.

EPILOGUE

"AOL's Case Won't Buy Jackie O's Early Home," *Washington Times*, August 31, 1999.

"A. Radziwill," *East Hampton Star*, August 19, 1999.

Auchincloss, Janet Lee. Codicil. Op. cit.

———. Last Will. Op. cit.

Burns. "At Miss Porter's School, Miss Bouvier Is Just Not for Sale." Op. cit.

Cassidy, Tina. "For Sale: A Piece of History," *Boston Globe*, July 10, 1995.

Christie's East. *Christie's Global Sales Results: English Furniture and Decorative Arts, including the Property of the Heirs of Janet Auchincloss*, October 10, 2000, Sale no. 8427.

———. *English Furniture and Decorative Arts, Including the Property of the Heirs of Janet Auchincloss*. New York: Christie's East, 2000.

Condon, Dianne Russell. *Jackie's Treasures: The Fabled Objects from the Auction of the Century*. New York: Clarkson Potter, 1996.

DuBois, Diana. *In Her Sister's Shadow: An Intimate Biography of Lee Radziwill*. Boston: Little, Brown and Company, 1995.

"Farewell for the Phillipses," *Washington Post*, September 6, 2000.

Grove, Lloyd. "Reliable Source: Mister Murphy's Neighborhood," *Washington Post*, December 19, 2000.

Herman, Robin, and Laurie Johnston. "Lobbying for Lever House," *The New York Times*, February 23, 1983.

"Janet Lee Auchincloss, 81, Mother of Jacqueline K. Onassis," *Boston Globe*, July 24, 1989.

Kaplan. *Gore Vidal*. Op. cit.

"Kennedy Items for Sale," *Cincinnati Post*, September 23, 2000.

Lacey, Marc. "After Greeting Mrs. Bush, Mrs. Clinton House Hunts," *The New York Times*, December 18, 2000.

Nicholls, Walter. "First the Senate, Now the House," *Washington Post*, December 18, 2000.

"On the Block: Merrywood Memories," *People*, November 8, 1999.

Price, Joyce. "Newly Rich Hillary Seeking Posh D.C. Pad," *Washington Times*, December 18, 2000.

Rainie, Harrison. "Jackie," *U.S. News & World Report*, May 30, 1994.

Rourke, Bryan. "Bit of Camelot Brings in Bit of Cash," *Providence Journal-Bulletin*, October 11, 2000.

———. "Hammersmith Furnishings to Be Sold at N.Y. Auction," *Providence Journal-Bulletin*, October 8, 2000.

"Sold: Jackie O's Home," *Washington Post*, October 2, 1999.

Sotheby Parke Benet. "The Estate of Jacqueline Kennedy Onassis," April 23–26, 1996, Sale 6834, 1996.

Trescott, Jacqueline. "Caroline Kennedy's Turn for the Arts," *Washington Post*, August 1, 2000.

Research Collection

Library of Congress, Prints and Photographs Division, Toni Frissell Collection, Washington, D.C.

Interviews

Hugh D. Auchincloss III, Newport, Rhode Island

James Lee Auchincloss, Ashland, Oregon

John R. Drexel III, Newport, Rhode Island

Michael Dupre, Newport, Rhode Island

Elisa (Mrs. Joseph J. Sr.) Sullivan, Newport, Rhode Island

*I*ndex

JAN POTTKER is the author of five previous books, including *Celebrity Washington*, as well as the coauthor of *Dear Ann, Dear Abby: The Unauthorized Biography of Ann Landers and Abigail Van Buren*. She first noted the public's interest in Janet Auchincloss while conducting walking tours through Georgetown, in Washington, D.C., where the Auchincloss house was a particular point of interest. Jan Pottker has a Ph.D. from Columbia University and lives in Potomac, Maryland, with her husband, Andrew S. Fishel.